Mood Disorders in People With Mental Retardation

Peter Sturmey (Editor)

Queens College and The Graduate Center,

City University of New York

Mood Disorders

Edited By:
Peter Sturmey

An association for persons with
developmental disabilities and
mental health needs.

NATIONAL ASSOCIATION FOR THE DUALLY DIAGNOSED

132 Fair Street
Kingston, New York 12401

LCCN: 2005928626
ISBN: 1-57256-019-3

1st Printing 2005

Printed in the United States of America

TABLE OF CONTENTS

Contents

Part I: Definitions, diagnosis, and risk factors

Part II: Assessment

Part III: Treatment issues

FOREWORD

Mood disorders, especially depression and dysthymia, are common problems that result in a large cost to the individual and to society. Their prevention, treatment, and management is important, not only to enhance the functioning and to reduce the suffering of individuals, their families, and others, but also to reduce the cost of disability to society generally. Since mood disorders are so common, they result in both enormous human suffering and unrealized human potential. They also result in large costs to all of us in lost productivity and the costs of treatment.

People with mental retardation have by definition established disabilities—reductions in everyday functioning—and associated handicaps—stigmatization and rejection by others, because of their disability. Mood disorders in people with mental retardation result in additional, potentially preventable disability and handicap. Hence, recognition and treatment of mood disorders is especially important and valuable.

Early research greatly underplayed the emotional lives of people with mental retardation. Some epidemiological papers reported very low prevalences or no examples of mood disorders in people with mental retardation. Some clinical papers even questioned whether people with mental retardation experienced mood disorders at all. Hence, papers in the 1970s and 1980s focused on simply establishing that mood disorders were present in this population.

There was an increasing interest in dual diagnosis in the 1980s. Several papers at this time identified depression as an important area for future work, perhaps paralleling the increasing interest in mood disorders in children and adolescents at that time. This increased attention to mood disorders was reflected in the publication in 1990 of Dosen and Menolascino's edited volume *Depression in Mentally Retarded Children and Adults.*

The 15 years since the publication of Dosen and Menolascino have seen extensive research and many new developments in the assessment and treatment of mood disorders in people with mental retardation, hence the present volume. The aims of this book are: (a) to provide both practitioners and researchers an overview of research in mood disorders in people with mental retardation; (b) to provide resources for practitioners to use; and (c) to identify areas for future research. This book should be of interest to practitioners in the fields of both mental health and mental retardation, such as case mangers, Masters and Doctoral psychologists, therapists, and psychiatrists.

Overview of the Present Volume

The present volume is in three parts. The first part reviews work on definitions, diagnosis, and risk factors. The second part reviews clinical interviews and psychometric assessment. Treatment issues are reviewed in the third part.

McDaniel and Gregory describe the basic features of mood disorders. They describe some of the common problems in applying DSM-IV criteria to people with mental retardation, including an account of some of their own clinical work and research on diagnosis.

One development over the past 15 years has been greater and greater attention to the notion of behavioral equivalents of psychiatric disorders, including behavioral equivalents of depression. This has culminated in the recent publication by the Royal College of Psychiatrists of behavioral equivalents for many psychiatric disorders in people with mental retardation. In Chapter 2, Charlot provides a careful analysis of the notion of behavioral equivalents. She points out the several different meanings of the term and goes on to review the evidence for the notion of behavioral equivalents. In the end she concludes that we must be cautious in the use of behavioral equivalents, as the evidence to support their validity is limited.

Rojahn and Esbensen review the epidemiology of mood disorders in the general population and in people with mental retardation. They note that there have only been two well-conducted epidemiological studies of psychiatric disorders in the general population, but that even these studies produced prevalence figures that vary by a factor of two to three. The more imperfect studies of the epidemiology of mood disorders in people with mental retardation have produced prevalence estimates that vary from 0% (!) to 10.9%. (See Table 3.3.) Hence, for a variety of practical and resource reasons, we do not have a good epidemiology of mood disorders in people with mental retardation. An important implication of their review is that although several authors have speculated that people with mental retardation are at special risk for mood disorders, there is not a substantial body of evidence to support this view at this time. Only one study was located that directly compared the prevalence of mood disorders in individuals with and without mental retardation (Emerson, 2003). Understanding the causes of mood disorders is important because of potential links to prevention and treatment.

Esbensen and Rojahn's chapter provides a comprehensive review of biological, inter-personal, cognitive, and genetic theories of depression and the kindling theory of mania. They found that although there is a very large body of research on the causes of mood disorders in the general population, the quantity of evidence is much smaller for people with mental retardation, and this is especially true for mania in people with mental retardation. Although some support was found for interpersonal, cognitive, and be-havioral theories of depression with people with mental retardation, Esbensen and Rojahn found contradictory evidence and no clear tests of one theory versus another. Hence, no one explanation can be favored at this time.

Epidemiology has the potential to point toward prevention of mood disorders and management of relapse in at-risk clients. Crilly, Cain, and Davidson review the risk factors for mood disorders. They identify biological and psychosocial risks for both depression and bipolar disorder both in the general population and in people with mental retardation. The implications for prevention are discussed.

There has been considerable interest in gender issues in mental retardation in recent years, including work on gender issues in dual diagnosis. Lunsky and Canrinus pro-vide a review of these issues as they relate to depression in people with mental retardation. These include higher rates of depression in women; differences in presen-tation of depression, trauma, and abuse; the costs of caring for women; and implications for therapy and selection of therapists.

As the lifespan of people with mental retardation has increased, so has the interest in aging in people with mental retardation. Patti presents an extensive review and data from his own clinical work on the differential diagnosis of depression and dementia in Down syndrome. The key questions of detection and interpretation of functional de-cline in older adults with Down syndrome and the importance of accurate detection of depression as the basis of treatment of preventable disability are the themes of this chapter. Patti's case presentations nicely illustrate these important issues.

Two chapters on assessment make up Part II of this volume: Deb and Iyer review clini-cal interviews, and Finlay reviews psychometric assessments. A clinical interview is where diagnostic hypotheses are tested. Many important subsequent treatment and other decisions are based on this information, gleaned during interviews with clients, their family, and staff. Deb and Iyer survey the various common components of clini-cal interviews, including various aspects of history, the presenting complaint, and the mental status examination. Their chapter goes on to review some of the challenges in clinical interviews, including both client and interviewer issues. The chapter concludes with a pragmatic and useful set of prescriptions for good practice guidelines for interviewing.

As noted above, the 1980s saw a burgeoning interest in dual diagnosis. One aspect of that was the development of some of the first instruments to screen for psychopathology in people with mental retardation. Reviews in the 1980s identified a manageable number of such instruments; Finlay's heroic and exhaustive review reveals that the number of instruments available has increased greatly. Finlay begins by making the important point that psychometric instruments are developed for different purposes—screening, diagnosis, and measurement of various kinds of change. Finlay goes on to review both self-report and informant-based measures. After outlining the criteria by which these instruments should be judged, Finlay provides an instrument-by-instrument review of measures of depression. In the last section of the chapter, Finlay makes explicit recommendations as to the best available instruments for screening and for comprehensive assessment of mood disorders. Although there has been considerable progress in the development of these instruments, Finlay notes that his recommendation were based primarily on the item content and form of the instruments, rather than on their reliability, validity, or other psychometric properties. Some instruments have a larger research base than others do, but none have yet been shown to be robustly reliable and valid.

Two players are absent from the stage of assessment, but for rather different reasons: biological assessment and applied behavior analysis. In the past, there was excitement about the possibility of biological assessments supplementing or even replacing clinical assessments. The Dexamethosone Suppression Test (DST) was one such assessment. However, as shown in other chapters in this volume, the DST did not prove to be a valid measure of depression in this population. Although there is considerable excitement about new biological assessments of depression, none has yet been extensively researched or adopted. Applied Behavior Analysis has its own technology of functional assessment and analysis that describes the functional relationships between behavior and the environment. This has been extensively developed and refined in the field of maladaptive behaviors, but, other than a small number of studies described in the final chapter of this volume by Sturmey, there have been few applications to mood disorders.

Intervention to improve functioning, reduce suffering, and reduce preventable disability is the focus of Part III. To this end, there are five chapters that review psychotropic medications, other biological treatments, cognitive behavior therapy, psychodynamic counseling and psychotherapy, and behavior therapy. A theme of these chapters is evidence-based practice: What is the evidence that a particular kind of therapy is effective, either for this specific person or for people more generally? (I will return to this issue later.)

Many people with depression and many people with dual diagnosis receive psychotropic medication. Stigler et al. show that perhaps one in twenty people with mental retardation and, surprisingly, perhaps to one in five people with autism take antidepressants. They go on to systematically survey the common classes of antidepressants and mood stabilizers used for the treatment of bipolar and related disorders and their side effects. Their review of the evidence of efficacy for both antidepressants and for mood stabilizers in people with mental retardation is that there is little good evidence available. This is surprising, given the common use of these medications for mood disorders!

Sturmey and Ghaziuddin review other less commonly used biological interventions for depression: phototherapy, dietary modifications, and electroconvulsive therapy (ECT). There is evidence for the effectiveness of phototherapy for seasonal affective disorder, for Saint-John's-wort but not other forms of dietary intervention, and for ECT to treat depression in the general population. However, although examples of the use of all three of these therapies with people with mental retardation can be found, there is little evidence for the efficacy of these therapies in people with mental retardation.

Lindsay, Stenfert Kroese, and Drew's review of cognitive behavior therapy for depression begins with a historical review of the development of cognitive behavior therapy as an outgrowth of behavior therapy, predominantly with adult disorders, in the 1960s. They go on to describe several forms of cognitive therapy. In subsequent sections they describe various cognitive-behavioral assessment and intervention strategies. The final section nicely illustrates the application of cognitive-behavioral interventions with two adults with mental retardation and mood disorders.

Beail and Newman review and illustrate the use of psychodynamic counseling and psychotherapy in people with mental retardation. They begin by noting the traditional prohibitions against psychotherapy with people of below-average intelligence. A review of the evidence base for the use of psychotherapy with people with mental retardation reveals that there has been increased attention to research in this area over the past 10 years, but no well-controlled studies were identified. The majority of this chapter is devoted to a careful description of psychotherapy techniques and extensive illustrative case material.

In the last chapter, Sturmey describes the use of behavioral formulations and treatments of depression. The first part of the chapter described Skinner's model of behavior with its emphasis on the three sources of behavior: biological evolution, cultural evolution, and evolution of the operant during the lifespan. Skinner's description of therapy as a controlling agency of society and the various functions that therapists and therapy can have are then described. Skinner's emphasis on the role of the therapist to induce clients to discover their own functional assessment and develop their own self-control strategies is then described. Sturmey then describes the elements in a behavioral formulation of depression and its implication for behavioral treatment of depression. Two promising approaches to treatment of depression are identified: activation therapy and environmental enrichment. Although there is fairly good evidence for the efficacy of activation therapy in the general population, no evidence was found for its application in people with mental retardation. In contrast, there is good evidence for the use of environmental enrichment using preferred stimuli improving mood in people with severe and profound mental retardation, although only one application was identified with someone with a mood disorder. Again, the absence of a strong evidence base for the application of behavioral interventions with mood disorders in people with mental retardation is notable.

What Has Happened in 15 Years?

The changes in research and practice over the past 15 years can be found by making a comparison between the present volume and Dosen and Menolascino's. A first observation is that the quantity of research that is available is much greater now than 15 years ago. Many of the contributors to Dosen and Menolascino's volume had relatively few papers and little data to work with. A second difference is that much of the research in dual diagnosis at that time was not focused on specific disorders, but was more concerned with psychiatric disorders generally. This trend toward a more narrow focus on specific disorders is also evident in the development of assessment instruments specifically designed for mood disorders. A third difference is that although behavioral equivalents had been proposed in 1990 (Sovner, 1990), there were little data to test the validity of these hypotheses. Charlot's review in this volume attests to the considerable interest that there has been in this question. In 1990, the possibility that the DST might be useful was a live issue (Ruedich, 1990), which has since expired.

Dosen and Menolascino's volume, like this one, devoted several chapters to therapy. Interestingly, several chapters were devoted to various kinds of psychotherapy. Comparing these chapters with Beail and Newman's in this volume, two observations can be made. The fundamental model and intervention techniques associated with psychotherapy have not changed. Whereas in the 1990s there was almost no evidence available as to the efficacy of psychotherapy with people with mental retardation, there has indeed been a modest accumulation of evidence on this question. Lund's (1990) chapter on psychopharmacology seems very dated. He reviewed tricyclic antidepressants for depression, lithium for mania, and little else. Contrast this with the chapter in this volume by Stigler et al. on psychopharmacology. There are currently a larger number of psychotropic agents available, tools available to monitor medication side effects, and, again, more evidence available as to efficacy. Contrasting Benson's (1990) chapter and the chapter in this volume by Lindsay et al. on cognitive and behavioral treatment is also illuminating. Although there are not any more well-controlled trials of cognitive or cognitive-behavior therapy for depression than there were in 1990, there is now a growing literature on cognitive processes and on methods to assess cognition. Finally, although Benson's chapter reviewed some behavioral interventions for depression, such as social skills training, a clear distinction between cognitive and behavioral formulations of depression was not made. The present volume makes this distinction explicit by devoting separate chapters to these two approaches.

Future Research

Future research should continue to address the issues of diagnosis of mood disorders. A number of important lacunae remain. Diagnosis by a well-qualified and trained psychiatrist or psychologist is often referred to as the "gold standard" by which other measures should be evaluated. Unfortunately, when it comes to diagnosis of mood disorders in people with mental retardation, we still do not know if this shining (or tarnished?) substance is gold or pyrites. Systematic evaluations of independent clinicians diagnosing mood disorders in people with mental retardation are absent from the literature. Can clinicians reliably apply DSM-IV criteria to people with mild or moderate mental retardation to distinguish major depression from dysthymia or to distinguish bipolar I from bipolar II from plain old learned aggression? We do not know! Without this gold standard, progress is not possible in a number of other important domains, such as the validation of psychometric screening instruments and the description of subjects in treatment trials.

Practice guidelines have been established in some areas of practice related to dual diagnosis and autism, but they have not been developed for mood disorders in people with mental retardation. The potential basis of such guidelines is detectable in a number of the chapters in this volume, such as Deb and Iyer's guidelines on clinical interviewing, Finlay's recommendations for assessment instruments, and some of the treatment chapters. However, at this time, these guidelines have not been consolidated and codified into a unified set of practice guidelines.

The treatment chapters in this volume are generally distinct from those in Dosen and Menolascino's because of the greater quantity of research. But quantity is not quality. Case studies can be useful in many ways. Case series and open label trials of psychotropic medications hint at efficacy, and perhaps tell us something about treatment safety. *Neither allows us to conclude whether the treatment caused the change in the participant's behavior.* All the treatment chapters pay considerable attention to the evidence base for the particular treatment, yet none is able to cite strong evidence for the efficacy of their particular approach. One well-controlled treatment trial will tell us more than 20 case descriptions and case series. The question of treatment efficacy can only be answered by well-designed single-subject experimental designs and randomized controlled trials. Unfortunately, these studies are lacking.

The past 15 years have seen considerable progress our understanding and treatment of mood disorders in people with mental retardation. Let us look forward to continuing progress in this field.

Note on Terminology

Terminology relating to developmental disabilities continues to evolve. In the United States, the term mental retardation *remains current, although many in the United States have expressed dissatisfaction with it. In Europe and many British Commonwealth countries, the term* intellectual disability (ID) *is preferred at the present time. Both terms are used throughout this book, reflecting the international group of contributors. Readers should regard these terms as interchangeable.*

References

Benson, B. A. (1990). Behavioral treatment of depression. In A. Dosen & F. J. Menolascino (Eds.), *Depression in mentally retarded children and adults* (pp. 309–330). Leiden, Netherlands: Logon Publications.

Dosen, A., & Menolascino, F. J. (1990). *Depression in mentally retarded children and adults.* Leiden, Netherlands: Logon Publications.

Emerson, K. (2003). Prevalence of psychiatric disorders in children and adolescents with and without intellectual disability. *Journal of Intellectual Disability Research, 47,* 51–58.

Lund, J. (1990). Psychopharmacological approaches in the treatment of depression in the mentally retarded. In A. Dosen & F. J. Menolascino, *Depression in mentally retarded children and adults* (pp. 331–339). Leiden, Netherlands: Logon Publications.

Ruedich, S. L. (1990). Biochemical findings in mentally retarded persons with depressive disorders. In A. Dosen & F. J. Menolascino, *Depression in mentally retarded children and adults* (pp. 219–233). Leiden, Netherlands: Logon Publications.

Sovner, R. J. (1990). Bipolar disorder in persons with developmental disorders: An overview. In A. Dosen & F. J. Menolascino, *Depression in mentally retarded children and adults* (pp. 175–198). Leiden, Netherlands: Logon Publications.

Contributors

Nigel Beail is a Consultant Clinical Psychologist and Head of Psychology Services for People with Learning Disabilities at Barnsley Learning Disability Services, UK. He is also an Honorary Professor of Psychology at the University of Sheffield, UK. His main clinical interest is in providing psychological therapies for people with mental retardation. His main research studies involve assessment of mental health, evaluation of psychological interventions, and forensic issues with people with mental retardation.

Nancy N. Cain is the Director of the Mental Retardation Dual Diagnosis Psychiatric Programs, Strong Behavioral Health, University of Rochester Medical Center, Department of Psychiatry, Rochester, New York. Her research interests are in bipolar disorders and individuals with mental retardation.

Maaike Canrinus is completing her Masters degree in child clinical psychology at the Unversity of Guelph, Ontario, Canada. Her research interests include developmental disabilities, adolescence, and family issues.

Lauren Charlot is an Assistant Professor in the Department of Psychiatry of the University of Massachusetts Medical School in Worcester, Massachusetts, where she is also Program Director of the Neuropsychiatric Disabilities Unit, a specialty inpatient psychiatric unit serving people with mental retardation and severe psychiatric problems. She has conducted investigations regarding the nature of mood disorders in people with mental retardation, focusing on the impact of developmental features on differential diagnosis. She is presently doing pilot studies using a semistructured interview tool based on behavioral equivalents

John Crilly is in the Long Term Care Division of the University of Rochester Department of Psychiatry. He is also a treatment team leader at Rochester Psychiatric Center and Clinical Assistant Professor at SUNY Buffalo School of Social Work.

Philip W. Davidson is Professor of Pediatrics, University of Rochester School of Medicine and Dentistry and Co-Director of the Mental Retardation /Dual Diagnosis Psychiatric Programs at the Strong Behavioral Health, University of Rochester Medical Center, Department of Psychiatry, Rochester, New York.

Shoumitro Deb is Clinical Professor of Neuropsychiatry and Intellectual Disability in the Division of Neuroscience at the University of Birmingham, UK. His clinical and research interests include studies of neuropsychiatric consequences of developmental and acquired brain injury in adult life. His team is studying the relationship between higher executive function and other neurobehavioral disorders in the context of various neuropsychiatric conditions, which includes functional neuro-imaging work.

Philippa Drew was trained as a clinical psychologist in Perth, Western Australia. She has worked in adult mental health and learning disability services and has recently been involved in setting up a systematic therapeutic service for adults with learning disabilities and their families and caregivers. She currently works in Perth.

Anna J. Esbensen is a Doctoral candidate at the Nisonger Center, Ohio State University. Her research interests include dual diagnosis, in particular the nature and development of depression and its associated features among individuals with mental retardation. Other research interests include the impact of stressors and life transitions on the development of psychopathology and the development of treatment models for individuals with dual diagnoses.

Mick Finlay is a social psychologist at the University of Surrey, UK. He works on the postgraduate training course in clinical psychology. His research interests include assessment, interaction, stigma, and intergroup conflict.

Alicia M. Gregory graduated from the University of Alabama, Tuscaloosa, in Theological Studies and completed a Masters degree in Clinical Psychology at the California State University, Fullerton. She is an Adjunctive Instructor in the Department of Psychology, Georgia College and State University. Her research and clinical interests lie in the treatment and diagnosis of adult and adolescent clients.

Anupama Iyer is a Specialist Registrar in Psychiatry of Learning Disabilities in Birmingham, UK. She has special interest in psychopathology among children who have intellectual disabilities.

Bill Lindsay is a consultant forensic clinical psychologist at the State Hospital, Carstairs; Head of Clinical Psychology Learning Disabilities Services, NHS Tayside; and the Chair of Learning Disabilities, University of Abertay, Dundee, Scotland. He has published extensively, including on the treatment of offenders with mental retardation, evaluation of therapies, and assessment of mental health issues in people with mental retardation.

Yona Lunsky is an Assistant Professor in the Department of Psychiatry at the University of Toronto, Canada. She works as a psychologist in the dual diagnosis program at the Centre for Addiction and Mental Health in Toronto. She is interested in women's health issues and developmental disabilities.

William F. McDaniel received his Ph.D. from the University of Georgia and is Professor of Psychology at Georgia College and State University. He is also the coordinator of Psychology Services, Comprehensive Health Care Division, at Central State Hospital, Milledgeville, Georgia. His research interests include psychological assessment, including assessment of dual diagnosis, functional neuroanatomy of the cerebral cortex, endocannabinoids and exercise, and animal models of fetal alcohol syndrome. His clinical interests include clinical neuropsychology.

Christopher J. McDougle is the Albert E. Sterne Professor and Chairman and Director of the Section of Child and Adolescent Psychiatry, Department of Psychiatry, Indiana University School of Medicine. Dr. McDougle is founder of the Christian Sarkine Autism Treatment Center at the James Whitcomb Riley Hospital for Children. His primary research interests include the neurobiology and psychopharmacology of childhood-onset disorders, such as autism and other pervasive developmental disorders, obsessive-compulsive disorder, and Tourette's disorder. He is the principal investigator at the Indiana University site of the Research Units on Pediatric Psychopharmacology—Psychosocial Interventions Autism Network.

David Newman is Clinical Psychologist in the Barnsley and Doncaster Learning Disability Services and Honorary Teacher at the University of Sheffield, UK. His main clinical interests are assessment and intervention for people with dual diagnosis and complex needs. His main research interests include practice-based evidence for psychological interventions, assessment of mental health, and assimilation of problematic experience.

Paul J. Patti is a research scientist at the Jervis Clinic, Institute for Basic Research, Staten Island, New York. He has research interests in aging, dementia, depression, and the efficacy of vitamin E for dementia.

David J. Posey is Assistant Professor, Department of Psychiatry, Indiana University School of Medicine. He is Chief of the Christian Sarkine Autism Treatment Center at the James Whitcomb Riley Hospital for Children. His primary research interests include the neurobiology and psychopharmacology of pervasive developmental disorders, including autism. He is the recipient of a Career Development Award from the National Institute of Mental Health, focused on the development of drug treatments for the social impairment of autism.

Johannes Rojahn is Professor of Psychology at George Mason University and has published over 100 scientific articles and book chapters. He has served as Associate Editor for *Research in Developmental Disabilities* and the *American Journal on Mental Retardation*. His main research interest has been in behavior disorders and mental illness in mental retardation.

Kimberly A. Stigler is Assistant Professor, Department of Psychiatry, Indiana University School of Medicine. Her primary research interests include the neurobiology and psychopharmacology of pervasive developmental disorders, including autism. She is a co-investigator at the Indiana University site of the Research Units on Pediatric Psychopharmacology—Psychosocial Interventions Autism Network.

Biza Stenfert Kroese is a Senior Lecturer in clinical psychology at the School of Psychology, University of Birmingham, United Kingdom. She is also a Consultant Clinical Psychologist in Shropshire County Primary Care Trust, where she is head of psychological services for adults with learning disabilities. She is the Psychology Advisor to the British Learning Institute of Learning Disabilities. Her research interests include consent to participate in research and cognitive therapy with people with learning disabilities.

Peter Sturmey is an Associate Professor of Psychology at Queens College and The Graduate Center, City University of New York. He is a member of the Doctoral programs in Learning Processes and Neuropsychology at Queens College. He has published widely on topics related to mental retardation and other developmental disabilities. His interests include applied behavior analysis, especially as applied to mental health issues, teaching skills, reduction of maladaptive behaviors and restrictive management practices, and staff and parent training.

This book is dedicated to the late John Jacobson.

Part I

Definitions, Diagnosis, and Risk Factors

1

Diagnostic Criteria for Mood Disorders and Applications to People With Mental Retardation

William F. McDaniel

and

Alicia M. Gregory

Mental Disorders and Mental Retardation

The 1990s were important years in the history of mental retardation, because it became increasingly appreciated that the incidence of comorbid mental disorders with mental retardation actually exceeded the incidence in the general population. For example, it is estimated in the *Diagnostic and Statistical Manual of Mental Disorders* (4th edition) (DSM-IV) of the American Psychiatric Association (1994, pp. 42–43) that comorbidity might be three to four times greater than that found in the general population. Furthermore, the DSM-IV emphasizes that almost all mental disorders can coexist with mental retardation, and that the symptoms defining a mental disorder can be the same for both the general population and people with mental retardation. It has been argued (Borthwick-Duffy, 1994; Matson & Sevin, 1994; Nezu, 1994) that failure by clinicians to recognize this fact in the past was likely due to an "overshadowing" effect. That is, the presence of mental retardation likely masked concerns about mental health issues. The term *dual diagnosis* is often used to indicate the coexistence of serious psychopathological disturbance and mental retardation in the same individual (Prout, 1993; Reiss, 1990). However, this term is also used in clinical psychology and psychiatry in a more general sense to indicate the comorbidity of two or more mental disorders in the same individual, such as a bipolar disorder combined with one or more of the substance abuse disorders.

DSM-IV Concepts of Mood Disorders

Several authors have emphasized that although we have evidence that mood disorders have long been common, they appear to be particularly prevalent in modern society (e.g., Cohen, 1994). Several mood disorders are presented in the DSM-IV, including manic episode, major depressive disorder, bipolar disorder (types I and II), cyclothymic disorder, dysthymic disorder, atypical mood disorder, mood disorder due to a medical condition, and substance-induced mood disorder. We have elected to add schizoaffective disorder to our review. This is because, while classified in the DSM-IV as one of the "Schizophrenia and Other Psychotic Disorders," it represents a combination of schizophrenic and mood symptoms. Also, according to Meyer and Deitsch (1996), it differs from most forms of schizophrenia by having a later age of onset, no increased familial expression, less requirement for hospitalization, and a better prognosis for recovery. The characteristics of this disorder, combined with our clinical experience, led us to include coverage of this disorder under the topic of mood disorders. *The Clinicians' Handbook* (Meyer & Deitsch, 1996) and the DSM-IV have been utilized heavily in developing what follows.

Manic Episode

Three features that are consistent with a manic episode include hyperactive motor behavior, extreme euphoria often coupled with irritability, and increased flight of ideas. All are created through the use of external stimuli, and this is unlike the affective disorders that can accompany schizophrenia and schizoaffective disorder. During a manic episode, most individuals desire an increased amount of contact with others, and they will have what may appear to the clinician as a thought disturbance. However, the thought disturbance is rooted in unusual combinations of topics often related to the extreme euphoria. That is, the person's experiencing a manic episode will quickly proceed from one topic to the next without discrimination. It is not uncommon for someone experiencing mania to report the ability to achieve such lofty goals as writing a novel, running for government office, or even stating that a special relationship exists between the individual and God. Given the level of euphoria coupled with unrealistic goal-related ideation, the individual can become easily irritated when goals are denied or placed into any realistic context.

According to the DSM-IV, a manic episode must occur for a period of at least 1 week with the initial elevated mood symptom and must co-occur with three or more of the following symptoms: an inflated self-esteem or grandiosity, a decreased need for sleep, an increased tendency to be more talkative than usual or a pressure to continue talking, a flight of ideas, distractibility, an increase in goal-directed behavior, or an excessive involvement in pleasurable activities with an increase in potential consequences. These symptoms must cause marked impairment in occupational, social, or relationship functioning. They may also cause the individual to need psychiatric stabilization to prevent harm to self or others. The symptoms cannot be coupled with depressive symptoms of a mixed episode or be caused by the use of such substances as medications, illegal substances, or alcohol.

Major Depressive Episode

The most important feature of a major depressive episode is that the individual experiences a significant increase in feelings of sadness, hopelessness, and discouragement. The origin of this mood change can be due to many possibilities, including genetic factors, trauma, or significant life changes. Many pharmaceutical companies and authors of psychopharmacology texts (e.g., Stahl, 2000) argue that diminished serotonergic and/or epinephrinergic mechanisms are responsible. During a depressive episode, an individual might increase or decrease the amount of sleep from the normal routine, increase or decrease the amount of food intake, and, at times, consider suicide as a means to end his or her "down in the dumps" feeling. Mood disorders are highly associated with suicide, and this is especially true for individuals diagnosed with major depressive disorder (Angst, Angst, & Stasssen, 1999).

According to the DSM-IV, a major depressive episode is characterized by either (a) a depressed mood most of the day, nearly all day, and/or (b) a marked diminished interest in previous activities for most of the day for a period of at least 2 weeks along with four other symptoms. These symptoms include a 5% increase or decrease in weight, insomnia or hypersomnia, psychomotor agitation or retardation (slowing of physical movement), fatigue, feelings of worthlessness or excessive guilt, a diminished ability to concentrate or make decisions, recurrent thoughts of death, and recurrent suicidal ideation or suicide attempts. These symptoms must occur most days, and nearly all day. These symptoms must cause marked impairment in occupational, social, or relationship functioning, and they cannot be secondary to bereavement or a similar emotional condition related to transient personal loss. Likewise, the symptoms cannot be related to a psychosis involving such symptoms as delusions or hallucinations, and these symptoms cannot be related to the use of such substances as medications, illegal substances, or alcohol.

Dysthymic Disorder

The essential component of dysthymic disorder is a low-grade depression that continues chronically for a period of 2 or more years for an adult and 1 year for an adolescent. Many symptoms are parallel to a major depressive episode but would be considered not as severe. Many individuals describe dysthymia as an overall feeling of dysphoria, where no activity is enjoyable and even small tasks such as dressing require an increased amount of motivation. Many individuals suffering with this disorder see themselves as incapable and/or as failures, and they are often extremely self-critical. In particular, you might hear the person say such things as, "I have just always been this way." This information is important in noting a major depressive episode versus dysthymia.

The DSM-IV characterizes dysthymic disorder as having a depressed mood for most days for a period of at least 2 years (1 year for adolescents). At least two of the following symptoms must also be present: poor appetite or overeating, insomnia or hypersomnia, fatigue or low energy, low self-esteem, poor concentration or decision-making difficulties, or a feeling of hopelessness.

The person cannot be without these symptoms for more than 2 months at a time, and major depressive episodes cannot have occurred during the criterion years. Likewise, no manic or mixed episodes, hypomanic episodes, or cyclothymic episodes can have been observed during the criterion years. The symptoms must cause marked impairment in occupational, social, or relationship functioning, and they cannot be due to the effects of the use of such substances as medications, illegal substances, or alcohol.

Bipolar Disorder

The essential features of a bipolar disorder include the coupling of more than one of the following four criteria: a major depressive episode, dysthymia, a manic episode, or a hypomanic episode. Bipolar disorders are broken down into bipolar I disorder and bipolar II disorder. The more severe of the two is bipolar I disorder, in which the individual has both a major depressive and manic episodes. Bipolar II disorder is characterized by either an episode of mania and dysthymia or an episode of major depression and hypomania. If psychotic features are present and endure, a multitude of specifiers can be used to explain current episodes, the level of severity, and rapid cycling. Approximately 90% of individuals who have a manic episode will continue to have future episodes, and up to 70% of individuals who have a manic episode experience this either before or after a major depressive episode.

According to the DSM-IV, nine different diagnostic criteria categories are present for both bipolar I and bipolar II disorders. Each criterion category has its own specifiers, dependent upon the most recent episode of manic, hypomanic, depressed, or mixed features, as well as the chronicity of the disorder. These symptoms must cause marked impairment in occupational, social, or relationship functioning, and they cannot be due to the effects of the use of such substances as medications, illegal substances, or alcohol.

Cyclothymic Disorder

The essential components of cyclothymic disorder are periods of hypomania and periods of depression that continue chronically for a period of 2 years for an adult and 1 year for an adolescent. Many symptoms are parallel to manic and depressive episodes, but they are not considered as severe. Again, the individual would experience symptoms due to external stimuli, and he or she may function well during periods of hypomania. However, significant impairment in the quality of life must be present to meet the criteria for this disorder. It should be noted that this disorder is considered more rare, with 0.4%–1.0% of the population potentially affected.

According to the DSM-IV, the criteria for cyclothymic disorder include hypomanic and depressive episodes for 2 years (1 year for adolescents), with no major depressive or manic episodes having occurred during that first 2 years of the disorder. Following this period of time, if a manic or depressive episode occurs, then a further diagnosis of bipolar I or II can be given. This disorder cannot be better explained by an affective disorders such a schizoaffective, delusional, or psychotic disorder. These symptoms must cause marked impairment in occupational, social, or relationship functioning, and they cannot be due to the effects of the use of such substances as medications, illegal substances, or alcohol.

Atypical Mood Disorders

"Bipolar Disorder, Not Otherwise Specified (NOS)" and "Mood Disorder, NOS" are diagnoses given when there is clear evidence of an affective disturbance, but the symptoms fail to clearly meet the criteria for a more specific diagnosis. That is, an individual might show many physical signs of a depression but report still being able to enjoy many pleasurable activities in his or her life.

Schizoaffective Disorder

Schizoaffective disorder is often characterized as the "in between" of schizophrenia and bipolar disorders. An individual will have the psychotic features of schizophrenia with one or more of the characteristics of a bipolar disorder. This disorder, more than any other psychotic disorder, has an acute onset, and, although it is more complicated than schizophrenia, it has a better prognosis for recovery and a shorter hospitalization probability. It is well documented that schizophrenia has a consistent genetic component (Gottesman, 1991, 1995). However, schizoaffective disorder is less likely, in comparison with other schizophrenic disorders, to be conferred genetically to offspring.

According to the DSM-IV, the essential features of schizoaffective disorder include the presence of manic, depressive, or mixed affective episodes that occur for at least 1 month but less than 6 months, coinciding with the criteria for schizophrenia. Schizophrenia criteria include the following onset of prominent psychotic symptoms: delusions or hallucinations for at least 2 weeks without prominent mood symptoms, mood symptoms present for a qualified amount of time, and the fact that the disturbance is not due to the effects of drugs, alcohol, or a general medical condition. Individuals with schizoaffective disorder should be given a specifier of "Bipolar" or "Depressive" type, to indicate the prominent mood symptoms present along with the delusions and/or hallucinations.

Advances in the Development of Objective Screening Tools

The development of valid screening instruments that might assist the clinician in the objective assessment of psychopathology and behavioral excesses represented an important step in the area of dual diagnosis. Aman (1991) drafted a thorough comparative evaluation of the various instruments available at that time. There were three screens considered well supported on the basis of studies of reliability and validity: the Psychopathology Inventory for Mentally Retarded Adults (PIMRA; Matson, 1988), the

Aberrant Behavior Checklist (Aman & Singh, 1986), and the Reiss Screen for Maladaptive Behavior (Reiss, 1994). The latter instrument also has forms for children and adolescents. These instruments are usually administered to caregivers well familiar with the behavioral history of the individual being assessed. Combined with information obtained from observation, a review of the medical and behavioral history, and a clinical interview with the client, these instruments can help refine the nature of the psychiatric disturbance.

Aman (1991) concluded that the psychometric properties of the Reiss Screen were superior to those of other assessment tools available at that time, and in the decade and more of research that has occurred since Aman's important review, the Reiss Screen has been shown to have good content validity and factor structure validity (Havercamp & Reiss, 1996; Reiss, 1997). We have elected to briefly describe the Reiss Screen as a representative example of such instruments. A much more thorough comparative analysis of all instruments purported to have value in screening for psychopathology in individuals with mental retardation, including such recently created tests as the Assessment of Dual Diagnosis (ADD; Matson, 1997) and the Glasgow Depression Scale (Cuthill, Espie, & Cooper, 2003), is offered in Chapter 9 by Finlay.

The Reiss Screen is a 38-item questionnaire, where 26 items contribute to one or more of the eight clinical subscales assessed. The questionnaire is completed by two caregivers. Each must have a long history of interacting with the individual being assessed. The instrument's total score, based on the 26 items indicated above, has been described as the best predictor of serious psychopathology (Sturmey & Bertman, 1994). The subscales of the Reiss Screen include putative measures of aggressive behavior, psychosis, paranoia, depression (behavioral signs), depression (physical signs), dependent personality disorder, avoidant behavior, avoidant behavior disorder, and autism. The pattern of elevations on various scales of the Reiss Screen can assist the clinician in formulating an official diagnosis and treatment protocol. Six additional experimental scales are available, and attention to elevations on these scales can also prove informative, at least in the experience of one of the authors (WFM). These include the Drug / Alcohol Abuse, Self-Injury, Stealing, Over-Activity, Sexual Problem, and Suicidal Tendencies portions of the screen. Prout (1993) critiqued the Reiss Screen for having so few items that weigh heavily on diagnostic decisions. This opinion is shared by the authors of this chapter, despite the utilitarian impact of the Reiss Screen in developing both psychopharmacological and behavioral programs to address problem behaviors in the institutional setting where we provide consultative services. Elevations on scales addressed by the Reiss Screen, or for that matter by any other instrument, nevertheless need to be considered along with direct observation, behavioral history, and perhaps a structured clinical interview with the client and/or the individual's primary caregiver to refine the precise diagnosis in DSM-IV terms.

Applications to Individuals With Mental Retardation

Differential diagnosis of mood disorders in individuals with mental retardation is a challenging process. As indicated in the DSM-IV, diagnosis becomes more difficult as the severity of the intellectual disability increases. Regardless of the level of mental retardation, screening tools can help the clinician develop testable hypotheses for further clinical evaluation. We have already reviewed the potential of the Reiss Screen to guide the clinician. Additionally, the scales addressed by the Assessment of Dual Diagnosis (ADD: Matson, 1997) reportedly correspond to DSM-IV diagnostic criteria. Scales that correspond to affective disturbance include "Depression," "Anxiety," and "Mania." There is also a scale labeled "Schizophrenia." An elevation on the Schizophrenia scale along with an elevation on the Depression scale might lead the clinician to further examine the possibility of schizoaffective disorder. Unfortunately, while inter-rater reliability of the ADD is good (Matson & Bamberg, 1998), little work has been published to address the diagnostic criterion-related validity, content validity, and test-retest reliability of the ADD. Matson, Anderson, and Bamburg (2000) have, however, shown that elevations on several scales of the ADD correlate with impaired social functioning.

We have found that an abbreviated version of the Minnesota Multiphasic Personality Inventory, the MMPI-168(L), is useful in developing diagnoses of both schizoaffective disorder and bipolar disorder and for tracking changes in mental health as a consequence of pharmacological and behavioral management in some clients with higher cognitive abilities (McDaniel, 1997; McDaniel & Harris, 1999). Results obtained by the administration of the MMPI-168 in non–mentally retarded individuals were shown by Overall and Gomez-Mont (1974) to correlate well with the results obtained through the administration of the entire MMPI. The MMPI-168(L) was an attempt to alter the phrasing of the questions without changing the underlying meaning of the question so that it could be understood by many individuals with borderline intellectual abilities or with mild to moderate mental retardation. The remaining four Lie Scale items of the original MMPI were added to the MMPI-168, and this is the reason our version of the test is labeled the MMPI-168(L). Good test-retest reliability and diagnostic criterion–related validity with respect to the presence of a psychosis or a serious personality disturbance were demonstrated (McDaniel, 1997), and content validity was demonstrated relative to severe behavioral excesses (McDaniel, Childers, & Compton, 1997). We have not, however, had much success showing a correspondence between the Depression scale of the MMPI-168(L) and Depression scales of other screens, such as the Reiss Screen (Johns & McDaniel, 1998), the PIMRA (McDaniel & Turner, 2000), or the ADD (McDaniel, Passmore, & Sewell, 2003). Also, we have not attempted to address the criterion-related validity of scales of the MMPI-168(L) that are related to affective disorders.

Regardless of the results obtained via administration of an instrument created to assess psychopathology or behavioral excesses, the role of direct observation and attention to behavioral history cannot be overemphasized. Chapter 2 considers "behavioral equivalents" to affective disturbance that might be operationally defined and measured empirically. Sovner and colleagues (e.g., Sovner & Lowry, 1990) might be considered pioneers in this area. They advocated the development of behavioral assessment procedures that correspond to the diagnostic criteria for an affective disorder. With respect to mania, which can be manifested by euphoria or irritable mood, Sovner and Lowry (1990, Table 1, p. 57) suggested that "boisterousness or excitement may be the predominant mood state" reflecting mania, whereas "self-injury may be associated with irritability." Behavioral measures of the frequency of smiling and/or laughing could be indicative of mania, whereas frequency and/or (implied) severity of self-injury could be indicative of irritability. They go on to argue that other diagnostic criteria could also be measured objectively. Examples include a decreased need to sleep (as measured by monitoring the sleep pattern in 30-minute intervals), being more talkative or having pressured speech (by counting the "rates of swearing, singing, screaming"), or increased psychomotor agitation (by measuring aggressive behaviors, pacing, and refusal to comply with requests). With respect to depression, Sovner and Lowry (1990, Table 2, p. 58) noted that depressed or irritable mood might be reflected in an apathetic facial expression and a lack of emotional reactivity. Behavioral equivalents that might be measurable include "rates of smiling, responses to preferred activities, and crying episodes." Examples of accompanying symptoms include decreased or increased appetite or body weight that could be measured by weight changes and/or meal refusals, and insomnia or hypersomnia that could easily be measured by recording the information about the sleep cycle for the individual client. Psychomotor hyperactivity or retardation can be reflected in measures of the amount of time spent in bed, the number of spontaneous verbalizations, or pacing behaviors. Again, this will be addressed in much greater detail in the next chapter.

Summary and Conclusions

Significant advances have been made in the appreciation that mental disorders can coexist with intellectual disabilities, and techniques for the objective diagnosis of mood disorders in individuals with mental retardation have improved in recent years. Yet, the validity of many instruments has yet to be completely appreciated. Nevertheless, as reviewed early in this chapter, several instruments are available that can guide the practitioner in the development of diagnostic hypotheses that might be further pursued through analyses of behavioral history, symptom analysis, observation, and/or a clinical interview. The diagnostic criterion-related validity of many of the individual scales of several instruments still needs to be tested. Nevertheless, recent developments have, in our experience, improved the diagnostic accuracy.

Accurate diagnosis is one of the most important first steps in identifying efficacious treatments. For example, it is well known that major depression, dysthymia, cyclothymia, and atypical mood disorders respond well to any of a variety of psychotropic medications, including, but not limited to, serotonin reuptake inhibitors and/or noradrenergic reuptake inhibitors, or a monoamine oxidase inhibitor, if the disorders are treatment-resistant (Sadock & Sadock, 2001; Stahl, 2000). Although much greater detail will be offered concerning pharmacological treatment of mood disorders later in this book, the point is that mood disorders can be successfully treated. This improves the quality of life both for the individual with an intellectual disability and for caregivers. As an example, Clarke and Gomez (1999) tracked 11 inpatient individuals with mental retardation and comorbid depression over a 12-month period after initiating antidepressant therapy. In all cases, remission from depression was observed by the fifth week of treatment and was maintained for the duration of the study.

We had hoped to bring to light more information concerning the diagnosis and treatment of mood disorders in children and young adolescents. Unfortunately, the literature concerning this area is in its infancy, and many clinicians find it necessary to resort to extrapolations that might be made based upon the literature available concerning older adolescents and adults (e.g., Aman, Collier-Crespin, & Lindsay, 2000). We encourage greater empirical study of diagnostic signs and independent objective criteria for the diagnosis of mood disorders in children and young adolescents. In the interim, we encourage practitioners to continue to extrapolate from the adult mental health literature concerning treatments for affective disorders, even though this literature is based upon studies of older adolescents and adults.

It is hoped that the foregoing brief review of the mood disorders and the remaining chapters in this book will prove valuable to mental health practitioners who address the needs of persons with mental retardation. The final message is, however, that multiple methods of assessment are required for the accurate diagnosis of mood disorders when addressing the needs of individuals with mental retardation. Once an accurate diagnosis is determined, this information should guide the practitioner's strategies for active treatment as well as provide caregivers with information concerning the nature of the dual diagnosis.

References

Aman, M. G. (1991). *Assessing psychopathology and behavior problems in persons with mental retardation: A review of available instruments.* Rockville, MD: U.S. Department of Health and Human Services.

Aman, M. G., Collier-Crespin, A., & Lindsay, R. L. (2000). Pharmacotherapy of disorders in mental retardation. *European Child & Adolescent Psychiatry, 9,* 198–207.

Aman, M. G., & Singh, N. N. (1986). *Test manual for the Aberrant Behavior Checklist.* East Aurora, NY: Slosson Educational Publications.

American Psychiatric Association. (1994). *Diagnostic and statistical manual of mental disorders* (4th ed.). Washington, DC: Author.

Angst, J., Angst, F., & Stassen, H. H. (1999). Suicide risk in patients with major depressive disorder. *Journal of Clinical Psychiatry, 60* (Suppl. 2), 57–62.

Borthwick-Duffy, S. A. (1994). Epidemiology and prevalence of psychopathology in people with mental retardation. *Journal of Consulting and Clinical Psychology, 62,* 17–27.

Clarke, D. J., & Gomez, G. A. (1999). Utility of modified ICD-10 criteria in the diagnosis of depression associated with intellectual disability. *Journal of Intellectual Disability Research, 43,* 413–420.

Cohen, D. (1994). *Out of the blue: Depression and human nature.* New York: W.W. Norton.

Cuthill, F. M., Espie, C. A., & Cooper, S. A. (2003). Development and psychometric properties of the Glasgow Depression Scale for people with a learning disability. Individual and carer supplement versions. *British Journal of Psychiatry, 182,* 347–353.

Gottesman, I. L. (1991). *Schizophrenia genesis.* New York: Freeman.

Gottesman, I. L. (1995). *Schizophrenia genesis: The origins of madness.* New York: Freeman.

Havercamp, S. M., & Reiss, S. (1996). Composite versus multiple-rating scales in the assessment of psychopathology in people with mental retardation. *Journal of Intellectual Disability, 40,* 176–179.

Johns, M. R., & McDaniel, W. F. (1998). Areas of convergence and discordance between the MMPI-168 and the Reiss Screen for Maladaptive Behavior in mentally retarded clients. *Journal of Clinical Psychology, 54,* 529–535.

Matson, J. L. (1988). *Psychopathology in mentally retarded adults: A test manual.* Overland Park, IL: International Diagnostic Systems.

Matson, J. L. (1997). *The Assessment of Dual Diagnosis (ADD).* Baton Rouge, LA: Disability Consultants, LLC.

Matson, J. L., Anderson, S. J., & Bamburg, J. W. (2000). The relationship of social skills to psychopathology for individuals with mild or moderate mental retardation. *British Journal of Developmental Disabilities, 90,* 15–22.

Matson, J. L., & Bamburg, J. W. (1998). Reliability of the Assessment of Dual Diagnosis (ADD). *Research in Developmental Disabilities, 19,* 89–95.

Matson, J. L., & Sevin, J. A. (1994). Theories of dual diagnosis in mental retardation. *Journal of Consulting and Clinical Psychology, 62,* 6–16.

McDaniel, W. F. (1997). Criterion-related diagnostic validity and test-retest reliability of the MMPI-168(L) in mentally retarded adolescents and adults. *Journal of Clinical Psychology, 53,* 485–489.

McDaniel, W. F., Childers, L. M., & Compton, D. C. (1997). Construct validity of the MMPI-168(L) with mentally retarded adults and adolescents. *Journal of Clinical Psychology, 53,* 724–732.

McDaniel, W. F., & Harris, D. W. (1999). Mental health outcomes in dually diagnosed individuals with mental retardation assessed with the MMPI-168(L): Case studies. *Journal of Clinical Psychology, 55,* 487–496.

McDaniel, W. F., Passmore, C. E., & Sewell, H. M. (2003). The MMPI-168(L) and ADD in assessing psychopathology in individuals with mental retardation: Between and within associations. *Research in Developmental Disabilities, 24,* 19–32.

McDaniel, W. F., & Turner, M. D. (2000). The MMPI-168(L) as an instrument for assessing the mental health of individuals with mental retardation. *Developmental Disabilities Bulletin, 28,* 67–85.

Meyer, R. G., & Deitsch, S. E. (1996). *The clinician's handbook: Integrated diagnostics, assessment, and intervention in adult and adolescent psychopathology* (4th ed.). Boston: Allyn and Bacon.

Nezu, A. M. (1994). Introduction to special section: Mental retardation and mental illness. *Journal of Consulting and Clinical Psychology, 62,* 4–5.

Overall, J. E., & Gomez-Mont, F. (1974). The MMPI-168 for psychiatric screening. *Educational and Psychological Measurement, 34,* 315–319.

Prout, H. T. (1993). Assessing psychopathology in persons with mental retardation: A review of the Reiss Scales. *Journal of School Psychology, 31,* 535–540.

Reiss, S. (1990). Prevalence of dual diagnosis in community-based day programs in the Chicago metropolitan area. *American Journal on Mental Retardation, 94,* 578–585.

Reiss, S. (1994). *The Reiss Screen for Maladaptive Behavior: Test Manual* (2nd ed.). Overland Park, IL: International Diagnostic Systems.

Reiss, S. (1997). Comments on the Reiss Screen for Maladaptive Behavior and its factor structure. *Journal of Intellectual Disability Research, 41,* 346–354.

Sadock, B. J., & Sadock, V. A. (2001). *Pocket handbook of psychiatric drug treatment.* Philadelphia: Lippincott Williams & Wilkins.

Sovner, R., & Lowry, M. A. (1990). A behavioral methodology for diagnosing affective disorders in individuals with mental retardation. *The Habilitative Mental Healthcare Newsletter, 9,* 55–61.

Stahl, S. M. (2000). *Essential psychopharmacology* (2nd ed.). New York: Oxford University Press.

Sturmey, P., & Bertman, L. J. (1994). Validity of the Reiss Screen for Maladaptive Behavior. *American Journal on Mental Retardation, 99,* 201–206.

2

Use of Behavioral Equivalents for Symptoms of Mood Disorders

Lauren Charlot

What Are Behavioral Equivalents?

 The term *behavioral equivalents* has been used in different ways. First, behavioral equivalents may be seen as operational definitions or descriptions of likely manifestations of psychiatric symptoms. In the case of people with ID and psychiatric disorders, behavioral equivalents are behaviors or statements that could be made or exhibited by the individual, or, more often, observed and reported by informants. Behavioral equivalents can be especially helpful in the psychiatric assessment of a person with ID who has a limited capacity to provide self-report of symptoms. When the term *behavioral equivalents* is used in this way, crying, having a sad facial appearance, smiling much less than usual, and saying such things as "I just don't care anymore" may all be viewed as manifestations or behavioral equivalents of a depressed affect that the client cannot report directly.

The term *behavioral equivalents* has also been used in a related but somewhat different way, to mean an actual alternative or atypical symptom of a psychiatric syndrome. For example, Clarke and Gomez (1999) suggested that self-injurious behavior, aggressive behavior, and screaming are atypical symptoms of depression in people with ID. These authors used a number of atypical symptoms identified among people with ID as substitutes for research diagnostic criteria for major depression. The symptom substitutes designed specifically for people with ID were used in place of diagnostic symptom criteria less commonly reported in studies of people with both ID and depression, such as excessive feelings of guilt (WHO, 1992). There may be some problems with this application of behavioral equivalents, however, because there may not be adequate data to decide if atypical symptoms described in people with ID are true, core symptoms of mood disorders. The issue of how such a determination could be made empirically is described in detail later in this chapter.

Sovner and Hurley (1982a, b, 1983) were the first to provide empirical evidence of major mood disorders in people with ID, though occasional case reports had appeared in the literature off and on for a number years (Sovner & Pary, 1993). Sovner and Hurley (1982a, b) were also the first to use the term *behavioral equivalents* for people with ID when they described possible manifestations of the symptom criteria for the DSM-III categories of major depressive disorder and bipolar disorder. In the intervening two decades, a number of investigations have confirmed the earlier observations of these authors: that people with ID can and do often meet DSM criteria for a major mood disorder. Sovner and Hurley emphasized the fact that neurological and developmental differences in functioning between typically developing individuals and people with ID could result in differences in clinical features of psychiatric illness. At the time, there was much concern that mood disorders were under-diagnosed in people with ID and that this was due in part to the fact that clinicians often failed to consider the impact of developmental variations on the clinical picture.

The behavioral descriptions first provided by Sovner and Hurley for each of the mood disorder symptom criteria were further elaborated by Lowry and Sovner (1992), who labeled them "symptomatic behaviors." Selection of the specific behavioral manifestations was based not only on the extensive clinical experiences of the authors and their comprehensive review of case reports, but also on the likely impact of developmental factors on the manifestations of mood disorders. New symptom areas were not suggested per se, but rather the unusual ways were described in which a person with ID might manifest depressed mood, anhedonia, psychomotor agitation, problems concentrating, excessive guilt, or hopelessness. The descriptions included statements that people with milder cognitive disabilities might make that would differ from the kinds of things a person without ID of a similar age might say, as well as such easily observed behaviors as the onset of or marked increase in pacing as a sign of psychomotor agitation. In each case, identification of the described symptom manifestation would provide evidence to the clinician of the presence of a given mood symptom.

Why Use Behavioral Equivalents?

There are special challenges in the assessment of mood problems in people with ID due to characteristic skill deficits in such areas as the ability to label and describe internal feeling states or to report personal and medical history reliably. People with mild ID are better able than are individuals with more severe cognitive impairments to provide reliable reports of internal states (Beck, Carlson, Russell, & Brownfield, 1987). However, this is not always the case. Some individuals, even with very mild cognitive disabilities, may not be able to describe feelings accurately. Consider the following interview of an inpatient with mild ID:

Dr. C.: Hi, M. I just wanted to ask you a few questions. Is that OK with you?

Mr. M.: You are a handsome woman. I like you.

Dr. C.: You are very kind. I like you, too. I was wondering how you have been feeling lately.

Mr. M.: I really do like you. Did you see my menu?

Dr. C.: Yes, I did. It looks good. So, I wanted to ask you: Have you been feeling happy lately?

Mr. M.: Yes! (*Mr. M. smiles broadly*).

Dr. C.: Have you been feeling sad at all lately?

Mr. M.: Yes! (*Mr. M. smiles broadly*).

In the case of people without expressive language skills, the concern is even more pronounced that a clinical interview will not yield reliable and valid information about the presence and history of mood symptoms. This concern is compounded by the fact people with ID rarely refer themselves for a psychiatric evaluation. In many cases, the reason for referral is based on the perceptions of others, and—more often than not—some form of a challenging behavior is the main precipitant to a referral (Charlot et al., 2002; Hurley, Folstein, & Lam, 2003). Because of this, studies of clinically referred individuals will almost always contain large numbers of people with ID and challenging behaviors. These challenging behaviors can become the sole focus of the assessment, since the chief complaint is really not what is troubling the patient, but what is troubling to caregivers. Frequently, psychiatric diagnostic assessment is based in large part on information provided by caregivers and family members. Research suggests that informants tend to over-report externalizing types of problems (Angold, 1988). If the focus of clinical evaluation is overly driven by the need to decelerate challenging behaviors, clinicians may miss signs and symptoms that would suggest an internalizing disorder.

Behavioral equivalents or descriptions may help to attenuate some of the difficulties associated with reliance on informant reports. The more observable or complete the operational definition of a given symptom is, the more likely people are to agree about what they saw or heard. Because of this, behavioral equivalents have the potential to greatly enhance reliability at the level of symptom identification in people with ID. If clinicians assessing people with ID are careful to review each symptom criteria and all of its potential manifestations with multiple informants, the quality of the clinical information obtained should be greatly enhanced.

There are several important caveats. First, informants must be people who have spent considerable amounts of time with the person about whom they are providing reports. The behavioral equivalents need to be clear, but also comprehensive, including multiple descriptions for each symptom criterion of the varied ways in which the symptom might be displayed. Though reliability is important, validity is a separate but equal concern. Reliability and validity of the behavioral equivalents recommended for mood disorders will be addressed in more detail later in this chapter.

Beyond Behavioral Equivalents

Using behavioral descriptions of diagnostic symptom criteria may provide an important methodology for finding out if mood symptoms are really present, and if certain clinical variations occur more in people with ID than in other clinical populations. However, behavioral equivalents must be viewed as providing only one piece of the diagnostic puzzle. To diagnose a mood disorder, the clinician must be certain that duration criteria are met. Mood problems that are transient in nature or constitute a response to a severe stressful event indicate the presence of a different clinical problem. (For further discussions of this issue, see Chapter 4, by Esbensen and Rojahn, and Chapter 5, by Crilly, Cain, and Davidson.) Symptoms should represent departures from previous levels of functioning. If a person has always had difficulty concentrating, and has no more difficulty at present than before, then difficulty concentrating should not be identified as a symptom of a depressive episode.

Mood disorders have a usual history and course, and they must be differentiated from other clinical problems of a similar nature. In the overall process of establishing these diagnoses, a comprehensive evaluation is necessary. All of the many varied factors that might contribute to the current clinical picture should be taken into account in the individual case formulation. A comprehensive diagnostic assessment includes a complete history and physical, observation and interview of the patient, informant interviews, review of labs and other medical studies, and a comprehensive review of documented medical, behavioral, and psychosocial history. Like any human behavior, mood symptoms occur in a context that must also be characterized, with consideration given to variables that may transact in complex ways to produce outcomes (Gardner, 2000; Harris, 1998).

Major Depressive Disorder and Bipolar Disorder in People With ID

Studies involving people with both ID and presumed mood disorders in which symptoms are described have helped guide the selection of behavioral equivalents. The phenomenology of mood disorders in people with ID has been investigated more extensively than that of most other Axis I psychiatric categories. However, DSM-IV field trials, and much of the research that has formed the basis for this and other major psychiatric nosologies, specifically excluded people with ID (American Psychiatric Association, 1968, 1994, 2000). The studies that have been conducted regarding the clinical picture of mood disorders in people with ID have used a wide variety of methods for sample selection, and different classification systems were used, including the DSM-IV or DSM-IV-TR systems and the ICD-10 system (American Psychiatric Association, 1994, 2000; WHO, 1992). In the majority of studies, these criteria were modified (Sturmey, 1993). Different changes were made in different studies. The rationale for changes was not always clear, nor were the changes empirically derived.

Most studies before 1993 involved descriptions of just a few cases, or reviews of case reports (see Davis, Judd, & Herrman, 1997a, b; Pawlarcyzk & Beckwith, 1987; Sovner & Hurley, 1983; Sovner & Pary, 1993; Sturmey, 1995). Investigations using larger samples appeared in the literature starting in 1993 (Charlot, Doucette, & Mezzacappa, 1993; Clark & Gomez, 1999; Davis et al., 1997a, b; Evans, Cotton, Einfield, & Florio, 1999; Johnson, Handen, Lubetsky, & Sacco, 1995; Marston, Perry, & Roy, 1997; McGuire & Chicoine, 1996; Meins, 1995; Meyers, 1998; Reiss & Rojahn, 1993, Tsiouris, 2001; Tsiouris, Mann, Patti, & Sturmey, 2003). Methods used to identify individuals as having major depression or bipolar disorder varied greatly, limiting the extent to which findings can be generalized. Despite these concerns, there were many similar reports of how depression and mania might manifest in people with ID.

Depressive Disorders

In Table 2.1, the percent rates for DSM-IV-TR symptom criteria for major depressive episode are reported for group studies in which these data were available. Rates for other symptoms such as anxiety, obsessive-compulsive behaviors, somatic complaints, and aggression are also provided. Several studies report irritable mood as a common symptom of people with ID who are diagnosed with depression (Charlot, 1997; Charlot et al., 1993; Davis et al., 1997a, b; McGuire & Chicoine, 1996; Meins, 1995; Reiss & Rojahn, 1993, Tsiouris, 2001; Tsiouris et al., 2003). Irritable mood is also common in childhood depression; as a result, it is an accepted alternative mood symptom criterion in the last three editions of the DSM in addition to depressed mood and anhedonia (American Psychiatric Association, 1980, 1987, 1994; Angold, 1988; Rutter, 1998). A lack of expressiveness or flat affect and a labile affect have been reported in depressed people with ID (Charlot, 1997; Cooper & Collacott, 1993; Sovner & Hurley, 1983). Both flat affect and labile affect have been described in studies of young children (Carlson & Kashani, 1988; Shafii & Shafii, 1992). Sovner and Hurley (1983) noted that it was often the informant rather than the individual with ID him or herself who was describing the individual as appearing sad, tearful, or crying.

A number of investigations found that people with ID had lost interest in things they had previously enjoyed (anhedonia), and many noted withdrawn behavior. It has been suggested by some investigators that psychomotor agitation may be more common than psychomotor retardation in individuals with both ID and depression (Meins, 1995; Sovner & Pary, 1993). Some individuals actually show a combination of both agitation and retardation (i.e., the individual is withdrawn and underactive at times, and then becomes restless or agitated in response to demands) (Charlot, 1997; Charlot et al., 1993; Johnson et al., 1995: Meins, 1995).

Depressed appearance, withdrawal, and somatic complaints have been found to differentiate children with both ID and mood disorders from a comparison group with other psychiatric diagnoses (Johnson et al., 1995). Similar findings have been described in studies of the phenomenology of mood problems in adults with ID (Charlot, 1997; Charlot et al., 1993; Lowry, 1998; Meins, 1995; Reiss & Rojahn, 1993). Withdrawal, fatigue, decreased appetite, and presence of an episodic pattern differentiated indi-

Table 2.1. Rates of symptoms of depression and associated symptoms in people with mental retardation and depression.

Study Symptom	Meyers 1998) n=19	Charlot 1997) n=70	Marston et al. 1997) n=36	Charlot et al. 1993) n=16	Hucker et al. (1979) n=11	Meins 1998) n=19	Clarke & Gomez 1999) n=11	Mcguire & Chicoine 1996) n=40	Johnson et al. 1995) n=50	Tsiouris (2001) n=22	Tsiouris et al. (2003) n=35
Depressed or sad	90	99	88	69	91	44	91	100		95	66
Anhedonia	79	84	66	69		53	91	100		54	23
Irritable Mood		93	28	100	36	47		78	22	40	66
Sleep problem	68	81	83	81		63	64	73	42	86	49
Wake early		40			82						
Weight change	58	45					45	55	10		
Weight loss			27	44	82	38				27	20
Weight gain						31					
Psychomotor	84					6	82				
Agitation		60	33			72		73		73	29
Retardation		49	16		82	22		83		36	46
Fatigue	26	89	28	69		34	91			32	18
Guilt	5	32	22	19		22	19			13	11
Hopelessness		24	16								
Decreased concentration	16	68	22	87	73	25	9	83			40
Suicidal ideations	32	34	16	6	55	22			42		3
Mood swings		53	17						24		
Withdrawn		76	33	81	91			88	29	45	54
Somatic		34		31	36						
Delusions		16	3	12	45					9	11
Hallucinations	10	13		0	9			70			
Anxiety	21	49	28					60		50	
Aggression	21	64	33	75		30	82		80	50	20
SIB	32	41				34	36		40	68	3

viduals with mood disorders from a matched sample of people with ID who had other psychiatric diagnoses (Charlot et al., 1993).

People with mild ID have been described with cognitive symptoms of depression, including suicidal ideation, excessive guilt, and hopelessness (Charlot, 1997; Davis et al., 1997a, b; Hurley, 1998; Paclawskyj & Beckwith, 1987; Sovner & Hurley, 1983; Sovner & Pary, 1993; Walters, Barrett, Knapp, & Borden, 1995). Cognitive symptoms of depression are rarely described in people with severe or profound ID, because these individuals typically have no way to communicate such things, and they likely do not have the cognitive developmental capacity to experience them (Charlot, 1997; Charlot et al., 1993; Clarke & Gomez, 1999; Meyers, 1998; Ross & Oliver, 2003).

Like many people without ID, depressed individuals with ID have been reported to present with anxiety, obsessive-compulsive disorder, psychotic features, catatonia, or mutism (Charlot, 1997; Hurley, 1996; Hurley & Moore, 1999; McGuire & Chicoine, 1996; Meyers, 1998; Sovner & Hurley, 1983). High rates of aggression and self-injurious behavior have been documented in studies of individuals with depression or mania. The nature of the relationship between challenging behaviors and mood syndromes in people with ID has been controversial, and it relates closely to the topic of how behavioral equivalents may be viewed as atypical core features of depression and mania in people with ID (see the discussion below).

DC-LD and Behavioral Equivalents.

In the United Kingdom, the faculty for the Psychiatry of Learning Disabilities of the Royal College of Psychiatrists (2001) adapted ICD-10 criteria known as *Diagnostic Criteria for Learning Disabilities (DC-LD)*. The recommended modifications and additions to ICD-10 in the guide are based on the consensus of many European experts in the field of ID as well as a review of the literature. In the DC-LD, variations in the clinical features of mania and depression are described. In the case of major depression, the ICD-10 requirements that the patient recognizes and communicates internal states, such as ideas of guilt and unworthiness, pessimistic views of the future, and ideas or acts of self-harm, were also eliminated. Two symptoms were added: (a) an increase in a specific maladaptive behavior and (b) onset of or increase in somatic symptoms or physical health concerns. In the DC-LD, loss of interest or pleasure in activities can be manifested by an apparent loss of self-care skills, a refusal to cooperate with the usual physical care provided by others, or a reduction in the quantity of speech or communication. It is emphasized that the individuals with both ID and depression may experience a loss of confidence, as manifested by an increase in reassurance-seeking behavior or by fearfulness.

Bipolar Disorder

Sovner and Hurley (1983) and Sovner and Pary (1993) reviewed case reports and case series in which bipolar disorder had been diagnosed in people with ID. They concluded that most individuals met DSM criteria for a manic episode. Several subsequent studies also found that people with ID who received a clinical diagnosis of a bipolar disorder displayed many of the DSM or ICD symptom criteria for bipolar disorder. Irritable mood, labile affect, overactivity, and decreased sleep are the most frequently reported features. Lowry and Sovner (1992) described two adults with severe to profound ID who were diagnosed with bipolar disorder. Both individuals showed symptoms of mania and depression, and both had aggression or self-injurious behavior that varied in intensity with the onset of acute mood symptoms.

Affective lability, usually referred to as mood swings, and irritable mood have been described in people with ID who were diagnosed with mania. Cognitive symptoms, such as inflated self-esteem or grandiosity, appear infrequently in individuals with severe or profound ID (Charlot et al., 1993). Pressured speech may be manifested as an increased rate of speech or an increased speech volume, and changes in ability level or skipping from one activity to another may be a sign of distractibility (Pary, Friedlander, & Capone, 1999).

Cain et al. (2003) conducted a retrospective chart review of 166 outpatients, and diagnosed 69 individuals with a bipolar disorder based on the clinical review of recorded information. A comparison group of people with ID and other psychiatric diagnoses was used. Aggression, self-injurious behavior, and other disruptive behaviors as well as irritable mood were most commonly described in the patients diagnosed with bipolar disorder. Having an episodic pattern of illness may also suggest the possibility of a mood disorder and has actually been found to differentiate people with both ID and a mood disorder from their peers with other psychiatric diagnoses (Charlot et al., 1993). Some authors have cautioned that cycles, frequently seen as a hallmark sign of bipolar disorder, may actually occur in relation to an array of other factors, including seasonal changes in staffing patterns, seasonal allergies, cluster headaches, or other episodic variables (Pary, Levitas, & Hurley, 1999).

Individuals with both ID and bipolar disorder have higher rates of rapid cycling when compared with other clinical populations (Charlot et al., 1993; Glue, 1989; Jones &

Berney, 1987; King, 1999; King, Fay, & Croghan, 2000; Reid & Naylor, 1976; Sovner & Pary, 1993; Vanstraelen & Tyrer, 1999). Vanstraelen and Tyrer (1999) reviewed a number of case reports, including a total of 40 individuals with ID who were diagnosed with rapid-cycling bipolar disorder. As in the general case reports of bipolar disorder in people with ID, irritability, overactivity, sleeplessness, and agitation were noted in most cases, whereas pressured speech was reported primarily in people with mild ID.

In the DC-LD section addressing mania, modifications to ICD-10 were described. Reduced sleep could sometimes be just "an hour less than usual" (Royal College of Psychiatrists, 2001). Pressured speech and increased talkativeness might appear as increased vocalization in people who have limited expressive language skills. "Loss of usual social inhibitions and inappropriate behavior" was described, including talking to strangers, over-familiarity, intrusiveness, and talking across others' conversation. Also included was engaging in nonsexual bodily functions in public (that is, urinating) when such behaviors are "out of keeping with the person's usual discretion." DC-LD noted that during an episode of mania, individuals may engage in reckless behavior or activities that would usually be avoided, including giving away possessions or getting into dangerous situations.

Dysthymia and Cyclothymia

Very little has been written about these less severe but more chronic variants of major depressive and bipolar disorders (Jancar & Gunaratne, 1994). Behavioral equivalents for these syndromes might also be developed in time, and it seems likely that these syndromes occur in people with ID but are missed and not attended to in studies of mood disorders in the populations. Comorbidity of dysthymia, anxiety, and depression are known to be high (Kovacs, Feinberg, Crouse-Novak, Paulauskas, & Finkelstein, 1984). Early onset of dysthymia may be a risk factor in major depressive disorder. Cyclothymia may be a precursor to bipolar disorder type I or II.

Since the majority of symptom criteria for the two syndromes are the same as for depression and mania, behavioral descriptions of the probable manifestations in people with ID could readily be applied. Key issues in differential diagnosis therefore focus on the chronic nature of the disorder and the intensity or severity of the symptoms. In most cases, documented reports about mania and depression assume episodes are intense whenever accompanied by challenging behavior, though this assumption may not be valid. On the other hand, cyclothymia and dysthymia may not be associated with aggression or other disruptive behaviors as often as seems to be the case for major depressive disorder and bipolar disorder. Thus, clinically referred populations may be less likely to contain individuals who have these syndromes.

Challenging Behaviors and Their Relationship to Mood Disorders

Recent research has provided important support for the notion that externalizing behaviors may co-occur with mood disorders at high rates in people with ID, but they are not specific to these disorders. In fact, some investigators have argued that such problems as aggression may be seen as a surface manifestation of a wide array of possible sources of distress in people with ID (Gardner, 2000). Aggression is the most frequently documented atypical manifestation of mood disorders, and a number of investigations have documented a relationship between irritability or anger, aggression, and depression or mania (Charlot et al., 1993; Johnson et al., 1995; Lowry & Sovner, 1992; Marston et al., 1997; Meins, 1995; Reiss & Rojahn, 1993). For example, Johnson et al. (1995) found that 80% of inpatient children with ID diagnosed with an affective disorder had comorbid aggression. However, though frequently reported, this relationship between aggression and depression does not appear to be specific to ID. In the Johnson et al. (1995) study, a comparison group of children with other psychiatric diagnoses also displayed high rates of aggression (84%).

Tsiouris et al., (2003) reported similar findings in an adult clinical sample including 93 people with ID who were clinically evaluated to determine psychiatric diagnosis. Thirty-three subjects met unmodified DSM-IV criteria for a major depressive disorder (MDD). Individuals with a diagnosis of MDD were then compared with subjects with ID who received different psychiatric diagnoses. Almost one-half of the subjects had either severe or profound cognitive disabilities. The investigators were interested in whether earlier findings by Marston et al. (1997), which had suggested that aggression was a common and diagnostically specific manifestation of depression in people with ID, would be replicated. In the Tsiouris et al. (2003) study, the most frequently reported symptoms in the depressed group included anxiety (86%), depressed affect (66%), irritability (66%), loss of interest (54%), social isolation (54%), lack of emotion (49%), sleep disturbance (49%), and loss of confidence (49%). A number of symptoms occurred at significantly higher rates in the depressed versus nondepressed group, including depressed affect, tearfulness, loss of interest, lack of emotion, sleep disturbance, diurnal variation, psychomotor retardation, loss of appetite, weight loss, loss of confidence, lack of energy, social isolation, and constipation. The authors performed a factor analysis that yielded a strong single-factor resolution. The items of depressed affect, loss of interest, loss of energy, psychomotor retardation, and lack of emotional response comprised the "depression" factors. Subjects were then separated into three groups: not depressed, mildly depressed (in remission), and depressed. Statistically significant differences were detected for the depression factor scale for the three groups. Of special note was the finding that challenging behaviors did not differ across the three groups, and did not correlate with the validated measure of depression.

Challenging Behaviors and Mood Disorders: Hypothesized Links

There are some theories about the ways in which challenging behaviors may be specifically linked to mood disorders. Individuals who are depressed or manic may learn to escape or avoid unwanted demands or situations by screaming, breaking things, assaulting others, or becoming self–injurious (Lowry & Sovner, 1992). Lowry and Charlot (1996) noted that escape-motivated aggression might emerge in situations in which it had not been seen before, because depression, especially anhedonia, may alter the response to a potential triggering event. For example, an individual might be described as enjoying his or her day program prior to the onset of depression. If acutely depressed, the same person might refuse activities and might experience requests to engage in routines as aversive events. The depressed individual might assault caregivers to escape demands to be active, particularly when he or she has a limited repertoire of possible responses. In this way, dysphoric mood acts as a setting event for aggression. Lowry and Sovner (1992) discuss how challenging behaviors appear to be state-dependent features of mood episodes in people with ID who might show either the onset of or an increase in challenging behaviors with the onset of an acute mood episode.

There has been an increasing recognition that internal states of distress can act as setting events (Gardner, 2000). People may first learn to aggress in the context of an acute mood episode. Later, even with the resolution of this phase of illness, the aggressive responding may be maintained. In this situation, escape-motivated aggression becomes a part of the individual's ongoing behavioral repertoire.

Challenging behaviors may emerge or escalate when an individual has physical discomfort or pain, especially if a person's ability to communicate about internal states is limited (Charlot et al., 2002; Cooper, 1999; McDermott et al., 1997; Ryan & Sunada, 1997). For example, Tsiouris et al. (2003) noted elevated rates of constipation in depressed versus nondepressed subjects with ID. Individuals with ID may suffer negative side effects from medications and may under-report or inaccurately report these internal effects (Charlot et al., 2002). Pary, Friedlander, and Capone (1999) and Sovner and Pary (1993) described cases in which akathisia was mistaken for mania, and drug-induced fatigue and withdrawal were mistaken for depression in people with ID.

A tendency for aggression or other impulsive behaviors to emerge in stressful circumstances or when a person is depressed or manic might also be linked to central nervous system deficits associated with ID. In many cases, the specific nature of brain impairment is not well characterized. The specific and varied ways in which brain functions are impaired may also impact on the manifestation of psychiatric syndromes and could predispose people with ID to become aggressive in the setting of an acute mood episode.

Charlot et al. (1993) suggested another link between depression and aggression. They argued that aggression may be a surface feature of irritability or anger in a person with a limited behavioral repertoire. The notion that people with ID are more prone to aggression when irritable corresponds well to Lowry and Sovner's (1992) observations. Based on this, one would predict that people with more severe ID or who have expressive language deficits would be more likely to become aggressive under stress, simply because fewer options for responding to problems are available. People with ID may be more likely to display challenging behaviors when depressed, manic, sick, frustrated, tired, or distressed in any way. In a similar vein, externalizing behaviors and dysphoric mood have been studied in children. Examination of developmental effects on features of mood syndromes may provide an additional important source of information for the selection of behavioral equivalents.

Lessons From the Past: Masked Depression

Important lessons might be learned from the study of childhood depression that parallel the current trend toward the use of behavioral equivalents in diagnosing mood disorders in people with ID (Charlot, 2003). In both clinical populations, there was previously much doubt that depression was even possible. In the case of children, it became clear that depression occurs, but it may look different in children than it does in adults. The concept of "masked depression" was introduced to account for these differences and to explain the under-diagnosis of depression in children (Carlson & Cantwell, 1983). It was commonly reported that depressed children expressed somatic complaints, had tantrums, ran away, refused to go to school, were restless, and often did not show the classic sad appearance so frequently described in depressed adults. These challenging behaviors and atypical features were said to mask the depression, which lay hidden beneath the surface.

New diagnostic criteria were suggested, and various atypical features were suggested as alternative symptom criteria for depression in children. Over time, however, serious problems emerged with the notion of a masked depression, because almost every psychopathologic state or trait was added to the list of possible behavioral equivalents of childhood depression (Cantwell, 1996). The eventual resolution can be seen in the DSM-IV (American Psychiatric Association, 1994). Adult-based criteria, which were subsequently validated in numerous studies of depression in children, are essentially retained with only minor modification. In their place is a section describing age effects on clinical features of the syndrome (American Psychiatric Association, 2000).

Similar concerns might be raised in regards to current trends in the study of depression in people with ID, because some researchers have advocated the use of aggression or other challenging behaviors as depressive equivalents. Others have argued that DSM-IV-TR mood disorder criteria need not be changed in significant ways. Rather, methods that can increase reliability in assessment of the existing criteria are needed. These authors point to research demonstrating that challenging behaviors are reported just as frequently in people with ID diagnosed with other psychiatric syndromes as they have been noted in individuals with ID and a mood disorder diagnosis (Cain et al., 2003; Charlot, 1998; McBrien, 2003; Tsiouris, 2001; Tsiouris et al., 2003).

Behavioral Equivalents As Atypical Symptoms of a Mood Disorder

Most authors and researchers agree that some people with ID present with different symptoms of depression and mania, when compared with individuals without ID. DSM-IV diagnostic criteria have been found to be reliable and valid for people without ID, but have not been studied in a systematic way in people with ID. How can investigators demonstrate empirically when a challenging behavior—or any behavior—should be regarded as a true atypical symptom of a mood disorder? When is it empirically justified to list a behavior as a new criterion that applies only to the diagnosis of mood disorders in a person with ID? One way in which investigators have selected symptom substitutes or added a new symptom criterion is to note a high rate of co-occurrence of symptoms of the psychiatric syndrome with a specific atypical symptom or problem. As discussed, many researchers have pointed to the fact that challenging behaviors, such as aggression, are reported at elevated rates in samples of people with ID diagnosed with depression or mania and may not be specifically associated with a mood disorder.

Meins (1995) adjusted depression criteria from the DSM-IV requiring a shorter duration (1 week versus 2 weeks) and fewer overall symptoms (4 of 9 versus 5 of 9) to diagnose the disorder in a sample of people with ID. If a subject had fewer symptoms, the MDD diagnosis was given only if he or she also displayed "atypical symptoms such as aggressive or self-injurious behavior." As noted earlier, Clarke and Gomez (1999) added new symptoms to the ICD-10 criteria for depression, based on a review of the literature showing these behaviors to occur at high rates among people with ID diagnosed with depression. New symptom criteria included "crying or sobbing" as a substitute for depressed mood, and decreased ability to care for self, decreased mobility, or marked reduction in communication as substitutes for decreased energy. An increase in or onset of self-injurious behavior or aggressive behavior was selected as a substitute symptom criterion in place of recurrent thoughts of death or suicide, while a "marked increase in screaming" was employed as a substitute symptom criterion for decreased ability to concentrate. Davis et al. (1997b) dropped certain DSM-IV items and added substitutes in their assessment of people with ID and possible depression. Loss of energy was dropped as a criterion for depression for people with ID, and "crying excessively" was added.

There are some significant problems with the methodologies employed to select symptom substitutes. In these investigations in which behavioral equivalents or symptom substitutes were employed, no comparison groups were studied including people with ID who suffered from other psychiatric syndromes. To decide empirically that a symptom is a core mood symptom, it would seem important to establish a more unique relationship to the disorder by demonstrating much higher rates of aggression in depression than in schizophrenia, generalized anxiety disorder, PTSD, etc. To the contrary, investigations in which comparison groups of people with other psychiatric diagnoses were studied, consistently reported challenging behaviors occur at high rates in people diagnosed with almost any psychiatric disorder.

More obvious problems with studies that have examined the phenomenology of mood disorder in people with ID is that sample selection techniques have not been rigorous, calling into question the extent to which results can be generalized to most people with ID. Even when clinical samples are used, an important concern is that people with ID are typically referred for psychiatric evaluation because of externalizing behavior problems, so clinical samples are *de facto* likely to contain large percentages of subjects with challenging behaviors. Finally, case ascertainment remains a difficult stumbling block if clinical diagnosis is made in the usual manner (Ross & Oliver, 2003). In studies to date, clinical assessments performed to establish cases have not been conducted in a controlled way—for example, with taped sessions and multiple raters to establish that the gold-standard clinical diagnosis is valid and reliable.

Although a given individual may become aggressive due to irritable or dysphoric mood at this time, there appears to be little empirical support for the contention that aggression is a core symptom of depression or mania in people with ID. On a case-by-case basis, clinicians may need to determine if challenging behaviors have a direct relationship to a mood syndrome. In future investigations, it will be important to systematically study the relationship between any suggested possible symptom substitutes and known core symptoms of mood disorder. Clinical samples should include matched comparison groups of people with ID and other psychiatric diagnoses. Rates of a large number of symptoms and observed behaviors should be contrasted between groups. Only after a set of symptoms has been reliably assessed and found to be significantly more common in groups of people with both ID and depression or mania than in matched samples of people with both ID and other psychiatric disorders, can symptom substitutes be recommended. In the interim, a parsimonious tactic may be to begin by using DSM-IV-TR symptom criteria providing clear descriptions or behavioral anchors for each symptom criterion, to suggest ways in which that symptom may manifest in people with ID. This would promote greater reliability at the level of symptom identification. The efficacy or validity of the behavioral descriptions can be empirically studied. Over time, data may support further modifications of the existing DSM-IV-TR or ICD-10 criteria. As noted, the process could parallel the one that occurred in relation to the study of the validity and reliability of DSM diagnostic criteria for mood disorders in children.

Using a Developmental Framework

In addition to closely examining the research on the phenomenology of mood disorders, use of a developmental perspective can enhance diagnostic assessment in people with ID (Charlot, 1998). A good deal of evidence exists to support the contention that many people with ID will pass through the same developmental stages as children without ID in a similar sequence (Zigler, Hodapp & Burack, 1990; Harris, 1998). Youth with ID do not progress through all of the typical stages, but, rather, they plateau at earlier developmental levels. Usually, people with ID also progress through these developmental stages more slowly (Zigler et al., 1990).

People with ID are a heterogeneous group, and there are important exceptions to these general rules about developmental effects. Certain individuals with specific ID syndromes or who have brain damage underlying intellectual impairment may present with variations in cognitive structures seen in typically developing children of a similar overall mental age (Cichetti & Ganeban, 1990). Some people with ID show a great deal of scatter in test batteries that measure an array of social and cognitive capacities. Most notable are people with pervasive developmental disorders. For example, a current patient of the author's who has autistic disorder and bipolar I disorder is capable of doing 50-piece puzzles independently, but he cannot sight-read most letters or very simple words. He can speak in sentences, albeit with poor syntax, but he has great difficulty making simple requests and has poor functional use of language. Most of the time, his language is scripted and repetitive. Familiar staff can tell when he is in a good or bad mood, but he rarely smiles or laughs, showing a very restricted range of affect. Mood is inferred from such facial expressions as a furrowed brow and such observable behaviors as withdrawing to bed and refusing things he usually likes to do or as screaming and loudly vocalizing.

Understanding the way that people with ID function developmentally at baseline can be of great help when looking for mood symptoms and trying to determine if a given behavior is really a departure from normal functioning. Research has been conducted regarding developmental effects on mood disorders in children and adolescents (Angold, 1988; Carlson & Kashani, 1988). Similarities to the findings reported about mood disorders in people with ID are striking. In young depressed children, sad appearance, irritable mood, labile affect, somatic complaints, and withdrawn behavior have been documented (Carlson & Kashani, 1988; Shafii & Shafii, 1992). Very young children do not tend to express hopelessness and guilt feelings, but they frequently show a more global pattern of deterioration and display externalizing behavior problems (Carlson & Kashani, 1988). These observations in regards to children seem consistent with the concept of cognitive disintegration introduced by Sovner and Hurley (1983).

Harris (1998) argues that clinicians should consider the developmental level of the individual with ID when performing a psychiatric assessment, because developmental level will affect which symptoms are likely or even possible. In the DSM-IV, age features of major depressive disorder and bipolar disorder are described. Irritable mood, withdrawn behavior, somatic complaints and associated conduct problems are developmental features seen in depressed children. Cognitive developmental differences between adults and children are thought to have an impact on these phenomenological differences between age groups. Young children characteristically process information differently from adults. These differences make some mood symptoms more or less likely. Developmental differences may be due in part to variations in the maturity of neural circuits that form the substrate for specific cognitive capacities. For example, very young children tend to show less of the cognitive symptoms of depression, such as guilt and hopelessness, possibly because even children with stable mood process information in a concrete manner tied primarily to the here and now. In some cases, the reasons for age variations in illness are unclear. Mixed episodes may be more common in youth with bipolar disorder who are often first misdiagnosed with schizophrenia, representing a phenomenon that has been well documented but remains poorly understood.

Psychotic symptoms can occur during a mood episode and have been reported in people with ID (Hurley, 1996; Hurley & Moore, 1999; Sovner & Pary, 1993). Recognition of thought disorder in people with ID and in children with language disorders can be difficult (Charlot, 1998; Hurley, 1996; Rapoport & Ismond, 1996). Hurley (1996) suggested that self-talk, imaginary friends, and fantasy, which are normally appearing phenomena at certain developmental stages, might be mistaken for psychotic symptoms in people with ID. Good operational definitions of symptoms can help make clear what has or has not been observed and what has been reported by the individual him or herself. These observations then must be viewed in light of the individual's developmental level, and what is typical behavior for a person with this level and quality of cognitive skill.

It is important to note that individual variations have a large impact on the nature of psychiatric syndromes. Using a developmental framework to help guide the process of thinking about behavioral equivalents does not imply in any way that the behavior of people with ID can be best understood as being a simple function of mental age. On the contrary, developmental psychologists emphasize that the complex nature of human behavior results from transactions among a wide array of factors, including psychological, psychosocial, genetic, physiological, and experiential factors (Sroufe & Rutter, 1984). One small part of the highly complex human behavior formula includes how people process information and interpret experiences, as well as how they communicate with others. Some of these specific processes are constrained by one's genetic plan, brain architecture, and cognitive developmental phenomena. An appreciation of the developmental domains of functioning and how these are altered in people with ID may help to inform the difficult task of differential diagnosis of psychiatric illness in the population, and suggest certain behavioral equivalents to select for further investigation.

Case Examples

Susan

Susan was a 28-year-old woman with Down syndrome and moderate ID referred for assessment due to a variety of significant changes in behavior. She lived in a group residence with three other people with ID, where she had resided for several years. Over a period of 4 months, she became increasingly irritable, stopped attending her day program, and lost 20 pounds. Her hygiene deteriorated, and she started to refuse activities she had formerly enjoyed, such as shopping and dining out. She began sleeping more, taking frequent naps throughout the day. She began sleeping in a chair in the living room, refusing to go to her bedroom to sleep. She was angry when people asked her to bathe, and once she assaulted staff when being prompted to shower. Her staff reported that Susan seemed to be exhausted by the smallest physical effort, even though she slept a lot, and that she was much less active than she had been in the past. Susan's sister, who was her legal guardian, was very concerned and described how Susan used to be social, often smiling and joking with others. Reportedly, Susan was previously able to talk in short sentences, but she had recently stopped speaking, apart from periodically muttering in low tones to her favorite stuffed animal (see table 22).

Her primary physician prescribed Risperdal® and suggested that she might be psychotic. She was found to have constipation and a fungal skin infection, and these problems were treated and resolved. Hypothyroidism had previously been detected, and she was started on Synthroid®, but she remained slowed and fatigued following normalization of her thyroid-stimulating hormone. When referred for the present psychiatric evaluation, she was diagnosed with major depressive disorder. Her sister asked if Susan might have dementia, and she described apparent memory problems that emerged after risperidone had been started. It was felt that the speed with which Susan's decline occurred was more consistent with a diagnosis of depression, and that risperidone may have caused sedative effects that might depress cognitive functions. Risperidone was tapered and stopped, because there were no clear symptoms of psychosis. Citalopram was started and was titrated to a dose of 40 mgs qd over a period of 1 month. A behavioral treatment plan was also started to promote her participation in activities. She gradually began to appear less fatigued. Her affect brightened. She was starting to smile, and she resumed attendance at her day program. At follow-up, 4 months after the initiation of her antidepressant treatment, she had returned to baseline levels of functioning.

Table 2.2. Behavioral equivalents for Susan's diagnosis of major depressive episode.

DSM-IV-TR criteria for major depressive episode	Behavioral equivalents or manifestations for Susan
A. five or more symptoms present during same 2 weeks and represent a change from previous functioning. At least one is either (1) depressed mood or (2) loss of interest or pleasure	*see below*
(1) Depressed mood most of the day, nearly every day, as indicated by either subjective report or observation made by other. Note: In children and adolescents, may be irritable mood.	• Never smiled or laughed anymore • Gave short angry answers to questions • Described by caregivers as irritable often • *Other times, her affect seemed "flat" (on real expression on her face)*
(2) Markedly diminished interest or pleasure in all, or almost all activities most of the day, nearly every day (as indicated by either subjective account or observation made by others)	• *Said "no" to almost anything she was asked to do* • *Refused going to all of the activities she used to greatly enjoy* • *Agitated when prompted to attend social activites she once enjoyed.* *Prior to these recent problem, she had been usually social. She had smiled a lot, laughed, and showed a sence of humor; spoke in full sentences; enjoyed going out to eat and shopping; and liked attending her day program.*
(3) Significant wight loss when not dieting or weight gain (e.g, a change of 5% of body wright per month), or decrease or increase in appetite nearly every day.	• *Started refusing meals* • *Lost 20 lbs in 3 months*
(4) Insomnia or hypersomnia nearly every day.	• *Began to sleep excessively* • *Slept in naps off and on all day*
(5) Psychomotor agitation or retardation nearly every day.(observed by others)	• *Decreased talking* • *Much less physically active than before* • *This was noted by caregivers and family*
(6) Fatigue or loss of energy nearly every day.	• *Refused, or becomes agitated about, activities that required physical effort.* • *Spent ecxessive amounts of time sitting in a chair in the living room*
(7) Feelings of worthlessness or excessive or inappropriate guilt (which may be delusional) nearly everyday.	Not observed or reported
(8) Diminished ability to think or concentrate.	• *Diminished self-care skills* • *Stopped attending work program*
(9) Recuurent thoughts of death, suicidal ideation without a specific plan or a suicide attempt or a specific plan to commit suicide.	Not observed or reported

B. The symptoms do not meet criteria for a mixed episode.	No manic syptoms were described during the period above when depressed symptoms were prominent.
C. The symptoms cause clinically significant distress ot impairment in social, occupational, or other important areas of functioning	• *Symptoms caused major disruption in her life* • *Stopped work program* • *Family expressed great concern* • *Symptoms present for 4 months*
D. The symptoms are not due to the direct physiological effects of a substance (e.g. a drug of abuse, medication) or a general medical condition.	*Patient has constipation, fungal skin infection, and hypothyroidism. Lethargy had been noted on Risperdal®. After Risperdal ® was stopped, hormone replacement lead to a euthyroid condition, constipation resolved, symptoms of depression persisted.*
E. Symptoms not better accounted for by bereavement—i.e., after loss of loved one, symptoms persist > 2 months or marked functional impairment, morbid preoccupation with worthlessness, suicidal ideation, psychotic symptoms, or psychomotor retardation.	• *Symptoms had been evident for about 4 months*

Tommy

Tommy was an 18-year-old male with moderate ID and autistic disorder referred for inpatient psychiatric admission due to an increase in severe aggressive outbursts. He was up at night demanding car rides, which his mother would take him on to avoid aggressive outbursts. He attacked his mother in the car and assaulted people at school. His aggressive behavior began to increase about 3 months prior to the admission, although aggression had been a problem for him since puberty for about the past 4 years. He had formerly engaged in some more minor and less frequent aggression, which increased in both frequency and intensity. He was started on Risperdal® in the fall, and this initially seemed to help. He had a generalized tonic clonic seizure after this, for the first time in his life. He was started on Depakene® at this time. He then looked sedated, acted lethargic, and he was drooling. He had decreased verbal output. He became incontinent. He was taken off of risperidone and his valproic acid dose was lowered. His past medical history included constipation as well as his seizure and abnormal EEG.

At the time of this admission, he was having difficulty sleeping. He was up much of the night, but he still did not appear tired during the day. Staff and family talked about his angry facial expression and what was described as a "dark look" on his face. At other times, he would seem less irritable, and he would begin to wrestle with staff or tickle in a playful manner. Unfortunately, this almost always turned into an aggressive episode. In general, he was sensitive to noise—in particular, he was bothered by such machines as the vacuum cleaner and the dishwasher. He would become very aggressive whenever peers on the unit were loud. He would also aggress when he was prompted to engage in tasks requiring him to focus his attention. At baseline, he had sat and enjoyed doing puzzles, but he had recently been pacing constantly. He seemed unable to focus on the tasks that had formerly been easy for him. His family asked if he was losing skills, because he also did not wash himself well anymore when he showered which was something he had formerly been able to do. At baseline, he had spoken in short sentences and phrases, but his speech was scripted and repetitive, and he had a limited functional use of language. During the past few weeks, he had been screaming frequently, and vocalizing more.

His mother reported that, as a child, he had delayed developmental milestones. He had been toilet-trained age 7–8 years. He had always had limited language skills. He had actually seemed to regress and lose some language skills about age 3–4 years. He did have some limited functional language use and seemed to have much better receptive versus expressive skills. There was a family history of major depressive disorder, anxiety disorder, bipolar disorder, and obsessive-compulsive disorder.

During his inpatient stay, he was able to tolerate a higher does of Depakene® when Risperdal® was tapered, and he did begin to sleep and showed less agitation, as well as a decrease in his extra-pyramidal symptoms. For a short time, he seemed improved, and he began to respond more to a high-density reinforcement plan encouraging his functional use of language and his completion of a structured daily schedule. He then gradually began to withdraw to his room, and his appetite decreased dramatically. He eventually stopped talking altogether. He refused any of the activities he had normally enjoyed, such as watching videos, coloring, or doing puzzles. Although he had usually spent time alone off and on, even when functioning well, he always had seemed to seek out ways to watch the other patients. He had enjoyed doing so, even though his social skills with peers were quite limited. During this time period, however, he rarely moved around, and after a while, he could not be encouraged to come out of his room. He began to assault staff who prompted him to engage in activities. He was sleeping off and on at night, and he was having episodes of assaultive behavior at night. He napped on and off through the day. He became constipated over time. After Zoloft® was added, his depression lifted, and he began to return to baseline levels of functioning. His appetite improved markedly. He started to talk again. He enjoyed activities and would seek out activities by going to get a puzzle and handing it to staff. He also began to have a more regular sleep pattern, though he still had some nights of wakefulness. His constipation was treated and resolved and was less of a problem when he became more physically active again. He did not have any further seizure activity. He was discharged home and remained stable at his 1-year follow-up, though he continued to have minor aggression and occasional sleep problems.

Tommy was diagnosed with bipolar disorder, and he also carried a diagnosis of autistic disorder. His symptoms of mania included his irritable mood, as shown by a lowered threshold for aggression that occurred, accompanied by clear facial expressions that many familiar caregivers labeled as angry-looking or "dark." He also sometimes displayed an over-excited mood, as shown by an increase in a baseline tendency to get over-stimulated and over-excited in a playful way that turned into aggression. There was also evidence from verbal behaviors, such as screaming and vocalizing much more than usual, of a decreased capacity to focus his attention (not being able to finish tasks he used to finish, decreased self-care skills), decreased sleep without loss of energy, and psychomotor agitation, shown through his pacing and restlessness. His illness had an episodic course, and after his mania was better controlled, he gradually slipped into a depression. His depression was characterized by anhedonia, shown through his decreased interest in games, puzzles, and movies; withdrawn behavior; a disrupted sleep pattern; fatigue, shown through his napping during the day and staying in bed a lot; psychomotor retardation, shown through a decreased motor activity level and speech; and decreased appetite.

When his case was further explored with his family, it became evident that he may have had earlier mood episodes, but changes in his behavior were attributed to his autistic disorder.

Summary

Behavioral equivalents, when defined as behavioral descriptions, can guide the clinician, providing concrete examples of what a person with ID might say or do when experiencing a particular mood symptom. The ultimate goal of using the behavioral descriptions of symptoms is to increase our ability to correctly identify mood and other psychiatric disorders in people with ID. People with ID may show some variations in the surface features of mood syndromes that are due to developmental level or to the effects of central nervous system impairments. Also, characteristic deficits in expressive language skills make it difficult to determine if symptoms that are usually self-reported by patients are present or not. Informants often provide the bulk of the information about symptoms experienced by people with ID. If multiple, familiar informants are carefully interviewed about the presence or absence of each mood symptom using behavioral descriptions for each, reliability is likely to be enhanced.

Even with this, many other sources of clinical data should be used to arrive at a complex, individual case formulation, including recorded information regarding the clinical history, family history of illness, laboratory data, physical examination, and ongoing observations and assessments of the individual.

Behavioral equivalents may be especially helpful in the assessment of people with severe and profound ID, as well as people with pervasive developmental disorders. Behavioral equivalents may also help in the development of research diagnostic criteria that could lead to a more valid and reliable system of diagnosing mood syndromes in people with ID. In much of the literature, the term *behavioral equivalents* has been used to refer to atypical symptoms or possible substitute symptoms for existing diagnostic symptom criteria. The most commonly cited behavioral equivalents of mood disorders in people with ID are aggression and self-injurious behaviors. At this time, the research that has formed the basis for the selection of behavioral equivalents as symptom substitutes has many methodological flaws. In more controlled investigations, challenging behaviors were found to be common in many conditions that cause distress for people with ID. For now, clinicians may need to decide on an individual case basis if a challenging behavior or other atypical feature is the direct result of a mood episode.

There are a number of plausible explanations for links between challenging behaviors and mood syndromes. People with ID may present more as young children do when suffering from a mood disorder, due to similarities in cognitive functioning and other developmental domains. Having a limited behavioral repertoire and less ability to identify and describe feelings, coupled with compromises in central nervous system functions associated with impulsivity, may increase the likelihood of the observed co-occurrence in people with ID. Also, variability in rates of challenging behaviors in samples of clinically referred individuals is likely to be low because most people with ID come to clinical attention due to the presence of these symptoms.

References

American Psychiatric Association. (1968). *Diagnostic and statistical manual of mental disorders* (2nd ed., rev.). Washington, DC: Author.

American Psychiatric Association. (1980). *Diagnostic and statistical manual of mental disorders* (3rd ed.,). Washington, DC: Author.

American Psychiatric Association. (1987). *Diagnostic and statistical manual of mental disorders* (3rd ed., rev.). Washington, DC: Author.

American Psychiatric Association. (1994). *Diagnostic and statistical manual of mental disorders* (4th ed.). Washington, DC: Author.

American Psychiatric Association. (2000). *Diagnostic and statistical manual of mental disorders* (4th ed., rev.).Washington, DC: Author.

Angold, A. S. (1988). Childhood and adolescent depression II: Research in clinical populations. *British Journal of Psychiatry, 153,* 476–492.

Beck, D. C., Carlson, G. A., Russell, A. T., & Brownfield, F. E. (1987). Use of depression rating instruments in developmentally and educationally delayed adolescents. *Journal of the American Academy of Child Adolescent Psychiatry, 26,* 97–100.

Cain, N. N., Davidson, P. W., Burhan, A. M., Andolsek, M. E., Baxter, J. T., Sullivan, L., et al. (2003). Identifying bipolar disorders in individuals with intellectual disability. *Journal of Intellectual Disability Research, 47,* 31–38.

Cantwell, D. P. (1996). Classification of child and adolescent psychopathology. *Journal of Child Psychology and Psychiatry, 17,* 3–12.

Carlson, G., & Cantwell, D. P. (1983). Case studies in prepubertal child depression. In D. P. Cantwell & G. Carlson (Eds.), *Affective disorders in childhood and adolescence* (pp. 39–59). Richmond, Victoria, Australia: Spectrum Publications.

Carlson, G., & Kashani, J. H. (1988). Phenomenology of major depression from childhood through adulthood: Analysis of three studies. *American Journal of Psychiatry, 145,* 1222–1225.

Charlot, L. R. (1997). Irritability, aggression, and depression in adults with mental retardation: A developmental perspective. *Psychiatric Annals, 27,* 190–197.

Charlot, L. R. (1998). Developmental effects on mental health disorders in persons with developmental disabilities. *Mental Health Aspects of Developmental Disabilities, 1,* 29–38.

Charlot, L. R. (2003). Mission impossible: Developing an accurate classification of psychiatric disorders in individuals with developmental disabilities. *Mental Health Aspects of Developmental Disabilities, 6,* 26–35.

Charlot, L. R., Abend, S., Silka, V. R., Kuropatkin, B. B., Garcia, O., Bolduc, M., et al. (2002). A short stay inpatient psychiatric unit for adults with developmental disabilities. In J. Jacobson (Ed.), *Model programs for individuals with developmental disabilities and psychiatric disorders* (pp. 35–53). Kingston, NY: NADD Press.

Charlot, L. R., Doucette, A. C., & Mezzecappa, E. (1993). Affective symptoms of institutionalized adults with mental retardation. *American Journal of Mental Retardation, 98,* 408–416.

Cicchetti, D., & Ganiban, J. (1990). The organization and coherence of developmental processes in infants and children with Down syndrome. In R. M. Hodapp, J. A. Burack, & E. Zigler (Eds.), *Issues in the developmental approach to mental retardation* (pp. 169–225). Cambridge, UK: Cambridge University Press.

Clarke, D. J., & Gomez, G. A. (1999). Utility of the DCR-10 criteria in the diagnosis of depression associated with intellectual disability. *Journal of Intellectual Disability Research, 43,* 413–420.

Cooper, S. A. (1999). The relationship between psychiatric and physical health problems in elderly people with intellectual disability. *Journal of Intellectual Disabilities Research, 43,* 54–60.

Cooper, S. A., & Collacott, R. A. (1993). Prognosis of depression in Down's syndrome. *Journal of Nervous and Mental Disease, 181,* 204–205.

Davis, J. P., Judd, F. K., & Herrman, H. (1997a). Depression in adults with intellectual disability. Part 1: A review. *Australia and New Zealand Journal of Psychiatry, 31,* 232–242.

Davis, J. P., Judd, F. K., & Herrman, H. (1997b). Depression in adults with intellectual disability. Part 2. A pilot study. *Australia and New Zealand Journal of Psychiatry, 31,* 243–251.

Evans, L. M., Cotton, M. M., Einfeld, S. L., & Florio, T. (1999). Assessment of depression in adults with severe or profound intellectual disability. *Journal of Intellectual & Developmental Disability, 24,* 147–160.

Gardner, W. (2000). Understanding challenging behaviors. In D. M. Griffiths, W. I. Gardner, & J. A. Nugent (Eds.), *Behavioral supports: Individual centered interventions: A multimodal functional approach* (pp. 7–17). Kingston, NY: NADD.

Glue, P. (1989). Rapid cycling affective disorders in the mentally retarded. *Biological Psychiatry, 26,* 250–256.

Harris, J. (1998). *Developmental neuropsychiatry, Volume II: Assessment, diagnosis, and treatment of developmental disorders.* New York: Oxford.

Hucker, S. J., Day, K. E., George, S., & Roth, M. (1979). Psychosis in mentally handicapped adults. In P. E. Snaith (Ed.), *Psychiatric illness and mental handicap* (pp. 52–76). London: Gaskell.

Hurley, A. D. (1996). The misdiagnosis of hallucinations and delusions in persons with mental retardation: A neurodevelopmental perspective. *Seminars in Clinical Neuropsychiatry, 1,* 122–133.

Hurley, A. D. (1998). Two cases of suicide attempt by patients with Down syndrome. *Psychiatric Services, 49,* 1618–1619.

Hurley, A. D., Folstein, M. F., & Lam, N. (2003). Patients with and without intellectualdisability seeking outpatient psychiatric services: Diagnoses and prescribing pattern. *Journal of Intellectual Disability Research, 47*, 39–50.

Hurley, A. D., & Moore, C. (1999). A review of erotomania in developmental disabilities and new case report. *Mental Health Aspects of Developmental Disabilities, 2*, 12–21.

Jancar, J., & Gunaratne, I. J. (1994). Dysthymia and mental handicap. *British Journal of Psychiatry, 164*, 691–693.

Johnson, C. R., Handen, B. L., Lubetsky, M. J., & Sacco, K. A. (1995). Affective disorders in hospitalized children and adolescents with mental retardation: A retrospective study. *Research in Developmental Disabilities, 16*, 221–231.

Jones, P. M., & Berney, T. P. (1987). Early onset rapid cycling bipolar disorder. *Journal of Child Psychology and Psychiatry and Allied Disciplines, 28*, 731–738.

King, R. (1999). Clinical implications of comorbid bipolar disorders and obsessive compulsive disorders in individuals with developmental disabilities. *The NADD Bulletin, 2*, 3–7.

King, R., Fay, G., & Croghan, P. (2000). Rapid cycling bipolar disorder in individuals with developmental disabilities. *Mental Retardation, 38*, 253–261.

Kovacs, M., Feinberg, T., Crouse-Novak, M., Paulauskas, S., & Finkelstein, R. (1984). Depressive disorders in children: I. A longitudinal prospective study of characteristics and recovery. *Archives of General Psychiatry, 41*, 643–649.

Lowry, M. A. (1998). Assessment and treatment of mood disorders in persons with developmental disabilities. *Journal of Developmental and Physical Disabilities, 10*, 387–406.

Lowry, M. A., & Charlot, L. (1996). Depression and associated aggression and self-injury. *NADD Newsletter, 13*, 1–5.

Lowry, M. A., & Sovner, R. (1992). Severe behaviour problems associated with rapid cycling bipolar disorder in two adults with profound mental retardation. *Journal of Intellectual Disabilities Research, 36*, 269–281.

Marston, G. M., Perry, D. W., & Roy, A. (1997). Manifestations of depression in people with intellectual disability. *Journal of Intellectual Disability Research. 41*, 476–480.

McBrien, J. A. (2003). Assessment and diagnosis of depression in people with intellectual disability. *Journal of Intellectual Disability Research, 47*, 1–13.

McDermott, S., Breen, R., Platt, T., Dhar, D., Shelton, J., & Krishnawaswami, S. (1997). Do behavior changes herald physical illness in adults with mental retardation? *Community Mental Health Journal, 33*, 85–97.

McGuire, D. E., & Chicoine, B. A. (1996). Depressive disorders in adults with Down syndrome. *The Habilitative Mental Healthcare Newsletter, 15,* 1–7.

Meins, W. (1995). Symptoms of major depression in mentally retarded adults. *Journal of Intellectual Disabilities Research, 39,* 41–45.

Meyers, B. A. (1998). Major depression in persons with moderate to profound mental retardation: Clinical presentation and case illustrations. *Mental Health Aspects of Developmental Disabilities, 1,* 57–68.

Pary, R. J., Friedlander, R., & Capone, G. T. (1999). Bipolar disorder in Down syndrome: Six cases. *Mental Health Aspects of Developmental Disabilities, 2,* 59–63.

Pary, R. J., Levitas A. S., & Hurley, A. D. (1999). Diagnosis of bipolar disorder in persons with developmental disabilities. *Mental Health Aspects of Developmental Disabilities, 2(2),* 37–49.

Pawlarcyzk, D., & Beckwith, B. (1987). Depressive symptoms displayed by persons with mental retardation: A review. *Mental Retardation, 25,* 323–330.

Rapoport, J. L., & Ismond, M. A. (1996). *DSM-IV training guide for diagnosis of childhood disorders.* New York: Brunner Mazel.

Reid, A. H., & Naylor, G. J. (1976). Short-cycle manic depressive psychosis in mental defectives: A clinical physiological study. *Journal of Mental Deficiency Research, 20,* 67–76.

Reiss, S., & Rojahn, J. (1993). Joint occurrence of depression and aggression in children and adults with mental retardation. *Journal of Intellectual Disabilities Research, 37,* 287–294.

Ross, E., & Oliver, C. (2003). The assessment of mood in adults who have severe or profound mental retardation. *Clinical Psychology Review, 23,* 225–245

Royal College of Psychiatrists. (2001). *DC-LD: Diagnostic Criteria for Psychiatric Disorders for Use With Adults With Learning Disabilities/Mental Retardation* (Occasional Paper OP48). London: Gaskell Press.

Rutter, M. (1998). Depressive disorders. In M. Rutter, A. H. Tuma, & I. S. Lann (Eds.), *Assessment and diagnosis in child psychopathology* (pp. 347–376). New York: Guilford Press.

Ryan, R., & Sunada, K. (1997). Medical evaluation of persons with mental retardation referred for psychiatric assessment. *General Hospital Psychiatry, 19,* 274–280.

Shafii, M., & Shafii, S. L. (1992). Clinical manifestations in developmental psychopathology of depression. In M. Shafii & L. S. Shafii (Eds.), *Clinical guide to depression in children and adolescents* (pp. 3–42). Washington, DC: American Psychiatric Press.

Sovner, R., & Hurley, A. D. (1982a). Diagnosing depression in the mentally retarded. *Psychiatric Aspects of Mental Retardation Reviews, 1,* 1–3.

Sovner, R., & Hurley, A. D. (1982b). Diagnosing mania in the mentally retarded. *Psychiatric Aspects of Mental Retardation Reviews, 1,* 9–11.

Sovner, R., & Hurley, A. D. (1983). Do the mentally retarded suffer from affective illness? *Archives of General Psychiatry, 40,* 61–67.

Sovner, R., & Pary, R. J. (1993). Affective disorders in developmentally disabled persons. In J. L. Matson & R. P. Barrett (Eds.), *Psychopathology in the mentally retarded* (2nd ed., pp. 87–147). Needham Heights, MA: Allyn and Bacon.

Sroufe, M., & Rutter, L. A. (1984). The domain of developmental psychopathology. *Child Development, 55,* 17–29.

Sturmey, P. (1993). The use of DSM and ICD diagnostic criteria in people with mental retardation: A review of empirical studies. *Journal of Nervous and Mental Disease, 181,* 38–41.

Sturmey, P. (1995). DSM-III-R and persons with dual diagnoses: Conceptual issues and strategies for future research. *Journal of Intellectual Disabilities Resreach, 39,* 357–364.

Tsiouris, J. A. (2001). Diagnosis of depression in people with severe/profound intellectual disability. *Journal of Intellectual Disability Research, 45,* 115–120.

Tsiouris, J. A., Mann, R., Patti, P. J., & Sturmey, P. (2003). Challenging behaviours should not be considered as depressive equivalents in individuals with intellectual disability. *Journal of Intellectual Disability Research, 47,* 14–21.

Vanstraelen, M., & Tyrer, S. P. (1999). Rapid cycling bipolar disorder in people with intellectual disability: A systematic review. *Journal of Intellectual Disability Research, 43,* 349–359.

Walters, A. S., Barrett, R. P., Knapp, L. G., & Borden, M. C. (1995). Suicidal behavior in children and adolescents with mental retardation. *Research in Developmental Disabilities, 16,* 85–96.

World Health Organization (WHO). (1992). *International Statistical Classification of Diseases and Health Related Problems (ICD-10), Volume 1: Classification of mental and behavioural disorders: Clinical description and diagnostic guidelines.* Geneva: Author.

Zigler. E., Hodapp, M., & Burack, J. A. (1990). Issues in the developmental approach to mental retardation. In R. M. Hodapp, J. A. Burack, & E. Zigler (Eds.), *The developmental perspective in the field of mental retardation* (pp. 27–48). New York: Cambridge University Press.

3

EPIDEMIOLOGY OF MOOD DISORDERS IN PEOPLE WITH MENTAL RETARDATION

Johannes Rojahn

and

Anna J. Esbensen

This chapter deals with the epidemiology of mood or affective disorders in individuals with mental retardation. Wherever possible, we shall adhere to the diagnostic criteria proposed in the fourth edition of the *Diagnostic and Statistical Manual of Mental Disorders* (DSM-IV; American Psychiatric Association, 1994). The term *affective disorders* used in the DSM-III (American Psychiatric Association, 1980) was later replaced by *mood disorders* in the DSM-III-R (American Psychiatric Association, 1987) and the DSM-IV. Both of these terms are used interchangeably in this chapter.

It should be noted that the presence mental retardation typically weakens the diagnostic accuracy for psychiatric disorders in general and mood disorders in particular, and the accuracy further deteriorates with declining levels of intellectual functioning (Rush & Frances, 2000). Therefore, we cannot expect reliable diagnostic differentiations into all mood disorder subcategories designated by the DSM-IV at the current state of affairs in the field of mental retardation. It is not surprising, therefore, that most studies on mood disorders among people with mental retardation deal only with such broad categories as depression and bipolar disorders.

Large-scale epidemiological surveys of mental illness in the general population with rigorous methodologies are a rather recent phenomenon. In particular, two studies are of note: the Epidemiologic Catchment Area (ECA) study (Robins & Regier, 1991) and the National Comorbidity Survey (NCS; Kessler et al., 1994). For the ECA study, interviews with over 18,000 residents in five health catchment areas in the U.S. were conducted with the Diagnostic Interview Schedule (DIS; Robins, Helzer, & Croughan, 1981). For the NCS, more than 8,000 individuals drawn from all contiguous states of the U.S. were interviewed with the Composite International Diagnostic Interview (WHO, 1990). These studies defined mental illness according to the then prevailing editions of the DSM, that is, the DSM-III and the DSM-III-R. Unfortunately, neither one of these large surveys provided explicit information on individuals with mental retardation. Table 3.1 presents the lifetime and 12-month prevalence rates of mood disorders from the ECA and NCS studies in the general population (ages 18–54).

Table 3.1. Lifetime and 12 month prevealnce rate in percentage of the ECA and NCS studies in the general population (ages 18-54).

	ECA[1]		ECA[2]	
	12 mo.	Lifetime	12 mo.	Lifetime
Any affective disorder	3.7	7.8	11.3	19.3
Major depressive episode	2.7	4.9	10.3	17.1
Manic episode	0.6	.08	1.3	6.4
Dysthymia		3.2	2.5	6.4
Bipolar I	0.7	0.8		
Bipolar II	0.3	0.5		

[1]*Weissman et al. (1991): Epidemiologic Catchment Area*
[2]*Kessler et al. (1994): National Comorbidity Survey*

The basis for the discussion of the prevalence of mood disorders in mental retardation is a systematic review of 16 international epidemiologic studies that were published between 1982 and 2004. *Prevalence* refers to the number of cases with a given condition at a particular point in time (*point prevalence*) or within a specified period of time (*period prevalence*). In contrast, *incidence* refers to the number of new cases that emerge within a specified period of time.

The selection of these studies was not intended to be exhaustive, but to be representative of the better-controlled surveys in this area. The main inclusion criterion for reviewed studies was the availability of specific data on mood disorders (depressive disorder, bipolar disorder, or both). Table 3.2 summarizes these studies with regard to the sampling methods employed, the samples that were screened for mood disorders, the instruments and diagnostic criteria used to classify individuals as having a mood disorder, and the results (prevalence estimates). The studies under review are for the most part descriptive rather than analytic, and focused on the prevalence of mood disorders in demographic or geographic subgroups of persons with mental retardation in general.

The quality of epidemiological data depends on the internal and external validity of the research protocol, which is influenced by an abundance of factors, including the adequacy of the survey sampling method, its representativeness of a meaningful theoretical population (that is, the population to which the data could be generalized), the equal or biased opportunity of each member of the sampling universe to be included in the classification process, the reliability of the data collection procedure, the expertise of the data collectors, and the sensitivity and specificity of the case classification criteria. To adjust our expectations of epidemiological data at this point, the reader should be reminded that this also means that the prerequisite for sound epidemiological data is usually a well-organized and well-trained team of researchers, a well-designed sampling method, and the availability of accurate classification criteria, such as the precision of the diagnosis in terms of sensitivity and specificity.

Mood Disorders in Mental Retardation Versus the General Population

Ever since the famed Isle of Wight study (Rutter, Tizard, Yule, Graham, & Whitmore, 1976), it has become a frequently reiterated assertion that people with mental retardation are at a disproportionate risk of developing a psychiatric disorder as compared with the general population (Dykens, 2000; Einfeld & Tonge, 1996a, b). To determine the extent to which there is empirical support for this assertion of an elevated prevalence of mood disorders in mental retardation, we will review the data of the 15 epidemiological prevalence studies on mental retardation (see Table 3.2).

Table 3.2. *Summary of selected epidemiological prevalence studies of mood disorders among people with mental retardation or developmental disabilities.* [a]

Authors and Year	Sampling Procedure	Sample Screened for Mood Disorder	Classification Criteria and Instruments	Prevalence of Mood Disorder

Eaton & Menolascino (1982)	Two-phase sampling:
	1. All 798 individuals from an MR community-based program from one catchment area (five counties in Nebraska)
	2. Of these, 114 were referred for psychiatric services over a 3-year period.
		▪ N = 114 individuals with a mental illness
		▪ Age
		  ○ between 6 and 76 years)
		  ○ < 10 = 6%
		  ○ 11–20 = 43%
		  ○ 2–29 = 32%
		  ○ 30–39 = 12%
		  ○ 40–50 = 5%
		  ○ 50+ = 2%
		▪ Sex
		  ○ M = 66%
		  ○ F = 34%
		▪ Other dual diagnoses
		  ○ Organic brain syndrome = 30%
		  ○ Personality disorder = 27%
		  ○ Adjustment reactions = 21%
		  ○ Schizophrenia = 21%
			▪ Diagnoses based primarily on DSM-III criteria
			▪ Specific diagnostic procedures unknown
			▪ Prevalence period not clearly discernable
				▪ Overall affective disorder = 0.0%

Jacobson (1982)	Total population study of individuals served by the public DD lead agency in New York State	▪ N = 27,023
		▪ Age
		  ○ 0–4 = 4%
		  ○ 5–20 = 25%
		  ○ 21–44 = 48%
		  ○ 45–64 = 18%
		  ○ 65+ = 5%
		▪ Sex
		  ○ M = 55%
		  ○ F = 45%
		▪ Other dual Diagnoses
		  ○ Delusions/hallucinations = 2.2%
		  ○ Disorientation = 3.8%
		  ○ Perseverations = 2.8%
		  ○ Echolalia = 1.3%
			▪ DDIS (informant based assessment instrument completed by informed clinical staff)
			▪ Point prevalence
				▪ Overall depression = 2.9%
				▪ By level of MR
				  ○ Mild = 5.0%
				  ○ Moderate = 2.9%
				  ○ Severe = 1.8%
				  ○ Profound = 1.1%
				▪ By age
				  ○ 0–21 = 1.6%
				  ○ 21+ = 2.1%
				▪ By residential setting
				  ○ Independent living = 10.0%
				  ○ Living with parents = 2.0%
				  ○ Family care = 1.6%
				  ○ Community residence = 4.0%
				  ○ Institution = 1.1%

Study	Sampling procedure	Sample characteristics	Method	Results
Lund (1985)	Two-phase sampling: 1. National registry of individuals with mental retardation in Denmark ($n \approx 22{,}500$) 2. A two-stage cluster sampling procedure identified 324 individuals in Aahrus County (Denmark) for psychiatric screening (302 valid cases)	■ $N = 302$ ■ Age o Between 20 and years 65+ ■ Sex o M = 170 o F = 132 ■ Level of MR o Borderline = 10.0% o Mild = 15.5% o Moderate = 28.1%% o Severe = 11.3% o Profound = 8.3% o Not clearly discernable = 26.8 ■ Other dual diagnoses o Schizophrenia = 1.3% o Dementia = 3.6 o Autism = 3.6% o Psychoses = 5.0% o Neuroses = 2.0%	■ MRC-HBC (standardized clinical interview) ■ Psychiatric diagnoses based on modified DSM-III criteria ■ Prevalence period not clearly discernable	■ Affective disorders (i.e., depression and mania): 1.7% ■ By age o 20–29 = 1.0% o 30–44 = 0.0% o 45–64 = 6.0% o 65+ = 0.0% ■ By sex o M = 2.4% o F = 0.8% ■ By level of MR o Borderline = 3.3% o Mild = 2.6% o Moderate = 1.2% o Severe = 2.9% o Profound = 0.0%
Gillberg, Persson, Grufman, & Themner (1986)	1. Screening and register searches among 24,498 youngsters (Göteborg, Sweden) 2. Identified 149 children and adolescents with MR	■ $N = 149$ ■ Age o Between 13 and 17 years ■ Sex o M = 92 o F = 57 ■ Level of MR o Mild = 56% (IQ = 50–70) o Severe = 44% (IQ < 50) ■ Other dual diagnoses o Emotional disorder = 7.4% o Conduct disorder = 8.7% o Psychotic behavior = 36.9% o Psychosomatic disorder = 3.4% o Hyperactive disorder = 6.0%	■ Individual diagnostic assessment by a child psychiatrist ■ DSM-III criteria ■ Structured interviews of a parent ■ 1-month period prevalence	■ Depressive syndrome = 2.7% ■ By level of MR o Mild = 3.6% o Severe = 1.5%

Table 3.2 continued

Study	Method	Measures / Sample	Results

Reiss (1990)	1. Mental health screening of 205 randomly chosen individuals from 17 participating community-based MR day programs (Chicago)
	2. Verification: psychological evaluations of 59 individuals by clinical psychologists blind to the screening data.
		- RSMB (informant-based rating scale reflecting DSM-III-R symptoms)
		- Point prevalence
		
		N = 205
		Age
		  o 12–20 = 3.7%
		  o 21–35 = 66.5%
		  o 35+ = 29.8%
		Sex
		  o M = 59.5%
		  o F = 40.5%
		Level of MR
		  o Mild = 45.8%
		  o Moderate = 36.0%
		  o Severe or profound = 17.1%
		Other dual diagnoses
		  o Overall = 39.0%
		  o Aggression = 6.8%
		  o Psychosis = 5.8%
		  o Paranoia = 7.8%
		  o Avoidant = 11.2%
		  o Dependent = 10.2%
		  o Overactive = 3.9%
			- Physical signs of depression = 8.3% (> 2-SD cutoff relative to a national sample)
			- Behavioral signs of depression = 8.3% (> 2-SD cutoff relative to a national sample)
			- About 3.4% were rated as having a "major problem" with affective disorder.

Charlot, Doucette, & Mezzacappa (1993)	Two-phase design:
	1. Residents of a large residential facility (Massachusetts) were regularly reviewed by psychiatrists and diagnosed when appropriate.
	2. Selection of 30 residents with affective disorder and 30 residents with other psychiatric diagnoses matched by level of MR
		- Psychiatric assessments by psychiatrists
		- Diagnosis: DSM-III-R
		- Prevalence period unclear
		
		N = 640[b]
		Mean age = 50 years
		Sex
		  o M = 57%
		  o F = 43%
		Level of MR
		  o Mild or moderate = 17%
		  o Severe or profound = 83%
		Other dual diagnoses
		  o Schizophrenia
		  o PDD/autism
		  o Organic brain syndrome
			- Affective disorder = 10.9%
			- Major depression = 6.9%
			- Bipolar disorder = 4.9%
			
			Prevalence of aggression, self-injury, and destruction:
			- Among persons with affective disorders 67%, 47%, and 43%, respectively
			- Among individuals with other psychiatric diagnoses 87%, 50%, and 63%, respectively.

Meins (1993)	Two-phase design:
	1. All 798 individuals with severe or profound MR from group homes, institutions, and psychiatric clinics (Hamburg, Germany) were screened.
	2. Thorough psychiatric examinations of
	  - Group home residents with a CDI score > 16
		- Screening instrument: CDI
		- Followed by a psychiatric examination for DSM-III-R diagnoses
		- Prevalence period not reported
		
		N = 798
		Age (means)
		  o Group homes = 37.1 years
		  o Institutions and psychiatric clinics = 37.5 years
		Sex
		  o M = 65.4% (group homes) to 49.1 (institutions)
		  o F = 34.6% (group homes) to 50.9% (institutions)
			- Depressive disorder total = 4.8%
			By residence
			  o Group homes = 2.0%
			  o Institutions = 1.8%–2.2%
			  o Psychiatric clinics = 3.0%–7.5%
			- Major depression = 2.5%
			- Dysthymia = 1.3%
			- Adjustment disorder = 0.8%

Study	Sampling procedures	Sample characteristics	Diagnostic method	Findings
	• Residents of clinics and institutions with an CDI score > 12 • Random selection of 124 individuals with a low CDI score (> 12)	• Level of MR 　o Severe 　　▪ 45.6% (group homes) 　　▪ 12.6% (institutions) 　o Profound 　　▪ 54.4% (group homes) 　　▪ 87.4% (institutions)	• RSMB (informant-based rating scale reflecting DSM-III-R symptoms) • Point prevalence	• Depression = 8.9% • Criterion levels of depression four times as high in people with aggressive behavior as compared with those without aggressive behavior.
Reiss & Rojahn (1993)	Two-step sampling procedures 1. Random selection of service agencies 2. Random selection or total sample of individuals to be screened Three groups of individuals served by 1 of 37 community-based service agencies in the Midwest (Illinois, Wisconsin, Ohio)	• N = 528 • Age 　o < 12 = 16.9% 　o 12–20 = 45.1% 　o 21–35 = 26.5% 　o 35+ = 11.5% • Sex 　o M = 63.4% 　o F = 36.6% • Level of MR 　o Mild or moderate = 60.6% 　o Severe or profound = 39.4%		
Rojahn, Borthwick-Duffy, & Jacobson (1993)	Total population studies involving everybody who received DD services from the California Department of Developmental Services and the New York State Office of MRDD in 1990	• California: N = 89,419 • New York: N = 45,683 • Other dual diagnoses (CA – NY) 　o ADHD = 0.6% – 0.3% 　o Conduct disorder = 0.4% – 1.2% 　o PDD = 0.3% – 1.7% 　o Adjustment disorder = 0.4% – 0.3% 　o Anxiety disorder = 0.3% – 0.5% 　o Organic brain disorder = 0.1% – 0.8% 　o Personality disorder = 0.3% – 0.2%	• California: 　o CDER (informant-based rating scale completed by agency staff) 　o DSM-III-R diagnosis by qualified clinical staff 　o Prevalence period unclear 　New York: 　o DDIS (informant-based assessment instrument) 　o DSM-III-R diagnosis by qualified clinical staff 　o Prevalence period unclear	• Depression 　o California = 0.7% 　o New York < 0.01%

Table 3.2 continued

Study	Sample description	Method	Results
Crews, Bonaventura, & Rowe (1994)	Total population (N = 1,273) screening of residents from a large residential facility (Virginia)	<ul><li>N = 189 (or 15.6% of 1,273 residents)</li><li>Age<ul><li>Between 10 and 80 years</li></ul></li><li>Sex<ul><li>M = 53.7%</li><li>F = 46.3%</li></ul></li><li>Level of MR<ul><li>Mild = 48.9%</li><li>Moderate = 28.9%</li><li>Severe = 22.7%</li><li>Profound = 10.7%</li></ul></li><li>*Other dual diagnoses*<ul><li>Total = 15.6%</li><li>Infancy, childhood, and adolescent disorders = 1.8%</li><li>Organic mental disorders = 0.5%</li><li>Schizophrenic disorder = 0.6%</li><li>Psychotic disorder not otherwise specified = 2.3%</li><li>Anxiety disorder = 0.63%</li><li>Impulse control disorder = 0.4%</li><li>Personality disorder = 0.86%</li></ul></li></ul>	<ul><li>Diagnoses by licensed psychologists, psychiatrists, or staff physicians using DSM-III-R criteria</li><li>Point prevalence</li></ul>	<ul><li>Overall affective disorder = 8.9%</li><li>*By sex*<ul><li>M = 8.8%</li><li>F = 9.0%</li></ul></li><li>*By level of MR*<ul><li>Mild = 24.4%</li><li>Moderate = 15.3%</li><li>Severe = 12.9%</li><li>Profound = 6.5%</li></ul></li><li>Major depression = 0.7%</li><li>Bipolar mixed = 3.7%</li><li>Bipolar manic = .03%</li><li>Bipolar depressed = 1.4%</li><li>Dysthymia = 0.2%</li></ul>
Cherry, Matson, & Paclawskyj (1997)	Selection of participants from an institutionalized population with not clearly discernable sampling procedure (Louisiana)	<ul><li>N = 168</li><li>Age<ul><li>Between 20 and 79 years</li></ul></li><li>Sex<ul><li>M = 54.2%</li><li>F = 45.8%</li></ul></li><li>Level of MR<ul><li>Severe = 48.2%</li><li>Profound = 51.8%</li></ul></li><li>*Other dual diagnoses*<ul><li>Anxiety</li><li>PDD/autism</li><li>Schizophrenia</li></ul></li></ul>	<ul><li>DASH-II (informant-based instrument for severe or profound MR reflecting DSM-III-R)</li><li>Prevalence period unclear</li></ul>	<ul><li>Depression = 0.6%</li><li>Mania = 11.3%</li></ul>
Maughan, Collishaw, & Pickles (1999)	Prospective study of all children in Britain born in 1 week in 1958 (~17,000 total)	<ul><li>N = 100–122 (depending on missing data)</li><li>Age<ul><li>33 years</li></ul></li></ul>	<ul><li>Malaise Inventory (self-report scale for affective symptoms)</li><li>Prevalence period unclear</li></ul>	<ul><li>Elevated levels of affective symptoms by sex<ul><li>M = 29.7%</li><li>F = 51.1%</li></ul></li></ul>

Study	Sample	Subject characteristics	Method	Findings

After birth surveys, follow-ups at 7, 11, 16, 23, and 33 years		- *Sex*
		  o Ratios varying (depending on missing data)
		- *Level of MR*
		  o Mild (i.e., IQ equivalent scores of < 70, excluding those who attended special schools for children with severe MR at ages 11 and 16)
				(as compared with 9.0% [M] and 15.9% [F] in the non-MR control sample)

Salvador-Carulla, Rodríguez-Blázquez, de Molina, Pérez-Marín, & Velázquez (2000)	Total population screening of 146 employees in a supported employment program (Spain); 130 met study criteria.	- *N* = 130
		- *Age*
		  o Between 18 and 65 years
		- *Sex*
		  o M = 92
		  o F = 38
		- *Level of MR*
		  o Mild = 64%
		  o Moderate = 26%
		  o Severe = 3%
		  o Profound = 7%
		- *Other dual diagnoses*
		  o Total = 32.3%
		  o Psychotic disorder total = 17.7%
		  o Adjustment disorder = 2.3%
		  o Anxiety disorder = 1.5%
			- AIRP (informant-based assessment tool)
			- Psychiatric interview using DSM-III criteria
			- CGI
			- GAF
			- Prevalence period unclear
				- Mood disorder = 4.6%
				- Major depression = 0.8%
				- Cyclothymia = 0.8%
				- Dysthymia = 3.1%

Deb, Thomas, & Bright (2001)	1. General population of persons in Vale of Glamorgan (South Wales, UK) between 16 and 64 years = 75,600
	2. 246 adults with MR known in the local social service registry
	3. Random selection of 120 for psychiatric interviews (30 dropped out)
	4. Psychiatric screening using the Mini PAS-ADD
	5. Semistructured interview with the full PAS-ADD
		- *N* = 90
		- *Age*
		  o Between 16 and 64 years
		- *Sex*
		  o M = 47
		  o F = 43
		- *Level of MR*
		  o Mild = 48%
		  o Moderate = 42%
		- *Other dual diagnoses*
		  o Total = 14.4%
		  o Schizophrenia = 4.4%
		  o Delusional disorder = 1.1%
		  o Generalized anxiety disorder = 2.2%
		  o Phobic disorder = 4.4%
		  o Panic disorder = 0.0%
			- Mini PAS-ADD screening in the home setting
			- PAS-ADD semistructured interview by a trained psychiatrist (ICD-10 diagnoses were rendered from PAS-ADD interviews)
			- Prevalence period not clearly discernable
				- ICD-10 depressive disorder = 2.2%
				- ICD-10 bipolar disorder = 0.0%

Table 3.2 continued

Emerson (2003)	1. Multistage, stratified, random sample of 10,438 children and adolescents (England, Scotland, and Wales).
	2. Identification of 264 children and adolescent with MR
		▪ N = 264 with MR
		▪ Age
		  ○ Between 5 and 15 years
		▪ Sex
		  ○ M = 192
		  ○ F = 72
		▪ Other dual diagnoses
		  ○ Total = 39%
		  ○ Anxiety disorder = 8.7%
		  ○ Conduct disorder = 25%
		  ○ Hyperkinesis = 8.7%
		  ○ PDD = 7.6%
		  ○ Tic disorder = 0.8%
		  ○ Eating disorder = 0.4%
		  ○ Psychotic disorder = 0.0%
			▪ DAWBA – consists of structured interviews with the primary caregiver or the children, questionnaire for the teacher and ICD-10–based diagnostic rating system
			▪ Prevalence period unclear
				▪ Depression = 1.5% (as compared with 0.9% in a non-MR control sample)

Taylor, Hatton, Dixon, & Douglas (2004)	Individuals who were either residents in hospitals or known to care management system within a county district (northeast England)	▪ N = 1,155
		▪ Age
		  ○ Mean 44.0 years
		  ○ Between 17 and 92 years
		▪ Sex
		  ○ M = 57.5%
		  ○ F = 42.5%
		▪ Level of MR
		  ○ Unavailable information
		▪ Other dual diagnoses
		  ○ Organic condition = 3.9%
		  ○ Psychotic disorder = 10.2%
			▪ PAS-ADD
			▪ Prevalence period unclear
				▪ Affective or neurotic disorder = 14.0%
				▪ By sex
				  ○ M = 12.3%
				  ○ F = 17.0%

Key to Acronyms: *AIRP: Assessment and Information Rating Profile (Bouras, 1995); CDER: Client Development Evaluation Report (Harris et al., 1982); CDI: Children's Depression Inventory (Helsel & Matson, 1984); CGI: Clinical Global Impressions (National Institute of Mental Health, 1985); DASH II: Diagnostic Assessment of the Severely Handicapped (Matson, Coe, Gardner, & Sovner, 1991); DAWBA: Development and Well Being Assessment (Goodman, Ford, Richards, Gatward, & Meltzer, 2000); DD: developmental disabilities; DDIS: New York Developmental Disabilities Information Survey (Jacobson, 1982); DSM-III-R: Diagnostic and Statistical Manual of Mental Disorders (3rd ed. rev.) (American Psychiatric Association, 1987); GAF: General Assessment of Functioning (American Psychiatric Association, 1994); ICD-10: International Classification of Diseases and Related Health Problems (10th ed.) (World Health Organization, 1992); Malaise Inventory (Rutter, Tizard, & Whitmore, 1970); MR: mental retardation; PAS-ADD: Psychiatric Assessment Schedule for Adults with Developmental Disabilities (Moss et al., 1993); PDD: pervasive developmental disabilities; RSMB: Reiss Screen for Maladaptive Behavior (Reiss, 1988).*

[a] To standardize the presentation format across studies, the authors had to recalculate figures of some of the published material.

[b] Information not provided by Charlot et al. (1993), but by Lowry (1998)

The only study of epidemiological mood disorders that directly compared individuals with and without mental retardation was Emerson (2003), who conducted a study in the United Kingdom on depression in children and adolescents. Using a structured interview with the primary caregivers, teachers, or the children themselves and questionnaires based on IDC-10 diagnostic criteria, he reported a relative higher rate of symptoms of depression among those with mental retardation (1.5%) as compared with those without (0.9%). This means that the odds for a child or adolescent with mental retardation to have depression was 1.7.

To compare the prevalence estimates of mood disorders in the adult population with and without mental retardation, we first examined the prevalence estimates for mood disorders in the general population, as yielded by the ECA and the NCS surveys. The 1-year prevalence of mood disorders in the general population in the U.S. was reported to be 3.7% in the ECA survey (Weissman, Livingston-Bruce, Leaf, Florio, & Holzer, 1991) and 11.3% in the NCS (Kessler et al., 1994) (see Table 3.1). To account for the remarkable prevalence differences between the ECA survey and the NCS, some have speculated that mood disorder may actually have become more common during the period between those two studies. It is more likely, however, that a good portion of the discrepancy can be attributed to methodological differences, such as the greater number of probe questions in the NCS (Lowry, 1998). The fact that even the most rigorously controlled and highly funded research endeavors in the mental health field yield outcomes with a 60% discrepancy speaks to the difficulty of epidemiological research of mental illness.

In contrast, prevalence estimates of an aggregate mood disorders category in mental retardation based on DSM definitions ranged from 0.0% (Eaton & Menolascino, 1982) to 10.9% (Charlot, Doucette, & Mezzacappa, 1993) (see Tables 3.2 and 3.3). The zero prevalence rate reported by Eaton and Menolascino is surprising and raises questions, particularly in the context of the substantial prevalence rates reported for organic brain syndrome, personality disorders, and schizophrenia. Considering the high rates of adjustment disorders (21%), one could speculate whether that label may actually incorporate some of the affective disorder cases. The Charlot et al. study, on the other hand, was restricted to the population of a large institutionalized population. Therefore, it is unclear to what broader population those results can be generalized. Some of the European studies may have a stronger claim to generalizability, because their screening samples tended to represent broader subgroups of individuals with mental retardation. The existence of national health registries in Europe certainly facilitates the case finding and sampling procedures. Lund (1985; Denmark), Gillberg, Persson,

Grufman, and Themner (1986; Sweden), Meins (1993; Germany), Deb, Thomas, and Bright (2001; Wales), and Emerson (2003; England, Scotland, Wales) found prevalence rates of mood disorders ranging from 1.5% to 4.8%. If we consider that the European studies in general have relatively stronger sampling features than their U.S. counterparts, we can conclude that prevalence rates of mood disorders in Europeans with mental retardation do not appear higher than the prevalence rates of mood disorders in the general population in the U.S. If this conclusion is true, it is inconsistent with the long-held assumption that individuals with intellectual disabilities are more vulnerable to mood disorders. (It should be noted that the prevalence of mood disorders in the general population varies widely cross-nationally and tends to be considerably higher in some European countries than in the U.S. [Weissman et al., 1996]). Similar discrepancies may be true for the population of people with mental retardation).

Table 3.3. Prevalence estimates of an omnibus mood disorder among individuals with mental retardation/developmental disabilities[1]

Authors and Year	Prevalence Estimates in %
Eaton & Menolascino (1982)	0.0
Rojahn et al. (1993)	0.0 (New York)
Rojahn et al. (1993)	0.7 (California)
Emerson (2003)	1.5
Lund (1985)	1.7
Gillberg et al. (1986)	2.7
Jacobson (1982)	2.9
Salvador-Carulla et al. (2000)	4.6
Meins (1993)	4.8
Crews et al. (1994)	8.9
Reiss & Rojahn (1993)	8.9
Charlot et al. (1993)	10.9

[1]Studies presented in Table 3.1 that are excluded in this table were (a) those that did not report the prevalence of one omnibus mood disorders category (Cherry et al., 1997; Deb et al., 2001; Reiss, 1990), and (b) one that combined mood and anxiety disorders (Taylor et al., 2004).

It is important, however, to keep in mind that the diagnosis of mood disorders in this population has posed great difficulties, and many researchers have suggested that mood disorders are likely to be under-diagnosed (e.g., Lowry, 1998; Salvador-Carulla, Rodríguez-Blázquez, de Molina, Pérez-Marín, & Velázquez, 2000). Furthermore, comparisons between the studies on mental retardation, on the one hand, and the ECA and NCS studies, on the other hand, have to be made with great caution, because of widely differing methodological features. The mental retardation studies were by and large methodologically much weaker than the ECA and NCS studies, and we do not really have the quality of information available to confirm or reject the notion that people with mental retardation have a higher risk of developing mood disorders than their counterparts in the general population.

Mood Disorders and Level of Mental Retardation

Several studies have indicated that the prevalence rates of psychiatric disorders in mental retardation decline with the level of intellectual and adaptive functioning (see Rojahn & Tassé, 1996). That means that the proportion of individuals with profound mental retardation who have a concurrent mood disorder is smaller than the proportion of individuals with mild mental retardation, and so forth (which is different from the observation that the proportion of individuals with profound mental retardation among those with mood disorders is smaller than the proportion of individuals with severe mental retardation, and so forth). We found 4 of the 15 reviewed studies that presented data on this issue (see Figure 3.1). Three of these 4 studies (with an exception of the Lund [1985]) confirmed that trend. In other words, there is accumulating evidence that people with severe mental retardation have a relatively lower rate of mood disorders than do those with mild and moderate mental retardation.

Whether this trend reflects actual differences in mood disorder prevalence and vulnerability or whether this is an artifact remains unanswered. It seems counterintuitive, however, that declining level of intellectual functioning, which is typically accompanied by a host of other vulnerabilities (such as neurological and behavior problems), would be a protective factor to mood disorders. It seems more likely that manifestations of mood disorders vary across levels of functioning. A consensus seems to emerge that DSM-like diagnostic criteria of mood disorders are valid for people mild and moderate mental retardation, but that they are of decreasing value for individuals with severe and profound mental retardation (McBrien, 2003). In addition, a declining ability in individuals with severe or profound mental retardation to talk about states of emotions and thoughts all but eliminates the use of key diagnostic criteria, which is probably one of the main reasons why the reliability of assessment of psychiatric conditions with decreasing levels of functioning deteriorates (Havercamp, 1996).

Figure 3.1. Prevalence of mood disorders by levels of mental retardation, as reported in four surveys.

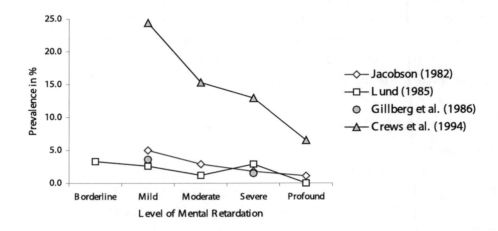

Mood Disorders and Sex

Affective disorders in the general population are more prevalent in females than in males (Weissman et al., 1991). Among the studies reviewed, only four reported specific prevalence figures for the sexes. The results were inconsistent. Lund (1985); Crews, Bonaventura, and Rowe (1994); Maughan, Collishaw, and Pickles (1999); and Taylor, Hatton, Dixon, and Douglas (2004) reported female:male odds ratios of having a mood disorder (or elevated affective levels) and mental retardation as 0.3 (0.8% versus 2.4%), 1.02 (9.0% versus 8.8%), 1.7 (51.1% versus 29.7%), and 1.4 (17.0% versus 12.3%).

Mood Disorders and Severe Behavior Problems

Challenging behaviors or such severe behavior disorders as self-injurious, aggressive, and destructive behavior are common phenomena among individuals with mental retardation (Emerson et al., 2001; Rojahn, Borthwick-Duffy, & Jacobson, 1993). There has been speculation as to whether behavior problems may be functionally related to psychiatric disorders. In an early study involving a small number of subjects with mental retardation, Laman and Reiss (1987) found that sadness and antisocial behavior were correlated. This led to a more extensive study by Reiss and Rojahn (1993), which produced confirming evidence of the association between mood disorders and aggressive behavior. Criterion levels of depression were four times as high in individuals with aggressive behavior as compared with those without aggressive behavior (see Table 3.1). More recent studies, however, have not been able to replicate evidence for a relationship between mood disorders and behavior disorders (Charlot et al., 1993; Holden & Gitlesen, 2003; Moss et al., 2000; Rojahn, Matson, Naglieri, & Mayville, 2004).

Summary and Discussion

In summary, there is ample evidence that many individuals with mental retardation suffer from mood disorders, which affirms the existence of an often-overlooked, grave public health concern. This is an important point to make, particularly since it was not that long ago that the very existence of mood disorders in this population had been questioned by professionals and clinicians. However, this is the only epidemiologic finding we can consider as being robust at this point. For instance, contrary to frequently encountered assertions, only the Emerson (2003) study provided empirical evidence that this population is at a greater risk of developing mood disorders as compared with the general population. Nor did the reviewed surveys reveal whether females with mental retardation are more likely to develop a mood disorder than are males, as is the case in the general population. And finally, epidemiological surveys have not been able to clarify the question whether mood disorders are associated with specific behavior problems, as some have observed (e.g., Reiss & Rojahn, 1993).

Most of the reviewed studies on mood disorders in mental retardation were marred by methodological weaknesses, which make it difficult to draw firm conclusions and to compare results between studies. Three of these should be highlighted here. First, all the studies were based on samples of convenience, rather than on scientific sampling procedures. Samples of convenience have practical advantages, no doubt, but they tend to be compromised by sampling errors and biases that are difficult to account for *a posteriori*—errors and biases that severely limit the generalizability of the data. As a consequence, it often remained unclear to which theoretical population the data of a respective study were supposed to generalize. A second concern is that most of the survey data came from screening tools rather than from clinical or research diagnoses. Instruments such as the Assessment and Information Rating Profile (Bouras, 1995), the Client Development Evaluation Report (Harris, Eyman, & Mayeda, 1982), the Children's Depression Inventory (Helsel & Matson, 1984), the Diagnostic Assessment of the Severely Handicapped (DASH-II; Matson, Coe, Gardner, & Sovner, 1991), the New York Developmental Disabilities Information Survey (Jacobson, 1982), the Psychiatric Assessment Schedule for Adults With Developmental Disabilities (PAS-ADD; Moss et al., 1993), and the Reiss Screen for Maladaptive Behavior (Reiss, 1988) were developed to reflect DSM or ICD criteria, but they are screening instruments that do not render actual diagnoses. Depending on the sensitivity and specificity of the screening tools they over-estimate or under-estimate the true prevalence. Finally, we noted that only a handful of studies explicitly stated the prevalence period during which symptoms of mood disorders had to occur. Obviously, as the ECA and NCS studies clearly showed, it makes a big difference whether we talk about 1-month, 12-month, or lifetime prevalence estimates. It is, therefore, possible that some studies with small prevalence periods underestimated the prevalence of mood disorders due to the fact that a person's mood disorder was in remission or that the client was temporarily asymptomatic.

Although it is unfortunate, it is not surprising that existing epidemiological studies on mood disorders in mental retardation lacked the methodological rigor and sophistication expected for contemporary survey research. But this cannot be blamed on the authors alone. The problem has many sources, including the lack of adequate funds to support the sampling of truly representative groups. In addition, the diagnostic precision of mood disorders in mental retardation—especially among those with lower levels of intelligence—has not reached a point yet that would justify the considerable investment for a state-of-the-art epidemiological study. Therefore, we ought to continue to refine our understanding of the nature of mood disorders in this population, to improve the reliability and validity of the screening and assessment instruments, and to sharpen the precision of our case classification. After this has been accomplished, nationally representative epidemiological surveys should be conducted to give us an accurate picture of the extent of the problem and to explore other issues that lend themselves to the epidemiological approach of inquiry.

References

American Psychiatric Association. (1980). *Diagnostic and statistical manual of mental disorders* (3rd ed.). Washington, DC: Author.

American Psychiatric Association. (1987). *Diagnostic and statistical manual of mental disorders* (3rd ed. rev.). Washington, DC: Author.

American Psychiatric Association. (1994). *Diagnostic and statistical manual of mental disorders* (4th ed.). Washington, DC: Author.

Bouras, N. (1995). Assessment and Information Rating Profile. *British Journal of Psychiatry, 166,* 262–263.

Charlot, L. R., Doucette, A. C., & Mezzacappa, E. (1993). Affective symptoms of institutionalized adults with mental retardation. *American Journal on Mental Retardation, 98,* 408–416.

Cherry, K. E., Matson, J. L., & Paclawskyj, T. R. (1997). Psychopathology in older adults with severe and profound mental retardation. *American Journal on Mental Retardation, 101,* 445–458.

Crews, W. D., Bonaventura, S., & Rowe, F. (1994). Dual diagnosis: Prevalence of psychiatric disorders in a large state residential facility for individuals with mental retardation. *American Journal on Mental Retardation, 98,* 688–731.

Deb, S., Thomas, M., & Bright, C. (2001). Mental disorder in adults with intellectual disability. I: Prevalence of functional psychiatric illness among a community-based population aged between 16 and 64 years. *Journal of Intellectual Disability Research, 45,* 495–505.

Dykens, E. M. (2000). Psychopathology in children with intellectual disability. *Journal of Child Psychology and Psychiatry, 41,* 407–417.

Eaton, L. F., & Menolascino, F. J. (1982). Psychiatric disorders in the mentally retarded: Types, problems, and challenges. *American Journal of Psychiatry, 139,* 1297–1303.

Einfeld, S. L., & Tonge, B. J. (1996a). Population prevalence of psychopathology in children and adolescents with intellectual disability. I: Rationale and methods. *Journal of Intellectual Disability Research, 40,* 91–98.

Einfeld, S. L., & Tonge, B. J. (1996b). Population prevalence of psychopathology in children and adolescents with intellectual disability. II: Epidemiological findings. *Journal of Intellectual Disability Research, 40,* 99–109.

Emerson, E. (2003). Prevalence of psychiatric disorders in children and adolescents with and without intellectual disability. *Journal of Intellectual Disability Research, 47,* 51–58.

Emerson, E., Kiernan, C., Alborz, A., Reeves, D., Mason, H., Swarbrick, R., et al. (2001). The prevalence of challenging behavior: A total population study. *Research in Developmental Disabilities, 22,* 77–93.

Gillberg, C., Persson, E., Grufman, M., & Themner, U. (1986). Psychiatric disorders in mildly and severely mentally retarded urban children and adolescents: Epidemiological aspects. *British Journal of Psychiatry, 149,* 68–74.

Goodman, R., Ford, T., Richards, H., Gatward, R., & Meltzer, H. (2000). The Development and Well-Being Assessment: Description and initial validation of an integrated assessment of child and adolescent psychopathology. *Journal of Child Psychology and Psychiatry, 41,* 645–656.

Harris, C., Eyman, R. K., & Mayeda, T. (1982). *An inter-rater reliability study of the Client Development Evaluation Report (Final Report).* Sacramento, CA: California Department of Developmental Services.

Havercamp S. M. (1996). *Psychiatric symptoms and mental retardation: Reliability of rating scales as a function of IQ.* Unpublished master's thesis. Columbus: Ohio State University.

Helsel, W. J., & Matson, J. L. (1984). The assessment of depression in children: The internal structure of the Child Depression Inventory (CDI). *Behaviour Research and Therapy, 22,* 289–298.

Holden, B., & Gitlesen, J. P. (2003). Prevalence of psychiatric symptoms in adults with mental retardation and challenging behavior. *Research in Developmental Disabilities, 24,* 323–332.

Jacobson, J. W. (1982). Problem behavior and psychiatric impairment within a developmentally disabled population. I: Behavior frequency. *Applied Research in Developmental Disabilities, 3,* 121–139.

Kessler, R. C., McGonagle, K. A., Zhao, S., Nelson, C. B., Hughes, M., Eshelman, S., et al. (1994). Lifetime and 12-month prevalence of DSM-III-R psychiatric disorders in the United States: Results from the National Comorbidity Survey. *Archives of General Psychiatry, 51,* 8–19.

Laman, D. S., & Reiss, S. (1987). Social skill deficiencies associated with depressed mood of mentally retarded adults. *American Journal of Mental Deficiency, 92,* 224–229.

Lowry, M. A. (1998). Assessment and treatment of mood disorders in persons with developmental disabilities. *Journal of Developmental and Physical Disabilities, 10,* 387–406.

Lund, J. (1985). The prevalence of psychiatric morbidity in mentally retarded adults. *Acta Psychiatrica Scandinavia, 72,* 563–570.

Matson, J. L., Coe, D. A., Gardner, W. I., & Sovner, R. (1991). A factor analytic study of the Diagnostic Assessment for the Severely Handicapped Scale. *Journal of Nervous and Mental Diseases, 179,* 553–557.

Maughan, B., Collishaw, S., & Pickles, A. (1999). Mild mental retardation: Psychosocial functioning in adulthood. *Psychological Medicine, 29,* 351–366.

McBrien, J. A. (2003). Assessment and diagnosis of depression in people with intellectual disabilities. *Journal of Intellectual Disability Research, 47,* 1–13.

Meins, W. (1993). Prevalence and risk factors for depressive disorders in adults with intellectual disability. *Australia & New Zealand Journal of Developmental Disabilities, 18,* 147–156.

Moss, S. C., Emerson, R., Kiernan, C., Turner, S., Hatton, C., & Alborz, A. (2000). Psychiatric symptoms in adults with learning disability and challenging behaviour. *British Journal of Psychiatry, 177,* 452–456.

Moss, S., Patel, P., Prosser, H., Goldberg, D., Simpson, N., Rowe, S., et al. (1993). Psychiatric morbidity in older people with moderate and severe learning disability. I: Development and reliability of the patient interview (PAS-ADD). *British Journal of Psychiatry, 163,* 471–480.

National Institute of Mental Health. (1985). Clinical Global Impression Scale. *Psychopharmacology Bulletin, 21(4),* 839–841.

Reiss, S. (1988). *The Reiss Screen for Maladaptive Behavior test manual.* Worthington, OH: IDS Publishing.

Reiss, S. (1990). Prevalence of dual diagnosis in community-based day programs in the Chicago metropolitan area. *American Journal on Mental Retardation, 94,* 578–585.

Reiss, S., & Rojahn, J. (1993). Joint occurrence of depression and aggression in children and adults with mental retardation. *Journal of Intellectual Disability Research, 37,* 287–294.

Robins, L. N., Helzer, J. E., & Croughan, J. L. (1981). The NIMH diagnostic interview schedule: Its history, characteristics, and validity. *Archives of General Psychiatry, 38,* 381–389.

Robins, L. N., & Regier, D. A. (1991). *Psychiatric disorders in America: The epidemiologic catchment area study.* New York: Maxwell Macmillan International.

Rojahn, J., Borthwick-Duffy, S. A., & Jacobson, J. W. (1993). The association between psychiatric diagnoses and severe behavior problems in mental retardation. *Annals of Clinical Psychiatry, 5,* 163–170.

Rojahn, J., Matson, J. L., Naglieri, J. A., & Mayville, E. (2004). Relationships between psychiatric conditions and behavior problems among adults with mental retardation. *American Journal on Mental Retardation, 109,* 21–33.

Rojahn, J., & Tassé, M. J. (1996). Psychopathology in mental retardation. In J. W. Jacobson & J. A. Mulick (Eds.), *Manual on mental retardation and professional practice* (pp. 147–156). Washington, DC: American Psychological Association.

Rush, A. J., & Frances, A. (Eds.). (2000). Treatment of psychiatric and behavioral problems in mental retardation [Special issue]. *American Journal on Mental Retardation, 105,* 159–228.

Rutter, M., Tizard, J., & Whitmore, K. (Eds.). (1970). *Education, health and behaviour.* London: Longman and Green.

Rutter, M., Tizard, J., Yule, W., Graham, P., & Whitmore, K. (1976). Isle of Wight studies, 1964–1974. *Psychological Medicine, 6,* 313–332.

Salvador-Carulla, L., Rodríguez-Blázquez, C., de Molina, M. R., Pérez-Marín, J., & Velázquez, R. (2000). Hidden psychiatric morbidity in a vocational programme for people with intellectual disability. *Journal of Intellectual Disability Research, 44,* 147–154.

Taylor, J. L., Hatton, C., Dixon, L., & Douglas, C. (2004). Screening for psychiatric symptoms: PAS-ADD Checklist norms for adults with intellectual disabilities. *Journal of Intellectual Disability Research, 48,* 37–41.

Weissman, M. M., Livingston-Bruce, M., Leaf, P. J., Florio, L. P., & Holzer III, C. (1991). Affective disorders. (1991). In L. N. Robins & D. A. Regier (Eds.), *Psychiatric disorders in America: The Epidemiologic Catchment Area study* (pp. 53–80). New York: Maxwell Macmillan International.

Weissman, M. M., Bland, R. C., Canino, G. J., Faravelli, K., Greenwald, S., Hwu, H. G., et al. (1996). Cross-national epidemiology of major depression and bipolar disorder. *Journal of the American Medical Association, 276,* 293–299.

World Health Organization (WHO). (1990). *Composite International Diagnostic Interview (CIDI), Version 1.0.* Geneva: Author.

World Health Organization (WHO). (1992). *International Statistical Classification of Diseases and Health Related Problems (ICD-10), Volume 1: Classification of mental and behavioural disorders: Clinical description and diagnostic guidelines.* Geneva: Author.

Author Note

Preparation of this chapter was supported in part by Grant # R215K010121 from the U.S. Department of Education.

4

Causes of Mood Disorders in People With Mental Retardation

Anna J. Esbensen

and

Johannes Rojahn

Understanding the etiology of a condition enhances the development of appropriate treatment techniques. Numerous theories explaining the etiology of mood disorders have been proposed, most of which stimulated the development of assessment and treatment methods. Since these theories were all developed for the general population, we need to ask whether and to what extent these theories may be applicable for mood disorders in individuals with mental retardation. This chapter reviews several of the most relevant etiological theories for depression and bipolar disorder and then evaluates on the basis of the available literature their respective utility for individuals with mental retardation.

Depressive Disorders

A number of etiological theories of depressive disorders have been formulated, which can be classified into four broad categories: biological, interpersonal, behavioral, and cognitive-behavioral theories.

Biological Theories of Depression

Among the biological theories that attempt to explain the etiology of depressive disorder, we can distinguish between the genetic and the endocrine theories.

Genetic Theories.

Genetic studies with twins and family members have produced strong evidence that an inherited, genetic predisposition to depression exists, notwithstanding the significant role played by social and environmental factors (Beardslee, Versage & Gladstone, 1998; Kendler & Prescott, 1999). Only a few studies have evaluated family members of individuals with a dual diagnosis of mental retardation and concurrent depression. However, some do discuss the incidence of psychopathology among family members of individuals with only developmental disabilities. Of a sample of autistic individuals, the incidence of bipolar disorders among first- and second-degree relatives was 4.2%, and the incidence of depressive disorder was 8.0% (DeLong & Dwyer, 1988). As compared with the general population, the incidence rate of bipolar disorder was higher in mental retardation, whereas the rate of depressive disorders was similar (Schwartz & Schwartz, 1993). A comparison of siblings and parents of children with pervasive developmental disorders (PDDs), children with Down syndrome, and a control group of typically developing children revealed that rates of parental distress and depression were higher among parents of children with PDDs and Down syndrome as compared with the control group (Fisman, Wolf, Ellison, & Freeman, 2000). Rossiter and Sharpe (2001) cited several papers that indicated that siblings of children with mental retardation exhibit such negative consequences as depression, loneliness, and low self-esteem. Their meta-analysis confirmed differences in levels of depression and psychological functioning among these siblings as compared with a control group. Together, these studies indicate that families of individuals with mental retardation and/or developmental disabilities are susceptible to depression; the duration and the cause of the depressive symptoms are variable at best, however, and depend on a variety of other factors (as reviewed in Krauss & Seltzer, 1998; Rossiter & Sharpe, 2001). In addition, since there is no mention of comorbid depression among individuals with mental retardation, no conclusions can be made about the genetic component of depression among individuals with mental retardation and depression based on family members.

Neuroendocrine Theories.

Empirical support of neurobiological theories of depressive disorder has been less conclusive. Neurobiological tests have been developed in an attempt to find biological markers that could be used to screen for depression. These include the Dexamethasone Suppression Test (DST), based on the functioning of the hypothalamic-pituitary-adrenal (HPA) axis, and the Thyrotropin-Releasing Hormone Suppression Test (TRHST), based on the functioning of the thyroid-stimulating hormone (TSH) on the hypothalamic-pituitary-thyroid (HPT) axis (Carroll, 1982; Pueschel, Jackson, Giesswein, Dean, & Pezzullo, 1991). Using different hormones, the HPA and HPT axes regulate such functions as sleep, appetite, and adaptation to stress, all characteristics symptomatic of depression. It was hoped that the DST or TRHST could serve as gold standards for the diagnosis of depression. Unfortunately, testing has revealed contradictory findings regarding the effectiveness of these tests. A high rate of false positives has led to the utility of the tests being questioned (American Psychiatric Association Task Force on Laboratory Tests in Psychiatry, 1987; Birmaher et al., 1992; Poznanski, Carroll, Banegas, Cook, & Grossman, 1982). False positives can result from various major medical conditions, autism, such medications as anticonvulsants and sedative hypnotics, endocrine disturbances, weight changes, alcohol abuse or withdrawal, thyroid abnormality, and other commonly used psychiatric medications, and they also vary with age and gender (Wolkowitz, 1990).

Evaluations of the DST with individuals with mental retardation have led to mixed results. Some were in favor of the test, whereas others concluded that it had limited diagnostic value (Beckwith et al., 1985; Keane & Soni, 1992; Mattes & Amsell, 1993; Mudford et al., 1995; Ruedrich, Wadle, Sallach, Hahn, & Menolascino, 1987; Soni, Keane, & Soni, 1992). Assessments of TSH among individuals with mental retardation have primarily focused on individuals with Down syndrome, because they are vulnerable to hypothyroidism and dementia of the Alzheimer's type (Pueschel et al., 1991). Again, results are mixed regarding the utility of the TSH (Bhaumik, Collacott, Garrick, & Mitchell, 1991; Christie et al., 1987; Prasher & Hall, 1996).

In general, the evidence regarding genetic and neurobiological theories of depression among individuals with mental retardation parallels the findings from the general population. With advances being made in such biological assessment as fMRIs and MRIs, it is hoped that these developments will also be applied to individuals with mental retardation and psychopathology.

Interpersonal Causes

Interpersonal theories take a multidimensional perspective, where social, environmental, and biological factors are all seen as potentially influencing depression (Klerman, Weissman, Rounsaville, & Chevron, 1984; Lewinsohn, 1974a; Lewinsohn, Mischel, Chaplin, & Barton, 1980; Schwartz & Schwartz, 1993). The main focus, however, is directed to the specific environmental and social circumstances that can cause depression. These causes include a poor social support system and stressful life events (for example, losing a job, or the loss of a significant relationship). A related assumption is that poor social skills contribute to negative social experiences and therefore to symptoms of depression. The interpersonal theories focus less on how interpersonal skills cause depression and more on how management of interpersonal skills can be used in the treatment of depression.

Empirical evidence among individuals with mental retardation that is consistent with interpersonal theories of depression has been found in studies of social skills, social support, and depression (Benson, Reiss, Smith, & Laman, 1985; Laman & Reiss, 1987; Reiss & Benson, 1985). For instance, Benson et al., (1985) and Reiss and Benson (1985) found that ratings of depressed mood were negatively correlated with global ratings of social skills and social support among individuals with mild mental retardation. A later extension of this work incorporated specific ratings of social skills to supplement the previous global ratings (Laman & Reiss, 1987) and replicated the negative association between depressed mood and social skills. Three of the four subscales of the measure of social skills negatively correlated with depression, and 53% of the social skills items differentiated high- and low-depressed groups. In a comparison of individuals diagnosed with depression and mental retardation and a control group with only mental retardation, Meins (1993) found a significant difference between these groups on measures of social support. Individuals with depression had lower levels of social support, as measured by the amount and quality of it. A study of loneliness, depression, and self-reports of social skills found a moderate negative correlation between depression and social skills among adolescents with mental retardation, further supporting the interpersonal theories (Heiman & Margalit, 1998).

Other study outcomes were inconsistent with the interpersonal theories of depression. Rojahn and Warren (1997) examined mood, social competence, and the ability to recognize facially expressed emotions. Because the link between depression and social skills was not an expressed interest of the study, depression was correlated only with the subscale of inappropriate assertion (a measure of aggression) on the social skills measure. Depression was not significantly associated with such other social skills subscales as empathy, self-centeredness, or sociopathic behaviors. This finding argues against the interpersonal theory of depression, in that depression was not associated with all features of social skills. Helsel and Matson (1988) also correlated measures of depression and social skills, and concluded that they were correlated. A closer look at the correlations, however, suggests that this conclusion may be debatable. The study included four depression measures and two measures of social performance, a self-report, and an informant-report measure. Informant-reported social skills were not significantly correlated with any of the depression measures, and self-reported social skills were significantly correlated with only one depression measure. Paradoxically, this correlation was positive, which means that more severe depression was associated with better social skills and vice versa.

Consistent with the interpersonal theories of mood disorders are findings from the social support literature among individuals with mental retardation (Lunsky & Benson, 2001). The impact of social support and social strain were examined using self-reports of individuals with mental retardation. Social strain was defined as interpersonal relations that lead to stress or negative outcomes. It was found that social strain rather than social support, as measured by self-report of perceived support, was predictive of depressive symptoms. Lunsky and Havercamp (1999) also found an association between depressive symptoms and social strain. No association between depressive symptoms and positive social support was found. Lunsky and Havercamp's findings are consistent with the interpersonal theories in that social strain is predictive of depressive symptoms.

Interpersonal theories of depression are generally supported by research among individuals with mental retardation. Despite the occasional study with deviating data, there does appear to be an association among social skills, social support, social strain, and depression in this population. It is not clear, however, whether there is a direct causal link between deficits in social skills and depression or vice versa or whether other variables cause both social skills deficits and depression.

Behavioral Causes

Inadequate Reinforcement Theory.

According to Lewinsohn (1974a), depression is a product of an unreinforcing environment and the person's interaction with that environment. Lewinsohn believed that the depressed person's inadequate social skills and inability to elicit positive interpersonal responses resulted in insufficient positive reinforcement from significant others, and a depressed pattern of responding. Low rates of "response-contingent positive reinforcement" (RCPR) in significant areas of one's life, or a high rate of aversive experiences, would lead to the reduction in behavior, and subsequently the development of depression. Three factors were suggested to contribute to low rates of RCPR. One involved deficits in behavioral skills, which resulted in the attainment of fewer reinforcers or a reduction in the individual's ability to behave effectively during aversive situations. The second factor concerned a lack of potential reinforcers in the individual's environment, and the last involved a decrease in the individual's ability to enjoy positive experiences. Lewinsohn's theory of depression focused on a reduction of contingently obtained social reinforcement from significant others.

Coyne's Model.

Coyne's (1976) theory of depression extended Lewinsohn's model by suggesting that individuals vulnerable to depression tend to arouse anger, rejection, and anxiety in others through their depressive behavior, such as constant complaints, negativistic statements, requests for support, and talking about personal problems. The depressed individual's behaviors gradually become increasingly demanding and aversive to their family and friends. The family and friends then feel guilty and inhibit expressions of anger at the depressed individual's repeated demands. To reduce their guilt, family and friends withdraw and display false reassurance or support, of which the individual becomes aware. This negative interpersonal feedback results in the individual becoming increasingly symptomatic, further deteriorating the social environment.

Empirical Evidence of Behavioral Models.

Among individuals with mental retardation, research has produced some empirical support for the behavioral theories of depression. For instance, in comparing verbal interactions between depressed and nondepressed individuals with mental retardation, Schloss (1982) found that the depressed subjects elicited fewer interactions than did the nondepressed participants, and that the interactions that were elicited were primarily requests. In other words, depressed individuals with mental retardation not only interacted less with others, but they also elicited fewer interactions. The reluctance of staff to initiate communications with the depressed individuals is consistent with Coyne's theory that interacting with an individual with depression is unpleasant and thus avoided by others (Schloss, 1982). Additional support comes from a study comparing children with mental retardation and depression or no depression (Kobe & Hammer, 1994). Differences were found on the Reinforcement of Parent subscale of the Parenting Stress Index. Although the directionality of this finding is unclear, it is consistent with Coyne's contention that individuals with depression are demanding of their friends and family.

Several studies have been conducted using treatments based on behavior therapy to reduce the symptoms of depression among individuals with mental retardation (Frame, Matson, Sonis, Fiaklov, & Kazdin, 1982; Matson, 1982; Matson, Dettling, & Senatore, 1981). The behavioral treatments targeted negative self-statements, suicidal statements, somatic complaints, overall word output, eye contact, and positive affect. The behavioral treatments were successful in changing the targeted behaviors in the desired direction, and also in reducing scores on self-report measures of depression. The studies are limited, however, in that they did not assess for generalization of treatment to other symptoms of depression or beyond the treatment sessions (Benson, 1990).

Although some studies have found evidence for an association between aggressive behavior and depressive symptoms in individuals with mental retardation (Bramston & Fogarty, 2000; Reiss & Rojahn, 1993), others have not (Benson & Ivins, 1992; Rojahn, Matson, Naglieri, & Mayville, 2004; Tsiouris, Mann, Patti, & Sturmey, 2003). Behavioral theories could explain that aggressive behaviors might be associated with depression among individuals with mental retardation, because aggressive behavior can be maintained by low rates of contingent positive reinforcement in the presence of high response effort (Lewinsohn, 1974b). Aggressive individuals tend to be avoided by others, which further isolates them and aggravates the severity of their depressive symptoms.

Cognitive Causes

The basic assumption of cognitive theories of depression is that depressive cognitive patterns cause individuals to interpret experiences in such a way as to develop, maintain, or exacerbate their depression. These cognitive patterns of thought are stable over the lifespan and predisposing to depressive episodes. Numerous theories have been posited over the years and differ in regard to the specific nature of the cognitions.

Cognitive Triad Model.

Aaron Beck (Beck, 1967, 1970, 1976) theorized that negative schemata and the development of a "cognitive triad" could characterize depressed individuals. Schemata are stable organizing rules and procedures that guide the processing of information. In the face of events the individual interprets as stressful, the negative schemata are activated and serve to influence the processing of subsequent information negatively. The depressed individual negatively interprets situations as an automatic reaction and has limited ability to generate rational and obvious explanations for the same event. The cognitive triad consists of "a negative conception of the self, a negative interpretation of life experiences, and a nihilistic view of the future" (Beck, 1967, p. 84). Negative self-views lead depressed individuals to consider themselves as inadequate and to believe that unpleasant experiences occur as a result of their own actions or characteristics. A depressed individual views the world as full of obstacles and interprets interactions with the environment in a negative manner. Further, the future is viewed as full of hardships, and the current difficulties are believed to continue endlessly. This distorted view functions to maintain the individual's depression.

Beck (1967, 1970) acknowledged that individuals with mental retardation could suffer from depression. In describing motivational changes in depression, Beck used a case example of a woman with depression and mental retardation. Her attempts to avoid undesirable activities were used as an instance of negative views of the environment. In presenting a cognitive theory and providing an example of an individual with mental retardation, Beck may have been the first to imply that his theory is applicable to individuals with mental retardation.

Self-Control Model of Depression.

Rehm (1977) adopted a self-control model of depression. This model was derived from a general model of self-control, describing adaptive processes of self-monitoring, self-evaluation, and self-reinforcement (Kanfer, 1970). Rehm speculated that depressed individuals suffered from important deficits in self-management skills. In regards to self-monitoring, depressed individuals exhibit selective attention to negative as opposed to positive events, and to immediate as opposed to delayed consequences of behavior. Deficits in self-evaluation included setting stringent self-evaluation standards and adopting a negative attributional style. In regards to self-reinforcement, depressed individuals provide insufficient contingent positive self-reinforcement and excessive self-punishment. Depressed individuals set standards for themselves that are unrealistic, and thus attainment of these standards is improbable.

Learned Helplessness Theory.

Originally, Seligman (Seligman, 1974, 1975) proposed that exposure to non-contingently delivered aversive events could result in *learned helplessness,* which could be a behavioral model of depression. Because the original theory was not empirically supported, the theory was revised to include cognitive explanations and was retitled the *reformulated learned helplessness theory of depression* (Abramson, Seligman & Teasdale, 1978). Here it was proposed that the development of depression would be influenced by an individual's attributions regarding a situation. These attributions would be a combination of attributions regarding negative events that were stable (unchanging), internal (due to characteristics of the individual), and global (generalized across many situations). The attributions were assumed to be dependent upon fixed characteristics of the individual. The learned helplessness theory was revised once again to include a *hopeless* subtype of depression (Abramson, Metalsky, & Alloy, 1989). Depression stemmed from negative expectations about the desired outcome of events and from thoughts of hopelessness regarding changing the likelihood of these undesired outcomes.

Cognitive Considerations.

Most studies examining cognitive causes of depression among individuals with mental retardation limit their findings to those functioning at the higher levels of intellectual functioning. Studies typically exclude individuals with severe, profound, and occasionally moderate mental retardation. However, it is still important to evaluate cognitive theories with individuals with mental retardation within a cognitive developmental framework. Developmental models of cognition conclude that the capability to encode information regarding the self begins to emerge during elementary school and solidifies in adolescence (Kaslow, Brown, & Mee, 1994). The ability to differentiate judgments regarding their own characteristics can be seen in children as young as 8 years. Self-reflection and self-evaluation are abilities developed in elementary school, although preschoolers can also make absolute self-evaluations; that is, they can set unrealistic and perfectionist standards for themselves. The ability to conceptualize temporal events is a prerequisite for having a negative view of the future. It appears that when children have achieved thinking in a concrete operational manner, they are also able to understand temporal features, such as time intervals between events and the sequencing of events (Rehm & Carter, 1990). Preschool children are capable of making attributions regarding their successes and failures (Kaslow et al., 1994). Still, the ability to differentiate between internal and external loci of control, similar to internal and external attributions, is not fully developed until children enter elementary school. These findings suggest that some of the cognitive processes required to support the cognitive theories of depression develop in elementary school or around 8 years of age. Among studies of depression in individuals with mental retardation, a similar level of cognitive ability should be taken into consideration when evaluating these theories.

Empirical Evidence of Cognitive Theories of Depression.

Very few studies have evaluated the cognitive theories of depression among individuals with mental retardation. (See Chapter 12, by Lindsay, Stenfert Kroese, and Drew, for a detailed, comprehensive review). In the examination of modified cognitive therapy for depression among two individuals with mild mental retardation, self-report scores on the Beck Depression Inventory (BDI) decreased with treatment (Lindsay, Howells, & Pithcaithy, 1993). It was concluded that the cognitive therapy could be effective with this population.

A study of depression among individuals with mental retardation assessed verbal behavior. No differences in negative self-statements were found between groups of depressed and nondepressed individuals with mental retardation (Matson, Senatore, Kazdin, & Helsel, 1983). The absence of negative self-statements among depressed individuals is not supportive of cognitive theories of depression. However, this study compared individuals with mental retardation with high scores versus low scores on the BDI, and did not report clinical diagnoses.

Support for the cognitive theories of depression among adults with mild mental retardation was found in a systematic study of self-report measures of depression, automatic thoughts, hopelessness, self-reinforcement, and social support (Nezu, Nezu, Rothenberg, DelliCarpini, & Groag, 1995). The self-report measures of depression, the BDI, and the Psychopathology Inventory for Mentally Retarded Adults (PIMRA) were all significantly correlated with the cognitive variables. Individuals with higher depressive scores on these instruments exhibited more negative automatic thoughts, lower rates of self-reinforcement, and greater feelings of hopelessness. The association between instruments measuring depression and cognitive variables was also confirmed with a group of individuals with mental retardation diagnosed with clinical depression as compared with a matched control group without depression.

Most recently, Glenn, Bihm, and Lammers (2003) examined the "cognitive specificity" of cognitions related to anxiety and depression among individuals with mental retardation. Assessments of automatic thoughts with self-report instruments confirmed a relationship between cognitions and measures of depression among individuals with mental retardation. In addition, the measured cognitive variables accounted for 79% of the variance in depression.

Although the construct of learned hopelessness has been extensively studied in the mental retardation, rarely has it been explored in the context of depression. An early report described individuals with mental retardation and depression as expressing feelings of hopelessness, helplessness, and unworthiness (Berman, 1967). Since then, studies have focused on assessing differences in learned helplessness among individuals with and without mental retardation, but not always in relation to depression. It was found that individuals with mental retardation, both institutionalized and noninstitutionalized, displayed more behaviors consistent with learned helplessness as compared with control individuals (Floor & Rosen, 1975). Individuals with mental retardation have been shown to experience more failure compared with their peers, which, according to the learned helplessness theory, would result in differing expectations of success (Raber & Weisz, 1981; Weisz, 1979). However, this conclusion has not always been supported (Gargiulo, O'Sullivan, & Barr, 1987). So far, studies have failed to demonstrate that individuals with mental retardation make attributions in the expected domains according to the learned helplessness theory. Individuals with increased learned helplessness would be expected to attribute failure to a lack of ability. However, while it was found that children with mental retardation were more likely to be helpless in the face of failure than were children without mental retardation, they were also more likely to attribute their failure to lack of effort rather than to a lack of ability (Raber & Weisz, 1981). Reports relating depression and hopelessness among individuals with mental retardation are few (Barnhill, 2001; Nezu et al., 1995; Reynolds & Miller, 1985). Adolescents with mental retardation were found to score significantly higher on self-report measures of depression and learned helplessness as compared with a matched group of adolescents without mental retardation (Reynolds & Miller, 1985). Barnhill (2001) assessed attributions and depression among adolescents with Asperger syndrome and found a positive relationship between depression and ability attributions for social failure. However, these adolescents were not diagnosed with mental retardation.

The diathesis-stress model is a major component of the cognitive theories of depression. Unfortunately, life events and stressors have received little attention in relation to depression among individuals with mental retardation. More attention has been focused on the relation of life events to behavioral problems. An examination of life events among adults with Down syndrome experiencing recurrent depression revealed that they were less likely than were individuals suffering a single episode to have significant life events prior to an occurrence (Cooper & Collacott, 1994). Of the cases of single episode depression, 44% exhibited an associated life event, as compared with only 14% in the recurrent depression group. The finding indicates that the association between depression and life events may be influenced by the duration and recurrence of the psychiatric illness, with life events playing a smaller role in predicting depression over time. An additional study examined children with pervasive developmental disorders (PDDs) and comorbid depression with a control group of nondepressed children with PDDs (Ghaziuddin, Alessi, & Greden, 1995). The mean number of life events for the 12 months prior to the onset of depression was significantly higher for the depressed group as compared with the nondepressed group. However, 45% of the depressed children and only 27% of the nondepressed children met the criteria for definition of mental retardation.

In measuring stressors in the diathesis-stress model, it has been suggested that individuals with mental retardation may be more vulnerable to daily life stressors, which then increases their risk for mental health disorders. The types of situations considered stressful by individuals with mental retardation have been compared with those reported by university students (Bramston, Fogarty, & Cummins, 1999). It was found that individuals with mental retardation reported more interpersonal stressors. The nature of stress, potentially related to the diathesis-stress in depression, is a new area of research currently receiving more attention. Given the work of Bramston and colleagues, it may be that life event stressors among individuals with mental retardation may be different from the general population. The relative influence of life events or daily stressors in the development of depression warrants further research.

Although no studies to date have explicitly tested the cognitive theories of depression among individuals with mental retardation, it appears that self-report measures of cognitions can be reliably reported among individuals with mild mental retardation. Preliminary work in mental retardation has supported the notion of an association between cognitive variables and depression, and that cognitive theories of depression in mental retardation should be examined further. However, how suitable the cognitive theories are for explaining depression among individuals functioning at moderate, severe, and profound levels of mental retardation remains to be seen.

Bipolar Disorder

Bipolar disorder is considered to be the most genetically influenced mental disorder, aside from schizophrenia. However, its mechanism is generally unknown. The field of neurobiology and genetics of bipolar disorder in the general population is in its infancy. New genetic innovations are providing some insight into the possible causes of the disorder; however they have received minimal attention in the field of mental retardation. A quick review of the potential causes of the disorder is provided, along with a review of the literature related to mental retardation and developmental disabilities.

Genetic Theories

Genetic vulnerability to bipolar disorder among the general population has been initially evaluated using family, twin, and genetic studies. Bipolar disorder is strongly tied to genetic causes with studies revealing family history to be a significant risk factor in its development (Kelsoe, 1997). Twin studies have reported high, but imperfect, concordance rates. This indicates that bipolar disorder is highly, but not exclusively, heritable.

Case reports of individuals with bipolar disorder and mental retardation provide marginal support for causal family history. Two of 5 case reports and 5 of 10 case reports show a family history of mood disorders among first-degree relatives (Glue, 1989; McCracken & Diamond, 1988). Several studies have examined the family history of individuals with autism and typically found higher prevalence of bipolar disorder than expected in the general population (DeLong & Dwyer, 1988; Gillberg, 1989). Some genetic studies have suggested a link between autism spectrum disorders and bipolar disorder (Gillberg & Wahlstrom, 1985; Kerbershian, Severud, Burd, & Larson, 2000). Replication is still warranted, however.

Evidence in support of the genetic theories of bipolar disorder in both the general population and among individuals with mental retardation is promising. Although the field is still in its infancy with both populations, initial evidence shows a strong genetic component of bipolar disorders.

Kindling Hypothesis

Recent neuroimaging studies are linking bipolar disorder to structural and functional abnormalities in the amygdala, cerebellar vermis, hippocampus, prefrontal cortex, thalamus, striatum, and white matter lesions (DelBello et al., 2000; reviewed in Strakowski, DelBello, Adler, Cecil, & Sax, 2000). A theory that has been proposed to explain the mechanism of bipolar disorder is the *kindling hypothesis* (Post, 1990). Frequent early episodes of bipolar illness predispose the individual to more frequent episodes later in the course of the disorder. In this view, responses to stress result in changes at the level of the individual neuron, thereby intensifying the individual's vulnerability to affective disorders.

Case-study reports of adolescents with mental retardation and bipolar disorder provide marginal support for the kindling hypothesis (McCracken & Diamond, 1988). Of the five case reports presented, three involved an identifiable stressor.

Circadian Rhythms

Circadian rhythms, such as the sleep-wake cycle and temperature rhythm, are commonly believed to play an important role in bipolar disorder (Barbini, Bertelli, Colombo, & Smeraldi, 1996; Colombo, Benedetti, Barbini, Campori, & Smeraldi, 1999). Sleep duration and timing have been reported to be influential in the onset of manic episodes (Wehr et al., 1998). Several theories have been presented over the years to explain the hypothesized mechanism of sleep-wake disturbances on mood disorders. The research in the general population has primarily focused on depression, however.

The influence of circadian rhythms on bipolar disorders has been acknowledged within the field of mental retardation. The amount of sleep is commonly measured along with other symptoms to help assess bipolar symptoms among individuals with mental retardation (Lowry, 1998; Lowry & Sovner, 1992). Glue (1989) reviewed a series of case reports of cyclical changes. The cyclical changes occurred in blood chemistry, however, and were not linked to cycles of mood.

Conclusion

Research regarding the causes of depression among individuals with mental retardation is still is its infancy. Although the causal theories of depression developed for the general population typically perform well for individuals with mental retardation, the theories have not been explicitly tested with this population. Research to date presents a trend toward support of the behavioral, interpersonal, and cognitive causes of depression among individuals with mental retardation. An evaluation of the theoretical causes of depression deserves more attention, however, in order to confirm their utility in designing assessments and treatment programs for this population. Presenting an accurate theory-driven causal basis of mood disorders tailored for individuals with mental retardation will provide great assistance in the development of treatment and prevention programs in order to relieve symptoms of depression.

Information about the causal nature of bipolar disorder is in its early years in both the general population and in the field of mental retardation. It is hoped that as advances are made in the neurobiology of bipolar disorder, researchers will continue to examine the causes in relation to individuals with mental retardation.

Implications for Practice

In order to provide the best treatment to a client with psychopathology, the treatment must be based on sound research. Sound research is driven by theory. These principles hold true both for the general population and for individuals with mental retardation. Clinicians treating individuals with mental retardation and mood disorders are advised (a) to understand the theory that drives the treatments developed for the general population, (b) to assess how the theories developed for the general population are appropriate for individuals with mental retardation (through reviewing or conducting research), (c) to apply theory to their practice, and (d) to share their theoretically driven treatment modifications with other clinicians. Based on the theories generated to explain mood disorders in the general population and the support of these theories in treating individuals with mental retardation, some implications can be drawn. Clinicians are advised to avoid using the DST or TRHST until these instruments have been provided with greater support. Behavioral, interpersonal, and cognitive theories all have some support with regard to depression and are worth applying in therapy, but they need more rigorous testing among individuals with mental retardation. Clinicians should stay aware of advances being made in regard to the development of bipolar disorder.

References

Abramson, L. Y., Metalsky, G. I., & Alloy, L. B. (1989). Hopelessness depression: A theory-based subtype of depression. *Psychological Review, 96,* 358–372.

Abramson, L. Y., Seligman, M. E. P., & Teasdale, J. (1978). Learned helplessness in humans: Critique and reformulation. *Journal of Abnormal Psychology, 87,* 49–74.

American Psychiatric Association Task Force on Laboratory Tests in Psychiatry. (1987). The Dexamethasone Suppression Test: An overview of its current status in psychiatry. *American Journal of Psychiatry, 144,* 1253–1262.

Barbini, B., Bertelli, S., Colombo, C., & Smeraldi, E. (1996). Sleep loss, a possible factor in augmenting manic episode. *Psychiatric Research, 65,* 121–125.

Barnhill, G. P. (2001). Social attributions and depression in adolescents with Asperger syndrome. *Focus on Autism and Other Developmental Disabilities, 16,* 46–53.

Beardslee, W. R., Versage, E. M., & Gladstone, T. R. G. (1998). Children of affectively ill parents: A review of the past 10 years. *Journal of the American Academy of Child and Adolescent Psychiatry, 37,* 1134–1141.

Beck, A. T. (1967). *The diagnosis and management of the emotional disorders.* Philadelphia: University of Pennsylvania Press.

Beck, A. T. (1970). *Depression: Causes and treatment.* Philadelphia: University of Pennsylvania Press.

Beck, A. T. (1976). *Cognitive therapy and the emotional disorders*. New York: International Universities Press.

Beckwith, B. E., Parker, L., Pawlarczyk, D., Couk, D. I., Schumacher, K. S., & Yearwood, K. (1985). The dexamethasone suppression test in depressed retarded adults: Preliminary findings. *Biological Psychiatry, 20,* 825–831.

Benson, B. A. (1990). Behavioral treatment of depression. In A. Dosen & F. J. Menolascino (Eds.), *Depression in mentally retarded children and adults* (pp. 309–330). Leiden, Netherlands: Logon Publications.

Benson, B. A., & Ivins, J. (1992). Anger, depression and self-concept in adults with mental retardation. *Journal of Intellectual Disability Research, 36,* 169–175.

Benson, B. A., Reiss, S., Smith, D. C., & Laman, D. S. (1985). Psychosocial correlates of depression in mentally retarded adults. II: Poor social skills. *American Journal of Mental Deficiency, 89,* 657–659.

Berman, M. I. (1967). Mental retardation and depression. *Mental Retardation, 5,* 19–21.

Bhaumik, S., Collacott, R. A., Garrick, P., & Mitchell, C. (1991). Effect of thyroid stimulating hormone on adaptive behaviour in Down's syndrome. *Journal of Mental Deficiency Research, 35,* 512–520.

Birmaher, B., Ryan, N. D., Dahl, R., Rabinovich, H., Ambrosini, P., Williamson, D. E., et al. (1992). Dexamethasone Suppression Test in children with major depressive disorder. *Journal of the American Academy of Child and Adolescent Psychiatry, 31,* 291–297.

Bramston, P., & Fogarty, G. (2000). The assessment of emotional distress experienced by people with an intellectual disability: A study of different methodologies. *Research in Developmental Disabilities, 21,* 487–500.

Bramston, P., Fogarty, G., & Cummins, R. A. (1999). The nature of stressors reported by people with an intellectual disability. *Journal of Applied Research in Intellectual Disabilities, 12,* 1–10.

Carroll, B. J. (1982). The Dexamethasone Suppression Test for melancholia. *British Journal of Psychiatry, 140,* 292–304.

Christie, J. R., Walley, J., Bennie, J., Dick, H., Blackburn, I. M., Blackwood, D. H. R., et al. (1987). Characteristic plasma hormonal changes in Alzheimer's disease. *British Journal of Psychiatry, 150,* 674–681.

Colombo, C., Benedetti, F., Barbini, B., Campori, E., & Smeraldi, E. (1999). Rate of switch from depression into mania after therapeutic sleep deprivation in bipolar depression. *Psychiatric Research, 86,* 267–270.

Cooper, S. A., & Collacott, R. A. (1994). Relapse of depression in people with Down's syndrome. *British Journal of Developmental Disabilities, 40,* 32–37.

Coyne, J. C. (1976). Toward an interactional description of depression. *Psychiatry,* *39,* 28–40.

DelBello, M.A., Soutullo, C.A., Ryan, P., Graman, S.M., Zimmerman, M.E., Getz, G.E., et al. (2000). MRI analysis of children at risk for bipolar disorder. *Biological Psychiatry, 47* (Suppl. 1), 135.

DeLong, G. R., & Dwyer, J. T. (1988). Correlation of family history with specific autistic subgroups: Asperger's syndrome and bipolar affective disease. *Journal of Autism and Developmental Disorders, 18,* 593–600.

Fisman, S., Wolf, L., Ellison, D., & Freeman, T. (2000). A longitudinal study of siblings of children with chronic disabilities. *Canadian Journal of Psychiatry, 45,* 369–375.

Floor, L., & Rosen, M. (1975). Investigating the phenomenon of helplessness in mentally retarded adults. *American Journal of Mental Deficiency, 79,* 565–572.

Frame, C., Matson, J. L., Sonis, W. A., Fiaklov, M. J., & Kazdin, A. E. (1982). Behavioral treatment of depression in a prepubertal child. *Journal of Behavior Therapy in Experimental Psychiatry, 13,* 239–243.

Gargiulo, R. M., O'Sullivan, P. S., & Barr, N. J. (1987). Learned helplessness in reflective and impulsive mentally retarded and nonretarded children. *Bulletin of the Psychonomic Society, 25,* 269–272.

Ghaziuddin, M., Alessi, N., & Greden, J. F. (1995). Life events and depression in children with pervasive developmental disorders. *Journal of Autism and Developmental Disorders, 25,* 495–502.

Gillberg, C. (1989). Asperger syndrome in 23 Swedish children. *Developmental Medicine and Child Neurology, 31,* 520–531.

Gillberg, C., & Wahlstrom, J. (1985). Chromosome abnormalities in infantile autism and other childhood psychoses: A population study of 66 cases. *Developmental Medicine and Child Neurology, 27,* 293–304.

Glenn, E., Bihm, E. M., & Lammers, W. J. (2003). Depression, anxiety and relevant cognitions in persons with mental retardation. *Journal of Autism and Developmental Disorders, 33,* 69–76.

Glue, P. (1989). Rapid cycling affective disorders in the mentally retarded. *Biological Psychiatry, 26,* 250–256.

Heiman, T., & Margalit, M. (1998). Loneliness, depression, and social skills among students with mild mental retardation in different educational settings. *Journal of Special Education, 32,* 154–163.

Helsel, W. J., & Matson, J. L. (1988). The relationship of depression to social skills and intellectual functioning in mentally retarded adults. *Journal of Mental Deficiency Research, 32,* 411–418.

Kanfer, F. H. (1970). Self-monitoring: Methodological limitations and clinical applications. *Journal of Consulting and Clinical Psychology, 35,* 148–152.

Kaslow, N. J., Brown, R. T., & Mee, L. L. (1994). Cognitive and behavioral correlates of childhood depression: A developmental perspective. In W. M. Reynolds & H. F. Johnston (Eds.), *Handbook of depression in children and adolescents* (pp. 97–121). New York: Plenum Press.

Keane, V., & Soni, S. (1992). Dexamethasone Suppression Test in mentally handicapped subjects. *Irish Journal of Psychological Medicine, 9,* 101–105.

Kelsoe, J. R. (1997). The genetics of bipolar disorder. *Psychiatric Annals, 27,* 285–292.

Kendler, K. S., & Prescott, C. A. (1999). A population-based study of lifetime major depression in men and women. *Archives of General Psychiatry, 56,* 39–44.

Kerbershian, J., Severud, R., Burd, L., & Larson, L. (2000). Peek-a-boo fragile site at 16D associated with Tourette syndrome, bipolar disorder, autistic disorder, and mental retardation. *American Journal of Medical Genetics (Neuropsychiatric Genetics), 96,* 69–73.

Klerman, G. L., Weissman, M. M., Rounsaville, B. J., & Chevron, E. S. (1984). *Interpersonal psychotherapy of depression.* New York: Basic Books.

Kobe, F. H., & Hammer, D. (1994). Parenting stress and depression in children with mental retardation and developmental disabilities. *Research in Developmental Disabilities, 15,* 209–221.

Krauss, M. W., & Seltzer, M. M. (1998). Life course perspectives in mental retardation research: The case of family caregiving. In J. A. Burack, R. M. Hodapp, & E. Zigler (Eds.), *Handbook of mental retardation and development* (pp. 504–520). New York: Cambridge University Press.

Laman, D. S., & Reiss, S. (1987). Social skill deficiencies associated with depressed mood of mentally retarded adults. *American Journal of Mental Deficiency, 92,* 224–229.

Lewinsohn, P. M. (1974a). A behavioral approach to depression. In R. M. Friedman & M. M. Katz (Eds.), *The psychology of depression: Contemporary theory and research* (pp.157–185). New York: John Wiley.

Lewinsohn, P. M. (1974b). Clinical and theoretical aspects of depression. In K. S. Calhoun, H. E. Adams, & K. M. Mitchell (Eds.), *Innovative treatment methods in psychopathology* (pp. 63–120). New York: John Wiley.

Lewinsohn, P. M., Mischel, W., Chaplin, W., & Barton, R. (1980). Social competence and depression: The role of illusory self-perceptions. *Journal of Abnormal Psychology, 89,* 203–212.

Lindsay, W. R., Howells, L., & Pitcaithly, D. (1993). Cognitive therapy for depression with individuals with intellectual disabilities. *British Journal of Medical Psychology, 66,* 135–141.

Lowry, M. A. (1998). Assessment and treatment of mood disorders in persons with developmental disabilities. *Journal of Developmental and Physical Disabilities, 10,* 387–406.

Lowry, M.A., & Sovner, R. (1992). Severe behaviour problems associated with rapid cycling bipolar disorder in two adults with profound mental retardation. *Journal of Intellectual Disability Research, 36,* 269–281.

Lunsky, Y., & Benson, B. A. (2001). Association between perceived social support and strain, and positive and negative outcomes for adults with mild intellectual disability. *Journal of Intellectual Disability Research, 45,* 106–114.

Lunsky, Y., & Havercamp, S. (1999). Distinguishing low levels of social support and social strain: Implications for dual diagnosis. *American Journal on Mental Retardation, 104,* 200–204.

Matson, J. L. (1982). The treatment of behavioral characteristics of depression in the mentally retarded. *Behavior Therapy, 13,* 209–218.

Matson, J. L., Dettling, J., & Senatore, V. (1981). Treating depression of a mentally retarded adult. *British Journal of Mental Subnormality, 26,* 86–88.

Matson, J. L., Senatore, V., Kazdin, A. E., & Helsel, W. T. (1983). Verbal behaviors in depressed and nondepressed mentally retarded persons. *Applied Research in Mental Retardation, 4,* 79–83.

Mattes, J. A., & Amsell, L. (1993). The Dexamethasone Suppression Test as an indication of depression in patients with mental retardation. *American Journal on Mental Retardation, 98,* 354–359.

McCracken, J. T., & Diamond, R. P. (1988). Bipolar disorder in mentally retarded adolescents. *Journal of the American Academy of Child and Adolescent Psychiatry, 27,* 494–499.

Meins, W. (1993). Prevalence and risk factors for depressive disorders in adults with intellectual disability. *Australia and New Zealand Journal of Developmental Disabilities, 18,* 147–156.

Mudford, O. C., Barrera, F. J., Murray, A., Boundy, K., Caldwell, K., & Goldberg, B. (1995). The Dexamethasone Suppression Test and the diagnosis of depression in adults with severe and profound developmental disabilities. *Journal of Intellectual Disability Research, 39,* 275–283.

Nezu, C. M., Nezu, A. M., Rothenberg, J. L., DelliCarpini, L., & Groag, I. (1995). Depression in adults with mild mental retardation: Are cognitive variables involved? *Cognitive Therapy and Research, 19,* 227–239.

Post, R. M. (1990). Sensitization and kindling perspectives for the course of affective illness: Toward a new treatment with the anticonvulsant carbamazepine. *Pharmacopsychiatry, 35,* 3–17.

Poznanski, E. O., Carroll, B. J., Banegas, M. C., Cook, S. C., & Grossman, J. A. (1982). The Dexamethasone Suppression Test in prepubertal depressed children. *American Journal of Psychiatry, 139,* 321–324.

Prasher, V. P., & Hall, W. (1996). Short-term prognosis of depression in adults with Down's syndrome: Association with thyroid status and effects on adaptive behaviour. *Journal of Intellectual Disability Research, 40,* 32–38.

Pueschel, S. M., Jackson, I. M., Giesswein, P., Dean, M. K., & Pezzullo, J. C. (1991). Thyroid function in Down syndrome. *Research in Developmental Disabilities, 12,* 287–296.

Raber, S. M., & Weisz, J. R. (1981). Teacher feedback to mentally retarded and nonretarded children. *American Journal of Mental Deficiency, 86,* 148–156.

Rehm, L. P. (1977). A self-control model of depression. *Behavior Therapy, 8,* 787–804.

Rehm, L. P., & Carter, A. S. (1990). Cognitive components of depression. In M. Lewis & S. M. Miller (Eds.), *Handbook of developmental psychopathology* (pp. 342–351). New York: Plenum Press.

Reiss, S., & Benson, B. A. (1985). Psychosocial correlates of depression in mentally retarded adults. I: Minimal social support and stigmatization. *American Journal of Mental Deficiency, 89,* 331–337.

Reiss, S., & Rojahn, J. (1993). Joint occurrence of depression and aggression in children and adults with mental retardation. *Journal of Intellectual Disability Research, 37,* 287–294.

Reynolds, W. M., & Miller, K. L. (1985). Depression and learned helplessness in mentally retarded and non-mentally retarded adolescents: An initial investigation. *Applied Research in Mental Retardation, 6,* 295–306.

Rojahn, J., Matson, J. L., Naglieri, J. A., & Mayville, E. (2004). Relationships between psychiatric conditions and behavior problems among adults with mental retardation. *American Journal on Mental Retardation, 109,* 21–33.

Rojahn, J., & Warren, V. J. (1997). Emotion recognition as a function of social competence and depressed mood in individuals with intellectual disability. *Journal of Intellectual Disability Research, 41,* 469–475.

Rossiter, L., & Sharpe, D. (2001). The siblings of individuals with mental retardation: A quantitative integration of the literature. *Journal of Child and Family Studies, 10,* 65–84.

Ruedrich, S. L., Wadle, C. V., Sallach, H. S., Hahn, R. K., & Menolascino, F. J. (1987). Adrenocortical function and depressive illness in mentally retarded patients. *American Journal of Psychiatry, 144,* 597–602.

Schloss, P. J. (1982). Verbal interaction patterns of depressed and non-depressed institutionalized mentally retarded adults. *Applied Research in Mental Retardation, 3,* 1–12.

Schwartz, A., & Schwartz, R. M. (1993). *Depression: Theories and treatments.* New York: Columbia University Press.

Seligman, M. E. P. (1974). Depression and learned helplessness. In R. J. Friedman & M. M. Katz (Eds.), *The psychology of depression: Contemporary theory and research* (pp. 83–113). New York: Winston-Wiley.

Seligman, M. E. P. (1975). *Helplessness: On depression, development and death.* San Francisco: Freeman.

Soni, S., Keane, V., & Soni, S. D. (1992). Dexamethasone Suppression Test and response to antidepressants in depressed mentally handicapped subjects. *Journal of Intellectual Disability Research, 36,* 425–433.

Strakowski, S. M., DelBello, M. P., Adler, C., Cecil, K. M., & Sax, K. W. (2000). Neuroimaging in bipolar disorder. *Bipolar Disorders, 2,* 148–164.

Tsiouris, J. A., Mann, R., Patti, P. J., & Sturmey, P. (2003). Challenging behaviours should not be considered as depressive equivalents in individuals with intellectual disability. *Journal of Intellectual Disability Research, 47,* 14–21.

Wehr, T. A., Turner, E. H., Shimada, J. M., Lowe, C. H., Barker, C., & Leibenluft, E. (1998). Treatment of a rapidly cycling bipolar patient by using extended bed rest and darkness to stabilize the timing and duration of sleep. *Biological Psychiatry, 43,* 822–828.

Weisz, J. R. (1979). Perceived control and learned helplessness among retarded and nonretarded children: A developmental analysis. *Developmental Psychology, 15,* 311–319.

Wolkowitz, O. M. (1990). Use of the Dexamethasone Suppression Test with mentally retarded persons: Review and recommendations. *American Journal on Mental Retardation, 94,* 509–514.

5

RISK FACTORS FOR MOOD DISORDERS IN PEOPLE WITH INTELLECTUAL DISABILITY

John Crilly,

Nancy N. Cain,

and

Philip W. Davidson

This chapter provides a comprehensive literature review on the risk factors for major depressive disorder and bipolar disorder in people with and without ID. The final sections of the chapter outline the clinical applications of this literature and the implications for prevention of mood disorder in people with mental retardation.

Risk Factors for Mood Disorder in the General Population

Major Depression

Major depressive disorder (MDD) is the most prevalent of the primary psychiatric diagnoses, with a current prevalence of about 5% and a lifetime estimate of about

17% (Blazer, Kessler, McGonagle, & Schwartz, 1994; Kessler et al., 1994). MDD is associated with both physical and emotional or mental changes (Hesdorffer, Hauser, Annegers, & Cascino, 2000; Musselman et al., 1996; Musselman, Evans, & Nemeroff, 1998; Schweiger et al., 1994; Zeiss, Lewinsohn, Rohde, & Seeley, 1996). The prevalence of depression may be as high as 65% in patients with acute myocardial infarction, 15%–22% of whom have MDD (Guck, Kavan, Elsasser, & Barone, 2001). Persons who are depressed and who have preexisting cardiovascular disease have a four-times-greater risk of death than do patients who are not depressed and have cardiovascular disease. Subclinical hypothyroidism may lower the threshold for the occurrence of depression (Haggerty et al., 1993). Level of education, severity of initial depressed mood, and comorbid medical conditions may predict unremitted depression (Swindle, Cronkite, & Moos, 1998), although gastrointestinal problems do not appear to play a role as a risk factor (Hochstrasser & Angst, 1996). However, acute and chronic stress from physical disabilities have been found to represent significant risk factors for both depressive symptomatology and MDD (Turner & Beiser, 1990).

Biomarkers for MDD.

Goodwin (1997) summarized data that appear to suggest the role of cognitive impairment as a risk factor for depression in older adults. This may likely be the result of both reversible and permanent loss of active neurons in frontal, temporal, and parietal brain areas, particularly in older men. Subjects with impoverished mental states appear more likely to have reductions in frontal lobe areas. Kumar et al. (1997) relate similar findings. Using MRI data, they found that both brain atrophy and comorbid medical illness are associated with an increased risk of developing MDD in late life. Kendler and Karkowski-Shuman (1997) linked genetic culpability for MDD by causing individuals to select themselves into high-risk environments. These findings coincide with those of Zlotnick, Warshaw, Shea, and Keller (1997), who found evidence suggesting that a history of trauma from stressful life events is a risk factor for chronic depression. Warner, Mufson, and Weissman (1995) found that the risk for MDD in offspring was increased by proband-recurrent early-onset MDD and co-parent alcohol abuse. A large twin study examining the interrelationship of six major Axis I psychiatric disorders found both genetic and individual-specific environmental factors loading on major depression and generalized anxiety disorder unconnected with phobia, panic disorder, bulimia, and alcoholism (Kendler et al., 1995). Krieg, Lauer, Schreiber, Modell, and Holsboer (2001) found differences in healthy first-degree relatives of subjects with major depression. These include signs of a hyperactive pituitary adrenocortical system, slow sleep wave deficit (first sleep cycle), increased eye movement in REM sleep, and such personality traits as increased rigidity, lability, and depressionlike features.

Theoretical Models for MDD Etiology.

In developing an exploratory integrated model of risk factors for depression, Kendler, Kessler, Neale, Heath, and Eaves (1993) reported that the strongest predictors of depression liability for women were stressful life events, genetic factors, previous history of MDD, and neuroticism. They recommended paying particular attention to four domains: traumatic experiences, genetic factors, temperament, and interpersonal relations. Lauer et al. (1997) found that autonomic lability may be an antecedent of major depression. Zwaigenbaum, Szatmari, Boyle, and Offord (1999) identified high levels of somatic symptoms in young adolescents as a significant risk factor for MDD within the following four years. Hayward, Killen, Kraemer, and Taylor (2000), confirming the results of other studies (Servant and Parquet, 1994), reported that a history of panic attacks predicted MDD. They also found that female sex and negative affectivity predicted onset of MDD. However, Kessler et al. (1998) concluded that the absence of a dose-response relationship suggests that panic attack is a marker rather than a risk factor of MDD.

Cultural and Social Markers for MDD: Life Events.

There is evidence that exposure to social and family disadvantages in childhood are risk factors for adult depression. Sadowski, Ugarte, Kolvin, Kaplan, and Barnes (1999) found that multiple family disadvantages, such as marital relationship instability, poor parenting and physical care, social welfare use, and overcrowding, substantially increased the risk of a MDD in adulthood. Physical abuse, neglect, and such traumatic events as a prolonged separation of children from parents or the death of parents have all been associated with increased risk for a lifetime diagnosis of MDD and such other social problems as anxiety, social phobias, and difficulty interacting with others (Gersten, Beals, & Kallgren, 1991; Kaplan et al., 1998; Kendler et al., 1993; Maes, Mylle, Delmeire, & Altamura, 2000; Oakley-Browne, Joyce, Wells, Bushnell, & Hornblow, 1995a, b; Servant & Parquet, 1994). Prolonged separation may also be a marker for other risk factors that affect emotional health, but it may not in itself be an independent risk factor. Hoff, Bruce, Kasl, and Jacobs (1997) used subjective ratings of emotional health (SEH) with the Epidemiologic Catchment Area data and found that SEH ratings had a significant relationship with MDD, suggesting that negative ratings increase risk for developing MDD. Excessive dependency, such as dependent personality disorder, does not appear to play a role as a risk factor with MDD (Skodol, Gallaher, & Oldham, 1996), but high neuroticism has been found to predict increases in depressive symptoms (Lozano & Johnson, 2001).

Other studies point to trends around certain variables or situations and require further follow-up. For example, Foley, Neale, and Kendler (2000) found that although lighter birth weight showed a trend toward predicting the occurrence of MDD, twins of varying weight at birth were not significantly more likely to develop a mental disorder. Bouhuys and Sam (2000) assessed recurrent and first-episode MDD subjects and found partial support for the "vulnerability-accumulation hypothesis" in interpersonal interaction. They found that subjects with recurrent MDD had accumulated more nonverbal vulnerability in social interactions than had those with only a first episode. This suggests that some longer-term damaging symptoms may not be immediately present in the person with first-episode MDD. Table 5.1 provides a compact summary of the MDD risk factors.

Table 5.1. Risk Factors for major depression in the general population.

Risk Factor	Symptoms	References
Biological Factors		
Comorbidity with medical conditions	• Acute myocardial infarction • Subclinical hypothyroidism • Stress from physical disabilities	Guck et al., 2001 Haggerty et al., 1993 Turner & Beiser, 1990 Kumar et al., 1997
Cognitive impairment	For older adults	Goodwin, 1997
Brain atrophy		Kumar et al., 1997
Trauma from stressful life events		Zlotnick et al., 1997
Comorbidity with psychiatric disorders	• Anxiety disorder and panic attacks • Social inhibition and avoidance	Kendler et al., 1995 Parker et al., 1999
Differences in first-degree relatives	• Hyperactive pituitary adrenocortical system • Slow sleep wave, increased eye movement in REM sleep • Personality traits	Kreig et al., 2001
Environmental and Social Factors		
Strong predictors (for women)	• Stressful life events • Genetic factors • Previous history of MDD • Neuroticism	Kendler et al., 1993
Problem domains (for women)	In addition to above: • Temperament • Interpersonal relationships	Kendler et al., 1993
Autonomic lability		Lauer et al., 1997
Chaotic family environment		Warner et al., 1995
High levels of somatic symptoms in teen years		Zwaigenbaum et al., 1999
Negative affectivity		Hayward et al., 2000
Through childhood: • Family disadvantages • Physical abuse and neglect • Traumatic events • Prolonged separation from or death of parents	• Marital problems or instability • Poor parenting • Social welfare use • Residential overcrowding	Sadowski et al., 1999 Gersten et al., 1991 Kendler et al., 1993 Servant & Parquet, 1994 Oakley-Browne et al., 1995a, b Kaplan et al., 1998 Maes et al., 2000
High neuroticism		Lozano & Johnson, 2001

Dysthymic Disorder

Dysthymia is a disorder closely related to depression. It is a chronic condition in which individuals experience a form of depressive malaise and anxiety that cause them to have lower levels of functioning (Klein & Santiago, 2003). Dysthymia has a prevalence rate of 6.2% in young adults (Jonas, Brody, Roper, & Narrow, 2003). Dysthymia is also a clinical factor for major depression and its relapse (Coryell et al., 1988; Faravelli, Ambonetti, Pallanti, & Pazzagli, 1986; Keller, Lavori, Endicott, Coryell, & Klerman, 1983; Keller, Lavori, Lewis, & Klerman, 1983; Levitt, Joffe, & MacDonald, 1991; Sherbourne & Wells, 1997) as well as a clinical risk factor associated with an increased risk for a first onset of major depression (Horwath, Johnson, Klerman, & Weissman, 1992).

Anxiety plays a role in both anxiety disorders and MDD (Parker et al., 1999; Warner et al., 1995). Parker et al. (1999) found that anxiety in the form of social inhibition or avoidance was particularly likely to precede or be a conduit to early onset nonmelancholic depression, or dysthymia. Kessler, Zhao, Blazer, and Swartz (1997) reported that subclinical depression or dysthymia may be a risk factor for MDD but also stressed the linear relationship between dysthymia and the risk of MDD.

Bipolar Disorder

Bipolar disorder (BD), also known as manic-depressive illness, is a brain disorder that causes unusual shifts in a person's mood, energy, and ability to function. Bipolar disorder is a disease that is projected to affect nearly 1% of the population (Kessler et al., 1994; Regier & Burke, 1987; Regier, Narrow, & Rae, 1993) with equal gender ratio (Blehar et al., 1998). Although less prevalent in the general population than such other diseases as schizophrenia and major depressive disorder, it is considered a major health problem (Hilty, Brady, & Hales, 1999).

Identification of risk factors has been facilitated by the Human Genome Project. Genetic linkage studies have revealed several chromosomal loci likely to contain genes that increase the risk of bipolar disorder (Blackwood & Muir, 2001). The most promising chromosomal regions have been localized on chromosomes 4, 5, 11, 12, 18, 21, and X (Souery, Rivelli, & Mendlewicz, 2001). By contrast, a study by Ginns et al. (1998) attempted to identify chromosomal loci that are protective against BD by studying those who are at high risk for developing BD and yet avoid the disease. They found evidence to suggest a locus on chromosomes 4p and 4q that may be linked to mental health wellness.

Other studies are more specific. Meira-Lima, Pereira, Mota, Krieger, and Vallada (2000) examined the association between functional polymorphisms in the angiotensin-converting enzyme (ACE) and angiotensinogen (AGT) genes in BD versus normal subjects. Though the ACE showed no difference between the groups, the AGT M235T polymorphism M allele was three times more likely to be in BD subjects than in controls, suggesting an increased susceptibility in this sample. A later study by the same group (Meira-Lima et al., 2001) did not support the hypothesis that variation at the polymorphic CAG/CTG repeat loci ERDA-1, SEFA2-1B, MAB21L, or KCNN3 influenced susceptibility to developing BD.

It remains unclear how transmission of BD occurs and the factors that account for the variance in some variables such as age of onset. The methodologies of epidemiology and molecular genetics are complimentary approaches that have been useful in beginning to identify risk factors for bipolar disorder. Genetic linkage may be hypothesized in tandem with the presence of other theorized predictive variables, such as demography, childhood experiences, exposure to adversity, and availability of social support. Such theories suggest a less endogenous process. Studies have found that the frequency of stressful events do not affect the BD patient's ability to cope with these events. Rather it may be the interaction of age, stress, and the onset of new episodes that contributes more to the ability to cope (Hlastala et al., 2000). Miklowitz and Alloy (1999) argued that stressful life events and disturbances in social-familial support systems affect the cycling of the disorder against the backdrop of genetic, biological, and cognitive vulnerabilities.

Early Life Risks.

Early life events may be risk factors for BD. Kinney, Yurgelun-Todd, Tohen, and Tramer (1998) reported that obstetric complication scores were significantly worse for BD patients compared with older siblings. Bipolar disorder is also prevalent in children, with between 20% and 40% of adults developing symptoms prior to age 18 years (Geller & Luby, 1997) and about 32% of children with major depressive disorder developing BD in later life (Geller, Fox, & Clark, 1994). Manzano and Salvador (1993) found that 31% of a sample of Swiss adults with serious affective disorders had accessed child psychiatry services and that patients had distinguishing psychopathology in childhood. The correlations between the childhood pathology and that of the adults were specific for BD. Expanding on this research, Kessing (1999) found in a large sample of Danish patients that 4.4% of patients whose first hospitalization was for a depression eventually developed a manic episode. These occurred at the same rate as those who presented initially with a BD diagnosis.

Twenty to 40% of adolescents with major depression will develop mania within 5 years (Birmaher et al., 1996). Robb (1999) cited population-based studies in which the annual incidence of BD per 100,000 children (10–19 years) is 1.5 and 1.9, respectively, for Finnish boys and girls, 3 to 5 times higher than the incidence in Europe, and 10 times higher in the United States. This coincides with Levitan et al.'s (1998) study of 8,000 children, which yielded a strong relationship between mania and early physical abuse. In a case-control study comparing BD with depressed adolescents, Sigurdsson, Fombonne, Sayal, and Checkley (1999) reported that BD cases were nearly six times more likely than depressed controls to experience delayed language, social, or motor development. Similarly, twin studies (Karkowski & Kendler, 1997) suggest that mania in one twin predicts major depression in the co-twin, suggesting a familial or genetic association between major depression and mania.

Later-Life Risks.

BD may also develop later in life. Hays, Krishnan, George, and Blazer (1998) found that adults with later-life onset BD reported less family history of psychiatric problems, more comorbid cardiovascular disease, and more instrumental and subjective social support. This study suggests that early-onset BD may be characterized by a psychosocial component, whereas organic factors may contribute to late-onset BD. Early predictors of illness may be gleaned from studies of children and adolescents. Egeland, Hostetter, Pauls, and Sussex (2000) found that prodromal symptoms of episodic changes in mood and energy as well as anger dyscontrol suggest the later development of BD.

Markers for BD.

Finding identifiable markers has been a circuitous process (Jones & Tarrant, 2000; Nurnberger et al., 1988). Stoll, Renshaw, Yurgelun-Todd, and Cohen (2000) proposed an increased use of brain imaging after identifying CNS morphological anomalies in individuals with BD. Goldberg, Harrow, and Whiteside (2001) conducted a 15-year prospective follow-up of a large, young cohort of persons originally hospitalized for unipolar major depression to determine prevalence of developing BD. Depressed patients with psychosis at the onset were significantly more likely to develop BD than those without psychosis. Those with family histories of BD showed a slightly higher propensity to develop BD symptoms. McElroy et al. (2001) found that 65% of their sample of the patients with BD also met DSM-IV criteria for at least one comorbid lifetime Axis I disorder. In their sample of 78 individuals, four times as many patients had comorbid anxiety disorders and substance-use disorders than had eating disorders. Prosser et al. (1997) found that aminobutric acid levels in plasma were low (below 100 pmol/mL) in 15% of patients with mood disorders and were not altered with treatment, suggesting a possibly stable trait marker for some affectively ill patients.

Other variables have also been explored as risk factors. Mirroring schizophrenia research, there is evidence that early onset of BD predicts a poorer prognosis. Pauls, Morton, and Egeland (1992) and Strober et al. (1988) both reported that the rate of BD was higher among first-degree relatives with early-onset disease. Schurhoff et al. (2000) found that early onset may be associated with greater severity and with more psychotic features, mixed episodes, greater comorbidity with panic disorder, and poorer response to lithium. First-degree relatives of early-onset patients also had a higher risk of affective disorders.

BD and attention-deficit/hyperactivity disorder (ADHD) have been linked (Geller & Luby, 1997; Pliska, 1998). Furthermore, Sachs, Baldassano, Truman, and Guille (2000) found in a small sample that ADHD in children of bipolar parents developed BD at about 12 years of age, whereas those without ADHD had a mean age of onset of 20 years. Lapalme, Hodgins, and LaRoche (1997) found that children of parents with BD are about three times more likely to develop a mental disorder and four times more likely to develop an affective disorder. McMahon, Stine, Meyers, Simpson, and DePaulo (1995) found a higher than expected frequency of affected mothers, increased risk of illness for maternal relatives, and increased risk of illness for the offspring of affected mothers. Fathers did not appear to transmit the affected phenotype to sons or daughters.

BD has been linked with schizophrenia. Torrey (1999) and Torrey and Yolken (1998) suggested that whereas both disorders gravitate toward similar factors that may suggest risk—such as winter-spring births, abnormal dermatoglyphics, and perinatal complications—patients with BD do not exhibit an excess of urban births and physical anomalies. However, BD patients may be found in higher socioeconomic groups, suggesting a geographic and presumably genetic isolate. Table 5.2 provides a compact summary of the BD risk factors.

Table 5.2. Risk factors for bipolar disorder in the general population.

Risk Factor	Symptoms	References
Biological Factors		
Chromosomal loci: Chromosomes 4,5,11,12,18,21,and X	Ginns et al. (1998) suggest that loci on chromosomes 4p and 4q are protective against mental illness.	Blackwood & Muir, 2001 Sourey et al., 2001 Ginns et al., 1998
AGT M235T polymorphism M allele	3 times more likely in BD	Meira-Lima et al., 2001
Stressful life events	These increase cycling with influence of genetic, biological, and cognitive issues.	Miklowitz & Alloy, 1999
Early onset	Studies indicate that early onset predicts poorer prognosis as well as greater severity of symptoms and poorer response to medications.	Pauls et al., 1992 Strober et al., 1988 Schurhoff et al., 2000
Obstetric complication scores	Significantly worse for BD	Kinney et al., 1998
Low plasma levels of aminobutric acid		Prosser et al., 1997
Environmental and Social Factors		
Development of symptoms prior to age 18	• These symptoms could include depression and mania. • Some symptoms may also be linked to early physical abuse and have been found between twins.	Geller et al., 1994 Geller & Luby, 1997 Manzano & Salvador, 1993 Kessing, 1999 Birmaher et al., 1996 Robb, 1999 Levitan et al., 1998 Karkowski & Kendler, 1997 Goldberg et al., 2001
Psychosocial component • Family psychiatric problems • Organic factors	• Early-onset BD is characterized by psychosocial components. • Late-life onset correlated with *fewer* family psychiatric problems.	Hays et al., 1998
Episodic changes in mood, energy, or anger control		Egeland et al., 2000
Depression with psychosis at onset		Goldberg et al., 2001
Family history of BD		Goldberg et al., 2001 Lapalme et al., 1997 McMahon et al., 1995
Comorbidity with other mental illnesses	ADHD, depression with psychosis, schizophrenia	McElroy et al., 2001 Geller & Luby, 1997 Torrey, 1999 Torrey & Yolken, 1999

Risk Factors for Affective Disorders in People With Intellectual Disabilities

Davis, Judd, and Herrman (1997) identified a number of risk factors that may make people with ID more prone than the general population to developing MDD. These include both physical factors, such as those linked with CNS disturbance and hypothyroidism, and psychosocial factors, such as poor communication skills, limited coping strategies, lack of social support, poor social skills, and poor self-esteem. Benson and Ivins (1992) found that self-reports of low self-concept in people with ID correlated with high levels of depression. Also contributing may be the effects of discrimination, labeling, rejection, ridicule, and stigma. Depressive symptoms in mothers may also contribute to poor adjustment and depression in the intellectually disabled child (Walker, Ortiz-Valdez, & Newbrough, 1989).

Biological Risk Factors

A limited literature is available on genetic risk factors. Gecz, Barnett, and Liu (1999) sequenced the entire gene GRIA-3 at Xq24 in a woman with both ID and bipolar disorder. GRIA-3 may be a potential link for ID and mental illness, and the fragile-X chromosome may be linked to major depression (Tranebjaerg & Orum, 1991). However, Deb and Weston (2000) report that there are many such links along the chromosome that may also account for a variety of disorders when mutated, so the work is inconclusive at present.

Environmental and Social Risk Factors

A number of environmental and social risk factors have been identified for affective disorders and for ID. Sovner and Pary (1993) and Szymanski (1994) state that the risk factors for such affective disorders as early childhood deprivation, impaired social learning, physical maturation, level of cognitive functioning, and psychosocial development are all linked and are even more relevant in people with ID. Ruedrich and Menolascino (1984) outlined similar influences or risk factors: medical fragility, reflections of parental concerns regarding ID, peer group expectations to perform, frustration from repeated failures, humiliation of being ridiculed, fears from trying to cope in society, dependency from overprotectiveness, and a push toward achieving beyond capabilities.

Kirkpatrick-Sanchez, Williams, Matson, and Anderson (1996) compared rates of psychopathology in people with severe versus profound ID. People with severe ID had more psychopathology than did people with profound ID. Charlot (1997) also found this difference in symptom prevalence across ID severity. A study by Morgan et al. (1997) examined the prevalence of one of the more predominant factors suspected of contributing to the development of these processes in the brain. They found that influenza epidemics had no effect on the development of schizophrenia or affective disorders. They did find, however, a possible effect for ID in males exposed during the first and second trimester.

Life Events

Stressful life events have been identified as potential risk factors for mood disorders. Emerson (2003) found that factors associated with an increased risk of psychopathology among children and adolescents with ID included age, gender, social deprivation, family composition, and the number of potentially stressful life events. These life events affect the person with ID whether the events happen to the person with ID directly or to caregivers (Rimmerman & Muraver, 2001). Hastings, Hatton, Taylor, and Maddison (2004) identified five of the most prevalent stressful life events occurring in depressed persons with ID during the preceding 12 months: moving to a new residence (15.5% of the sample); a serious illness of a close relative or friend (9.0%); a serious problem with a close friend, neighbor, or relative (8.8%); a serious illness or injury to self (8.5%); and the death of a close family friend or other relative (8.3%). It is important, however, to be aware of the role of stressful life events on behavioral problems in addition to their risk factor potential (Coe et al., 1999). Table 5.3 provides a compact summary of the affective disorder risk factors for people with ID.

Table 5.3. Risk factors for affective disorders in people with intellectual disabilities.

Risk Factor	Symptoms	References
Biological Factors		
Potential genetic markers	• Gene GRIA-3 at Xq24 (bipolar) • Fragile-X chromosome (major depression)	Gecz et al., 1999 Tranebjaerg & Orum, 1991
Physical and cognitive functioning markers	• Impaired social learning • Slower physical maturation • Early childhood deprivation • Medical fragility • Dependency from overprotectiveness • Push to achieve beyond capabilities • Hypothyroidism • CNS disturbance	Sovner & Pary, 1993 Szymanski, 1994 Ruedrich & Menolascino, 1984 Davis et al., 1977
Environmental and Social Factors		
Low self-concept	Effects of discrimination, labeling, stigma, rejection, ridicule	Benson & Ivins, 1992
Depressive symptoms in mother		Walker et al., 1989
Psychosocial factors	• Poor communication skills • Limited coping strategies • Lack of social support • Poor social skills • Poor self-esteem	Davis et al., 1997
Differences in age and level of ID	Severe ID has more psychopathology than profound ID	Kirkpatrick-Sanchez et al., 1996 Charlot, 1997
Possible effect of exposure to influenza	In males, first and second trimester influenza in mother has associated risk	Morgan et al., 1997

Clinical Applications and Diagnostic Considerations

Studies consistently find similarities between affective symptoms exhibited in patients who have ID and those of patients who do not have ID (Charlot, 1997; Johnson, Handen, Lubetsky, & Sacco, 1995; Matson, Barrett, & Helsel, 1988). This same phenomenon was found by Heiman and Margalit (1998) in their study of loneliness and depression in students with mild ID in general educational settings. They found that preadolescent differences between students with ID and normal students faded as the students entered adolescence.

These types of studies encourage researchers and clinicians to utilize such current mainstream diagnostic tools as the latest DSM to identify diagnoses (Matson & Smiroldo, 1997; Meins, 1995; Pawlarcyzk & Beckwith, 1987; Reynolds & Baker, 1988). Balboni, Battagliesi, and Pedrabissi (2000) found that the Psychopathology Inventory for Mentally Retarded Adults (PIMRA) also has good construct validity. Bramston and Fogarty (2000) recommend caution in methods to determine this assessment in their comparison of self-report, clinical interview, or report of a significant other, particularly in light of the wide disparity in prevalence rates between various studies. This was further assessed by Masi, Brovedani, Mucci, and Favilla (2002), who determined that such general instruments as the PIMRA can be used both as screening tools and as assessments of overall severity of disturbance. They also found that self-report and rating scales are inconsistent diagnostic measurements and that structured interviews with subjects and parents are more reliable. Although this concern occurs in other areas of the literature, a well-constructed study by Manikam, Matson, Coe, and Hillman (1995) presents findings indicating that self-report scales for depression can be valid.

Strategies for Preventing Mood Disorders in Individuals With Intellectual Disability

At the present, there is little that can be done to address the organic causes of mood disorders. However, adjustment of the environment and interpersonal interactions can decrease the severity of the symptoms and the frequency of relapse. Families can be under a great deal of stress when caring for an individual with a mood disorder. In addition, the stigma of mental illness can lead to isolation of the family and thus decreased social supports. Help for families, whether through parent groups, family counseling, or family therapy, can prevent many of the dysfunctional interactions that can develop. Families should be helped to accept the limitations or decreased functioning that may occur, to grieve the loss of the prior abilities as well as some of their dreams for their loved one, and to deal with the sense of guilt or the belief that they may have caused the disorder. Without resolving these issues, caregivers may foster unnecessary dependence, develop resentful feelings, and behave unintentionally in ways that may make the individual feel rejected. It is important for the individual's self-esteem that caregivers provide an environment that gives the individual the sense that people care about him or her and will support the individual in functioning at his or her best.

An Individual with ID generally has decreased coping skills, limited social skills, and difficulty communicating. His or her functioning in these areas may be further impaired by a mood disorder, which may manifest itself behaviorally. This can affect the caregiver's ability to respond positively. Techniques that help increase coping strategies are important. Role-playing difficult situations can be helpful in increasing coping skills. Repeated practice helps the individual to draw upon these skills when in a stressful situation, leaving him or her feeling better prepared to cope independently. It is also important to continually work to increase the individual's communication skills and to ensure that there is no hearing impairment. This can help prevent isolation or misunderstanding, which can worsen symptoms.

Efforts to provide opportunities to succeed are important. Identification of an individual's talents, such as sports, music, or cooking, can greatly assist in increasing self-esteem. Participation in community-based activities (Special Olympics, organized sports, Scouts, camp) can enhance feelings of accomplishment and self-worth. In addition, these activities provide the added benefit of developing friendships and increasing social skills. To the extent possible, activities that lead to failure should be avoided. Attentiveness to the individual's ability to master a task can help identify problem areas that may require a different teaching approach. Vigilance is needed to deter or avoid destructive situations of ridicule, rejection, labeling, or teasing so that a positive learning environment can be maintained.

Periods of transition are difficult and can lead to increased stress and possible relapse of the mood disorder. Awareness of these situations can trigger caregivers to provide extra support and encouragement to the individual to use his or her coping skills. Temporarily decreasing expectations around the normal daily routine can compensate for the individual's lower ability to concentrate. During these periods, it is appropriate to give extra help with daily activities and chores until the individual regains his or her ability. Giving more organization to the individual's life at these times and keeping things as simple as possible is also helpful.

References

Balboni, G., Battagliese, G., & Pedrabissi, L. (2000). The Psychopathology Inventory for Mentally Retarded Adults: Factor structure and comparisons between subjects with or without dual diagnosis. *Research in Developmental Disabilities, 21,* 311–321.

Benson, B. A., & Ivins, J. (1992). Anger, depression and self-concept in adults with mental retardation. *Journal of Intellectual Disability Research, 36,* 169–175.

Birmaher, B., Ryan, N. D., Williamson, D., Brent, D., Kaufman, J., & Dahl, R. (1996). Childhood and adolescent depression: A review of the past 10 years. Part I. *Journal of the American Academy of Child and Adolescent Psychiatry, 35,* 1427–1439.

Blackwood, D., & Muir, W. (2001). Molecular genetics and the epidemiology of bipolar disorder. *Annals of Medicine, 33,* 242–247.

Blazer, D., Kessler, R., McGonagle, K., & Swartz, M. (1994). The prevalence and distribution of major depression in a national community sample: The National Comorbidity Survey. *American Journal of Psychiatry, 151,* 979–986.

Blehar, M., DePaulo, J., Jr., Gershon, E., Reich, T., Simpson, S., & Nurnberger, J. (1998). Women with bipolar disorder: Findings from the NIMH Genetics Initiative sample. *Psychopharmacology Bulletin, 34,* 239–243.

Bouhuys, A., & Sam, M. (2000). Lack of coordination of nonverbal behavior between patients and interviewers as a potential risk factor to depression recurrence: Vulnerability accumulation in depression. *Journal of Affective Disorders, 57,* 189–200.

Bramston, P., & Fogarty, G. (2000). The assessment of emotional distress experienced by people with an intellectual disability: A study of different methodologies. *Research in Developmental Disabilities, 21,* 487–500.

Charlot, L. R. (1997). Irritability, aggression, and depression in adults with mental retardation: A developmental perspective. *Psychiatric Annals, 27,* 190–197.

Coe, D., Matson, J., Russell, D. W., Slifer, K., Capone, G., Baglio, C., et al. (1999). Behavior problems of children with Down syndrome and life events. *Journal of Autism and Developmental Disorders, 22,* 149–156.

Coryell, W., Endicott, J., Andreasen, N. C., Keller, M. B., Clayton, P. G., Hirschfeld, R. M. A., et al. (1988). Depression and panic attacks: The significance of overlap as reflected in follow-up and family study data. *American Journal of Psychiatry, 145,* 293–300.

Davis, J., Judd, F., & Herrman, H. (1997). Depression in adults with intellectual disability. Part 1: A review. *Australian and New Zealand Journal of Psychiatry, 31,* 232–242.

Deb, S., & Weston, S. (2000). Psychiatric illness and mental retardation. *Current Opinion in Psychiatry, 13,* 497–505.

Egeland, J., Hostetter, A., Pauls, D., & Sussex, J. (2000). Prodromal symptoms before onset of manic-depressive disorder suggested by first hospital admission histories. *Journal of the American Academy of Child and Adolescent Psychiatry, 39,* 1245–1252.

Emerson, E. (2003). Prevalence of psychiatric disorders in children and adolescents with and without intellectual disability. *Journal of Intellectual Disability Research, 47,* 51–58.

Faravelli, C., Ambonetti, A., Pallanti, S., & Pazzagli, A. (1986). Depressive relapses and incomplete recovery from index episode. *American Journal of Psychiatry, 143,* 888–891.

Foley, D., Neale, M., & Kendler, K. (2000). Does intra-uterine growth discordance predict differential risk for adult psychiatric disorder in a population-based sample of monozygotic twins? *Psychiatric Genetics, 10,* 1–8.

Gecz, J., Barnett, S., & Liu, J. (1999). Characterization of the human glutamate receptor subunit 3 gene (GRIA-3), a candidate for bipolar disorder and nonspecific X-linked mental retardation. *Genomics, 62,* 356–368.

Geller, B., Fox, L., & Clark, K. (1994). Rate and predictors of prepubertal bipolarity during follow-up of 6- to 12-year-old depressed children. *Journal of the American Academy of Child and Adolescent Psychiatry, 33,* 461–468.

Geller, B., & Luby, J. (1997). Child and adolescent bipolar disorder: A review of the past 10 years. *Journal of the American Academy of Child and Adolescent Psychiatry, 36,* 1168–1176.

Gersten, J., Beals, J., & Kallgren, C. (1991). Epidemiology and preventive interventions: Parental death in childhood as a case example. *American Journal of Community Psychology, 19,* 481–500.

Ginns, E., St. Jean, P., Philibert, R., Baldzicka, M., Damschroder-Williams, P., Thiel, B. et al. (1998). A genome-wide search for chromosomal loci linked to mental health wellness in relatives at high risk for bipolar affective disorder among the Old Order Amish. *Proceedings of the National Academy of Sciences of the United States of America, 95,* 15531–15536.

Goldberg, J., Harrow, M., & Whiteside, J. (2001). Risk for bipolar illness in patients initially hospitalized for unipolar depression. *American Journal of Psychiatry, 158,* 1265–1270.

Goodwin, G. (1997). Neuropsychological and neuroimaging evidence for the involvement of the frontal lobes in depression. *Journal of Psychopharmacology, 11,* 115–122.

Guck, T., Kavan, M., Elsasser, G., & Barone E. (2001). Assessment and treatment of depression following myocardial infarction. *American Family Physician, 64,* 641–648.

Haggerty, J., Jr., Stern, R., Mason, G., Beckwith, J., Morey, C., & Prange, A., Jr. (1993). Subclinical hypothyroidism: A modifiable risk factor for depression? *Archives of General Psychiatry, 150,* 508–510.

Hastings, R., Hatton, C., Taylor, J., & Maddison, C. (2004). Life events and psychiatric symptoms in adults with intellectual disabilities. *Journal of Intellectual Disability Research, 48,* 42–46.

Hays, J., Krishnan, K., George, L., & Blazer, D. (1998). Age of first onset of bipolar disorder: Demographic, family history, and psychosocial correlates. *Depression and Anxiety, 7,* 76–82.

Hayward, C., Killen, J., Kraemer, H., & Taylor, C. (2000). Predictors of panic attacks in adolescents. *Journal of the American Academy of Child and Adolescent Psychiatry, 39,* 207–214.

Heiman, T., & Margalit, M. (1998). Loneliness, depression, and social skills among students with mild mental retardation in different educational settings. *The Journal of Special Education, 32,* 154–165.

Hesdorffer, D., Hauser, W., Annegers, J., & Cascino, G. (2000). Major depression is a risk factor for seizures in older adults. *Annals of Neurology, 47,* 246–249.

Hilty, D., Brady, K., & Hales, R. (1999). A review of bipolar disorder among adults. *Psychiatric Services, 50,* 201–213.

Hlastala, S., Frank, E., Kowalski, J., Sherrill, J., Tu, X. & Anderson, B. (2000). Stressful life events, bipolar disorder, and the "kindling model." *Journal of Abnormal Psychology, 109,* 777–786.

Hochstrasser, B., & Angst J. (1996). The Zurich Study: XXII. Epidemiology of gastrointestinal complaints and comorbidity with anxiety and depression. *European Archives of Psychiatry and Clinical Neuroscience, 246,* 261–272.

Hoff, R., Bruce, M., Kasl, S., & Jacobs, S. (1997). Subjective ratings of emotional health as a risk factor for major depression in a community sample. *British Journal of Psychiatry, 170,* 167–172.

Horwath, E., Johnson, J., Klerman, G. L., & Weissman, M. M. (1992). Depressive symptoms as relative and attributable risk factors for first onset major depression. *Archives of General Psychiatry, 49,* 817–823.

Johnson, C., Handen, B., Lubetsky, M., & Sacco, K. (1995). Affective disorders in hospitalized children and adolescents with mental retardation: A retrospective study. *Research in Developmental Disabilities, 16,* 221–231.

Jonas, B., Brody, D., Roper, M., & Narrow, W. (2003). Prevalence of mood disorders in a national sample of young American adults. *Social Psychiatry and Psychiatric Epidemiology, 38,* 618–624.

Jones, P., & Tarrant, C. (2000). Developmental precursors and biological markers for schizophrenia and affective disorders: Specificity and public health implications. *European Archives of Psychiatry and Clinical Neuroscience, 250,* 286–291.

Kaplan, S., Pelcovitz, D., Salzinger, S., Weiner, M., Mandel, F., & Lesser, M. (1998). Adolescent physical abuse: Risk for psychiatric disorders. *American Journal of Psychiatry, 155,* 954–959.

Karkowski, L., & Kendler, K. (1997). An examination of the genetic relationship between bipolar and unipolar illness in an epidemiological sample. *Psychiatric Genetics, 7,* 159–163.

Keller, M. B., Lavori, P. W., Endicott, J., Coryell, W., & Klerman, G. L. (1983). "Double depression": A two-year follow-up. *American Journal of Psychiatry, 140,* 689–694.

Keller, M. B., Lavori, P. W., Lewis, C. E., & Klerman, G. L. (1983). Predictors of relapse in major depressive disorder. *Journal of the American Medical Association, 250,* 3299–3304.

Kendler, K., & Karkowski-Shuman, L. (1997). Stressful life events and genetic liability to major depression: Genetic control of exposure to the environment? *Psychological Medicine, 27(3),* 539–547.

Kendler, K., Kessler, R., Neale, M., Heath, A., & Eaves, L. (1993). The prediction of major depression in women: Toward an integrated etiologic model. *American Journal of Psychiatry, 150,* 1139–1148.

Kendler, K., Neale, M., Kessler, R., Heath, A., & Eaves, L. J. (1993). Childhood parental loss and adult psychopathology in women: A twin study perspective. *Archives of General Psychiatry, 49,* 109–116.

Kendler, K., Walters, E., Neale, M., Kessler, R., Heath, A., & Eaves, L. (1995). The structure of the genetic and environmental risk factors for six major psychiatric disorders in women: Phobia, generalized anxiety disorder, panic disorder, bulimia, major depression, and alcoholism. *Archives of General Psychiatry, 52,* 374–383.

Kessing, L. (1999). The effect of the first manic episode in affective disorder: A case register study of hospitalized episodes. *Journal of Affective Disorders, 53,* 233–239.

Kessler, R. C., McGonagle, K. A., Zhao, S., Nelson, C. B., Hughes, M., Eshleman, S., et al. (1994). Lifetime and 12-month prevalence of DSM-III-R psychiatric disorders in the United States: Results from the National Comorbidity Survey. *Archives of General Psychiatry, 51,* 8–19.

Kessler, R. C., Stang, P., Wittchen, H., Ustun, T., Roy-Burne, P., & Walters, E. (1998). Lifetime panic-depression comorbidity in the National Comorbidity Survey. *Archives of General Psychiatry, 55,* 801–808.

Kessler, R. C., Zhao, S., Blazer, D., & Swartz, M. (1997). Prevalence, correlates, and course of minor depression and major depression in the National Comorbidity Survey. *Journal of Affective Disorders, 45,* 19–30.

Kinney, D., Yurgelun-Todd, D., Tohen, M., & Tramer, S. (1998). Pre- and perinatal complications and risk for bipolar disorder: A retrospective study. *Journal of Affective Disorders, 50,* 117–124.

Kirkpatrick-Sanchez, S., Williams, D., Matson, J., & Anderson, S. (1996). An evaluation of age and intellectual functioning on rates of psychopathology. *Journal of Developmental and Physical Disabilities, 8,* 21–27.

Klein, D., & Santiago, N. (2003). Dysthymia and chronic depression: Introduction, classification, risk factors, and course. *Journal of Clinical Psychology, 59,* 807–816.

Krieg, J., Lauer, C., Schreiber, W., Modell, S., & Holsboer, F. (2001). Neuroendocrine, polysomnographic, and psychometric observations in healthy subjects at high familial risk for affective disorders: The current state of the Munich Vulnerability Study. *Journal of Affective Disorders, 62,* 33–37.

Kumar, A., Miller, D., Ewbank, D., Yousem, D., Newberg, A., Samuels, S., et al. (1997). Quantitative anatomic measures and comorbid medical illness in late-life major depression. *American Journal of Geriatric Psychiatry, 5,* 15–25.

Lapalme, M., Hodgins, S., & LaRoche, C. (1997). Children of parents with bipolar disorder: A meta-analysis of risk for mental disorders. *Canadian Journal of Psychiatry, 42,* 623–631.

Lauer, C., Bronisch, T., Kainz, M., Schreiber, W., Holsboer, F., & Krieg, J. (1997). Premorbid psychometric profile of subjects with high familial risk for affective disorder. *Psychological Medicine, 27,* 355–362.

Levitan, R., Parikh, S., Lesage, A., Hegadoren, K., Adams, M., Kennedy, S., et al. (1998). Major depression in individuals with a history of childhood physical or sexual abuse: Relationship to neurovegetative features, mania, and gender. *American Journal of Psychiatry, 155,* 1746–1752.

Levitt, A. J., Joffe, R. T., & MacDonald, C. (1991). Life course of depressive illness and characteristics of current episode in patients with double depression. *Journal of Nervous and Mental Disease, 179,* 678–682.

Lozano, B., & Johnson, S. (2001). Can personality traits predict increases in manic and depressive symptoms? *Journal of Affective Disorders, 63,* 103–111.

Maes, M., Mylle, J., Delmeire, L., & Altamura, C. (2000). Psychiatric morbidity and comorbidity following accidental man-made traumatic events: Incidence and risk factors. *European Archives of Psychiatry and Clinical Neuroscience, 250,* 156–162.

Manikam, R., Matson, J. L., Coe, D. A., & Hillman, N. (1995). Adolescent depression: Relationships of self-report to intellectual and adaptive functioning. *Research in Developmental Disabilities, 16,* 349–364.

Manzano, J., & Salvador, A. (1993). Antecedents of severe affective (mood) disorders: Patients examined as children or adolescents and as adults. *Acta Paedopsychiatrica, 56,* 11–18.

Masi, G., Brovedani, P., Mucci, M., & Favilla, L. (2002). Assessment of anxiety and depression in adolescents with mental retardation. *Child Psychiatry and Human Development, 32,* 227–237.

Matson, J. L., Barrett, R. P., & Helsel, W. J. (1988). Depression in mentally retarded children. *Research of Developmental Disabilities, 9,* 39–46.

Matson, J. L., & Smiroldo, B. B. (1997). Validity of the Mania Subscale of the Diagnostic Assessment for the Severely Handicapped-II (DASH-II). *Research in Developmental Disabilities, 18,* 221–225.

McElroy, S., Altshuler, L., Suppes, T., Keck, P., Frye, M., Denicoff, K., et al. (2001). Axis I psychiatric comorbidity and its relationship to historical illness variables in 288 patients with bipolar disorder. *The American Journal of Psychiatry, 158,* 420–426.

McMahon, F., Stine, O., Meyers, D., Simpson, S., & DePaulo, J. (1995). Patterns of maternal transmission in bipolar affective disorder. *American Journal of Human Genetics, 56,* 1277–1286.

Meins, W. (1995). Symptoms of major depression in mentally retarded adults. *Journal of Intellectual Disability Research, 39,* 41–45.

Meira-Lima, I., Pereira, A., Mota, G., Krieger, J., & Vallada, H. (2000). Angiotensinogen and angiotensin converting enzyme gene polymorphisms and the risk of bipolar affective disorder in humans. *Neuroscience Letters, 293,* 103–106.

Meira-Lima, I., Zhao, J., Sham, P., Pereira, A., Krieger, J., & Vallada, H. (2001). Association and linkage studies between bipolar affective disorder and the polymorphic CAG/CTG repeat loci ERDA-1, SEFA2-1B, MAB21L, and KCNN3. *Molecular Psychiatry, 6,* 565–569.

Miklowitz, D., & Alloy, L. (1999). Psychosocial factors in the course and treatment of bipolar disorder: Introduction to the special section. *Journal of Abnormal Psychology, 108,* 558–588.

Morgan, V., Castle, D., Page, A., Fazio, S., Gurrin, L., Burton, P., et al. (1997). Influenza epidemics and incidence of schizophrenia, affective disorders, and mental retardation in Western Australia: No evidence of a major effect. *Schizophrenia Research, 26,* 25–39.

Musselman, D., Evans, D., & Nemeroff, C. (1998). The relationship of depression to cardiovascular disease: Epidemiology, biology, and treatment. *Archives of General Psychiatry, 55,* 580–592.

Musselman, D., Tomer, A., Manatunga, A., Knight, B., Porter, M., Kasey, S., et al. (1996). Exaggerated platelet reactivity in major depression. *American Journal of Psychiatry, 153,* 1313–1317.

Nurnberger, J., Jr., Berrettini, W., Tamarkin, L., Hamovit, J., Norton, J., & Gershon, E. (1988). Supersensitivity to melatonin suppression by light in young people at high risk for affective disorder: A preliminary report. *Neuropsychopharmacology, 1,* 217–223.

Oakley-Browne, M., Joyce, P., Wells, J., Bushnell, J., & Hornblow, A. (1995a). Adverse parenting and other childhood experience as risk factors for depression in women aged 18-44 years. *Journal of Affective Disorders, 34,* 13–23.

Oakley-Browne, M., Joyce, P., Wells, J., Bushnell, J., & Hornblow, A. (1995b). Disruptions in childhood parental care as risk factors for major depression in adult women. *Australian and New Zealand Journal of Psychiatry, 29,* 437–448.

Parker, G., Wilhelm, K., Mitchell, P., Austin, M., Roussos, J., & Gladstone, G. (1999). The influence of anxiety as a risk to early onset major depression. *Journal of Affective Disorders, 52,* 11–17.

Pauls, D., Morton, L., & Egeland, J. (1992). Risks of affective illness among first-degree relatives of bipolar I Old-Order Amish probands. *Archives of General Psychiatry, 49,* 703–708.

Pawlarcyzk, D., & Beckwith, B. (1987). Depressive symptoms displayed by persons with mental retardation: A review. *Mental Retardation, 25,* 325–330.

Pliska, S. (1998). Comorbidity of attention-deficit hyperactivity disorder with psychiatric disorder: An overview. *Journal of Clinical Psychiatry, 59,* 50–58.

Prosser, J., Hughes, C., Sheikha, S., Kowatch, R., Kramer, G., & Rosenbarger, N. (1997). Plasma GABA in children and adolescents with mood, behavior, and comorbid mood and behavior disorders: A preliminary study. *Journal of Child and Adolescent Psychopharmacology, 7,* 181–199.

Regier, D., & Burke, J. (1987). Psychiatric disorders in the community: The Epidemiologic Catchment Area study. In R. Hales & A. Frances (Eds.), *American Psychiatric Association annual review* (Vol. 6, Chap. 27, pp. 580–605). Washington, DC: American Psychiatric Association.

Regier, D., Narrow, W., & Rae, D. (1993). The de facto mental and addictive disorders service system. Epidemiologic Catchment Area prospective 1-year prevalence rates of disorders and services. *Archives of General Psychiatry, 50,* 85–94.

Reynolds, W. M., & Baker, J. A. (1988). Assessment of depression in persons with mental retardation. *American Journal on Mental Retardation, 93,* 93–103.

Rimmerman, A., & Muraver, M. (2001). Undesired life events, life satisfaction and well-being of ageing mothers of adult offspring with intellectual disability living at home or out-of-home. *Journal of Intellectual and Developmental Disability, 26,* 195–204.

Robb, A. (1999). Bipolar disorder in children and adolescents. *Current Opinion in Pediatrics, 11,* 317–322.

Ruedrich, S. L., & Menolascino, F. J. (1984). Dual diagnosis of mental retardation and mental illness: An overview. In F. J. Menolscino & J. A. Stark. (Eds.), *Handbook of mental illness in the mentally retarded* (pp. 45–81). New York: Plenum Press.

Sachs, G., Baldassano, C., Truman, C., & Guille, C. (2000). Co-morbidity of attention deficit hyperactivity disorder with early- and late-onset bipolar disorder. *American Journal of Psychiatry, 157,* 466–468.

Sadowski, H., Ugarte, B., Kolvin, I., Kaplan, C., & Barnes, J. (1999). Early family life disadvantages and major depression in adulthood. *British Journal of Psychiatry, 174,* 112–120.

Schurhoff, F., Bellivier, F., Jouvent, R., Moren-Simeoni, M., Bouvard, M., Allilaire, J., et al. (2000). Early and late onset bipolar disorders: Two different forms of manic-depressive illness? *Journal of Affective Disorders, 58,* 215–221.

Schweiger, U., Deuschle, M., Korner, A., Lammers, C., Schmider, J., & Gotthardt, U. (1994). Low lumbar bone mineral density in patients with major depression. *American Journal of Psychiatry, 151,* 1691–1693.

Servant, D., & Parquet, P. (1994). Early life events and panic disorder: Course of illness and comorbidity. *Progress in Neuro-Psychopharmacology and Biological Psychiatry, 18,* 373–379.

Sherbourne, C. D., & Wells, K. B. (1997). Course of depression in patients with comorbid anxiety disorders. *Journal of Affective Disorders, 43,* 245–250.

Sigurdsson, E., Fombonne, E., Sayal, K., & Checkley, S. (1999). Neurodevelopmental antecedents of early-onset bipolar affective disorder. *British Journal of Psychiatry, 174,* 121–127.

Skodol, A., Gallaher, P., & Oldham, J. (1996). Excessive dependency and depression: Is the relationship specific? *Journal of Nervous and Mental Disease, 184,* 165–171.

Souery, D., Rivelli, S., & Mendlewicz, J. (2001). Molecular genetic and family studies in affective disorders: State of the art. *Journal of Affective Disorders, 62,* 45–55.

Sovner, R., & Pary, R. (1993). Affective disorders in developmentally disabled persons. In J. L. Maton & R. P. Barrett (Eds.), *Psychopathology in the mentally retarded* (2nd ed., pp. 87–147). Needham Heights, MA: Allyn and Bacon.

Stoll, A., Renshaw, P., Yurgelun-Todd, D., & Cohen, B. (2000). Neuroimaging in bipolar disorder: What have we learned? *Biological Psychiatry, 48,* 505–517.

Strober, M., Morrell, W., Burroughs, J., Lampert, C., Danforth, H., & Freeman, R. (1988). A family study of bipolar I disorder in adolescence: Early onset of symptoms linked to increased familial loading and lithium resistance. *Journal of Affective Disorders, 15,* 255–268.

Swindle, R., Jr., Cronkite, R., & Moos, R. (1998). Risk factors for sustained nonremission of depressive symptoms: A 4-year follow-up. *Journal of Nervous and Mental Disease, 186,* 462–469.

Szymanski, L. (1994). Mental retardation and mental health: Concepts, aetiology, and incidence. In N. Bouras (Ed.), *Mental health and mental retardation: Recent advances and practices* (pp. 19–33). Cambridge, UK: Cambridge University Press.

Torrey, E. (1999). Epidemiological comparison of schizophrenia and bipolar disorder. *Schizophrenia Research, 39,* 101–106.

Torrey, E., & Yolken, R. (1998). At issue: Is household crowding a risk factor for schizophrenia and bipolar disorder? *Schizophrenia Bulletin, 24,* 321–324.

Tranebjaerg, L., & Orum, A. (1991). Major depressive disorder as a prominent but underestimated feature of fragile X syndrome. *Comprehensive Psychiatry, 32,* 83–87.

Turner, R., & Beiser, M. (1990). Major depression and depressive symptomatology among the physically disabled: Assessing the role of chronic stress. *Journal of Nervous and Mental Disease, 178,* 343–350.

Walker, L., Ortiz-Valdez, J., & Newbrough, J. (1989). The role of maternal employment and depression in the psychological adjustment of chronically ill, mentally retarded, and well children. *Journal of Pediatric Psychology, 14,* 357–370.

Warner, V., Mufson, L., & Weissman, M. (1995). Offspring at high and low risk for depression and anxiety: Mechanisms of psychiatric disorder. *Journal of the American Academy of Child and Adolescent Psychiatry, 34,* 786–797.

Zeiss, A., Lewinsohn, P., Rohde, P., & Seeley, J. (1996). Relationship of physical disease and functional impairment to depression in older people. *Psychology and Aging, 11,* 572–581.

Zlotnick, C., Warshaw, M., Shea, M., & Keller, M. (1997). Trauma and chronic depression among patients with anxiety disorders. *Journal of Consulting and Clinical Psychology, 65,* 333–336.

Zwaigenbaum, L., Szatmari, P., Boyle, M., & Offord, D. (1999). Highly somatizing young adolescents and the risk of depression. *Pediatrics, 103,* 1203–1209.

6

GENDER ISSUES, MENTAL RETARDATION, AND DEPRESSION

Yona Lunsky

and

Maaike Canrinus

Why a Chapter on Gender and Depression?

Depression is expected to be the second most significant cause of global disease burden by 2020, and it is the most frequently encountered women's mental health problem (Astbury & Cabral, 2000). An enormous amount of research attention has been paid to issues of gender and depression within the general population. In contrast, depression in individuals with mental retardation has typically been understood as a genderless problem. Little is known about how men and women differ with regard to risk factors for, symptoms of, and treatment for depression. This chapter considers how gender is relevant to understanding depression as it affects people with mental retardation. It begins by reviewing gender differences in prevalence rates. Next, it considers how various risk factors for depression (biological and psychosocial) have relevance for women compared with men with mental retardation. Finally, it explores several gender-related assessment and treatment issues.

Prevalence

In the general population, depression is twice as common in women as in men across culture and social class (Stoppard, 2000). Such gender differences do not seem to be present in childhood (Nolen-Hoeksema, Girgus, & Seligman, 1991; Petersen, Sarigiani, & Kennedy, 1991). During adolescence, however, there is consistent evidence of a higher prevalence of depression in girls than in boys (Compas, Ey, & Grant, 1993). This gender difference begins to emerge between ages 13 and 14, and by the age of 15, females are twice as likely as males to be depressed (Nolen-Hoeksema & Girgus, 1994).

Several research studies on depression and mental retardation have explored whether gender differences exist. Research with children has not reported a gender difference (Einfeld & Tonge, 1996; Hardan & Sahl, 1999), according to informant and clinician perspectives. Two studies measuring self-reported symptoms of depression in adolescents with mild mental retardation reported that girls with mental retardation exhibited more depressive symptoms than did either boys with mental retardation (Heiman & Margalit, 1998; Reynolds & Miller, 1985) or girls without mental retardation (Heiman & Margalit, 1998), lending some support to the idea that gender differences emerge with puberty in this population, as has been found in the general population (at least for adolescents with mild disabilities). Hardan and Sahl (1999) reported a similar increase in rates of suicidal behavior in female adolescents with mental retardation versus children.

As with the general population, women with mental retardation have been reported to experience depression or depressed moods at higher rates than did men (Benson, 1985; Lunsky, 2003; Lunsky & Benson, 2001; Meins, 1993, 1996; Reiss, 1982; Reiss & Trenn, 1984). In exception to this, two studies adopting self-report methodology and nonclinical samples did not find a gender difference in the level of depressed mood in individuals with mild to moderate mental retardation (Dagnan & Sandhu, 1999; Reynolds & Baker, 1988). Studies involving gender and clinical samples of inpatients with mental retardation who have depression are based on individuals with more mild disabilities. Whether gender is a relevant variable in individuals with more severe mental retardation is an important issue to address, because the social explanations for different prevalence rates are less applicable to them. Three recent studies included individuals with severe to profound mental retardation in their samples and reported a gender difference, but they did not report findings separately for those with severe or profound mental retardation from the rest of the sample (Lunsky et al., 2003). However, inpatient samples are biased, in that there are typically more men than women, and the predominant problem is aggression, not depression (for further discussion, see Lunsky et al., 2003).

Most research on in this area focuses on mild mental retardation (Marston, Perry & Roy, 1997; Meins, 1996). Tsiouris's (2001) study of depression in individuals with severe to profound mental retardation is an exception to this. He reviewed case files of 150 adults with severe or profound mental retardation who received psychiatric evaluations. Although more men than women received psychiatric evaluations, there was a nonsignificant trend for more women than men (13 versus 9) to meet criteria for major depressive disorder. Therefore, it is possible that a gender difference holds for those with more severe mental retardation, but more research is required. Specifically, epidemiological studies are necessary that look at the incidence of depressive disorder and dysthymia in males and females of all levels of mental retardation, across the lifespan. In addition to documenting rates of depressive disorder by age group and functioning level, gender differences must be explored.

Gender-Relevant Risk Factors for Depression

In this section, gender-relevant risk factors for depression will be reviewed in the general population and in those with mental retardation.

Biological Explanations

Important gender differences have been found in the development, organization, and degeneration of the human brain. However, such differences have not been directly linked to differential rates of depression. In fact, the current viewpoint is that differences in depression rates cannot be well explained by brain-based differences (Nolen-Hoeksema, 2002). Brain-based differences between men and women with mental retardation and their potential influence on such disorders as depression have not been studied.

Differences have also been found in the endocrine system of women and men with depression. Such differences have been linked to a higher frequency of mental health difficulties prior to, during, or following such reproductive events as menstruation, pregnancy, childbirth, abortion, and menopause (Kulkarni & Fink, 2000). The current consensus in the field is that hormonal fluctuations in women related to the menstrual cycle can trigger changes in the central nervous system, such as serotonin dysregulation, which can lead to a change in mood, particularly in women who are already vulnerable to depression (Nolen-Hoeksema, 2002). There is also some support for a relationship between levels of activation of ovarian hormones in puberty and the onset of depression in adolescent girls (Brooks-Gunn & Warren, 1989, as cited in Nolen-Hoeksema & Girgus, 1994). However, although women in the general population tend to report changes in depressed mood associated with changes in levels of sex hormones (puberty, menopause, hormone replacement therapy), systematic reviews have failed to find that rates of major depression are associated with any of these experiences (Yonkers et al., 2000, as cited in Kessler, 2003). Hormonal changes appear to play a role only for those women who already have a vulnerability to depression, genetic or otherwise (Nolen-Hoeksema, 2002). Although specific mental retardation syndromes do have associated hormonal abnormalities (for example, Down syndrome, Prader-Willi syndrome), whether such endocrine abnormalities could be related to depression has not yet been studied.

Family history studies show that genetics clearly play a role in susceptibility to depression, and some researchers argue that the genetic link is stronger in female than in male family members (MacKinnon, Jamison, & DePaulo, 1997). Some twin studies also suggest a heavier genetic link for women than for men (for example, Jacobson & Rowe, 1999). However, not all studies show a heritability gender difference. More research is needed before conclusions can be made about gender differences in genetic predisposition (Nolen-Hoeksema, 2002). There is no research on gender, genetics, depression, and mental retardation.

Psychosocial Explanations

Social Support.

Social support has been identified as important buffer of depression in the general population. Having social support in one's life can greatly minimize or even prevent depression in someone when confronted with difficulty (Cohen & Wills, 1985). Women tend to receive more social support than do men (Leavy, 1983) and also tend to have better social skills (Seeman & Fitzgerald, 2000).

In three studies, women with mental retardation received more social support than did men, according to caregivers (Krauss, Seltzer, & Goodman, 1992; Lunsky, 1996; Lunsky & Benson, 1999). This gender difference was not found according to self-report, however (Lunsky, 1996; Lunsky, 1999). In fact, two studies noted just the opposite trend: women with mental retardation reported experiencing more loneliness (the absence of social support) than did men (Lunsky, 1999; Petrovski & Gleeson, 1997). Although loneliness and lack of social support have been linked to depression in this population, it is not clear how men and women might differ. In the one study that examined all three variables according to self and informant ratings, men and women with mental retardation reported differences in depressive symptoms, but they did not report differences in terms of social support or loneliness, and informants did not report any gender differences (Lunsky, 2003).

Social Expectations and Failure to Meet Them.

Men and women often have gender-specific social expectations, and the failure to meet such expectations has been linked to emotional distress. Typically, women fulfill multiple life roles: as a wife, as a mother, and as a working woman. These roles give women a sense of self-worth and competence. If a woman finds herself unable to satisfactorily fulfill a role, her self-image is damaged. Women who experience severe mental illness have been reported to struggle emotionally with their inability to meet societal standards (Kulkarni & Fink, 2000).

Failure to take on one's gender role may be particularly relevant to women with mental retardation. These women are often discouraged if not prevented from marrying and having children because of their intellectual limitations, and such limitations may be very stressful to them (Burns, 2000; Scior, 2000; Traustadottir & Johnson, 2000). Some researchers have argued that women with mental retardation tend to overly embrace traditional stereotypical roles of women, and they suffer more so because of their inability to fulfill these roles (Burns, 2000; Scior, 2000). Some women may be at risk for depression because they get pregnant and try to fulfill the role of mother but lose custody of their children due to their limited parenting skills. In this situation, they are vulnerable to depression because of both social failure and postpartum influences.

For men with mental retardation, traditional role fulfillment may still be important and linked to depression but has not been well researched. Edgerton (1967), for example, discussed the value that deinstitutionalized men placed in being able to work and earn an income, sometimes to support a partner or family, and other times just to be independent. Men may espouse the belief that for them to be a success, they need to be able to do such things as take care of their girlfriend or wife, have a job, or be able to read or drive. Not meeting such expectations may be a threat to their self-esteem and put them at risk for depression.

Therefore, both men and women can be vulnerable to depression when they place great value in achieving gender-specific stereotyped milestones and fail at meeting such milestones. The milestones themselves may differ, depending on gender. It would be valuable to examine unmet goals or milestones identified by men and women with mental retardation, and explore how they feel because of not meeting such goals. More research in this area is warranted.

Trauma and Abuse.

The relationship between the experience of abuse and mental illness, including depression, has been well documented in the general population (Martin, Morris, & Romans, 1998), with women experiencing significantly more abuse than did men. As many as 50% of women who were abused in their past suffer from depression in their lifetime, leading researchers to theorize that gender differences in abuse prevalence are an important explanation for differential rates of depression in men and women (Kessler, 2003).

Women with mental retardation are more likely to be abused physically and sexually than are women in the general population, and they are also at higher risk for abuse than are men with mental retardation. Of the reported sexual abuse cases in the mental retardation population, between two thirds and three quarters are women (Furey, 1994; Turk & Brown, 1993). Beail and Warden (1995) argued that such abuse is under-reported and undetected in women, because they are less likely to display behavior problems or sexualized behavior that lead caregivers to refer them for treatment than are men in similar circumstances. In their study, more men (19) than women (3) received psychotherapy following sexual abuse, because more men than women were referred for psychotherapy. The impact of abuse experiences on the mental health of men and women with mental retardation is severe (Carlson, 1997) and has been linked to psychiatric such difficulties as depression and post-traumatic stress disorder (Ryan, 1994).

Therefore, both men and women with mental retardation are vulnerable to being abused, which can lead to depression. Women may be more likely than men to suffer from abuse, and the abuse may go unnoticed, because women tend to respond to it in a passive manner. Men, in contrast, may display behavior problems or sexualized behavior, receive treatment for these behavior problems, and in that process disclose sexual abuse (Beail & Warden, 1995). It is therefore relevant to consider whether abuse has occurred in both men and women with mental retardation, and to consider potential gender differences in the expression of their response to this abuse.

Stress and Coping.

Potential differences in rates of depression as well as differences in presentation may be understood in terms of differences between men and women in how they cope with stress. In the general population, men differ from women in that they tend to deal with stress actively or by distracting themselves. Women, in contrast, tend to ruminate about their difficulties, a more passive style of coping. Research has found that ruminating about sad mood leads to a more negative and hopeless outlook, contributing to depression. Women are more likely to do this than are men (Nolen-Hoeksema, 2002). They are less likely to take action and try to improve their situation.

Although no direct research on coping style, gender, and mental retardation exists, there are some preliminary reports suggesting potential gender differences. In one study, Benson and Fuchs (1999) reported that men and women with mental retardation differed in terms of what made them angry as well as in how they coped with their anger. In another study, women with mental retardation reported more passive means of dealing with conflict than did men (Jahoda, Pert, Squire, & Trower, 1998), and aggressive women wanted to be seen as passive, in accordance with the female stereotype. In a more recent study of depressed and nondepressed men and women with mental retardation, depressed women were able to list fewer adaptive coping strategies than were nondepressed women, but this difference was not found with men (Lunsky, 2003). Therefore, there is some supportive evidence that women with mild mental retardation may cope less actively with stress than do men and that depressed women may be the least active coping group. It is also the case, however, that both men and women with mental retardation are less active problem solvers than the general population, even when not depressed.

Costs of Caring.

One unique risk factor for depression faced by women in the general population has been termed the "cost of caring" (Kessler & McLeod, 1984). Women are more likely than are men to feel strong emotional ties to others in their lives and to be emotionally affected by events that happen to those people (see Nolen-Hoeksema, 2002). In addition, some women may worry too much about their relationships and may ignore their own needs in order to maintain a positive emotional tone with others (see Nolen-Hoeksema, 2002). Both of these tendencies have been linked to higher rates of depression in women than in men.

How such tendencies come into play with women compared with men with mental retardation remains relatively unexamined. Preliminary research, however, has high-lighted the vulnerability of women in two situations. The first situation is caring for an aging parent. Women with mental retardation may tend to be more often responsible for their aging parent, and are then more traumatized at the parent's death or illness than are men (Walmsley, 1996). In Walmsley's study, this was an issue for 50% of women surveyed compared with 13% of men. One woman, Eileen, was gradually given more and more responsibility for her ailing father. She suffered from depression and was eventually hospitalized as a result. The second situation involves women with mental retardation staying in unhealthy relationships with abusive men. Such women may have difficulty extricating themselves from the relationship because of the value they place in being in a romantic relationship with a man (Carlson, 1997).

Assessment

Gender Differences in Symptom Presentation

The studies just reviewed looked simply at whether rates of depressive symptoms or endorsement of depressive symptoms were higher for women than for men. Limited research exists how the symptoms of depression in women differ from those of men with mental retardation. It may be that men are more likely to express their depression in a more outward, aggressive, or agitated manner, which could account for lower rates of depression in this group. However, the studies that have examined the overlap between aggression and depression in mental retardation did not consider gender (for example, Reiss & Rojahn, 1993; Tsiouris, Mann, Patti, & Sturmey, 2003). Lunsky (2003) reported a gender difference on three items of a depression scale, in two separate samples of adults with mental retardation (99 and 80 individuals): Women were more likely than were men to endorse having stomach aches, feeling lonely, and experiencing a lack of energy. Further research is warranted on potential gender differences in symptom expression, because it may lead to a more accurate assessment of depression in men and women.

Men and women also differ in terms of comorbid conditions associated with depression. Women tend to have more somatic complaints as well as higher levels of anxiety. Men, in contrast tend to have more difficulties with alcohol or abuse of other substances as well as other antisocial behavior (see Lunsky & Havercamp, 2002). Comorbidity has not been studied extensively in men compared with women with mental retardation. Only a few case studies exist that consider these overlapping conditions.

One potentially important gender difference in symptom presentation relates to suicidal behavior. In the general population, men are more likely than are women to succeed in killing themselves (3:1), because they tend to use more lethal and immediate means. Women, in contrast, are more likely to attempt suicide but less likely to succeed, because they use nonlethal means more often (Skegg, 1998). One study of people with mental retardation reported that women were more likely to make repeated suicide attempts than were men (Benson & Laman, 1988). The majority of clinical case studies on potentially lethal suicide attempts or successes tend to focus on men (for example, Hurley, 2002; Walters, 1990). However, few systematic reviews of suicides or suicide attempts by gender have been completed. More research is necessary, based on large community and clinical samples, documenting suicidal behavior by age group, gender, and level of mental retardation.

Clinical Biases Related to Gender

Depression is often construed as a largely subjective experience and is therefore most often assessed in the general population using self-report methodology. This poses a challenge for clinicians working with people with mental retardation, when informant data and clinical observation and judgment are more heavily relied upon. Dependence on clinician and informant perspectives may lead to gender-specific biases.

Several researchers have noted, for example, that informants have difficulty rating subjective feelings of depression (e.g., Moss, Prosser, Ibbotson, & Goldberg, 1996), and it may be, as was suggested above, that women may be more likely to endorse such subjective symptoms (for example, loneliness). If this is the case, informants may miss symptoms of depression in women more frequently. Also, informants tend to refer individuals for treatment who are experiencing more outward difficulties, such as aggression, which are more commonly expressed by men. This could stop women from being assessed for depression, and/or lead men to be more frequently treated for behaviors (aggression) and not any underlying depression that might be there.

Treatment of Depression: Clinical Concerns With Regard to Gender

Gender Matching of Therapist to Client

Particularly in situations where the depression may be related to previous abuse, one should be sensitive to the gender matching of therapist to client. Women may be more comfortable in a women-only setting, or by working with a female therapist, who can approach therapy by virtue of her gender in a less threatening manner than can a man.

A man who was abused by a man in his past may also appreciate receiving services from a female therapist.

There is no research to suggest that women with mental retardation should have a female therapist or that men with mental retardation should be counseled by men. However, a given individual, based on his or her experiences with men and women, combined with gender-based beliefs, may be more comfortable with one gender over another. When possible, matching gender should assist in enhancing the therapeutic alliance, which is critical to successful therapy.

Focusing on Gender Issues

Both men and women may benefit from focusing in therapy on gender issues and how they can lead to difficulty. For example, someone like Sam (see case example) can learn that it is OK to cry or to feel sad and that being sad does not make a person less masculine. Women like Grace (see case example) can learn that it is OK to feel angry about something and that anger can be expressed in a healthy manner and does not have to be handled inwardly. Other women may need to learn that even without children or a husband a woman can be a worthwhile individual, and that—though all relationships are important—it is equally important to advocate for oneself and not just do what the boyfriend or husband says.

Empowerment

Feminist therapy focuses on empowerment and the reduction of power imbalances for women with depression (Gammell & Stoppard, 1999). Empowerment is an issue for both men and women with mental retardation. Some aspects of feminist therapy, therefore, have relevance to both genders. If woman with mental retardation struggles with depression in part because of a power imbalance in the relationship with her male partner, for example, the feminist therapy approach may be appropriate. Several papers have documented the effectiveness of a feminist approach in group therapy for women with mental retardation (Barber, Jenkins, & Jones, 2000; Millard, 1994). One paper has documented the effectiveness of a psychoanalytic approach for men with mental retardation (Beail, 1998). No research comparing different therapeutic approaches for men and women with mental retardation has been completed, however.

Case Examples

Grace

Grace was a 22-year-old woman who was recently hospitalized after taking a bottle of her mother's acetaminophen. When asked why she did this, she said that nobody really cares about her. She would never have a boyfriend, because she was stupid, fat, and ugly. She wanted to be skinny like the girls in the dance videos she saw on television. In hospital it became evident that Grace felt very angry about her situation but was uncomfortable expressing this anger to either her mother or sister.

Prior to her suicide attempt, Grace was living with her mother and her mother's boyfriend, as well as her sister and her sister's children in a two-bedroom apartment. Her sister moved in 3 months prior to the suicide attempt after the breakup of her marriage. She and her children moved into Grace's room, and Grace was given the couch in the living area, where she could sleep only after everyone else went to bed. According to her case files, Grace had been sexually abused by her father, who had left when she was 12 years old, but she had never received therapy.

In hospital, Grace began attending a women's group and learned about sexuality, personal boundaries, and how to keep herself safe. She also began individual therapy to process the abuse experience and learn to express her anger in a healthy manner. After 3 months, she moved from the hospital to a supported living setting. She now has her own apartment and regularly schedules visits to see her mother (without her mother's boyfriend) and her sister, niece, and nephew.

Sam

Sam was a 35-year-old man with Down syndrome living with two roommates in a supportive living setting that provides 10 hours of staff support a week. He was referred for psychiatric consultation because of his refusal to get up in the morning, his neglect of hygiene, and his argumentativeness with staff. The staff also voiced concern that he began drinking beer in his apartment and on the street.

Sam's father had been in the military, and strong gender stereotypes were promoted when Sam was growing up. His mother was described as emotional, but he and his brother had been restricted from crying or acting in a stereotypically feminine way. Two years prior to the psychiatric evaluation, one of Sam's roommates became very ill and died. There had been little discussion about this, and Sam had been prevented from visiting his roommate in the hospital before his death.

Sam was interviewed by a young female psychiatrist about his difficulties. He denied feeling sad and said he was not having any problems except that he had been thinking about changing jobs. He admitted to drinking beer because it made him feel good. When she questioned him about the death of his roommate, he became tearful and said he had to go to the washroom. He did not return to the assessment. He came to the next session with a male support staff, who was invited to stay for the interview. The psychiatrist asked questions to both of them this time, and the male support staff used the opportunity to offer his perspective and remind Sam of conversations they had had in the past about Sam feeling unhappy. Part of Sam's therapy focused on helping him to come to terms with loss in his life, normalizing his negative emotions. He learned that drinking beer when he feels sad can make him feel worse and that a better way to help himself feel better is to talk about it. He set a goal of returning to work at a job that did not threaten his self-esteem or his concept of manliness. He learned that strong men can cry and can ask for help in personal situations and at work without feeling ashamed.

Comments

In both of these cases, patients had gender-related difficulties coping, which led to their depression. Grace was angry but had difficulty expressing her anger, turning it inward instead. Sam was sad but felt ashamed to be sad, so he self-medicated with alcohol and did not seek help from others. Each had ideas about how their gender should act in their situation, which made coping with their interpersonal experiences more challenging. Although treatment for Grace and Sam had many components, one piece involved seeing them as women or men with gender-specific concerns or issues, and addressing such issues. Grace, because of her sexual abuse history, felt more comfortable working with women, and she benefited from being in a women's group, particularly through learning that she was not alone in her concerns and issues. Sam may have preferred to work with a male therapist, but he learned to be comfortable with a woman and to display "womanly" emotions, perhaps through receiving the additional support of his male caregiver.

Summary

Gender and depression is not well studied but is relevant to understanding the causes of, assessment, and treatment of depression for individuals with mental retardation. There is some research suggesting that women with mental retardation, like women in the general population, experience depression more often than do men, but how gender and functioning level interact has not been well researched. Gender-related risk factors for depression, such as coping with stress, social support, social expectations, and trauma, have relevance to individuals with mental retardation and may be linked to gender differences in prevalence rates or symptom presentation. The topic of gender, depression, and mental retardation is in its infancy, however. More research attention is required linking gender to depression's cause and treatment, based on clinical and community samples of individuals across functioning levels.

When working with individuals with mental retardation and depression, it is important to be alerted to potential gender biases in assessment, and to be sensitive to gender issues in treatment. Men and women can be better treated if an understanding of how their gender influences their self-concept, their goals in life, their coping strategies, and their expectations of others is integrated into the case formulation and subsequent therapy. Clinicians should be educated on gender issues as they relate to individuals with mental retardation who are depressed, as well as those who are not depressed.

References

Astbury, J., & Cabral, M. (2000). *Women's mental health: An evidence based review.* Geneva: World Health Organization.

Barber, M., Jenkins, R., & Jones, C. (2000). A survivor's group for women who have a learning disability. *The British Journal of Developmental Disabilities, 46,* 31–41.

Beail, N. (1998). Psychoanalytic psychotherapy with men with intellectual disabilities: A preliminary outcome study. *British Journal of Medical Psychology, 71,* 1–11.

Beail, N., & Warden, S. (1995). Sexual abuse of adults with learning disabilities. *Journal of Intellectual Disability Research, 39,* 382–387.

Benson, B. A. (1985). Behavior disorders and mental retardation: Associations with age, sex, and level of functioning in an outpatient clinic sample. *Applied Research in Mental Retardation, 6,* 79–85.

Benson, B. A., & Fuchs, C. (1999). Anger-arousing situations and coping responses of aggressive adults with intellectual disability. *Journal of Intellectual and Developmental Disability, 24,* 207–214.

Benson, B. A., & Laman, D. S. (1988). Suicidal tendencies of mentally retarded adults in community settings. *Australia and New Zealand Journal of Developmental Disabilities, 14,* 49–54.

Burns, J. (2000). Gender identity and women with learning disabilities: The third sex. *Clinical Psychology Forum, 137,* 11–15.

Carlson, B. E. (1997). Mental retardation and domestic violence: An ecological approach to intervention. *Social Work, 42,* 79–89.

Cohen, S., & Wills, T. A. (1985). Stress, social support, and the buffering hypothesis. *Psychological Bulletin, 98,* 310–357.

Compas, B. E., Ey, S., & Grant, K. E. (1993). Taxonomy, assessment, and diagnosis of depression during adolescence. *Psychological Bulletin, 114,* 323–344.

Dagnan, D., & Sandhu, S. (1999). Social comparison, self-esteem and depression in people with intellectual disability. *Journal of Intellectual Disability Research. Special Issue: Mental Health and Intellectual Disability, V, 43,* 372–379.

Edgerton, R. B. (1967). *The cloak of competence: Stigma in the lives of the mentally retarded.* Berkeley: University of California Press.

Einfeld, S. L., & Tonge, B. J. (1996). Population prevalence of psychopathology in children and adolescents with intellectual disability. II: Epidemiological findings. *Journal of Intellectual Disability Research, 40,* 99–109.

Furey, E. M. (1994). Sexual abuse of adults with mental retardation: Who and where. *Mental Retardation, 32,* 173–180.

Gammell, D. J., & Stoppard, J. M. (1999). Women's experiences of treatment of depression: Medicalization or empowerment? *Canadian Psychology. Special Issue: Women and Depression: Qualitative Research Approaches, 40,* 112–128.

Hardan, A., & Sahl, R. (1999). Suicidal behavior in children and adolescents with developmental disorders. *Research in Developmental Disabilities, 20,* 287–296.

Heiman, T., & Margalit, M. (1998). Loneliness, depression, and social skills among students with mild mental retardation in different educational settings. *Journal of Special Education, 32,* 154–163.

Hurley, A. D. (2002). Potentially lethal suicide attempts in persons with developmental disabilities: Review and three new case reports. *Mental Health Aspects of Developmental Disabilities, 5,* 90–95.

Jacobson, K. C., & Rowe, D. C. (1999). Genetic and environmental influences on the relationships between family connectedness, school connectedness, and adolescent depressed mood: Sex differences. *Developmental Psychology, 35(4),* 926–939.

Jahoda, A., Pert, C., Squire, J., & Trower, P. (1998). Facing stress and conflict: A comparison of the predicted responses and self-concepts of aggressive and non-aggressive people with intellectual disability. *Journal of Intellectual Disability Research, 42,* 360–369.

Kessler, R. C. (2003). Epidemiology of women and depression. *Journal of Affective Disorders. Special Issue: Women and Depression, 74,* 5–13.

Kessler, R. C., & McLeod, J. D. (1984). Sex differences in vulnerability to undesirable life events. *American Sociology Review, 9,* 620–631.

Krauss, M. W., Seltzer, M. M., & Goodman, S. J. (1992). Social support networks of adults with mental retardation who live at home. *American Journal on Mental Retardation. Special Issue: Social Skills, 96,* 432–441.

Kulkarni, J., & Fink, G. (2000). Hormones and psychosis. In D. J. Castle et al. (Eds.), *Women and schizophrenia* (pp. 51–66). New York: Cambridge University Press.

Leavy, R. L. (1983). Social support and psychological disorder: A review. *Journal of Clinical Child and Adolescent Psychology, 11,* 3–21.

Lunsky, Y. (1996). *Perceived social support in adults with mild mental retardation.* Unpublished master's thesis, The Ohio State University, Columbus.

Lunsky, Y. (1999). *Social support as a predictor of well-being for adults with mild mental retardation.* Unpublished doctoral dissertation, The Ohio State University, Columbus.

Lunsky, Y. (2003). Depressive symptoms in intellectual disability: Does gender play a role? *Journal of Intellectual Disability Research, 47,* 417–427.

Lunsky, Y., & Benson, B. A. (1999). Social circles of adults with mental retardation as viewed by their caregivers. *Journal of Developmental and Physical Disabilities, 11,* 115–129.

Lunsky, Y., & Benson, B. A. (2001). Association between perceived social support and strain, and positive and negative outcome for adults with mild intellectual disability. *Journal of Intellectual Disability Research. Special Issue: Mental Health and Intellectual Disability, VIII, 45,* 106–114.

Lunsky, Y., Bradley, E., Durbin, J., Koegl, C., Canrinus, M., & Goering, P. (2003). *Dual diagnosis in provincial psychiatric hospitals—A population based study. Year 1 summary report.* Toronto: Centre for Addiction and Mental Health.

Lunsky, Y., & Havercamp, S. (2002). Mental health and women with intellectual disabilities. In P. Noonan Walsh & T. Heller (Eds.), *Women's health and intellectual disability.* Oxford, UK: Blackwell Publishing.

MacKinnon, D. F., Jamison, K. R., & DePaulo, J. R. (1997). Genetics of manic depressive illness. *Annual Review of Neuroscience, 20,* 355–373.

Marston, G. M., Perry, D. W., & Roy, A. (1997). Manifestations of depression in people with intellectual disability. *Journal of Intellectual Disability Research. Special Issue: Mental Health and Intellectual Disability, 41,* 476–480.

Martin, J., Morris, E., & Romans, S. E. (1998). Violence against girls and women: Its relevance to mental health. In S. E. Romans (Ed.), *Folding back the shadows: A perspective on women's mental health* (pp. 147–162). Dunedin, New Zealand: University of Otago Press.

Meins, W. (1993). Prevalence and risk factors for depressive disorders in adults with intellectual disability. *Australia and New Zealand Journal of Developmental Disabilities. Special Issue: Ninth World Congress on Intellectual Disability, 18,* 147–156.

Meins, W. (1996). A new depression scale designed for use with adults with mental retardation. *Journal of Intellectual Disability Research, 40,* 222–226.

Millard, L. (1994). Between ourselves. Experiences of a women's group on sexuality and sexual abuse. In Ann Craft (Ed.), *Practice issues in sexuality and learning disabilities* (pp. 35–55). London: Routledge Press.

Moss, S., Prosser, H., Ibbotson, B., & Goldberg, D. (1996). Respondent and informant accounts of psychiatric symptoms in a sample of patients with learning disability. *Journal of Intellectual Disability Research, 40,* 457–465.

Nolen-Heoksema, S. (2002). Gender differences in depression. In I. H. Gotlieb & C. L. Hammen (Eds.), *Handbook of depression* (pp. 492–509). New York: Guilford Press.

Nolen-Hoeksema, S., & Girgus, J. S. (1994). The emergence of gender differences in depression during adolescence. *Psychological Bulletin, 115,* 424–443.

Nolen-Hoeksema, S., Girgus, J. S., & Seligman, M. E. P. (1991). Sex differences in depression and explanatory style in children. *Journal of Youth and Adolescence, 20,* 233–245.

Petersen, A. C., Sarigiani, P. A., & Kennedy, R. E. (1991). Adolescent depression: Why more girls? *Journal of Youth and Adolescence, 20,* 247–271.

Petrovski, P., & Gleeson, G. (1997). The relationship between job satisfaction and psychological health in people with an intellectual disability in competitive employment. *Journal of Intellectual and Developmental Disability, 22,* 199–211.

Reiss, S. (1982). Psychopathology and mental retardation: Survey of a developmental disabilities mental health program. *Mental Retardation, 203,* 128–132.

Reiss, S., & Rojahn, J. (1993). Joint occurrence of depression and aggression in children and adults with mental retardation. *Journal of Intellectual Disability Research, 37,* 287–294.

Reiss, S., & Trenn, E. (1984). Consumer demand for outpatient mental health services for people with mental retardation. *Mental Retardation, 22,* 112–116.

Reynolds, W. M., & Baker, J. A. (1988). Assessment of depression in persons with mental retardation. *American Journal of Mental Retardation, 93,* 93–103.

Reynolds, W. M., & Miller, K. L. (1985). Depression and learned helplessness in mentally retarded and nonmentally retarded adolescents: An initial investigation. *Applied Research in Mental Retardation, 6,* 295–306.

Ryan, R. (1994). Posttraumatic stress disorder in persons with developmental disabilities. *Community Mental Health Journal, 30,* 45–54.

Scior, K. (2000). Women with disabilities: Gendered subjects after all? *Clinical Psychology Forum, 137,* 6–10.

Seeman, M. V., & Fitzgerald, P. (2000). Women and schizophrenia: Clinical aspects. In D. J. Castle et al. (Eds.), *Women and schizophrenia* (pp. 35–50). New York: Cambridge University Press.

Skegg, K. (1998). Women and suicide. In S. E. Romans (Ed.), *Folding back the shadows: A perspective on women's mental health* (pp. 193–202). Dunedin, New Zealand: University of Otago Press.

Stoppard, J. M. (2000). *Understanding depression: Feminist social constructionist approaches.* Florence, KY: Taylor & Frances/Routledge.

Traustadottir, R., & Johnson, K. (Eds.). (2000). *Women with intellectual disabilities: Finding a place in the world.* London: Jessica Kingsley Publishers.

Tsiouris, J. A. (2001). Diagnosis of depression in people with severe/profound intellectual disability. *Journal of Intellectual Disability Research. Special Issue: Mental Health and Intellectual Disability, VIII, 45,* 115–120.

Tsiousis, J. A., Mann, R., Patti, P. J., & Sturmey, P. (2003). Challenging behaviours should not be considered as depressive equivalents in individuals with intellectual disability. *Journal of Intellectual Disability Research, 47,* 14–21.

Turk, V., & Brown, H. (1993). The sexual abuse of adults with learning disabilities: Results of a two-year incidence survey. *Mental Handicap Research, 6,* 193–216.

Walmsley, J. (1996). Doing what mum wants me to do: Looking at family relationships from the point of view of people with intellectual disabilities. *Journal of Applied Research in Intellectual Disabilities, 9,* 324–341.

Walters, R. M. (1990). Suicidal behaviour in severely mentally handicapped patients. *British Journal of Psychiatry, 151,* 444–446.

7

Depression, Dementia, and Down Syndrome

Paul J. Patti

This chapter discusses the incidence of depression and dementia in older people with Down syndrome, and it reviews some of the behavioral and psychiatric features that distinguish these two conditions. The issue of differential diagnosis of dementia, mood disorders, and physical health problems is discussed. Data on challenging behaviors, psychiatric signs and symptoms, and the accompanying psychiatric disorders from 300 adults with and without Down syndrome and several case studies illustrating differential diagnosis of mood disorders in people with Down syndrome are presented.

Introduction

Depression, one of the most common illnesses in the older adult population, can be difficult to distinguish from dementia, and it often coexists with dementia. According to the *Diagnostic and Statistical Manual of Mental Disorders* (4th edition) (DSM-IV; American Psychiatric Association, 1994), there must be impairment in multiple cognitive domains, not solely memory, for a diagnosis of dementia to be made. Similarly, changes in memory, attention, and the ability to make and carry out activities are indicative of depression. It is therefore important for health care providers to differentiate between normal aging, dementia, and depression, because depression and some of the causes of dementia can be treated to eliminate or greatly improve cognitive performance (U.S. Department of Health and Human Services, 1996).

It has been 2 decades since studies reported the prevalence of psychiatric disorders in people with intellectual disabilities (ID) to be higher than in the general population (Benson, 1985; Eaton & Menolascino, 1982; Reiss, 1990; Russell & Tanguay, 1981). The higher prevalence of behavioral disturbances in the ID population (Day, 1985), and the lack of differentiation between psychiatric disorders and challenging behaviors within the ID population (Day & Jancar, 1994), were two possible explanations for this greater incidence when compared with the general population. Age and size of the ID samples, however, can result in sampling biases; the reliability of the interview instruments used and the interpretation of clinical data can also influence the reporting of prevalence rates in psychiatric disorders (Jacobson, 2003).

The psychopathology of psychiatric illness and associated behavioral disorders in people with ID over age 60 show similarities to the general population, with dementia and depression being the most common psychiatric disorders (Jacobson, 2003; Tyrrell & Dodd, 2003). The spectrum of clinical features associated with depression in people with ID is similar to those seen in the general population. However, adults with Down syndrome (DS), a major subgroup of the population of persons with ID, may be predisposed to depression more than to other disorders (Prasher, 2003).

The prevalence of dementia among people with ID without DS was found to be about the same as in the general population—about 6% for individuals age 60 and older (Janicki & Dalton, 2000). It is now generally agreed that people with DS over age 50 are at higher risk to develop Alzheimer disease than are people in the general or ID populations (Dalton & Crapper-McLachlan, 1986; Oliver & Holland, 1986; Visser et al., 1997; Zigman, Schupf, Zigman, & Silverman, 1993). Neuropathological studies have established that marked changes in the brain seen in Alzheimer disease occur with increasing age in people with DS (Wisniewski, Silverman, & Wegiel, 1994; Wisniewski, Wisniewski, & Wen, 1985). In a population study, the prevalence of dementia, Alzheimer type (DAT), among persons with DS was reported to be much higher than among other people with ID—about 25% for adults with DS age 40 and older and about 60% for those with DS age 60 and older (Janicki & Dalton, 2000).

Lai and Williams (1989) described the course of dementia for people with DS and divided it into three stages. During initial stages, memory impairment, temporal disorientation, and a decrease in communication occur. During the middle stages, there is a loss of self-help skills, a decline in work performance, and often disturbances in gait. Late-onset seizures may also occur during this stage. In the late stages, the person may become nonambulatory, completely incontinent, and bedridden, and they exhibit pathological reflexes. Holland's (2000) review indicated that there is convincing evidence of an age-related increase in the prevalence of dementia in persons with DS, which matches that found in the general population, but it occurs anywhere from 30 to 40 years earlier. It should be stressed, however, that the rates of dementia in people with DS do not reach 100%, even with advancing age.

The Behavioral Phenotype of People With Down Syndrome

People with DS display a different spectrum of behavioral and psychiatric disorders than do people with ID without DS. Reports of psychiatric conditions in people with ID indicated depression and other mood-related disturbances to be the predominant disorders seen in people with DS (Haveman, Maaskant, van Schrojenstein Lantman, Urlings, & Kessels, 1994; McGuire & Chicoine, 1996; Myers & Pueschel, 1995a; Pary, Loschen, & Tomkowiak, 1996). Others noted that depression, along with DAT and hypothyroidism, were the primary conditions that can distinguish adults with DS from age-matched or developmentally matched control groups (Chapman & Hesketh, 2000). Smith (2001) reported that thyroid disease, diabetes, hearing loss, atlantoaxial subluxation, and Alzheimer disease were more likely to occur in adults with DS. These medical illnesses and sensory deficits were thought to contribute to the display of some challenging behaviors and psychiatric disorders, such as depression and obsessive-compulsive disorder often seen in people with DS. The effects of overt hypothyroidism on cognition and mood in the general population have been well established and are considered to be a common cause of reversible dementia (Davis, Stern, & Flashman, 2003). There is increasing evidence now to suggest that subclinical hypothyroidism may be a predisposing factor for depression, cognitive decline, and dementia. Normalization of thyroid function, however, can result in the successful reversal of depression after treatment (Jackson, 1998). This is especially important in people with DS, because they are at higher risk for all of these conditions.

It has been proposed that people with DS possess a different behavioral phenotype in comparison with people with ID but without DS (Chapman & Hesketh, 2000; Collacott, Cooper, Brandford, & McGrother 1998; Levitas, 2000). The types of challenging behaviors, psychiatric signs and symptoms, and the accompanying psychiatric disorders in people with DS differed from the people with ID without DS (Patti & Tsiouris,

2003). Cooper and Prasher (1998) went so far as to indicate that though people with DS as a group are commonly "excessively uncooperative," they display a lower prevalence of aggression than do controls; they also have higher incidences of restlessness, low mood, and disturbed sleep than do controls.

Other idiosyncratic behaviors and conditions have been reported in persons with DS. They include self-talk (Glenn & Cunningham, 2000; McGuire & Chicoine 2002; McGuire, Chicoine, & Greenbaum, 1997), repetitive behaviors (Evans & Gray, 2000), obsessive slowness (Charlot, 2002), obsessive-compulsive disorder, (Prasher, 1995; Prasher & Day, 1995), and Tourette's disorder (Kerbeshian & Burd, 2000; Myers & Pueschel, 1995b). Further studies are necessary, however, to determine with confidence the prevalence of these behaviors and conditions in the DS population.

Within the diagnostic category of affective/mood disorders, bipolar disorder, especially with manic features, was less common in people with DS than it was in the ID or the general population (Craddock & Owen, 1994; Pary, Strauss, & White, 1996). This finding suggests that unipolar rather than bipolar depression can be a characteristic of the DS behavioral phenotype. Suicidal ideation, one of the three subjective criteria for major depression, was an infrequent phenomenon in people with DS. In a large population survey on suicide attempts, people with DS had significantly fewer incidences of suicidal behavior compared with the ID control group without DS (Pary, Strauss, & White, 1997).

Because the behavioral phenotype in DS includes a higher incidence of depression and DAT, it conversely includes a lower incidence of other psychiatric disorders. Studies have reported a low prevalence of schizophrenia and other psychotic disorders in people with DS (Collacott, Cooper, & McGrother, 1992; Collacott et al., 1998; Cooper, Duggirala, & Collacott, 1995; Day & Jancar, 1994; Myers & Pueschel, 1991, 1994; Prasher, 1995). Collacott et al., (1992) speculated that people with DS are in some way protected against the development of schizophrenia, paranoid states, conduct disorders, and personality disorders. In addition, the presence of hallucinations and delusions was low in people with DS (Prasher, 1995, 1997), which lends support to the low incidence of psychotic disorders in the DS population. In one study, however, hallucinations were reported to be a prominent feature in a small group of individuals with DS and major depression (Myers & Pueschel, 1995a). The reporting and classification of hallucinations and the small sample size is a limiting factor (Hurley, 1996; Patti & Tsiouris, 2003). It is therefore important to observe and assess the presenting signs and symptoms in order to make an accurate psychiatric diagnosis.

Functional Decline

Age-associated functional decline in depression and dementia has been another area of investigation. A change in one's general level of functioning and behavior can be due to normal aging, factors related to dementia, or to depression. Prasher (1996) and Prasher and Chung (1996) reported an age-related decline in adaptive skills that can be seen in the people with ID over 50 years of age. This observed decline was found to be a function of age, the presence of dementia, and the level of ID. For adults with DS, functional decline was greater in comparison with age-specific controls with ID but without DS (Prasher, 1996; Prasher & Chung, 1996). The principal factor causing this differential decline in those with DS was the increased incidence of dementia (Prasher, 1999). A decline or loss in adaptive functioning, especially in adults with DS below age 50, may be due to depression rather than to dementia and can be effectively treated with positive results (Tsiouris & Patti, 1997). Furthermore, in order to arrive at a definitive differential diagnosis, it is necessary to have an accurate baseline measure of the individual's adaptive and cognitive level prior to the reported decline, for comparison before a definitive diagnosis of dementia is made. A careful history of whether the change in functioning is a steady decline or has a fluctuating course is also important in making a differential diagnosis of depression or dementia.

Although Alzheimer disease is a major part of the behavioral phenotype of DS, it is neither as universal in people with DS as was once thought, and it rarely has an onset before the fifth decade of life (Levitas, 2000). For some adults with DS, a decline in functioning associated with depression was labeled as "pseudo-dementia"; when treated with antidepressants, the symptoms can be reversed (Tsiouris & Patti, 1997). A differential diagnosis of age-related decline in people with DS is crucial, because sensory impairments, depression, and thyroid disorder can all mimic dementia and are nonetheless treatable (Holland, 2000). Therefore, a functional decline in adaptive skills, regardless of its causative factor or factors, is another distinguishing feature (as well as thyroid disorders) in the behavioral phenotype of people with DS who are at higher risk for both depression and dementia after the fourth decade of life. With this in mind, it is important for clinicians to formulate an accurate diagnosis whenever a functional decline occurs in an adult with DS, so proper treatment strategies can be implemented.

Challenging Behaviors and Psychiatric Symptoms in Dementia and Depression

The main focus of mental health research in people with DS has been depression and dementia. It is often unclear, however, how these diagnoses are determined. Less attention has been devoted to investigating the presence or absence of challenging behaviors, and the psychiatric signs and symptoms that accompany these two diagnoses (Patti & Tsiouris, 2003). Such behavioral problems as agitation, aggression, and screaming are commonly displayed by individuals suffering from dementia, especially by those in the late stages of the disease. Difficulties in managing behavioral problems rather than cognitive decline were the main reasons why family members in the general population seek placement into nursing homes (Stoppe, Brandt, & Staedt, 1999). This is less often the case for people with ID, because many reside in group homes, where the level of care and supervision is greater than that provided in a private home by only one or two caregivers. Moreover, even with the loss of mobility and the need for increased medical care, such as feeding tubes, people with ID and dementia can continue to receive good care in group homes when increased residential supports are provided (Udell, 1999).

Prasher and Chung (1996) found that a diagnosis of dementia was a predictive factor for increased maladaptive behavior. Even when dementia was present, however, the prevalence of aggressive behaviors was lower in individuals with DS than in individuals with other forms of ID (Cooper & Prasher, 1998; Cosgrave, Tyrrell, McCarron, Gill, & Lawlor, 1999). The most common symptoms in those with DS and dementia were the lack of energy, low mood, and behavioral problems (Cooper & Prasher, 1998).

In depression, the presence of such challenging behaviors as aggression, stereotyped behavior, and self-injurious behavior in people with ID are nonspecific indicators of distress and dysfunction and not a criterion for any specific psychiatric diagnosis (Tsiouris, 2001). Tsiouris, Mann, Patti, and Sturmey (2003) reported that the types and frequency of challenging behavior was lower overall in a group with DS than in a group with other forms of ID.

According to Tsiouris (2001), a diagnosis of major depression following the DSM-IV criteria (American Psychiatric Association, 1994) can be made in verbal and nonverbal adults with ID when at least five of the nine criteria are present. Of the nine necessary criteria for depression, six are observable signs and include depressed affect or irritable mood, sleep disturbances, appetite disturbance or weight loss or gain, social isolation/ loss of interest, psychomotor retardation or agitation, and loss of energy or fatigue. The remaining three criteria are subjective signs (feelings of worthlessness, diminished ability to think, and recurrent thoughts of death) and are less common, because they require expressive language to be observed (Tsiouris, 2001).

The common signs and symptoms of dementia follow a similar pattern of decline but are more strongly associated with age. Cognitive deterioration initially occurs in short-term memory, learning, and orientation. Other accompanying symptoms include irritability, low energy, and the loss of self-care skills. As dementia progresses into the late stages, the loss of ability to recognize people and objects (agnosia), difficulty performing a learned movement or coordinated motor activity (apraxia), and the inability to name objects (anomia) develop and lead to a vegetative state. In people with ID, dementia may not present with the typical deficits in memory, judgment, or loss in cognitive functions as seen in the general population. Instead, the early stages of dementia may present as a general slowing, a change in personality, apathy, and a loss of motivation (Tyrrell & Dodd, 2003). What is distinctive in people with DS is that the overall decline occurs much earlier than in the general or ID populations (Holland, 2000).

Difficulties in Differential Diagnosis

A major challenge to both clinicians and researchers is that depression and dementia, especially DAT, have similar presentations in older adults with DS (Burt, Loveland, & Lewis, 1992; Khan, Osinowo, & Pary, 2002; McGuire & Chicoine, 1996). Difficulties in making a differential diagnosis arise when clinicians confuse depression and dementia, which can lead to over-diagnosing dementia in people with DS. In addition, the reliance on informant-based ratings alone has its own limitations and must be used with caution when formulating a diagnosis (Burt, 1999).

For adults with DS, two commonly reported symptoms for DAT—apathy or inactivity and loss of self-help skills—are also typical of depression. Other overlapping behavioral features and signs were reported by Burt (1999) and include depressed mood, urinary incontinence, irritability, slowing, becoming uncooperative, and losing housekeeping skills. Although some of these features are not unique to depression, they indicate to clinicians that a change or decline in behavior has occurred. Some reports have demonstrated an association between age and depressed mood in DS and have suggested that low mood may even be a prodromal feature of dementia in DS (Burt et al., 1992; Meins, 1995). Nonetheless, a diagnosis of dementia in persons with or without ID and with or without DS is a difficult one to make in the early stages. It can be made, however, through exclusion of other disorders and close follow-up over time to observe the changing course of symptoms.

Clinical Data From an Outpatient Sample

The remainder of this chapter discusses clinical data from a cohort of 300 people with ID with and without DS to highlight some of the differences between these two groups. The types of challenging behaviors (CBs), the presenting psychiatric signs and symptoms (PSSs), and the occurrence of dementia, depression, or other psychiatric disorders are discussed.

The Sample

The sample represented a non-population-based cohort of 300 adults with and without DS between ages 40 and 86 who were evaluated at a diagnostic and research clinic in a major metropolitan area over a 10-year period. Sample characteristics are presented in Table 7.1. There were no persons with DS over age 71, and the group between 60 and 69 represented a smaller number of individuals (N=18). Likewise, those without DS over age 70 also represented a modest number of individuals (N=23). Previous studies have reported on similar smaller numbers of cases (Cooper & Prasher, 1998; Myers & Pueschel, 1995a). The specific cognitive tests and diagnostic procedures used have been described elsewhere (Tsiouris & Patti, 1997; Tsiouris et al., 2000). Referrals for evaluation were made because of (a) a change in behavior or personality; (b) a decline in cognitive or adaptive functioning; or (c) forgetting or memory decline.

The presenting behavioral and psychiatric complaints were obtained from interviews with the primary caregiver or group home staff. The informants completed the Behavior Problem Inventory (Rojhan, 1986) and a Psychiatric Signs Profile (Tsiouris, Korosh, Patti, & Pfadt, 1998) to determine the frequency and severity of the reported problems. Staff recorded the frequency of occurrence and the severity of the behavior or sign. Twelve CBs and 13 PSSs were identified from caregiver ratings and tabulated for each age group. (See Tables 7.2 and 7.3).

After the initial interview and assessment were completed, the psychiatric diagnosis was formulated using DSM-IV criteria (American Psychiatric Association, 1994). If the diagnosis could not be made after the initial contact, follow-up visits were arranged in order to complete the diagnostic process. The diagnoses were grouped into seven DSM-IV categories. Lower incidence diagnoses were listed under "Other disorders" (see Table 7.4). A category "Rule out dementia" was added if it remained uncertain

Table 7.1. Characteristics of individuals with and without Down syndrome referred to an outpatient clinic.

	No. of Cases	Age Range	Gender		Functioning Levels				
			Males	Females	Borderline	Mild	Moderate	Severe	Profound
DS[1]	56	40–49	27	29	0	9	17	19	11
NDS[2]	51	40–49	29	22	2	17	10	13	9
DS	84	50–59	45	39	2	11	34	26	11
NDS	36	50–59	21	15	0	10	12	8	6
DS	18	60–71	14	4	0	1	6	10	1
NDS	32	60–69	14	18	3	15	8	5	1
NDS	15	70–79	11	4	0	7	2	5	1
NDS	8	80–86	5	3	0	1	2	5	0

1. DS- Down Syndrome
2. NDS- Non-Down Syndrome

Table 7.2. Challenging behaviors by age group in a clinic sample of individuals with and without Down syndrome.

	40–49		50–59		60–69		70–79	80–86
Group:	DS[1]	NDS[2]	DS	NDS	DS	NDS	NDS	NDS
	(N=56)	(N=51)	(N=84)	(N=36)	(N=18)	(N=32)	(N=15)	(N=8)
Challenging Behaviors Percent (%) CBs								
Physical aggression	54	43	24	36	33	34	40	38
Verbal aggression	14	29	14	14	22	47	40	38
Property destruction	11	14	7	11	6	0	7	0
Tantrum behaviors	23	37	20	31	22	44	53	63
Disruptive behaviors	38	55	25	50	22	50	53	75
Self-injurious behavior (SIB)	18	29	13	39	6	16	7	13
Difficulty with transitions	20	22	24	31	11	22	53	38
Noncompliance	54	41	57	44	56	47	47	75
Inappropriate sexual behaviors	4	12	1	8	0	3	7	0
Stealing (food or objects)	9	8	14	8	0	19	33	0
Other (e.g., pica, fecal smearing)	11	12	10	6	0	6	20	0
Percent (%) CBs absent	27	16	30	25	39	19	27	13

Note: The frequency of each challenging behavior was converted to a percentage in each age group.

1. DS- Down Syndrome
2. NDS- Non-Down Syndrome

Table 7.3. Psychiatric signs and symptoms by age group in individuals with and without Down syndrome.

	Age Groups							
	40–49		50–59		60–69		70–79	80–86
Group:	DS[1] (N=56)	NDS[2] (N=51)	DS (N=84)	NDS (N=36)	DS (N=18)	NDS (N=32)	NDS (N=15)	NDS (N=8)
Psychiatric Signs and Symptoms								
Appetite disturbances	21	14	20	22	22	25	27	25
Sleep disturbances	59	41	67	61	56	47	40	38
Weight loss	41	12	45	31	39	34	27	25
Low energy	30	25	37	22	56	38	40	38
Mood disturbance	63	57	67	64	78	56	47	88
Social avoidance	23	25	27	31	11	25	40	25
Loss of self-help skills	32	14	55	31	61	34	13	38
Forgetfulness or disorientation	38	35	67	22	72	44	27	50
Hallucinations or hearing voices	5	8	5	6	17	19	0	13
Delusions	2	6	4	0	0	6	7	0
Talking to self	25	29	21	31	28	34	20	13
Behavior rituals	34	31	42	31	56	25	27	25
Tics or involuntary movements	21	14	5	22	0	41	33	13

Note: The frequency of each psychiatric sign or symptom was converted to a percentage in each age group.

1. DS- Down Syndrome
2. NDS- Non-Down Syndrome

Table 7.4. Psychiatric diagnoses by age group in a clinic sample of individuals with and without Down syndrome.

Psychiatric Disorders (%)	40–49		50–59		60–69		70–79	80–86
Group:	DS [1] (N=56)	NDS [2] (N=51)	DS (N=84)	NDS (N=36)	DS (N=18)	NDS (N=32)	NDS (N=15)	NDS (N=8)
Anxiety disorders	41	45	40	61	33	38	60	38
Tic disorders	16	2	2	3	0	3	7	0
Stereotypic movement disorder	9	6	5	6	0	3	7	13
Mood disorders (totals)	55	49	48	61	56	66	60	38
Depressive disorders	41	20	33	22	44	31	20	13
Bipolar disorders	7	22	6	31	6	16	33	13
Mood disorder, NOS	7	8	8	8	6	19	7	13
Impulse control disorders	21	8	14	14	6	25	20	25
Psychotic disorders	4	22	7	8	0	16	7	13
Dementia (totals)	23	8	63	3	62	22	20	63
Probable dementia, Alzheimer type	23	0	63	3	56	3	7	25
Dementia, vascular type	0	0	0	0	0	6	13	13
Amnestic disorder, NOS	0	6	0	0	6	3	0	0
Dementia, mixed type /NOS	0	2	0	0	0	9	0	25
Rule out dementia	4	2	13	3	33	6	13	0
Misdiagnosed as dementia	9	2	0	0	0	0	0	0
Other disorders	7	6	0	6	0	9	0	13

Note: The frequency of each psychiatric diagnosis was converted to a percentage in each age group.

1. DS- Down Syndrome
2. NDS- Non-Down Syndrome

if dementia was present in an individual showing some type of decline. A second category, "Misdiagnosed as dementia," was also added if there was disagreement with a diagnosis of dementia that had been made prior to evaluation. Such was the case for five adults with DS who were below age of 50. There were none in any of the groups without DS. For these cases, evaluation and follow-up ruled out the presence of dementia, and with proper treatment, their previous level of functioning returned.

To maintain uniformity, the number of individuals who displayed each of the identified CB or PSS in each DS and NDS age group were summed, and then divided by the total number for that group. This yielded a percentage for each CB and PSS by group and age. The same procedure was followed for the reported psychiatric diagnoses in the sample.

Challenging Behaviors

For many individuals in the sample, more than one CB was present in their behavioral repertoire. Noncompliance, such as refusing to follow directions or daily routines, was displayed in more than half the individuals with DS. For groups without DS, noncompliance behaviors were also present but less frequently than in the DS groups. Behavioral descriptions that people with DS are "excessively uncooperative" or have a temperament characterized by "stubbornness" have previously been made (Charlot, 2002; Cooper & Prasher, 1998). The data support that impression.

For other CBs, group differences (DS versus NDS) rather than age differences were evident in the data, with one other exception. Physical aggression was present in more than half the group with DS below age 50, and in most cases it was the presenting reason for the initial referral. The incidence of physical aggression, however, decreased in those with DS after age 50 and remained at a similar but lower frequency of occurrence when compared with those in the sample without DS.

A review of the data revealed that CBs were absent on average in 32% of those with DS and in 20% of those without DS. The lower incidence of aggression and other CBs in those with DS over age 50 suggests that they may be responding in a different manner to people and events in their surroundings. The data also support previous reports that aggression is lower in adults with DS and dementia (Cooper & Prasher, 1998; Cosgrove et al., 1999), and for those with DS and depression (Tsiouris et al., 2003). It would be important to investigate the types and incidence of CBs further in younger adults (below age 40) with and without DS to determine if these apparent differences are also present.

Psychiatric Signs and Symptoms

Group differences were also evident when comparing PSSs in the DS and NDS groups. The signs and symptoms that occur in depression and dementia were higher in the three groups with DS. In most instances the PSSs increased with age (see Table 7.3). Sleep disturbances, weight loss, low energy, and mood disturbances were consistently higher in the groups with DS. Appetite disturbances and social avoidance were also present but revealed fewer group differences. The loss of self-help skills and forgetfulness or disorientation, as found in dementia, were significantly higher in the groups with DS and increased twofold after age 50. The data coincided with the expected ages for functional decline when the early and middle stages of dementia are first reported in people with DS (Prasher & Chung, 1996).

For other PSSs, tics and involuntary movements, excluding tremors or myoclonus, were higher in the groups without DS over age 50 and may be related to the side effects of psychotropic medications. It was also interesting that there was a low incidence of hallucinations and delusions in both groups. There was a moderate but consistent incidence of talking to oneself across all age groups, which was only slightly higher for those without DS. If misinterpreted as a hallucination, self-talk may lead one to suspect psychosis (Hurley, 1996). Glenn and Cunningham (2000) studied self-talk in a younger group with DS (ages 17–24 years) and viewed it as an *adaptive* behavior rather than as an indication of pathology.

Behavior rituals were exhibited in over 40% of the people with DS, and in 28% of those without DS. The reported rituals typically involved compulsive hoarding of objects or food, clothing obsessions, and bathroom rituals. Such behaviors can be driven by anxiety and stress, or they may be a personality characteristic or trait. On the other hand, the hoarding of objects is also a common behavior in persons with Alzheimer disease (Stoppe et al., 1999), and its expression may be an adaptive means to limit forgetting where one's personal effects are in the environment. Evans and Gray (2000) suggested that repetitive behaviors may be a part of the behavioral phenotype of individuals with DS and the present data supports this view.

Psychiatric Diagnoses

Depressive disorders and dementia, Alzheimer type, were the principal psychiatric diagnoses made across all age groups with DS. The depressive disorders made up the majority of the reported mood disorders (39%) and included major depression, dysthymic disorder, and depression, NOS. The incidence of bipolar disorders was low

(6%). In comparison, the reported mood disorders for those in the cohort without DS were more equally divided between depressive and bipolar disorders in each age grouping.

The incidence of anxiety disorders were about equal in both groups for ages 40–49 and 60–69 but were notably higher for those without DS in the 50–59 age group. Other psychiatric disorders were higher in those individuals without DS over the age of 50. For those below age 50 with DS, however, behavioral problems and issues resulted in more psychiatric disorders other than depression or dementia. Some of the reported conditions in those with DS below age 50 included Tourette's or chronic tic disorder, obsessive-compulsive disorder, kleptomania, and schizoaffective disorder. Overall, the data were consistent with reports indicating that people with DS have higher prevalence rates of depression and a lower incidence of psychotic and other psychiatric disorders (Collacott et al., 1992; Pary, Loschen, & Tomkowiak, 1996; Prasher, 1995).

The incidence and types of dementia showed significant differences between the DS and NDS groups. A diagnosis of possible or probable dementia, Alzheimer type, was made in 76 (48%) of the 158 adults with DS. All were above age 40 and presented with some decline in cognition, memory, or adaptive functioning. One individual, a 67-year old man with DS, did not display the characteristic signs and symptoms of DAT and was diagnosed with amnestic disorder, based upon his presenting signs (see case #2). Although the present cohort represented a non-population-based sample, the high incidence of DAT and low incidence of vascular or other dementias in the group with DS supported the prevalence findings reported by Janicki and Dalton (2000). For those without DS, a diagnosis of dementia was made in only 20 (14%) of the 142 adults. When dementia was present, it included Alzheimer type, vascular type, mixed type and amnestic disorder.

The 40–49 year age group with DS had a lower frequency of occurrence (23%) for dementia, which increased threefold for the two age groups above age 50. Five adults with DS below age 50 received a diagnosis of dementia prior to referral. After comprehensive assessment, however, none were found to possess any clear signs or symptoms of dementia. These adults were reported to have displayed a sudden and vegetative decline in their behavior and functioning within a 1- to 2-year period. Cognitive testing did not reveal memory or psychomotor skills deficits, as are seen in individuals with dementia. In most cases, the change in behavior was due to an undiagnosed mood or anxiety disorder, which responded to prescribed medications.

Finally, no adults in either the DS or NDS groups were misdiagnosed for dementia after age 50. It was speculated that if a change or decline occurred, it was more recognizable to caregivers and the evaluating clinician. Older adults with DS also experienced increased medical problems, which may exacerbate the dementia process and make it easier to recognize. Examples include late-onset seizures, spinal cord compression, incontinence, thyroid disease, and diabetes (Smith, 2001).

Illustrative Cases of Psychiatric Disorders in People With Down Syndrome

Case #1: Delusional Disorder and Onset of Dementia

DL was a 50-year-old man with mild ID who lived in a community group home. Referral was made due to the onset of paranoid ideation and possible auditory hallucinations. Other presenting complaints included periods of agitation, suspiciousness, mental confusion, memory deficits, clothing compulsions, and an altered time concept. After the death of his only remaining relative, he fabricated the delusion that he was married and had a wife and an older son. He consistently maintained this delusion and freely spoke about them when asked about his family.

Initial evaluation found cognitive impairment, confabulation, poor insight, and paranoid ideation. A diagnosis of delusional disorder, mixed type, was given. The diagnosis of DAT was added at the 6-month follow-up, when a further decline in memory and general functioning was observed. Continued follow-up over a 5-year period noted a gradual loss of cognitive and adaptive skills. As mental confusion and disorientation increased, talk about his family and paranoid ideations decreased, and were no longer expressed by age 54. Late-onset seizures developed at this time, and a loss of ambulation resulted in him being moved to another group home that provided increased care and supervision. A loss of all self-help skills and total dependence in all areas by age 55 led to his eventual placement in a nursing home, where he died at age 56.

Comment.

DL had been a personable and very independent individual who took pride in his personal appearance. The declines in his cognitive and adaptive functioning were indicative of dementia, and they were a source of frustration and irritability because of the increasing confusion and resulting loss of independence. Although there were no signs of psychosis, DL created the idea of a family for himself, which gave him a role and purpose when other areas were becoming too difficult for him. The suspected auditory hallucinations were actually his engaging in self-talk dialog about daily activities. As his memory and general functioning declined, he became more dependent on group home staff and accepted their help and assistance.

Case # 2: Functional Decline in an Older Man With DS

RM was a 67-year-old man with severe ID who had been living in a community residence. Referral was first made at age 60 to evaluate for DAT, which was ruled out. A second assessment was done at age 67 to reevaluate his status due to a change in behavior and a decline in functioning. The recent complaints included mild aggression, irritability, compulsive behavior rituals, noncompliance, and weight loss. Reports of mild memory loss occurred after he experienced two infarcts at age 59 in the left hemisphere involving the frontal and parietal lobes. Based upon the clinical findings, a diagnosis of amnestic disorder was made. Follow-up evaluations and cognitive testing over a 4-year period revealed a gradual decline in sensory and self-care skills. No progressive decline in memory or communication skills was evident, however, and a diagnosis of DAT was not made. RM had a history of arthritis, duodenal ulcer, hypothyroidism, and seizures in adolescence. He was described as an alert, interactive, and cooperative individual, and he displayed mild irritability when daily routines were interrupted. By age 70, a gradual loss of ambulation skills and the reoccurrence of seizures developed. He remained active and responsive with few behavioral problems, however—the exception being his behavior rituals with water. Due to frailty, he could no longer be cared for in his community residence, and he was admitted to a nursing home at age 71, where he died within 2 months of placement.

Comment.

Although a gradual functional decline in all areas occurred over an 8-to-10-year period, RM did not clinically demonstrate signs of apraxia, agnosia, or increasing memory loss that are necessary for a diagnosis of probable DAT to be made. Likewise, there were no signs or symptoms of depression, and he remained an active and social person. Also significant, RM had two ApoE 2 alleles, which has been reported to be a protective factor against Alzheimer disease more than the ApoE 3 or 4 alleles (Farrer, et al., 1997; Cummings, Vinters, Cole, & Khachaturian, 1998). In addition, there was a positive family history for longevity (RM's mother lived until age 86, and his brother lived until age 95), which may have delayed his age-related functional decline.

Case #3: Major Depression, Single Episode, Misdiagnosed as Dementia

ML was a 42-year-old woman with DS and moderate ID who lived at home with her mother when the initial referral was made for a second opinion to rule out dementia.

A sudden change in behavior characterized by depressed mood, insomnia, talking about the devil, and difficulties interacting with others were displayed shortly after the death of a close relative (her aunt). A diagnosis of dementia with psychosis was made at two different medical centers prior to her referral. Haloperidol was prescribed, which produced a severe dystonic reaction, and was discontinued. She had talked to herself for many years when she was alone. However with the change in behavior, the quality and manner of her self-talk changed and she presented with suspiciousness and fears about death and dying.

The initial evaluation ruled out dementia, and a diagnosis of major depression, single episode, was made. Desipramine was started with positive results and was later replaced by sertraline. Follow-up observations revealed normal mood, intact memory, and cognitive functioning, and no further behavioral difficulties. When alone, ML continued to talk to herself as a means of reviewing the day's events. Follow-up over the next 10 years noted major depression to remain in full remission.

Comment.

ML displayed a sudden change in behavior shortly after the death of a close relative. During this same time, other psychosocial stressors occurred, which appeared to have added to the change in behavior. Also noteworthy, she had always talked to herself, which allowed her mother to be aware of what she was thinking and feeling at the time. During the onset of depression, ML stopped talking out loud to herself. Her mother became concerned, because she was no longer able to discern her daughter's emotional state and led to her seeking help. With the proper diagnosis of depression being made and treatment with sertraline, there was a return in functioning with no further reports of functional decline over a 10-year period.

Case #4: Major Depression and Dementia, Alzheimer Type, in an Older Man With DS

HK was a 61-year-old man with DS and moderate ID who lived in a group home. Referral was made for a differential diagnosis due to a decline in his cognitive and adaptive functioning. Presenting complaints included weight loss, forgetting, misplacing objects, reduced interest in such favorite activities as pipe smoking, general disorientation, increased noncompliance, episodes of moaning and crying, regression in self-help skills, and toileting accidents. HK had been an independent person, but due to his increasing confusion and forgetfulness, group home staff were concerned about his safety especially when he was smoking his pipe. Cognitive testing revealed significant deficits in memory and awareness indicative of dementia. In addition, visual deficits (cataracts) and hearing loss contributed to his disorientation. A diagnosis of major depression, severe, and DAT was made, and treatment with paroxetine was started. An improvement in general mood, appetite, and sleep, a gain in weight, and decreased toileting accidents were noted within a 3-month period. Staff reported HK to be more socially responsive and cooperative when paroxetine was prescribed. His aggressive and defiant behaviors were significantly reduced. Memory deficits and reduced independence in self-help skills remained present. Treatment was maintained on a low dose of paroxetine, and his depression was in remission. Vitamin E was added at age 63 and donepezil at age 64 for his cognitive decline. As HK progressed from the middle to late stages of DAT, he continued to be cared for in his group home. By age 65, he was no longer able to ambulate and was totally dependent on staff for all levels of care. Transfer to a nursing home was done at age 66, where he died at age 67.

Comment.

Although HK presented with functional decline that commonly occurs in DAT, he was displaying disturbed sleep patterns, loss of appetite, weight loss, and irritability, which are also common signs of depression. When depression, which is treatable and reversible, is recognized, the prognosis can be improved for some individuals who also have dementia (Tsiouris & Patti, 1997). Although HK still required increasing care and assistance in all areas, the staff in his group home reported a definite improvement in mood and social interactions when paroxetine was prescribed and maintained. Consequently, staff were able to provide good care for HK within the group home until the very end of his life.

Summary

There is widespread agreement that adults with DS are more prone to depression and dementia; however, the incidence of challenging behaviors and other psychiatric disorders remains low. The clinical features of depression in people with ID are similar to those in the general population, although people with DS show a higher incidence of depression compared with persons with ID but without DS. The prevalence of dementia was also similar in the general and ID populations when people with DS are excluded. However, dementia was reported to occur in more than half the DS population between the ages of 50 and 60, with Alzheimer type being the predominant form. In an attempt to explain these differences, some have suggested that people with DS possess a different behavioral phenotype than do people with ID but without DS.

Among the behavioral features that appear to show a higher incidence in persons with DS were noncompliance and behavior rituals. An earlier expression of functional decline was also evident in adults with DS and depression below age 50, and with dementia and depression after age 50.

The supporting clinical data presented in this chapter were consistent with previous findings that people with DS display a different behavioral phenotype and pattern of psychiatric disorders from people with ID without DS. It is imperative for clinicians to recognize the similarities and differences in depression and dementia, especially in people with DS over age 40, because it relates to functional decline. Failure to do so can result in misdiagnosis and improper treatment. More studies are needed to explore age-related differences in the incidence and types of specific challenging behaviors, the psychiatric signs and symptoms, and the presenting psychiatric disorders in younger people with DS.

References

American Psychiatric Association. (1994). *Diagnostic and statistical manual of mental disorders* (4th ed.). Washington, DC: Author.

Benson, B. (1985). Behavioural disorders and mental retardation. *Applied Research in Mental Retardation, 84,* 465–469.

Burt, D. B. (1999). Dementia and depression. In M. P. Janicki & A. J. Dalton (Eds.), *Dementia, aging, and intellectual disabilities: A handbook,* (pp. 198–216). Philadelphia: Taylor and Francis.

Burt, D. B., Loveland, K. A., & Lewis, K. R. (1992). Depression and the onset of dementia in adults with mental retardation. *American Journal on Mental Retardation, 96,* 502–511.

Chapman, R. S., & Hesketh, L. J. (2000). Behavioral phenotype of individuals with Down syndrome. *Mental Retardation and Developmental Disabilities, 6,* 84–95.

Charlot, L. R. (2002). Obsessional slowness in Down syndrome: Severe variant of OCD or separate disorder? *Mental Health Aspects of Developmental Disabilities, 5,* 53–56.

Collacott, R. A., Cooper, S-A., Brandford, D., & McGrother, C. (1998). Behaviour phenotype for Down's syndrome. *British Journal of Psychiatry, 172,* 85–89.

Collacott, R. A., Cooper, S.-A., & McGrother, C. (1992). Differential rates of psychiatric disorders in adults with Down's syndrome compared with other mentally handicapped adults. *British Journal of Psychiatry, 161,* 671–674.

Cooper, S.-A., Duggirala, C., & Collacott, R. A. (1995). Adaptive behaviour after schizophrenia in people with Down's syndrome. *Journal of Intellectual Disability Research, 39,* 201–204.

Cooper, S.-A., & Prasher, V. P. (1998). Maladaptive behaviours and symptoms of dementia in adults with Down's syndrome compared with adults with intellectual disability of other aetiologies. *Journal of Intellectual Disability Research, 42,* 293–300.

Cosgrave, M. P., Tyrrell, J., McCarron, M., Gill, M., & Lawlor, B. A. (1999). Determinants of aggression, and adaptive and maladaptive behaviour in older people with Down's syndrome with and without dementia. *Journal of Intellectual Disability Research, 43,* 393–399.

Craddock, N., & Owen, M. (1994). Is there an inverse relationship between Down's syndrome and bipolar affective disorder? Literature review and genetic implications. *Journal of Intellectual Disability Research, 38,* 613–620.

Cummings J. L., Vinters H. V., Cole G. M., & Khachaturian Z. S. (1998). Alzheimer's disease: Etiologies, pathophysiology, cognitive reserve, and treatment opportunities. *Neurology, 51,* 2–17.

Dalton, A. J., & Crapper-Mc Lachlan, D. R. (1986). Clinical expression of Alzheimer's disease in Down syndrome. *Psychiatric Clinic of North America, 9,* 659–670.

Davidson, P. W., Prasher, V. P., & Janicki, M. P. (Eds.). (2003). *Mental health, intellectual disabilities and the aging process.* Oxford. UK: Blackwell Publishing.

Davis, J. D., Stern, R. A., & Flashman, L. A. (2003). Cognitive and neuropsychiatric aspects of subclinical hypothyroidism: Significance in the elderly. *Current Psychiatry Reports, 5,* 384–390.

Day, K. (1985). Psychiatric disorder in the middle-aged and elderly mentally handicapped. *British Journal of Psychiatry, 147,* 660–667.

Day, K., & Jancar, J. (1994). Mental and physical health and ageing in mental handicap: A review. *Journal of Intellectual Disability Research, 38,* 241–256.

Eaton, L. F., & Menolascino, F. J. (1982). Psychiatric disorders in the mentally retarded: Types, problems, and challenges. *American Journal of Psychiatry, 139,* 1297–1303.

Evans. D. W., & Gray, F. L. (2000). Compulsive-like behavior in individuals with Down syndrome: Its relation to mental age level, adaptive and maladaptive behavior. *Child Development, 71,* 288–300.

Farrer L. A., Cupples L. A., Haines J. L., Hyman B., Kukull W. A., Mayeux R., et al. (1997). Effects of age, sex, and ethnicity on the association between apolipoprotein E genotype and Alzheimer disease. A meta-analysis. ApoE and Alzheimer Disease Meta Analysis Consortium. *Journal of the American Medical*

Association, 278, 1349–1356.

Glenn, S. M., & Cunningham, C. C. (2000). Parents' reports of young people with Down syndrome talking out loud to themselves. *Mental Retardation, 38,* 498–505.

Haveman, M. J., Maaskant, M. A., van Schrojenstein Lantman, H. M., Urlings, H. F. J., & Kessels, A. G. H. (1994). Mental health problems in elderly people with and without Down's syndrome. *Journal of Intellectual Disability Research, 38,* 341–355.

Holland, A. J. (2000). Down's syndrome and dementia. In J. O'Brien, D. Ames, & A. Burns (Eds.), *Dementia* (2nd ed., pp. 813–819). London: Arnold.

Hurley, A. D. (1996). The misdiagnosis of hallucinations and delusions in persons with mental retardation: A neurodevelopmental perspective. *Seminars in Clinical Neuropsychiatry, 1,* 122–133.

Jackson, I. M. (1998). The thyroid axis and depression. *Thyroid, 8,* 951–956.

Jacobson, J. W. (2003). Prevalence in mental and behavioral disorders. In P. W. Davidson, V. P. Prasher, & M. P. Janicki (Eds.), *Mental health, intellectual disabilities and the aging process* (pp. 9–21). Oxford, UK: Blackwell Publishing.

Janicki, M. P., & Dalton, A. J. (2000). Prevalence of dementia and impact on intellectual disability services. *Mental Retardation, 38,* 277–289.

Kerbeshian, J., & Burd, L. (2000). Comorbid Down's syndrome, Tourette syndrome and intellectual disability: Registry prevalence and developmental course. *Journal of Intellectual Disability Research, 44,* 60–67.

Khan, S., Osinowo, T., & Pary, R. J. (2002). Down syndrome and major depressive disorder: A review. *Mental Health Aspects of Developmental Disabilities, 5,* 46–52.

Lai, F., & Williams, R. S. (1989). A prospective study of Alzheimer disease in Down syndrome. *Archives of Neurology, 46,* 849–853.

Levitas, A. (2000, Spring/Summer). Behavioral and psychiatric phenotype of genetic syndromes: Part 1. *Healthy Times, 12,* 5–8.

McGuire, D., & Chicoine, B. A. (1996). Depressive disorders in adults with Down syndrome. *The Habilitative Mental Healthcare Newsletter, 15,* 1–7.

McGuire, D., & Chicoine, B. A. (2002). Life issues of adolescents and adults with Down syndrome. In W. Cohen, L. Nadel, & M. Madnick (Eds.), *Down syndrome: Visions for the 21st Century* (pp. 221–236). New York: Wiley-Liss.

McGuire, D., Chicoine, B., & Greenbaum, E. (1997). Self-talk in adults with Down syndrome. *Disability Solutions 2,* 1–4.

Meins, W. (1995). Are depressive mood disturbances in adults with Down's syndrome an early sign of dementia? *Journal of Nervous Mental Disorders, 183,*

663–664.

Myers, B. A., & Pueschel, S. M. (1991). Psychiatric disorders in a population with Down syndrome. *Journal of Nervous and Mental Disease, 179,* 609–613.

Myers, B. A., & Pueschel, S. M. (1994). Brief report: A case of schizophrenia in a population with Down syndrome. *Journal of Autism and Developmental Disorders, 24,* 95–98.

Myers, B. A., & Pueschel, S. M. (1995a). Major depression in a small group of adults with Down syndrome. *Research in Developmental Disabilities, 16,* 285–299.

Myers, B. A., & Pueschel, S. M. (1995b). Tardive or atypical Tourette's disorder in a population with Down syndrome? *Research in Developmental Disabilities, 16,* 1–9.

Oliver, C., & Holland, A. J. (1986). Down's syndrome and Alzheimer's disease: A review. *Psychological Medicine, 16,* 307–322.

Pary, R. J., Loschen, E. L., & Tomkowiak, S. B. (1996). Mood disorders and Down syndrome. *Seminars in Clinical Neuropsychiatry, 1,* 148–153.

Pary, R. J., Strauss, D., & White, J. F. (1996). A population survey of bipolar disorder in persons with and without Down syndrome. *Down Syndrome Quarterly, 1,* 1–4.

Pary, R. J., Strauss, D., & White, J. F. (1997). A population survey of suicide attempts in persons with and without Down syndrome. *Down Syndrome Quarterly, 2,* 12–13.

Patti, P. J., & Tsiouris, J. A. (2003). Emotional and behavioral disturbances in adults with Down syndrome. In P. W. Davidson, V. P. Prasher, & M. P. Janicki (Eds.), *Mental health, intellectual disabilities and the aging process* (pp. 81–93). Oxford, UK: Blackwell Publishing.

Prasher, V. P. (1995). Prevalence of psychiatric disorders in adults with Down syndrome. *European Journal of Psychiatry, 9,* 77–82.

Prasher, V. P. (1996). Age-associated functional decline in adults with Down's syndrome. *European Journal of Psychiatry, 10,* 129–135.

Prasher, V. P. (1997). Psychotic features and effect of severity of learning disability on dementia in adults with Down syndrome: Review of literature. *British Journal of Developmental Disabilities, 43,* 85–92.

Prasher, V. P. (1999). Adaptive behavior. In M. P. Janicki & A. J. Dalton (Eds.), *Dementia, aging, and intellectual disabilities: A handbook* (pp. 157–178). Philadelphia: Taylor and Francis.

Prasher, V. P. (2003). Depression in aging individuals with intellectual disabilities. In P. W. Davidson, V. P. Prasher, & M. P. Janicki (Eds.), *Mental health, intellectual disabilities and the aging process* (pp. 51–66). Oxford, UK: Blackwell Publishing.

Prasher, V. P., & Chung, M. C. (1996). Causes of age-related decline in adaptive behavior of adults with Down syndrome: Differential diagnoses of dementia. *American Journal on Mental Retardation, 101,* 175–183.

Prasher, V. P., & Day, S. (1995). Brief report: Obsessive-compulsive disorder in adults with Down syndrome. *Journal of Autism and Developmental Disorders, 25,* 453–458.

Reiss, S. (1990). Prevalence of dual diagnosis in community-based day programs in the Chicago metropolitan area. *American Journal of Mental Retardation, 94,* 578–585.

Rojahn, J. (1986). Self-injurious and stereotypic behavior on non-institutionalized mentally retarded people: Prevalence and classification. *American Journal of Mental Deficiency, 91,* 268–276.

Russell, A., & Tanguay, P. (1981). Mental illness and mental retardation: Cause or coincidence? *American Journal of Mental Deficiency, 85,* 570–574.

Smith, D. S. (2001). Health care management of adults with Down syndrome. *American Family Physician, 64,* 1031–1038.

Stoppe, G., Brandt, C. A., & Staedt, J. H. (1999). Behavioural problems associated with dementia: The role of newer antipsychotics. *Drugs & Aging, 14,* 41–54.

Tsiouris, J. A. (2001). Diagnosis of depression in people with severe/profound intellectual disability. *Journal of Intellectual Disability Research, 45,* 115–120.

Tsiouris, J. A., Korosh, W., Patti, P. J., & Pfadt, A. (1998). *Psychiatric Signs Profile* (unpublished informant-rating scale). Staten Island, NY.

Tsiouris, J. A., Mann, R., Patti, P. J., & Sturmey, P. (2003). Challenging behaviours should not be considered depressive equivalents in individuals with intellectual disability. *Journal of Intellectual Disabilities Research, 47,* 14–21.

Tsiouris, J. A., Mehta, P. D., Patti, P. J., Madrid, R. E., Raguthu, S., Barshatzky, M. R., et al. (2000). Alpha2 macroglobulin elevation without an acute phase response in depressed adults with Down syndrome: Implications. *Journal of Intellectual Disabilities Research, 44,* 644–653.

Tsiouris, J. A., & Patti, P. J. (1997). Drug treatment of depression associated with dementia or presented as "pseudodementia" in older adults with Down syndrome. *Journal of Applied Research in Intellectual Disabilities, 10,* 312–322.

Tyrrell, J., & Dodd, P. (2003). Psychopathology in older age. In P. W. Davidson, V. P. Prasher, & M. P. Janicki (Eds.), *Mental health, intellectual disabilities and the aging process* (pp. 22–37). Oxford, UK: Blackwell Publishing.

Udell, L. (1999). Supports in small group home settings. In M. P. Janicki & A. J.

Dalton (Eds.), *Dementia, aging, and intellectual disabilities: A handbook* (pp. 157–178). Philadelphia: Taylor and Francis.

U.S. Department of Health and Human Services. (1996). *Early Alzheimer disease: Recognition and assessment. Guideline Number 19* (AHCPR Publication No. 97-R123). Rockville, MD: Author.

Visser, F. E., Adenkamp, A. P., van Huffelen, A. C., Kuliman, M., Overweg, J., & van Wijk, J. (1997). Prospective study of the prevalence of Alzheimer-type dementia in institutionalized individuals with Down syndrome. *American Journal on Mental Retardation, 101,* 400–412.

Wisniewski, H. M., Silverman, W., & Wegiel, J. (1994). Ageing, Alzheimer disease and mental retardation. *Journal of Intellectual Disability Research, 38,* 233–239.

Wisniewski, K. E., Wisniewski, H. M., & Wen, G. Y. (1985). Occurrence of Alzheimer's neuropathology and dementia in Down syndrome. *Annals of Neurology, 17,* 278–282.

Zigman, W. B., Schupf, N., Zigman, A., & Silverman, W. (1993). Aging and Alzheimer's disease in people with mental retardation. *International Review of Research in Mental Retardation, 19,* 41–70.

Acknowledgment

The author would like to thank Dr. John Tsiouris and the staff of the George Jervis Clinic for their assistance in the research that contributed to this chapter. This research was supported by funds from the New York State Office of Mental Retardation and Developmental Disabilities.

PART II

ASSESSMENT

8

Clinical Interviews

Shoumitro Deb

and

Anupama Iyer

Clinical interviews with the client and with other informants, along with the direct observation of the client's behavior, remain vital in recognizing, diagnosing, and treating mood disorders among people who have mental retardation. Although the basic principles of clinical interviews with individuals with mental retardation are similar to those that apply to individuals who do not have mental retardation, certain important modifications may be necessary. In this chapter we highlight these differences. Given the wide spectrum of abilities among people with mental retardation, however, it is unlikely that a standard set of rules for clinical interview apply across the whole population. Therefore, the clinician needs to exercise his or her discretion in applying the rules and principles of interviewing people who have mental retardation.

Introduction

It is important to differentiate between symptoms that are part of a psychiatric disorder from those that could be manifestations of developmental disability. Certain signs and symptoms, such as social withdrawal, excessive agitation, lack of concentration, stereotyped movement disorders, and altered sleep, could be explained by an underlying brain damage and are not necessarily symptoms of a psychiatric disorder. Reiss and Szyszko (1983) refer to this as *diagnostic overshadowing*. It is therefore important to establish a baseline of what the subject was like before the index illness started and to look for any change since. For example, a patient may have a longstanding history of sleep difficulty. However, if caregivers have noticed in recent months that she has been waking earlier than usual—a change from the baseline—altered sleep in this case may be the manifestation of a mood disorder. Sovner and Hurley (1983) have called this *baseline exaggeration*. It is important not to over-interpret symptoms and behaviors, however. For instance, irritability and aggression may be manifestations of a mood disorder, but a diagnosis of a mood disorder cannot always be made when these behaviors are present. It would be a mistake to depend on behaviors alone in making a diagnosis of mood disorder in a person with mental retardation in the absence of other putative features of mood disorders.

History Taking

Traditionally the clinical interview is divided into history taking and mental status examination. History taking represents a process of maximizing information collected in order to arrive at a diagnosis and to understand an individual's situation and antecedents. Traditionally history taking is divided up into the following sections.

Family History

Family history of intellectual disability, psychiatric illness, such neurological illnesses as epilepsy or dementia, and other relevant illnesses, including physical illnesses, may provide information about familial and genetic predisposition to disorders. The family history may also be an indicator for possible aberrant family dynamics. The quality of important relationships between the patient and other family members is a key to assessing support the family may need in order to provide the optimum quality of care.

Personal and Developmental History

Information about the pregnancy, birth, and attainment of developmental milestones provides a rough guide to the cause and the extent of the individual's developmental difficulties. Inquiry into the family's management of a child with mental retardation, as well as the child's response to educational interventions, are essential components of the assessment. An overview of day placements and employment establishes a baseline level of functioning that the client has attained, which may have deteriorated following the illness. It may also provide clues to the client's relationships outside the family setting and his or her reactions to structure and authority. Caregivers are usually able to provide at least a rough assessment of the individual's personality and behavior prior to the development of the psychiatric illness. Notable life events—especially loss, abuse, and changes in placement or caregivers—may have particular bearing on the development of mood disorders. It is always important to note the highest level of functioning that the client reached during any time in his or her life. This will allow a comparison with the present state of affairs.

Medical History

The medical history should include information about the cause of mental retardation, including a genetic cause if known, past and present physical illnesses (for example, epilepsy, sleep apnea, or thyroid disorder), and past and present physical disability (for example, limb weakness or spasticity). It is always important to gather information on impairment in vision, hearing, speech, or mobility as well as to establish how the individual communicates pain or any other bodily discomfort. It is important to record any history of recurrent physical illnesses (for example, chest infection, toothache, or constipation). The presence of chronic physical conditions may explain such psychological symptoms as depression.

Psychiatric History

It is necessary to gather information about the history of contact with services and any previous diagnoses, because a previous diagnosis could be wrong. It is better, if possible, to find out the exact clinical picture of the previous illness. Assessment of risk, including any risk to the individual and others, is an essential component of history taking.

Social History

Information on the current and previous level of functioning in different areas of adaptive behaviors is important. It is also important to gather information on current and previous social circumstances (for example, marital and employment status), current and previous living arrangements (for example, group home or family home), current and previous social support (for example, quality and quantity of caregiver support, daytime activities, or social and leisure activities). Going through an individual's daily and weekly routines may be a good way of gathering information on these areas.

Drug History

Information regarding past and present medication—such as psychotropic, other prescribed, over-the-counter, and illicit drugs, including dosage, drug reactions, and allergies—can guide the current prescription. Any recent change in medication and its results may be of particular value. Knowledge regarding the use of illicit substances and alcohol use may provide diagnostic pointers and can substantially influence management. (See Sturmey, Reyer, Lee, & Robek, 2004, for a review).

Forensic History

Past and present history of involvement with the law, both of the client and of his or her friends and relations, must be sought. (See Mikkelsen, 2004, for a review).

History of the Presenting Complaint

This includes a detailed description of current problems for which the client has been referred to the services. It is also important to gather information on possible predisposing, precipitating, and perpetuating factors that may underlie the symptoms.

Biological Factors

These include genetic liability associated with behavioral phenotypes (Deb & Ahmed, 2000; Murphy, Jones, & Owen, 1999; O'Brien & Yule, 1995). Structural brain abnormalities that may be present in some people with mental retardation may cause behavioral and psychological symptoms (Deb, 1995). Other biological factors that may precipitate psychiatric symptoms are physical disabilities, including sensory difficulties. Epilepsy may affect between 14% and 24% of adults who have mental retardation (Deb, 2000), and the relationship between epilepsy and psychopathology is complex in this population (Deb, 1997). There is an association between thyroid abnormalities and Down syndrome (Deb, 2001), and thyroid disorder may predispose psychological symptoms. Similarly, certain drugs may cause psychologically adverse effects.

Psychological Factors

Psychological factors that may predispose or precipitate psychiatric symptoms in people who have mental retardation include impaired intelligence, impaired memory, impaired judgment, lack of initiative, a lower threshold for stress tolerance, immature psychological defenses, impaired problem-solving capacity, learned dysfunctional coping strategies, and a lack of emotional support.

Social Factors

Social factors include under- or over-stimulation within the immediate environment of the client, conflicts with family or caregivers, lack of social support, difficulties in forming relationships, difficulties with employment, physical and psychological abuse, lack of integration into the community, stigmatization, bereavement, caregiver stress, and immediate life events. Crilly, Cain, and Davidson describe these risk factors in more detail in Chapter 5 of this book.

Mental Status Examination

A key component of the clinical assessment is the determination of the client's current mental state (Sturmey, in press). The following are the standard headings for a psychiatric mental status examination: (a) appearance and behavior; (b) speech; (c) thought processes; (d) perceptual abnormalities; (e) cognitive assessment, including an assessment of intelligence, attention, and memory; and (f) rapport with the clinician as well as the client's own insight into his or her problems. In the general adult population, making a psychiatric diagnosis depends primarily on the account given by the subject. Many psychiatric diagnoses rely on the patient's describing quite complicated internal, subjective feelings or cognitions, such as thought broadcasting, obsessions, or derealization. Although many subjects with mild mental retardation and some with moderate mental retardation can describe such phenomena, those with severe or profound mental retardation either may not have such experiences or may be unable to adequately describe them. It is important at the outset to assess the subject's communication abilities, hearing, vision, memory, and ability to concentrate, because these can all affect the subject's responses during the assessment.

In most assessments, history taking and mental status examination need to be supplemented by a well-judged use of physical examination and investigations to rule out physical disorders. Multidisciplinary working reports from other professionals and caregivers add considerably to the information derived from the clinical interview. It is often useful to observe the client's behavior directly, especially when feasible in settings familiar to him or her. Structured methods of direct client observations include behavior recordings using a hand-held computer and a functional analysis of behaviors organized among clients, caregivers, and therapists.

Clinical interviews of individuals with mental retardation present certain unique features. These include greater role of the caregivers' accounts, the issues arising from the individual's own experiences, and the challenges for the interviewer in this varied settings. The next section explores some of these issues.

Informant Issues

Informant accounts are very useful in describing observable behaviors (Prosser & Bromley, 1998). However, a caregiver may not have complete awareness regarding subjective mood states such as depression. There may also be concerns if there is a marked discrepancy between the accounts of the caregiver and the client and also among different caregivers. Different caregivers may observe the client in varied situations and give a differing account of behavior. Moss and colleagues have therefore emphasized the need for interviewing both clients and caregivers to optimize the diagnosis (Moss, Prosser, Ibbotson & Goldberg, 1996; Patel, Goldberg, & Moss, 1993). Training and experience in interview skills increase the consistency of reporting (Moss et al., 1996). The interview also relies on the caregivers' understanding of mental illness (Borthwick-Duffy & Eyman, 1990) and their confidence in making the referral. There may be difference in the perception among caregivers regarding what constitutes a symptom (that is, how severe a behavior has to be before it becomes a symptom) (Moss & Patel, 1993). The existence of such prior labels as challenging behaviors may also influence caregiver reports. The nature of the client's relationship with the caregiver or a change in the care circumstances and caregiver coping might be more pertinent to the current referral than any change in the client's mental state. However, informant accounts may be vitally important in order to date the onset of a mood change and also in linking it to external events, which the client may not remember or be aware of. Clear accounts from caregivers of behaviors, such as social withdrawal, lack of interest, and irritability, as well as information about sleep and appetite, may be vital in establishing a diagnosis of mood disorder. Caregivers may also be more aware of the impact of mood changes on the client's functioning, especially his or her social functioning. To improve the validity of informant accounts, training materials have been designed to raise awareness and understanding of mental illness among caregivers (Bouras & Holt, 1997).

Client Issues

Individuals with mental retardation may have had negative experiences with the interview process. Difficulties in comprehension may result in the client not fully understanding the purpose of the consultation. They may also be concerned about the consequences of the interview (Prosser & Bromley, 1998). They might have limited understanding of their own difficulties or their impact on others. An assessment set in an unfamiliar location may pose its own anxieties and may also involve a change in routine, which may be distressing, especially to clients with pervasive developmental disorders.

Some clients may have a better expressive skill than comprehension, and as a result they may appear quite able even though in practice they may not be able to follow the interview questions properly. Sensory difficulties, especially those involving hearing and vision, may affect their ability to respond to set formats. In addition, persons with mental retardation may have limited attention spans and may need to hear the same message repeated and summarized.

Research into interviews conducted with clients with mental retardation has highlighted their more frequent use of response sets. These are set ways of responding to questions irrespective of their content, ways that threaten the validity of the responses (Sudman & Bradburn, 1974). There is now an extensive evidence base for acquiescence ("yea-saying") as being a frequent response bias (Finlay & Lyons, 2002; Heal & Sigelman, 1995). This is a tendency to say yes to questions regardless of their content (Gudjonsson, 1990; Sudman & Bradburn, 1974). Related to these are other response sets such as compliance (agreeing with the interviewer despite personal beliefs) and suggestibility (accepting information as true). Yea-saying has been explained in both social terms as a need to please the interviewer and as social submissiveness. Yea-saying may also be a product of cognitive factors, such as not knowing the answers to ambiguous questions (Cronbach, 1942; Ray, 1983), and not spending adequate time on answers (Knowles & Nathan, 1997). Less commonly, people with mental retardation also respond with self-contradictory "nay-saying," especially in response to taboo questions. This reflects a desire to present oneself in a socially acceptable way (Budd, Sigelman, & Sigelman, 1981; Heal & Sigelman, 1995). These response sets may come into play especially if clients have a differing point of view from caregivers. An interview with clients with mental retardation therefore needs to have checks and balances built into it in order to avoid response sets (Sigelman, Budd, Winer, Schoenrock, & Martin, 1982).

Interviewer Issues

The interviewer may have to accommodate to a "triangular interview space" with clients who are often seen with caregivers. This may be the case when clients have limited ability to communicate or require interpreters if they are using nonverbal sign systems, such as Makaton sign language (Prosser & Bromley, 1998). The assessment may take place in a nontraditional setting, such as a client's day care center or home in order to minimize client's distress (Edgerton, Bollinger, & Herr, 1984). The interviewer may also find him or herself spending more time putting the client at ease. It is always useful to ascertain the extent of the client's comprehension from caregivers. Asking a client to rephrase or summarize the purpose of the interview—for example, "Do you know why you are here to see me?"—may also be a gauge of the client's comprehension.

Qualitative research into client interviews has demonstrated that there exists a very significant power asymmetry, in that interviewers were subtly directive in their conversations with clients with mental retardation (Rapley, 1995). The most extreme form of this is asking leading questions, which presupposes an answer (usually a "yes"). For example, "You don't like living there, do you?" may be better phrased as "What is it like in your home?" The interviewer needs to avoid asking questions couched in complex phrasing and those involving such abstract concepts as "extent" and "all the time" questions. Such questions pose special difficulties for clients with mental retardation (Malin, 1980). For example, a question such as "Do you feel unhappy to the same extent throughout the day?" is better when phrased in more concrete terms, such as "Do you feel better in the mornings or in the evenings?"

The communication barrier may not be restricted to language alone. Altered phonation and varied cadences may often affect the interviewer's interpretation of the meaning of client's answers (Moss et al., 1996). Corroborative checks with caregivers who know the client may well be invaluable in these circumstances.

The interviewer needs to be more sensitive to nonverbal signs, especially those of distress and discomfort, and tailor the situation flexibly. For example, during an assessment of a child with autism for a mood disorder, the mother noticed that during the discussion of a recent bereavement, the boy had started to rock back and forth in his chair, a behavior she recognized as an early sign of distress, and she asked for the topic to be deferred.

In the context of the communication barrier, it becomes crucially important for the interviewer to optimize the therapeutic interactions and to avoid such inappropriate styles as condescension or excessive jocularity (Duckworth, Radhakrishnan, Nolan, & Fraser, 1993). The experienced interviewer realizes the value of observation of behavior ideally over a period of time to supplement and inform the interview, though such observation may not always be feasible. The interviewer also learns to recognize the individual value of both caregiver and client accounts in achieving a complete assessment. Table 8.1 lists the advantages and disadvantages of each approach.

Table 8.1. Advantages and disadvantages of informant versus client accounts.

Informant Account	Client Account

Advantages:
    Detailed information
    Different perspective
    Observed behavior
    Change from baseline
    Dates and times
    Correlation with life events
    Impact on functioning
	Advantages:
	    Subjective account of mental states
	    Ability to voice the extent of distress
	    (Dyadic) therapeutic relationship

Disadvantages:
    Cannot always report subjective
        symptoms
    May be influenced by prior labels
    Subject to diagnostic overshadowing
    Influenced by interpersonal
        relationships
    Dependent on awareness and training
    Influenced by personality and coping
        styles
	Disadvantages:
	    Limited communication
	    May be unable to describe complex mood
	        states
	    Unable to date onset
	    Unable to connect mood states with
	        external events
	    Response bias
	    Limited insight
	    Anxiety may influence interviews

Good Practice Guidelines

Optimum Use of Time and Setting

Qualitative research has highlighted the substantial benefits of interviewing clients with mental retardation in settings they are familiar with, such as their residence or day center (Edgerton et al., 1984). Interviews in varied setting also facilitate information gathering from different professionals and caregivers. It is important to ensure that clients and caregivers are both given adequate time and opportunity, and ideally for the client to be seen alone wherever appropriate. It may be helpful if the client knows the assessor, though this may not always be possible. Issues of confidentiality need to be borne in mind. Flexibility with regard to the length of interviews, such as using several shorter interviews rather than one long interview, may result in more meaningful responses and at the same time be more responsive to the needs of clients.

Framework Statements

Clear introductions and the use of framework statements explaining the nature, purpose, and consequences are important in minimizing client distress. For example:

"Hello, Mr. Jones. I am Dr _____ [this statement could be accompanied by an appropriate symbol for a doctor if necessary]. Your social worker, Mrs. E., is worried about your health. She told me that you are not eating properly. She has asked me to see you. I may be able to help you. I need to ask you and your mother some questions. Is it all right with you? This may take about an hour."

Varying the Type of Questions and Minimizing Response Sets

Easy questions at the start of the interview (and indeed throughout the interview process) may be useful in improving the client's confidence. The knowledge of the client's communication ability is necessary at the outset of the assessment. Some clients may appear superficially more capable of expressing themselves but may actually have significant problems with comprehension. Caregivers who know the client well may be aware of this. The use of open-ended questions at the start of the interview is also a fair guide to the client's communicative abilities. For example, start the interview with such statements as "How are you feeling today?"; "What do you like doing in the (day) center?"; "Tell me about…."

However, responses to open-ended questions also depend on the person's cognitive abilities and may produce fewer and sparser, though perhaps more valid, responses. Close-ended questions tend to produce more specific responses and are useful in clarifying particular issues. Close-ended questions in particular, however, are prone to the problem of response sets. Among the more studied response sets is acquiescence ("yea-saying"). Finlay and Lyons (2002) have reviewed several methods suggested for minimizing acquiescence, including the use of "either/or" questions instead of "yes/no" questions (Sigelman, Budd, Spanhel, & Schoenrock, 1981). For example: "Do you feel happy or sad?" rather than "Are you sad?" or "Are you happy?"

It has been suggested that the choices should be limited to two items and that these be kept short (Wehmeyer, 1994). The tendency of the client to echo the last option can be minimized by asking the client to confirm both options and choose one (Sigelman et al., 1981). The use of reverse wording further on in the interview could also be used. For example, the question "Do you have trouble sleeping?" can be followed by "Do you sleep well?" in a later part of the interview. The use of multiple-choice questions especially using pictures may improve responses (Sigelman et al., 1982).

Using Pictures and Symbols

The use of pictures improves responsiveness to multiple-choice questions and reduces the last-option effect. It also allows for such nonverbal responses as nodding or shaking (Sigelman et al., 1982). For example, appropriate pictures can accompany questions relating to various mood states such as "happy," "sad," "angry." Some clients, however, may find choosing from options stressful, and this method may have to be restricted to key questions.

Clarifying, Probing, and Prompting

Asking clients to clarify statements using examples is useful while interviewing persons with mild to moderate mental retardation. Judicious and sensitive probing may also improve the validity of answers (Prosser & Bromley, 1998). For example: "When you say you don`t like to go out, do you mean the day center?" or "Don`t you like to go out to the movies now?" The need to clarify has to be balanced against appearing intrusive or insistent.

Summarizing and Recapping

An individual with mental retardation may have a very short attention span. The interviewer can engage the individual's attention by recapping and summarizing important details. This helps the individual to reengage and also enables him or her to clarify any unclear issues (Moss, 1999). A fluid structure and multiple short interviews in the place of longer one also minimize the effect of client distractibility. For example: "You have said that you feel weepy all the time. You do not want to talk to anyone and you feel that everyone dislikes you. You have trouble sleeping. Things have not felt good even on your birthday."

Tailoring Questions to Cognitive Capacity

Prosser and Bromley (1998) recommend the use of simple sentences with short words in the present tense. You should avoid sentences with more than one dependent clause. You should also avoid double negatives. For example: "You do not refuse medication, do you?" is better recast as "Do you take your meds?" Avoid abstract or idiomatic language (for example, "low spirits").

Anchoring Events

For a client who may otherwise have difficulty with recalling times and dates, events that he or she can be expected to remember may be a useful device in deriving a time frame of events (Prosser & Bromley, 1998). These can include birthdays, personal events of note, or festive occasions. For example: "Have you been feeling sad even over Christmas?"

Informant Checks

Subtle differences of phonation and prosody may pose an additional information barrier. Clarifications from caregivers who know the client well are very useful in this respect. For example, BJ, a 13-year-old boy assessed for depression, talked about having his "tummy cut." His mother clarified that this referred to his preoccupation with his weight of late. He had recently watched a program on television about surgical treatments for obesity.

Informants are also able to corroborate factual data and provide dates. However, a potentially conflicting version from the client and the caregiver does need careful and impartial consideration and should sensitize the interviewer to relationship difficulties and a possible conflict of interest.

Behavioral Observation and Multidisciplinary Opinions

Interviewing should be supplemented by direct observation of the client's behavior preferably over a period of time and in different settings (Cain et al., 2003; Moss, 1999). Given the complexity of needs of clients with dual diagnosis, an assessment using more than one technique and gathering information from more than one source, such as from paid caregivers, relatives, and other professionals, is valued. The use of hand-held, palm-top computers for immediate recording of observed behavior in a continuous time frame is a useful tool for an objective assessment and analysis of behavior over a defined time period.

KT, a 36-year-old lady with Down syndrome, was seen following caregiver concerns about her increasing isolation from friends and peers. A day service staff reported that on being shown a photograph of KT being happy at a party, KT had responded with "not like now." Parents had been very upset on her weekend visit home when she had attempted to hit one of her young nieces. Her mother mentioned that she herself had suffered from postpartum depression that needed treatment. KT had also seen her local doctor, who had ruled out thyroid problems.

Use of Rating Scales

The judicious use of rating scales and other psychiatric instruments supplement and inform the clinical interview. They may be used to detect disorders, assess their severity, and monitor progress over time. They may also be useful to monitor the outcome of interventions and to standardize information over time and across assessors. (See Chapter 9 by Finlay for further details).

Transference and Counter-Transference

The issues of transference and counter-transference are pertinent, particularly with the unusual triangulation of the interview. The interviewer should actively avoid being condescending or more subtly directive with the client or directing questions predominantly to caregivers (Rapley, 1995).

Summary

While interviewing people with mental retardation, the interviewer needs to take into account key characteristics of the persons and settings. To maximize the validity of the client response, specific techniques can be used, including framework statements, obviating the effects of response sets, anchoring events, and pictures. Information from informants and direct observation of behaviors further help to clarify the client's mental state. The judicious use of varied settings and the gathering of information from more than a single source optimize the information obtained from interviewing. Clinical interviewing, used properly, remains a reliable means for accessing distress. Consistent and informed practice of this skill remains the cornerstone in diagnosis and management.

References

Borthwick-Duffy, S. A., & Eyman, R. K. (1990). Who are the dually diagnosed? *American Journal on Mental Retardation, 94,* 586–595.

Bouras, N., & Holt, G. (Eds.). (1997). *Mental health in learning disabilities: A training pack for staff working with people who have a dual diagnosis of mental health needs and learning disabilities* (2nd ed.). Brighton, UK: Pavilion Press.

Budd, E. C., Sigelman, C. K., & Sigelman, L. (1981). Exploring the outer limits of response bias. *Sociological Focus, 14,* 297–307.

Cain, N. N., Davidson, P. W., Burhan, A. M., Andolsek, M. E., Baxter, J. T., Sullivan, L., et al. (2003). Identifying bipolar disorders in individuals with intellectual disability. *Journal of Intellectual Disability Research, 47,* 31–38.

Cronbach, L. J. (1942). Studies of acquiescence as a factor in true and false test. *Journal of Educational Psychology, 60,* 151–174.

Deb, S. (1995) Neuroimaging in mental retardation. *Current Opinions in Psychiatry, 8,* 280–285.

Deb, S. (1997). Mental disorder in adults with mental retardation and epilepsy. *Comprehensive Psychiatry, 38,* 179–184.

Deb, S. (2000). Epidemiology and treatment of epilepsy in patients who are mentally retarded. *CNS Drugs, 13,* 117–128.

Deb, S. (2001). Medical conditions in people with intellectual disability. In L. Hamilton-Kirkwood, Z. Ahmed, D. Allen, S. Deb, B. Fraser, B. Lindsay, et al. (Eds.), *Health evidence bulletins—learning disabilities (intellectual disability* (pp. 48–55). Cardiff, UK: NHS Wales. Retrieved February 20, 2004 from http://hebw.uwcm.ac.uk

Deb, S., & Ahmed, Z. (2000). Special conditions leading to mental retardation. In M. G. Gelder, N. Adreasen, & J. J. Lopez-Ibor, Jr. (Eds.), *New Oxford textbook of psychiatry* (pp. 1953–1963). Oxford, UK: Oxford Press.

Duckworth, M. S., Radhakrishnan, G., Nolan, M. E., & Fraser, W. I. (1993). Initial encounters between people with a mild mental handicap and psychiatrists: An investigation of a method for evaluating interview skills. *Journal of Intellectual Disability Research, 37,* 263–276.

Edgerton, R. B., Bollinger, M., & Herr, B. (1984). The cloak of competence: After two decades. *American Journal of Mental Deficiency, 88,* 345–351.

Finlay, W. M. L., & Lyons, E. (2002). Acquiescence in interviews with people who have mental retardation. *Mental Retardation, 40,* 14–29.

Gudjonsson, G. H. (1990). The relationship of intellectual skills to suggestibility, compliance and acquiescence. *Personality and Individual Differences, 11,* 227–231.

Heal, L. W., & Sigelman, C. K. (1995). Response biases in interviews of individuals with limited mental abilities. *Journal of Intellectual Disability Research, 39,* 331–340.

Knowles, E. S., & Nathan, K. T. (1997). Acquiescent responding in self-reports: Cognitive styles or social concern? *Journal of Research in Personality, 31,* 293–301.

Malin, N. (Ed.). (1980). *Group homes for the mentally handicapped adults* (E.R.G. Report No: 9). Sheffield, UK: University of Sheffield.

Mikkelsen, E. J. (2004). The assessment of individuals with developmental disabilities. In W. R. Lindsay, J. L. Taylor, & P. Sturmey, (Eds.), *Offenders with developmental disabilities* (pp. 111–130). New York: Wiley.

Moss, S. (1999). Assessment: Conceptual issues. In N. Bouras (Ed.), *Psychiatric and behaviour disorders in developmental disabilities* (pp.18–37). Cambridge, UK: Cambridge University Press.

Moss, S. C., & Patel, P. (1993). Prevalence of mental illness in people with learning disabilities over 50 years of age, and the importance of diagnostic information from carers. *Irish Journal of Psychiatry, 14,* 110–129.

Moss, S., Prosser, H., Ibbotson, B., & Goldberg, D. (1996). Respondent and informant accounts of psychiatric symptoms in a sample of patients with learning disability. *Journal of Intellectual Disability Research, 40,* 457–465.

Murphy, K. C., Jones, L. A., & Owen, M. J. (1999). High rates of schizophrenia in adults with velo-cardio-facial syndrome. *Archives of General Psychiatry, 56,* 940–945.

O'Brien, G., & Yule, W. (Eds.). (1995). *Behavioural phenotypes.* Cambridge, UK: Cambridge University Press.

Patel, P., Goldberg, D. P., & Moss, S. (1993). Psychiatric morbidity in older people with moderate and severe learning disabilities (mental retardation). Part II: The prevalence study. *British Journal of Psychiatry, 163,* 481–491.

Prosser, H., & Bromley, J. (1998). Interviewing people with intellectual disabilities. In E. Emerson, C. Hatton, & J. Bromley (Eds.), *Clinical psychology and people with intellectual disabilities* (pp. 99–113). London: Wiley and Sons.

Rapley, M. (1995) Black swans: Conversation analysis of interviews with people with learning disabilities. *Clinical Psychology Forum, 84,* 17–23.

Ray, J. J. (1983). Reviewing the problem of acquiescent response bias. *Journal of Social Psychology, 121,* 81–96.

Reiss, S., & Szyszko, J. (1983). Diagnostic overshadowing and professional experience with the mentally retarded persons. *American Journal of Mental Deficiency, 87,* 396–402.

Sigelman, C. K., Budd, E. C., Spanhel, C. L., & Schoenrock, C. J. (1981). Asking questions of mentally retarded persons: a comparison of yes-no and either-or format. *Applied Research in Mental Retardation, 2,* 347–357.

Sigelman, C. K., Budd, E. C., Winer, J. L., Schoenrock, C. J., & Martin, P. W. (1982). Evaluating alternative techniques of questioning mentally retarded persons. *American Journal of Mental Deficiency, 86,* 511–518.

Sovner, R., & Hurley, A. D. (1983). Do the mentally retarded suffer from affective illness? *Archives of General Psychiatry, 40,* 61–67.

Sturmey P. (in press). Psychosocial and mental status assessment. In A. James Mulick & J. Jacobson (Eds.), *Handbook of mental retardation and developmental disabilities.* New York: Kluwer.

Sturmey, P., Reyer, H., Lee, R., & Robek, A. (2004). *Substance-related disorders in persons with mental retardation.* Kingston, NY: NADD Press.

Sudman, S., & Bradburn, N. M. (Eds.). (1974). *Response effects in surveys: A review and synthesis.* Chicago: Aldiss.

Wehmeyer, M. L. (1994). Reliability and acquiescence in the measurement of locus of control with adolescents and adults with mental retardation. *Psychological Reports, 75,* 527–537.

9

PSYCHOMETRIC ASSESSMENT OF MOOD DISORDERS IN PEOPLE WITH INTELLECTUAL DISABILITIES

W. Mick L. Finlay

This chapter discusses the psychometric assessment of mood disorders in people with intellectual disabilities and describes some of the commonly used scales. The majority of instruments assess depression, although several instruments that assess mania or bipolar disorders are also described. A number of these instruments perform quite well with people with mild or moderate mental retardation. It is important, however, to note that none of the instruments reviewed in the chapter perform particularly well with people with more severe impairments. For diagnosis and evaluation of treatment in these groups, the type of systematic recording of symptomatic behaviors described by Lowry (1998) and Pfadt, Korosh, and Wolfson (2003) is recommended.

Types of Instruments

Assessment instruments vary depending on what they are supposed to do. Screening instruments usually cover a wide range of psychiatric disorders, with depression and bipolar disorders being only part of the overall schedule. As a result, the sections on these disorders tend to be brief, with not all the symptoms covered that are described as diagnostic schemes in the *Diagnostic and Statistical Manual of Mental Disorders* (fourth edition) (DSM-IV; American Psychiatric Association, 1994), or the *International Classification of Diseases (Mental and Behavioural Disorders: Clinical Description and Diagnostic Guidelines* (*ICD-10*; WHO, 1992). Most of the better-known instruments designed specifically for people with intellectual disabilities—such as the *Psychopathology Inventory for Mentally Retarded Adults* (*PIMRA*; Matson, 1988), the *Reiss Screen* (Reiss, 1988), the *Diagnostic Assessment for the Severely Handicapped* (*DASH*; Matson, 1995b), and the *Assessment of Dual Diagnosis* (*ADD*; Matson, 1995a)—fall into this category. Some of these instruments are designed to be used by support staff or family members with no specific training in mental-health problems, and they are relatively quick to use. If the person being assessed scores above a certain threshold level, this indicates that he or she should be referred for a full psychiatric evaluation. Screening instruments are also used for studies of prevalence rates in large populations. On the other hand, only professionals with psychiatric training use instruments designed to permit psychiatric diagnosis. These instruments are longer and more complex, assessing a full range of symptoms for each disorder, and detailed rules for deciding when a person fulfills the criteria for diagnosis are provided. The *Psychiatric Assessment Schedule for Adults with Developmental Disabilities* Interview (*PAS-ADD*; Moss, 2002a) is the only such instrument reviewed here that is designed specifically for people with intellectual disabilities. A third type of instrument is designed to assess severity, to monitor change over time or following treatment, and for research purposes. Because these instruments focus on only one particular disorder, they contain a more comprehensive range of symptoms than do screening instruments and can assess severity in more detail.

Instruments can also be divided into those that rely on self-report—that is, the person with intellectual disabilities provides responses to the questions him or herself—and those in which an informant, such as a family member or support staff, provides the responses. Those that rely on self-report have been used mostly with people with mild or moderate disabilities, whereas those relying on reports from informants have been used with people with all levels of impairment. Instruments designed for the general population can be used with some of those with mild disabilities, but because of the potential problems described in the section on content validity, they should be used with caution.

Judging the Quality of Assessment Instruments

Instruments are judged on the basis of their validity and reliability. Validity refers to

Table 9.1. Reliability and validity: definitions.

Term		Definition
Validity	*Content validity*	The extent to which the questions in the measure represent an adequate sample of the construct (e.g., do the questions on a depression measure reflect the DSM-IV criteria?). Content validity also concerns whether the questions are appropriate for the population in question and the purpose of the instrument.
	Criterion validity	The extent to which a person's score is consistent with an independent psychiatric diagnosis.
	Convergent validity	The extent to which a person's score is correlated with their score on other measures of depression/mania.
	Construct validity	The extent to which a person's score is correlated with their score on a measure of something that is supposed to be theoretically related (e.g., hopelessness, negative cognitions).
Reliability	*Internal reliability*	The extent to which the items in the scale correlate with each other (i.e., are all questions measuring the same thing?). Alpha coefficients of 0.6 are usually taken as poor, 0.7 as adequate, and 0.8 as good.
	Inter-rater reliability	The extent to which different informants provide similar scores when rating the same person.
	Test-retest reliability	The extent to which a person's score is consistent over time.

whether the instrument measures what it is supposed to measure, whereas reliability refers to the accuracy or precision of the measure. (See Table 9.1).

Content Validity

Diagnostic Criteria and Behavioral Equivalents

The DSM-IV (American Psychiatric Association, 1994) provides diagnostic criteria for a range of mood disorders in the general population that are based on the identification of major depressive episodes and manic episodes. The symptom criteria are presented in simplified form in Table 9.2. Although standard diagnostic criteria have often been found to be adequate for people with mild intellectual disabilities, some of the criteria cannot be reported by people with severe or profound impairments, including suicidal ideation, feelings of hopelessness or guilt, and (in depression) diminished ability to concentrate or (in mania) flight of ideas and grandiosity. In these cases behavioral equivalents have been suggested, such as self-injury, frequent crying, screaming, and social isolation. (For reviews of depression, see McBrien, 2003; Ross & Oliver, 2003a; Smiley & Cooper, 2003. For reviews of mania, see Ruedrich, 1993. See also Chapter 2 by Charlot in this volume). Although there is no consensus on some of these criteria, such as self-injury and aggression, others, such as reduction in activity and increased crying, are more widely accepted, as is the use of the criteria "irritability" as an alternative to depressed mood. Lowry (1998) provides a set of "symptomatic behaviors" that operationalize depressive symptoms so that they can be recorded by untrained staff and caregivers. The new *Diagnostic Criteria – Learning Disabilities (DC-LD)*, developed in the UK by the Royal College of Psychiatrists (2001; Smiley & Cooper, 2003), are perhaps the most comprehensive criteria for the diagnosis of affective disorders in people with intellectual disabilities. The DC-LD include subcategories of depressive episodes, manic episodes, and mixed affective episodes. It is likely that revisions of the criteria will be necessary after they become widely adopted. A good scale (the Glasgow Depression Scale, described in this chapter), based on this set of criteria, has recently been published.

Some of the earlier informant scales developed for this population (for example, the Reiss Screen or the DASH) use modified diagnostic criteria based on reports of depressive symptoms in this population that had been published prior to the development of the scale in question, including such items as somatic complaints, anxiety, and tension. The content validity of such scales depends on the quality of these items: The older the scale, the less evidence would have been available to scale developers on symptoms in this population. If the modified items are subsequently not found to be widespread symptoms of depression in this group, or if they are not specific to affective disorders, then the validity of the scale is compromised and revisions are necessary. In screening instruments, where there are only a small number of items assessing each disorder, such items as these have a greater potential to interfere with the validity of the scale. A number of newer instruments, which have had less opportunity for validation, have been designed to assess depressive symptoms in particular. Not only do these instruments assess a wider range of symptoms, but they also reflect a more recent consensus on modifications of the standard diagnostic criteria. It is important to recognize, therefore, that judgments of the content validity of a particular instrument will change when the consensus over what count as symptoms of depression in this population changes.

Table 9.2. DSM-IV symptoms of depressive and manic episodes (simplified).

Major Depressive Episode	Manic Episode
Five or more of the following (including at least one of 1 or 2) must be present during a 2-week period:	A period of abnormally elevated, expansive or irritable mood lasting 1 week. During this period, 3 or more of the following (4 if the mood is only irritable) must be present:
1. Depressed mood (or irritability in children)	1. Inflated self-esteem or grandiosity
2. Diminished pleasure or interest in activities	2. Decreased need for sleep
3. Significant weight loss or gain	3. More talkative than usual
4. Insomnia or hypersomnia	4. Flight of ideas
5. Psychomotor agitation or retardation	5. Distractibility
6. Fatigue or loss of energy	6. Increase in goal-directed activity or agitation
7. Feelings of worthlessness or excessive guilt	7. Excessive involvement in pleasurable activities that have potential for painful consequences
8. Diminished ability to think or concentrate	
9. Recurrent thoughts of death or suicidal ideation	

Target Population

Instruments designed for the general population are often not valid for people with intellectual disabilities. Clearly self-report measures, the normal method of assessment in the general population, cannot be used with those who cannot communicate verbally. For those who can, instruments are often still not valid for three reasons. First, the content of the items may be too abstract or conceptually difficult. Second, the question phrasing may be too long or complex for the person to understand as intended. Third, the response format may require too many demands on memory (in the case of multiple-choice options) or judgment (in the cases of comparisons or judgments of degree, duration, or frequency). (For a review, see Finlay & Lyons, 2001). For these reasons, self-report instruments must always be used with care, the interviewer taking time to check that questions have been understood and answers have been given as intended. Moss et al. (1997), in discussing the use of the PAS-ADD, make the point that whereas flexibility and rewording are crucial to good clinical interviewing with this population, this requires a good deal of skill on the part of the interviewer to maintain validity. Unfortunately, for most self-report instruments, the degree of verbal ability required by respondents is not clearly specified.

Some test developers have used innovative techniques to facilitate self-reports. These include using focus groups during item development in order to phrase questions in appropriate language (Cuthill, Espie, & Cooper, 2003); providing scripted rephrasings and probes (Moss, 2002a); using screening tests to ensure that respondents can respond to both yes-or-no and Likert-type response formats (Kazdin, Matson, & Senatore, 1983); and using visual aids to enable people to respond to Likert scales (Glenn, Bihm & Lammers, 2003; Kazdin et al., 1983). Although these approaches are to be encouraged, further evidence on their validity is needed (Sturmey, Reed, & Corbett, 1991).

For informant measures, where the information is provided by family or staff members, care must be taken to include only items that can be assessed. Many scales for people with severe and profound disabilities contain items that assume the person is able to communicate to a certain level (Ross & Oliver, 2003a), which may often not be the case. In such cases, clear instructions should be provided for how total scores can be recalculated, taking into account inapplicable items.

Since different contents may be suitable for different populations, factor structures (the way in which items on a scale can be grouped) may depend on the characteristics of the sample in question (Reiss, 1997). This is certainly true when comparing self-report and informant versions of the same instrument, which may reveal different factor structures because of the different visibility of items to the self or an observer, but it is also true when considering samples with different linguistic abilities. For this reason, caution should be exercised in the interpretation of factor analytic studies.

Instruments have suffered from the assumption that they should be applicable to people with all levels of disability. There are two common results, neither of which is a good compromise. In some cases, item content gets reduced severely to include only easily observable behaviors so that the instrument can be used for people with severe and profound disabilities. When used with those with mild or moderate intellectual disabilities, then, sensitivity is compromised, because potentially important symptoms do not get assessed. In other cases, a full range of symptoms is included, many of which cannot be assessed in those with severe or profound disabilities, and validity is again compromised. As a general rule, instruments that attempt to specify more precise target populations, either in terms of verbal ability or degree of overall impairment, are to be encouraged.

Function

Both the ICD-10 and the DSM-IV provide rules regarding how many symptoms must be observed for a diagnosis to be made. Diagnostic instruments need to include all the symptoms identified in the diagnostic criteria, as well as providing decision rules for diagnosis. Most instruments are not designed for diagnosis, however. Screening instruments usually cover a broad range of psychopathology, with only a small number of items for each disorder. These instruments are not designed to cover the full range of symptoms that may be found in depression or bipolar disorders, and they need to be judged with this limitation in mind. The content of these instruments should include items that are both the most easily identifiable and are most indicative of the disorder in question.

Criterion Validity

Independent psychiatric diagnosis is the main criterion used to judge the performance of instruments that assess affective disorders. Validity statistics based on such criteria depend on the quality of psychiatric diagnosis. Because psychiatric diagnosis is often difficult in this population, particularly for those with more severe disabilities, there is good reason to take these statistics with caution. Moss et al. (1997) also point out that instruments based on the present state are likely to disagree with psychiatric diagnosis if the latter is based on retrospective diagnosis. Agreement would only be expected if the condition were active at the time of the interview or during the time period covered by the schedule.

For screening instruments, quality depends on whether the instrument identifies everyone it should (sensitivity) while not identifying large numbers of people incorrectly (specificity). When assessing these two aspects of criterion validity, it is important to consider how the instrument makes screening decisions. For example, the Reiss Screen has three routes to referral. A study to judge its ability to identify those suffering from depression needs to find out which proportion of the people diagnosed independently as suffering from depression are identified from any aspect of the screen, not just from the depression subscale (Reiss, 1997). The assumption is that the psychiatrist will be able to identify depression irrespective of which disorder the screen has suggested.

Convergent Validity

The quality of an instrument is also judged by its agreement with other self-report or informant measures of the disorder in question. When the new measure is not found to correlate with a parallel measure, as is often the case, the problem may lie with the new measure or with the comparison or with both, and it is often difficult to judge why they have failed to agree. (For a general discussion of this issue, see Bramston and Fogarty [2000]). Moss, Prosser, Ibbotson, and Goldberg (1996) found that respondents reported subjective retardation, such as slowing, significantly more than did informants. However, informants reported loss of concentration, loss of interest, social withdrawal, and irritability more than did respondents. Earlier informant measures often used in validity studies included items that could not legitimately be assessed by informants because they referred to private perceptions or emotions. This situation is improving with the development of measures that only tap behavioral equivalents of depressive symptoms, and which give detailed explanations of each item. Also, informants who have contact with the person in different settings may produce different ratings depending on which areas of the person's life they are involved in. Responses to this problem include the use of two or more informants, as recommended by the Reiss Screen (Reiss, 1993), and the use of both self-report and informant instruments to increase sensitivity, as used by the PAS-ADD (Patel, Goldberg, & Moss, 1993).

A similar problem exists when the parallel instrument is a self-report scale, many of which have not had encouraging results in this population for the reasons just described. This is particularly the case when scales developed for the general population are used with those with moderate or severe disabilities.

Reliability

Moss et al. (1998) discuss two reasons why measures of internal reliability may not be informative for psychopathology scales. First, individuals might be diagnosed with a disorder on the basis of having only a small number from a list of symptoms. Inter-correlations between other items may therefore be low. Second, the smaller scales have a smaller internal reliability coefficient, given the same average inter-item correlations. If affective disorder scales are only a small part of a general psychopathology instrument and contain only a few items, internal reliability coefficients would be expected to be lower. Finally, the usefulness of test-retest indices is questionable in assessing such disorders as depression and mania, which may be episodic and which may respond to treatment (Cooper & Collacott, 1996). For this reason, test-retest reliabilities will not be considered in this review unless the administrations were carried out within a very short time period.

Instruments Assessing Affective Disorders

This section reviews commonly used instruments for the assessment of mood disorders in people with intellectual disabilities. Attempting to form an overall judgment on the quality of different instruments is difficult, particularly in cases where studies appear to contradict one another. Problems often arise because of different samples and different analytic strategies. Studies may include different proportions of people with mild or severe and profound disabilities, and this often has important effects on the results. Similarly, studies that include people with a full range of psychiatric disorders may produce different results from those that do not (Reiss, 1997). Many decisions all have important effects on the validity indices that result from a study. These decisions include whether a stricter or a more relaxed significance level is used, which type of factor analysis has been performed, and whether group comparisons based on high versus low scorers or correlations have been carried out. A further factor that makes it difficult to assess screening instruments in particular is that validity statistics are often reported for the instrument overall, making it hard to judge the quality of individual affective disorders subscales.

Instruments With Both Self-Report and Informant Versions

Children's Depression Inventory (CDI)

Details.

The Children's Depression Inventory (CDI; Kovacs, 1985) includes 27 items and is modeled on the Beck Depression Inventory. It was developed for children in the general population and uses a three-option multiple-choice format.

Reliability and Validity.

The informant version has been used with both adults (Meins, 1993) and children (Benavidez & Matson, 1993; Matson, Barrett, & Helsel, 1988) with all levels of intellectual disabilities. Good relationships with other informant and self-report depression scales have been found in the child samples. Meins (1993) found good evidence of criterion validity, with one cutoff score identifying five of the six people with a clinical diagnosis. He found a specificity of 123 out of 132 negatives, good internal reliability (0.86), and moderate inter-rater reliability. Despite these encouraging results, many items concern complex subjective states and cognitions, and it is unclear how such items could be assessed by informants. Meins found that all 24 items could be assessed for only 81% of the sample, and he used an adjustment procedure to obtain total scores.

The self-report version has been used with adolescents (Benavidez & Matson, 1993; Heiman, 2001) and adults with mild and moderate intellectual disabilities (Bramston & Fogarty, 2000), the latter using a pictorial response scale and probes to check understanding. These studies found moderate to good relationships with other self-report and informant scales, good internal reliability (0.79–0.80), and some evidence of construct validity. Given the complexity of some of the items, it is important to determine the level of linguistic and cognitive ability needed to complete the scale.

Glasgow Depression Scale for People With a Learning Disability (GDS-LD)

Details.

The Glasgow Depression Scale for People With a Learning Disability (GDS-LD; Cuthill et al., 2003) contains 20 items that are based on DC-LD diagnostic criteria. It was designed for self-report for people with mild or moderate intellectual disabilities. It uses a two-stage response format with symbols. A screening test and anchoring event used and alternative phrasings are provided. Excellent procedures were followed to ensure coverage of symptoms and that language is appropriate to the target population. Both versions of the scale are published and are free (Cuthill et al., 2003).

Reliability and Validity.

Cuthill et al. (2003) found that those with an independent diagnosis of depression scored significantly higher than a group with no such diagnosis. They also found good levels of sensitivity and specificity. It also had a strong relationship with the informant version ($r = 0.93$). Test-retest reliability at the beginning and end of a single session (0.97) and internal reliability (0.90) were good.

The *GDS-CS* is a 16-item informant version of this scale. It has excellent test-retest reliabilities after 2 days ($r = 0.98$). Good internal reliability (0.88) and inter-rater reliability ($r = 0.98$) were found. It was also highly correlated with the self-report version. (See above).

Only one study has been published on these measures, but the care taken in designing them for a specific population gives them great potential. Further independent research is urgently required to provide evidence of validity and reliability, and to investigate whether different interviewers and raters produce consistent scores.

Psychopathology Inventory for Mentally Retarded Adults (PIMRA)

Details.

The Psychopathology Inventory for Mentally Retarded Adults (PIMRA; Matson, 1988) is a 56-item screening tool covering a range of disorders. The items were adapted from the DSM-III and include one affective disorders section with 7 items. It is sold for use with people within an IQ range of 60–80, although the informant version has often been used in studies with people with more severe impairments. It uses a yes-or-no response format. The authors of the scale suggest that it be used as a general measure of psychopathology rather than as an assessment of specific disorders (Senatore, Matson, & Kazdin, 1985). The items on the affective disorders scale are selected for simplicity and omit the more abstract subjective symptoms of the DSM. The scale covers symptoms of both depression and mania and is therefore not homogeneous. Some of the self-report questions are relevant to both disorders. It is unclear in these cases how a yes-or-no format can provide a clear picture (for example, "Do you have lots of energy?").

Reliability and Validity.

The self-report version (PIMRA-S) has been used in several studies with people with moderate to borderline intellectual disabilities, although quite high proportions are sometimes excluded on the basis of screening tests or clinical judgment (van Minnen, Savelsberg, & Hoogduin, 1994). The evidence of convergent validity is mixed (Helsel & Matson, 1988; Kazdin et al., 1983; McDaniel & Turner, 2000; Nezu, Nezu, Rothenberg, DelliCarpini, & Groag, 1995; Watson, Aman, & Singh, 1988). Significant, but generally small or medium, relations have been found with some parallel depression measures but not others. There are contradictory results between studies. Senatore et al. (1985) found that those diagnosed as suffering from depression on the basis of this scale did not score significantly higher on any of the five other depression measures used in the study. Van Minnen et al. (1994) found a general dual diagnosis group (including a range of disorders) scored significantly higher on the subscale. There is some evidence of construct validity, however, with significant relationships being found with neglect as a child (Tymchuk, 1993), hopelessness, automatic thoughts, self-reinforcement, and social support (Nezu et al., 1995). Studies of the factor structure have found different structures for the complete self-report and informant versions and no affective disor-der/depression factor in the self-report version (Matson, Kazdin, & Senatore, 1984; Watson et al., 1988). Internal reliabilities for this scale have been barely acceptable (0.63–0.68; van Minnen et al., 1994; Watson et al., 1988).

The informant version of the PIMRA (PIMRA-I) has been used in many studies using samples, including people with severe and profound disabilities. There is mixed evidence of convergent validity (Helsel & Matson, 1988; Kazdin et al., 1983; Masi, Brovedani, Mucci, & Favilla, 2002; Sturmey & Bertman, 1994; Sturmey & Ley, 1990; van Minnen et al., 1994; Watson et al., 1988). Significant relations have been found between the affective disorders scale and other depression scales in some studies but not in others. Evidence for criterion validity is also mixed. In a sample of 163 people of all levels of intellectual disability, Linaker (1991) found no cases of affective disorder identified by the scale. Van Minnen et al. (1994) found that a general psychiatric diagnosis group, including a range of disorders, scored significantly higher on the subscale. Balboni, Battagliese, and Pedrabissi (2000) found that those with an independent diagnosis of depression scored significantly higher on the total PIMRA scale and the three factors that emerged from their sample, which contained items from the affective disorders subscale. (Comparisons were not made on the affective disorders subscale). Factor analyses either have identified factors of affective disorders but found that different items load onto these factors (Matson et al., 1984; Watson et al., 1988), or have found no affective disorder factor at all (Balboni et al., 2000; Linaker, 1991). Levels of internal reliability for the affective disorders scale have ranged from virtually nonexistent to almost acceptable (Sturmey & Bertman, 1994; Sturmey & Ley, 1990; van Minnen et al., 1994; Watson et al., 1988), and one study found moderate to good levels of inter-rater agreement (Iverson & Fox, 1989).

Psychiatric Assessment Schedule for Adults With a Developmental Disability Interview (PAS-ADD 10 Interview)

Details.

The Psychiatric Assessment Schedule for Adults With a Developmental Disability Interview (PAS-ADD-10 Interview; Moss et al., 1993) contains 145 questions covering a range of psychiatric disorders. It is a semistructured clinical interview designed to produce ICD-10 research diagnoses based on the "schedules for clinical assessment in neuropsychiatry" (SCAN) scoring algorithm, and hence it requires training. The PAD-ASS 10 has comprehensive coverage of psychiatric symptoms. It assumes the same psychiatric symptoms are found in people with intellectual disabilities as in the rest of the population. It can be carried out with both the patient and an informant. A diagnosis is made if the information from either meets diagnostic criteria. The new edition of the PAS-ADD includes measures of both depression and hypomania. There is a series of questions and probes for each symptom, which the interviewer rates on 4-point scales. There is a clinical glossary, and rephrasings are provided. It is designed for use with people with all levels of intellectual disability. It uses a three-tier interview structure depending on the linguistic abilities of the respondent; it also uses anchoring events for historical events.

The PASS-ADD is a detailed and comprehensive instrument that aims to maximize sensitivity by using both informants and self-reports and by providing in-depth exploration of the full range of possible symptoms. The instrument is less sensitive in both self-report and informant versions for those with more severe disabilities (Moss et al., 1997; Patel et al., 1993).

Reliability and Validity.

Limited validity statistics are available on the affective disorders sections. In a sample of people with mild to profound intellectual disabilities, Moss et al. (1997) found that the PAS-ADD correctly identified only 6 of the 16 cases of depression identified by psychiatrists. Specificity was better. Of the 9 cases identified by the instrument, 6 were confirmed by a psychiatrist, 2 were diagnosed as mania/hypomania (not then assessed by the PAS-ADD), and 1 was diagnosed as schizophrenia/schizoaffective. Factor analysis found two factors related to depression, both of which included symptoms outside the DSM criteria but which correlated significantly with referrer ratings of depression ($r = 0.22$ and 0.41). Although generally good inter-rater reliabilities have been found for raters coding the same videotaped interview (Costello, Moss, Prosser, & Hatton, 1997; Patel et al., 1993), some items, such as loss of interest and delayed sleep, were less reliable. The authors highlighted the need for good clinical interviewing skills, training to ensure the validity of the instrument, and the need for research into reliability in more realistic clinical settings.

Mini PAS-ADD Interview

Details.

The Mini PAS-ADD Interview (Moss, 2002a) is an 86-item informant instrument assessing a range of disorders. It is used as an aid to gathering detailed information on psychiatric symptoms as part of multidisciplinary assessment, but not for diagnosis. It includes subscales for depression and expansive mood. Some training is required to use it. The items, which are rated on a 4-point scale, are drawn from the PAS-ADD Interview, and a scoring algorithm is provided. There is comprehensive range of symptoms, a good glossary of symptom definitions, and an excellent instruction manual.

Reliability and Validity.

In a sample of people with moderate to profound intellectual disabilities, Prosser et al. (1998) found acceptable internal reliabilities for the depression (0.84, 0.88) and expansive mood (0.77, 0.81) scales, but less encouraging inter-rater reliabilities ($r = 0.62$ and $r = 0.37$, respectively). Inter-rater agreement over case-noncase identification for those cases that had a diagnosis assessed by the PAS-ADD was good (91% agreement, kappa = 0.74). Reasonable evidence of criterion validity was found: 81% correct classification as measured against psychiatric diagnosis was obtained by nonpsychiatric professional raters. It should be noted, however, that these results apply to the instrument overall and are not specific to the two affective disorders scales. Further research is needed into the validity of this instrument.

PAS-ADD Checklist (Revised)

Details.

The PAS-ADD Checklist (Revised) (Moss, 2002b; Moss et al., 1998) is a 25-item informant instrument covering a range of disorders. It is used for screening and monitoring at-risk individuals and designed for caregivers and family members to complete. There is no glossary, but it is phrased in everyday language and requires no special training. It was developed by selecting items most predictive of psychiatric diagnosis from the PAS-ADD interview. Threshold scores are provided. One scale combines affective and neurotic disorders and includes items on depression and hypomania. The authors suggest that two raters be used. Items are rated on 4-point scales. There is good coverage of depressive symptoms for a screening instrument, but less coverage of hypomania.

Reliability and Validity.

Moss et al. (1998) report statistics from a sample of people with moderate to profound intellectual disabilities. Factor analysis did not confirm the three disorder groupings used for the algorithm, but produced eight factors, one of which was labeled depression and one was labeled hypomania. The affective/neurotic subscale has been found to have good internal reliability (0.84) and moderate to good inter-rater reliability. Criterion validity was assessed against psychiatric diagnoses for the whole instrument. Reasonable sensitivity was obtained for those with severe disorders (22/24), less so for those with mild disorders (9/16). Specificity was 4 false positives out of 13. Further research into validity is needed. One currently unresolved issue is the ability of untrained raters to use the checklist (Moss et al., 1998).

Clinical Behaviour Checklist for Persons With Intellectual Disabilities (CBDPID)

Details.

The Clinical Behaviour Checklist for Persons With Intellectual Disabilities (CBDPID; Marston, Perry, & Roy, 1997) is a 30-item checklist including symptoms of depression from the ICD-10 (WHO, 1992), other psychiatric symptoms, and challenging behaviours. Tsouris, Mann, Patti, & Sturmey (2003) developed a 5-item scale from the original 30 items, which had a good level of internal reliability (0.89) and some evidence of criterion validity based on psychiatric diagnosis, although this was compromised due to the psychiatrist having input into the CBPID score. The items include depressed affect, loss of interest, lack of emotional response, psychomotor retardation, and loss of energy. Further work is needed to assess whether this might form a useful brief scale for the assessment of depression.

Self-Report Instruments

Beck Depression Inventory

Details.

There are both an unmodified 21-item and a modified 13-item version of the Beck Depression Inventory (Beck & Steer, 1987), which have been used with people with borderline to moderate intellectual disabilities. It includes most but not all DSM-IV symptoms. A screening test and bar graph display has been used to represent response format (Kazdin et al., 1983). The unmodified version uses a multiple-choice format.

Reliability and Validity.

Evidence of convergent validity is generally good, with studies finding relationships with many parallel measures of depression (Helsel & Matson, 1988; Kazdin et al., 1983, Nezu et al., 1995, Prout & Schaefer, 1985). There is some evidence of construct validity (for example, relationships with hopelessness, automatic thoughts, self-reinforcement; Nezu et al., 1995). One study found a poor internal reliability coefficient of 0.59 (Helsel & Matson, 1988). While these results are relatively encouraging, more research is needed into the levels of linguistic and cognitive ability necessary for this scale.

Minnesota Multiphasic Personality Inventory-168 (MMPI[168]-L)

Details.

The Minnesota Multiphasic Personality Inventory-168 (MMPI[168]-L; Overall, Butcher, & Hunter, 1975) includes 168 items that cover a range of conditions. It was developed for the general population, but a modified version using a yes-or-no format has been used with people with mild and moderate intellectual disabilities. It includes depression and hypomania scales. The items do not closely match DSM-IV criteria. The questions are rephrased and simplified "when necessary." McDaniel and Turner (2000) suggest that validity is increased if the test is administered by an experienced clinician. Inspection of the items of the original MMPI suggests that a considerable degree of explanation and rephrasing would be necessary due to their complexity.

Reliability and Validity.

Although there is some evidence for some of the other subscales of this instrument, there is little evidence for either the reliability or the validity of the depression scale in people with intellectual disabilities. Studies have found no significant correlations with a range of other depression measures, although a small correlation was found with the BDI in one study (Johns & McDaniel, 1998; Kazdin et al., 1983; McDaniel, Passmore, & Sewell, 2003). There is also little evidence for the validity of the hypomania scale (McDaniel & Turner, 2000). One study has shown evidence of construct validity (McDaniel et al., 2003), with significant internal correlations between the depression and anxiety subscales on the MMPI(168)-L. Clearly, stronger evidence regarding the validity of this scale is necessary before it can be advocated for the assessment of mood disorders.

Reynolds Adolescent/Child Depression Scale (RADS/RCDS)

Details.

The Reynolds Adolescent/Child Depression Scale (RADS/RCDS; Reynolds, 1987) includes 30 items. It has been used with adolescents and adults with borderline to moderate intellectual disabilities. The items are consistent with the DSM-IV. A 4-point response format is used. Glenn et al. (2003) used cards with differing numbers of dots to represent the response format.

Reliability and Validity.

Studies of adolescents with mild or borderline intellectual disability have found good internal reliability (0.87–0.92: Benavidez & Matson, 1993; Glenn et al, 2003; Reynolds

& Miller, 1985). There is good evidence of convergent validity with parallel depression measures and some evidence of construct validity (for example, learned helplessness in the academic domain, anxiety, negative thoughts). Although these results are relatively encouraging, more research is needed into the levels of linguistic and cognitive ability necessary for this scale.

Self-Report Depression Questionnaire

Details.

The Self-Report Depression Questionnaire (Reynolds & Baker, 1988) contains 32 items. It was developed for adults with mild or moderate intellectual disability. It should be used for screening and assessing the depth of depressive symptomatology, but not for diagnosis. Studies have found 10–40% of samples could not respond to the items. Thirty-one items use a yes-or-no format and 1 item involves selection from five "smiley" faces. The items provide good coverage of basic DSM-IV symptoms, with additional items addressing possible behavioral equivalents (crying, social withdrawal) and associated symptoms (anger, somatic complaints).

Reliability and Validity.

Reynolds and Baker (1988), in a study with people mainly with mild and moderate disabilities, found good internal reliability (0.9). There is mixed evidence of convergent validity, one study finding good convergence with a clinical interview (Reynolds & Baker, 1988) while another found no agreement with the Reiss Screen or a diagnostic interview (Rojahn, Warren, & Ohringer, 1994). More research is needed into the levels of linguistic and cognitive ability necessary for this scale.

Zung Depression Inventory

Details.

There are 20 items on the Zung Depression Inventory (Zung, 1965). Both modified and unmodified versions have been used with adults and adolescents with borderline to moderate intellectual disabilities. The instrument includes most but not all DSM-IV symptoms. A 4-point scale is used.

Reliability and Validity.

The results are mixed, with good convergent validity being found with some depression measures and no correlations being found with others (Helsel & Matson, 1988; Kazdin et al., 1983; Lindsay, Michie, Baty, Smith, & Miller, 1994; Masi et al., 2002; Prout & Schaefer, 1985). Evidence of construct validity is mixed, a relationship being found with some variables (for example, self-esteem, anxiety, social support, and neuroticism) but not others (for example, stigma and social performance) (Dagnan & Sandhu, 1999; Lindsay et al., 1994; Reiss & Benson, 1985). One study found a poor internal reliability coefficient of 0.54 (Helsel & Matson, 1988). More research is needed into the levels of linguistic and cognitive ability necessary for this scale.

Informant Reports

Anxiety, Depression and Mood Scale (ADAMS)

Details.

The Anxiety, Depression and Mood Scale (ADAMS; Esbensen, Rojahn, Aman, & Ruedrich, 2003) is a 28-item screening instrument assessing depression (7 items), manic/hyperactive behavior (5 items), anxiety, social avoidance, and compulsive behavior. It was designed to be used with people with all degrees of intellectual disability. The items focus on observable behaviors and moods. Each item is rated on 4-point scale. Subscales were derived from factor analysis. The depression subscale content has considerable overlap between items: Three items tap depression or sadness, and three tap lack of energy. The ADAMS could be improved if a wider range of symptoms were assessed. The manic behavior subscale lacks items on expansive mood and irritability. Cutoff scores have not yet been developed. This scale might prove useful in the future, but further research and development is needed.

Reliability and Validity.

The internal reliability is good for the depression scale (0.80) and adequate for the manic behavior scale (0.75). The inter-rater reliability was not encouraging—0.39 and 0.37, respectively. There is some evidence of criterion validity: People with a clinical diagnosis of bipolar disorder scored significantly higher on the manic behavior subscale than did controls, and those with a diagnosis of depression scored significantly higher on the depression scale.

Assessment of Dual Diagnosis (ADD)

Details.

The Assessment of Dual Diagnosis (ADD; Matson, 1995a) is a 79-item psychopathology screening instrument assessing 13 diagnostic categories, including subscales for depression (8 items) and mania (6 items). It was designed for people with mild or moderate intellectual disability and should be used as part of a comprehensive assessment. Items are rated on duration, frequency, and severity. Cutoff scores are not provided. The manual states that investigators should be supervised by an appropriate professional. The mania scale covers six of the seven core DSM-IV symptoms of a manic episode. The depression scale covers seven of the nine core symptoms of a depressive episode (in the cases of sleep and appetite, only partially).

Reliability and Validity.

The ADD has excellent levels of internal and inter-rater reliability (over 0.90) for the depression and mania scales (Matson & Bamburg, 1998). There is limited evidence of validity. McDaniel et al. (2003) found no correlation between the depression and mania subscales of the modified self-report version of the MMPI-168(L) and the corresponding subscales of the ADD. However, this may be due to the problems with the MMPI (see above). Given the good reliability statistics and content validity of the depression and mania scales of this instrument, further evidence of validity is urgently needed.

Bipolar Mood Tracking Sheet

Details.

The Bipolar Mood Tracking Sheet (Pfadt et al., 2003) was designed to allow caregivers to monitor changes in mood over time and to assess the effects of treatment. It lists possible indicators of activation and withdrawal. Caregivers choose the most appropriate indicators to the person in question. Chosen indicators are assessed daily over a period of time. Reliability and validity statistics are not available

Diagnostic Assessment for the Severely Handicapped (DASH/DASH II)

Details.

The Diagnostic Assessment for the Severely Handicapped (DASH/DASH-II; Matson, 1995b; Matson, Gardener, Coe, & Sovner, 1991) is an 84-item screening instrument. It covers 13 diagnostic categories, including scales on depression (15 items) and mania (7 items). It was designed for use with people with severe or profound intellectual disability. Its items are scored on frequency, duration, and severity. Provisional cutoff scores are given. The authors stress that it should be used only with a comprehensive psychiatric assessment (Matson & Smiroldo, 1997), and the investigator should have a Masters degree. The items focus on observable behaviors. Symptoms concerning subjective states and cognitions are not included. Some items are atypical symptoms or behavioral equivalents not found in standard DSM criteria (for example, complaining about disabilities or the social environment), and further evidence is therefore required of their validity. Several items cannot be assessed in those who have limited communicative abilities.

Reliability and Validity.

Although studies have found good average statistics for inter-rater reliability across the whole instrument (Matson 1995b; Sevin, Matson, Williams, & Kirkpatrick-Sanchez, 1995), agreement for the depression and mania subscales were either low or only just acceptable. Poor internal reliabilities have been found in three studies for both the depression (0.48–0.58) and mania scales (0.52–0.61) (Matson, 1995b; Paclawskyj, Matson, Bamburg, & Baglio, 1997), although a good level of reliability (0.79) was found on the mania scale in one study (Matson & Smiroldo, 1997). A large-factor analytic study yielded no factor relating to affective disorders (Matson, Coe, Gardener, & Sovner, 1991). The depression and mania subscales were found to be correlated to most of the subscales of the Aberrant Behavior Checklist (Paclawskyj et al., 1997). Significant overall differences were found between three groups on the depression scale (depression, autism, and no psychiatric diagnosis), although follow-up tests are not reported (Matson et al., 1999). The DASH II mania scale has been found to differentiate those with and without a clinical diagnosis of mania (Matson & Smiroldo, 1997). Two prevalence studies have found rates of below 1% for depression and between 7% and 12% for mania (Cherry, Matson & Paclawskyj, 1997; Matson, 1995b), leading Matson, Gardener, et al., (1991) to question whether the scale is able to assess depression accurately. The mania scale appears to be performing better, although criterion validity studies addressing sensitivity and specificity are needed.

Mental Retardation Depression Scale (MRDS)

Details.

The Mental Retardation Depression Scale (MRDS; Meins, 1996) contains 9 items and was developed from the Comprehensive Psychopathological Rating Scale (Asberg, Perris, Schalling & Sedvall, 1978). Factor analysis revealed two factors: agitated/irritable (inner tensions, reduced sleep, hostility, agitation, muscular tension) and retarded/depressive (inability to feel, lassitude, apparent sadness, withdrawal). Several items are not specific to depression, and some would be difficult to assess in people who have limited communicative abilities.

Validity.

Meins (1996) found that a group diagnosed with depressive disorder scored significantly higher than a no-diagnosis group who were high scorers on the CDI.

Mood, Interest and Pleasure Questionnaire (MIPQ)

Details.

The Mood, Interest and Pleasure Questionnaire (MIPQ; Ross & Oliver, 2003b) has 25 items rated on a 5-point scale and was developed to assess behaviors relating to the definitions of low mood and anhedonia in the DSM-IV. It was designed for people with severe or profound intellectual disability. It contains two subscales: mood and interest/pleasure. It is used to aid diagnosis and assess change. Unqualified staff can use it. The authors warn that the scale may not be appropriate for people with very limited movement, for those with autism, or for those taking certain forms of medication. The scale is published free (Ross & Oliver, 2003b).

Reliability and Validity.

Good inter-rater (0.69 to 0.76) and internal (0.89 to 0.94) reliabilities were found. There is some evidence of convergent validity with the ABC lethargy/social withdrawal, irritability, agitation, and crying scales. Further work is required in independent samples to establish the validity of this new scale, and to further develop the items. However, it is potentially a very useful addition for people for whom it is difficult to assess internal states.

Reiss Screen for Maladaptive Behavior

Details.

The Reiss Screen for Maladaptive Behavior (Reiss, 1988) is a 36-item screening instrument rated on 3-point scales covering a range of disorders and maladaptive behaviors. There are versions for adults and children with mild to severe levels of disability. It contains two depression subscales (behavioral and physical signs, 5 items each) based on a factor analysis, with an additional single item concerning suicidal tendencies.

More than one informant must be consulted and the scores averaged. Each item includes a description and behavioral examples. Cutoff points are provided. Some of the items are behavioral equivalents or atypical symptoms not found in the DSM (for example, anxiety, fear, body stress) and therefore require further validation.

Reliability and Validity.

Although studies generally show the Reiss Screen is reasonably good overall for identifying people who have been given dual diagnoses by psychiatrists (Gustafsson & Sonnander, 2002; Reiss, 1990; Sturmey & Bertman, 1994), evidence for the two depression scales is mixed. Reiss (1993) reported that the manual provides evidence that those with specific diagnoses scored higher on the scales corresponding to their diagnosis. Van Minnen, Savelsberg, and Hoogduin (1995) found a composite group of people with any dual diagnosis scored higher on the two depression subscales. Gustafsson and Sonnander (2002) found that the depression subscales identified 6 of 10 people with a clinical diagnosis of depression, but also identified 17 of 32 people who did not have a diagnosis, indicating poor specificity. It should be noted that in this study the item content of the scales differed from the standard version, as did the cutoff scores. Sturmey and Bertman (1994) found that although there was a relation between total scores and having a psychiatric diagnosis, there was no relation between having a diagnosis and the two depression scales. Finally, Chitty, Boo, and Jamieson (1993) found the Reiss identified 14 of the 19 people in their sample who had a previous diagnosis in their case file, and 8 of the 10 people identified by a current psychiatric assessment. Within this, there was no agreement over specific diagnoses of depression. Specificity was poor, with the Reiss Screen identifying over twice as many cases as either past diagnoses or current psychiatric evaluation. Poor specificity statistics are partly due to the instrument also identifying people with maladaptive behaviors.

Evidence of convergent validity is inconsistent, with the two depression scales being related to the same parallel depression measures in some studies but not in others (Johns & McDaniel, 1998; Sturmey & Bertman, 1994; van Minnen et al., 1994; Walsh & Shenouda, 1999). Rojahn, Warren, and Ohringer (1994), in a study of people with mild and moderate disabilities, found almost no agreement on who scored highly based on the Reiss Screen, the Reynolds SRDQ, and a diagnostic interview carried out by a psychiatrist. Studies have found some evidence for construct validity, with correlations between the depression scale and measures of aggression and maladaptive behavior (Chitty et al., 1993; Reiss & Rojahn, 1993).

The original seven-factor structure (Reiss, 1988) has been confirmed in one study

(Havercamp & Reiss, 1997). In another study similar factors were found, although only two of the original items loaded onto the physical depression scale (Gustafsson & Sonnander, 2002), and in another different structures were found, with no depression factor identified (Sturmey, Jamieson, Burcham, Shaw, & Bertman, 1996). Reiss (1997) states that factor structure is not of central importance, because 75% of those who would be diagnosed on the basis of individual subscales (in general) would be detected through either the total score or the special maladaptive behavior items.

Internal reliabilities for the depression (physical) (between 0.54 and 0.76) and behavior (0.58 to 0.83) scales have ranged from poor to acceptable, depending on the study, with inter-rater reliabilities (r) ranging from 0.61 to 0.84, with most being over 0.7 (Gustafsson & Sonnander, 2002; Reiss, 1988; Sturmey & Bertman, 1994; Sturmey, Burcham & Perkins, 1995; van Minnen et al., 1995).

Reiss Screen for Children's Dual Diagnosis

Details.

The Reiss Screen for Children's Dual Diagnosis (Reiss & Valenti-Hein, 1994) is a 60-item screening instrument. There is one depression subscale (5 items), including sadness, loss of enjoyment, pessimism, sleep, and social inadequacy. The authors suggest that it less useful for a detailed assessment of specific disorders.

Reliability and Validity.

There is more evidence for the validity of the total scale score than for the depression subscale. Factor analysis did not reveal a depression factor. The depression scale was found to have a low level of internal reliability (0.57), but it did distinguish between children with and without a dual diagnosis of any type. Descriptive statistics revealed that those with a diagnosis of affective disorder scored higher on the depression scale than did those with no diagnosis, those with autism, and those with conduct disorder, but lower than did those with psychosis. No statistical tests were carried out on these differences. Reiss and Rojahn (1993) found some evidence of construct validity, with significant correlations between depression scores and aggression.

Recommendations

Table 9.3 provides details of the instruments recommended from this review. It should be noted, however, that these recommendations are based mainly on the item content and form of the instruments, and therefore they are tentative. Because many of the instruments recommended are relatively new, further work on their validity is necessary before we can be more confident of their quality.

Concluding Remarks

This chapter has described issues in the psychometric assessment of affective disorders in people with intellectual disabilities, and has reviewed the most commonly used instruments. Though there are encouraging results, it is clear that further work is required to validate and develop existing instruments. Psychometric assessment of people with intellectual disabilities is difficult and has only been seriously addressed relatively recently. Before 1983 there were no instruments designed to assess affective disorders

Table 9.3. Recommended instruments for assessing affective disorders in people with intellectual disabilities.

Population	Screening Instruments	Comprehensive Instruments
People with mild or moderate intellectual disability	ADD; PAS-ADD Checklist; ADAMS might be useful when further developed.	Bipolar Mood Tracking Sheet; GDS; PAS-ADD Interview; Mini PAS-ADD. The following can be useful but must be used with caution, considering the linguistic and cognitive abilities of the respondents: BDI, CDI, RADS/RCDS, SRDQ.
People with severe or profound intellectual disability	DASH (for mania only); PAS-ADD Checklist; ADAMS might be useful when further developed.	Systematic recording of behaviors (Lowry, 1998; Pfadt et al., 2003) preferable. Also MIPQ, PAS-ADD Interview, Mini-PAS-ADD.

in these populations (Sovner & Hurley, 1983). The earlier instruments need to be seen as first attempts at assessment, and they have provided an important step in our understanding of depression in this population. More recent instruments have often been able to take advantage of developments in our understanding of both symptomatology and assessment issues in people with intellectual disabilities. If high-quality instruments are to be developed, however, a long-term agenda needs to be adopted by test developers and publishers, an agenda that encourages research and allows for revised instruments to be published. Inconsistent findings and weaknesses in individual instruments should be regarded as a challenge, to encourage further refinement.

Many researchers stress the importance of comprehensive multidisciplinary assessments (Dosen & Gielen, 1993). Such assessments are particularly important for people with severe or profound disabilities, where it is generally recognized that identification of affective disorders is more difficult and where reliance on informant reports is the norm. This problem is reflected in the poorer validity statistics obtained when the instruments described above are assessed in these groups. Although better instruments can and should be developed for this population, it will probably always be necessary for comprehensive assessments and detailed behavioral observations to be carried out.

Recommended Reading

Smiley and Cooper (2003) and Sovner and Pary (1993) provide good reviews of diagnostic criteria and general diagnostic issues, respectively, in this population. Ross and Oliver (2003a) provide a discussion of methodological issues in the assessment of depression, and Finlay and Lyons (2001, 2002) review general issues in interviewing and developing self-report scales with people with intellectual disabilities. Moss et al. (1997) give a good overview of the PAS-ADD and an excellent discussion of issues in present state examinations with people with intellectual disabilities. The Glasgow Depression Scale is provided in Cuthill et al. (2003), whose article can also be used as a model for good self-report scale development. Finally, Lowry (1998) describes systematic behavioral recording of depressive symptoms, and Pfadt et al. (2003) provide a chart for recording bipolar symptoms.

Obtaining the Instruments

Table 9.4 provides details of where some of the more widely used instruments can be obtained. For availability of instruments not listed here, as well as for details of modifications to instruments developed for the general population, the authors of the publications cited should be contacted.

References

Table 9.4. Where to find instruments assessing mood disorders in people with intellectual disabilities.

Instrument	Free or Purchase?	Where to Find It
ADD	Purchase	JOHNMATSON@aol.com
BDI	Purchase	http://marketplace.psychcorp.com/PsychCorp.com/Cultures/en-US/default.htm
Bipolar Mood Tracking Sheet	Free	Pfadt et al. (2003)
CBDPID	Free	Marston et al. (1997)
CDI		Items are given in Meins (1993)
DASH-II	Purchase	JOHNMATSON@aol.com
GDS-LD	Free	Cuthill et al. (2003)
MIPQ	Free	Ross & Oliver (2003b)
PAS-ADD instruments	Purchase	http://web.onetel.com/~drplee/ and http://www.pasadd.co.uk (also has details of training courses)
PIMRA	Purchase	http://www.idspublishing.com/index/html
RADS/RCDS	Purchase	http://www.parinc.com
Reiss Screen for Children's Dual Diagnosis	Purchase	http://www.idspublishing.com/index.html
Reiss Screen for Maladaptive Behavior	Purchase	http://www.idspublishing.com/index/html
Zung Depression Inventory	Free	Zung (1965)

American Psychiatric Association. (1994). *Diagnostic and statistical manual of mental disorders* (4th ed.). Washington, DC: Author.

Asberg, M., Perris, C., Schalling, D., & Sedvall, G. (1978). The CPRS—development and applications of a psychiatric rating scale. *Acta Psychiatrica Scandinavica, 271* (Suppl.).

Balboni, G., Battagliese, G., & Pedrabissi, L. (2000). The Psychopathology Inventory for Mentally Retarded Adults: Factor structure and comparisons between subjects with or without dual diagnosis. *Research in Developmental Disabilities, 21*, 311–321.

Beck, A. T., & Steer, R. A. (1987). *Beck Depression Inventory manual.* San Antonio,

TX: The Psychological Corporation.

Benavidez, D. A., & Matson, J. L. (1993). Assessment of depression in mentally retarded adolescents. *Research in Developmental Disabilities, 14*, 179–188.

Bramston, P., & Fogarty, G. (2000). The assessment of emotional distress experienced by people with an intellectual disability: A study of different methodologies. *Research in Developmental Disabilities, 21*, 487–500.

Cherry, K. E., Matson, J. L., & Paclawskyj, T. R. (1997). Psychopathology in older adults with severe and profound mental retardation. *American Journal on Mental Retardation, 101*, 445–458.

Chitty, D. J., Boo, S. S., & Jamieson, J. (1993). Prevalence of dual diagnosis in an institution for individuals who are developmentally handicapped. *Behavioral Residential Treatment, 8*, 55–66.

Cooper, S. A., & Collacott, R. A. (1996). Depressive episodes in adults with learning disabilities. *Irish Journal of Psychological Medicine, 13*, 105–113.

Costello, H., Moss, S., Prosser, H., & Hatton, C. (1997). Reliability of the ICD-10 version of the Psychiatric Assessment for Adults With Developmental Disabilities (PAS-ADD). *Social Psychiatry and Psychiatric Epidemiology, 32*, 339–343.

Cuthill, F. M., Espie, C. A., & Cooper, S. (2003). Development and psychometric properties of the Glasgow Depression Scale for people with a learning disability. Individual and carer supplement versions. *British Journal of Psychiatry, 182*, 347–353.

Dagnan, D., & Sandhu, S. (1999). Social comparison, self-esteem and depression in people with intellectual disability. *Journal of Intellectual Disability Research. Special Issue: Mental Health and Intellectual Disability, V, 43*, 372–379.

Dosen, A., & Gielen, J. J. M. (1993). Depression in persons with mental retardation: Assessment and diagnosis. In R. J. Fletcher & A. Dosen (Eds), *Mental health aspects of mental retardation: Progress in assessment and treatment* (pp 70–97). New York: Lexington.

Esbensen, A. J., Rojahn, J., Aman, M. G., & Ruedrich, S. (2003). Reliability and validity of an assessment instrument for anxiety, depression and mood among individuals with mental retardation. *Journal of Autism and Developmental Disorders, 33*, 617–629.

Finlay, W. M. L., & Lyons, E. (2001). Methodological issues in interviewing and using self-report scales with people with mental retardation. *Psychological Assessment, 13*, 319–335.

Finlay, W. M. L., & Lyons, E. (2002). Acquiescence in interviews with people with mental retardation. *Mental Retardation, 40*, 14–29.

Glenn, E., Bihm, E. M., & Lammers, W. J. (2003). Depression, anxiety and relevant cognitions in persons with mental retardation. *Journal of Autism and Developmental Disorders, 33,* 69–76.

Gustafsson, C., & Sonnander, K. (2002). Psychometric properties of a Swedish version of the Reiss Screen for Maladaptive Behavior. *Journal of Intellectual Disability Research, 46,* 218–229.

Havercamp, S. M., & Reiss, S. (1997). The Reiss Screen for Maladaptive Behavior: Confirmatory factor analysis. *Behaviour Research and Therapy, 35,* 967–971.

Heiman, T. (2001). Depressive mood in students with mild intellectual disability: Students' reports and teachers' evaluations. *Journal of Intellectual Disability Research, 45,* 526–534.

Helsel, W. J., & Matson, J. L. (1988). The relationship of depression to social skills and intellectual functioning in mentally retarded adults. *Journal of Mental Deficiency Research, 32,* 411–418.

Iverson, J. C., & Fox, R. A. (1989). Prevalence of psychopathology among mentally retarded adults. *Research in Developmental Disabilities, 10,* 77–83.

Johns, M. R., & McDaniel, W. F. (1998). Areas of convergence and discordance between the MMPI-168 and the Reiss Screen for Maladaptive Behavior in mentally retarded clients. *Journal of Clinical Psychology, 54,* 529–535.

Kazdin, A. E., Matson, J. L., & Senatore, V. (1983). Assessment of depression in mentally retarded adults. *American Journal of Psychiatry, 140,* 1040–1043.

Kovacs, M. (1985). The Children's Depression Inventory (CDI). *Psychopharmacology Bulletin, 21,* 995–998.

Linaker, O. (1991). DSM-III diagnoses compared with factor structure of the Psychopathology Instrument for Mentally Retarded Adults (PIMRA), in an institutionalized, mostly severely retarded population. *Research in Developmental Disabilities, 12,* 143–153.

Lindsay, W. R., Michie, A. M., Baty, F. J., Smith, A. H. W., & Miller, S. (1994). The consistency of reports about feelings and emotions from people with intellectual disability. *Journal of Intellectual Disability Research, 38,* 61–66.

Lowry, M. A. (1998) Assessment and treatment of mood disorders in persons with developmental disabilities. *Journal of Developmental and Physical Disabilities, 10,* 387–406.

Marston, G. M., Perry, D. W., & Roy, A. (1997). Manifestations of depression in people with intellectual disability. *Journal of Intellectual Disability Research. Special Issue: Mental Health and Intellectual Disability, 41,* 476–480.

Masi, G., Brovedani, P., Mucci, M., & Favilla, L. (2002). Assessment of anxiety and depression in adolescents with mental retardation. *Child Psychiatry and Human Development, 32,* 227–237.

Matson, J. L. (1988). *The PIMRA manual*. Worthington, OH: IDS Publishing.

Matson, J. L. (1995a). *Assessment of dual diagnosis*. Baton Rouge, LA: Scientific Publishers.

Matson, J. L. (1995b). *Diagnostic assessment for the severely handicapped, II*. Baton Rouge, LA: Scientific Publishers.

Matson, J. L., & Bamburg, J. W. (1998). Reliability of the Assessment of Dual Diagnosis (ADD). *Research in Developmental Disabilities, 19*, 89–95.

Matson, J. L., Barrett, R. P., & Helsel, W. J. (1988). Depression in mentally retarded children. *Research in Developmental Disabilities, 9*, 39–46.

Matson, J. L., Coe, D. A., Gardener, W. I., & Sovner, R. (1991). A factor analytic study of the Diagnostic Assessment for the Severely Handicapped Scale. *Journal of Nervous and Mental Diseases, 179*, 553–557.

Matson, J. L., Gardener, W. I., Coe, D. A., & Sovner, R. (1991). A scale for evaluating emotional disorders in severely and profoundly mentally retarded persons: Development of the Diagnostic Assessment for the Severely Handicapped (DASH) scale. *British Journal of Psychiatry, 159*, 404–409.

Matson, J. L., Kazdin, A. E., & Senatore, V. (1984). Psychometric properties of the Psychopathology Instrument for Mentally Retarded Adults. *Applied Research in Mental Retardation, 5*, 81–89.

Matson, J. L., Rush, K. S., Hamilton, M., Anderson, S. J., Bamburg, J. W., Baglio, C. S., et al. (1999). Characteristics of depression as assessed by the Diagnostic Assessment for the Severely Handicapped-II (DASH-II). *Research in Developmental Disabilities, 20*, 305–313.

Matson, J. L., & Smiroldo, B. B. (1997). Validity of the Mania Subscale of the Diagnostic Assessment for the Severely Handicapped-II (DASH-II). *Research in Developmental Disabilities, 18*, 221–225.

McBrien, J. A. (2003). Assessment and diagnosis of depression in people with intellectual disability. *Journal of Intellectual Disability Research, 47*, 1–13.

McDaniel, W. F., Passmore, C. E., & Sewell, H. M. (2003). The MMPI-168(L) and ADD in assessing psychopathology in individuals with mental retardation: Between and within instrument associations. *Research in Developmental Disabilities, 24*, 19–32.

McDaniel, W. F., & Turner, M. D. (2000). The MMPI-168(L) as an instrument for assessing the mental health of individuals with mental retardation. *Developmental Disabilities Bulletin, 28*, 67–85.

Meins, W. (1993). Assessment of depression in mentally retarded adults: Reliability and validity of the Children's Depression Inventory (CDI). *Research in Developmental Disabilities, 14*, 299–312.

Meins, W. (1996). A new depression scale designed for use with adults with mental retardation. *Journal of Intellectual Disability Research, 40,* 222–226.

Moss, S. (2002a). *The Mini PAS-ADD Interview Pack.* Brighton, UK: Pavilion Publishing.

Moss, S. (2002b). *The PAS-ADD Checklist (revised).* Brighton, UK: Pavilion Publishing.

Moss, S., Ibbotson, B., Prosser, H., Goldberg, D., Patel, P., & Simpson, N. (1997). Validity of the PAS-ADD for detecting psychiatric symptoms in adults with learning disability (mental retardation). *Social Psychiatry and Psychiatric Epidemiology, 32,* 344–354.

Moss, S., Patel, P., Prosser, H., Goldberg, D., Simpson, N., Rowe, S., et al. (1993). Psychiatric morbidity in older people with moderate and severe learning disability. I: Development and reliability of the patient interview (PAS-ADD). *British Journal of Psychiatry, 163,* 471–480.

Moss, S., Prosser, H., Costello, H., Simpson, N., Patel, P., Rowe, S., et al. (1998). Reliability and validity of the PAS-ADD Checklist for detecting psychiatric disorders in adults with intellectual disability. *Journal of Intellectual Disability Research, 42,* 173–183.

Moss, S., Prosser, H., Ibbotson, B., & Goldberg, D. (1996). Respondent and informant accounts of psychiatric symptoms in a sample of patients with learning disability. *Journal of Mental Retardation Research, 40,* 457–465.

Nezu, C. M., Nezu, A. M., Rothenberg, J. L., DelliCarpini, L., & Groag, I. (1995). Depression in adults with mild mental retardation: Are cognitive variables involved? *Cognitive Therapy and Research, 19,* 227–239.

Overall, J. E., Butcher, J. N., & Hunter, S. (1975). Validity of the MMPI-168 for psychiatric screening. *Educational and Psychological Measurement, 35,* 393–400.

Paclawskyj, T. R., Matson, J. L., Bamburg, J. W., & Baglio, C. S. (1997). A comparison of the Diagnostic Assessment for the Severely Handicapped–II (DASH-II) and the Aberrant Behavior Checklist (ABC). *Research in Developmental Disabilities, 18,* 289–298.

Patel, P., Goldberg, D. P., & Moss, S. (1993). Psychiatric morbidity in older people with moderate and severe learning disabilities (mental retardation). Part II: The prevalence study. *British Journal of Psychiatry, 163,* 481–491.

Pfadt, A., Korosh, W., & Wolfson, M. S. (2003). Charting bipolar disorder in people with developmental disabilities: An informant-based tracking instrument. *MentalHealth Aspects of Developmental Disabilities, 6,* 1–10.

Prosser, H., Moss, S., Costello, H., Simpson, N., Patel, P., & Rowe, S. (1998). Reliability and validity of the Mini PAS-ADD for assessing psychiatric disorders in adults with intellectual disability. *Journal of Intellectual Disability Research, 42,* 264–272.

Prout, H. T., & Schaeffer, B. M. (1985). Self-reports of depression by community-based mildly mentally retarded adults. *American Journal of Mental Deficiency, 90,* 220–222.

Reiss, S. (1988). *The Reiss Screen for Maladaptive Behavior test manual.* Worthington, OH: IDS Publishing.

Reiss, S. (1990). Prevalence of dual diagnosis in community-based day programs in the Chicago metropolitan area. *American Journal on Mental Retardation, 94,* 578–585.

Reiss, S. (1993). Assessment of psychopathology in persons with mental retardation. In J. L. Matson & R. P. Barrett (Eds.), *Psychopathology in the mentally retarded* (2nd ed., pp. 17–39). Boston: Allyn and Bacon.

Reiss, S. (1997). Comments on the Reiss Screen for Maladaptive Behavior and its factor structure. *Journal of Intellectual Disability Research, 41,* 346–354.

Reiss, S., & Benson, B. A. (1985). Psychosocial correlates of depression in mentally retarded adults. I: Minimal social support and stigmatization. *American Journal of Mental Deficiency, 89,* 331–337.

Reiss, S., & Rojahn, J. (1993). Joint occurrence of depression and aggression in children and adults with mental retardation. *Journal of Intellectual Disability Research, 37,* 287–294.

Reiss, S., & Valenti-Hein, D. (1994). Development of a psychopathology rating scale for children with mental retardation. *Journal of Consulting and Clinical Psychology, 62,* 28–33.

Reynolds, W. M. (1987). *Reynolds Adolescent Depression Scale: Professional manual.* Odessa, FL: Psychological Assessment Resources.

Reynolds, W. M., & Baker, J. A. (1988). Assessment of depression in persons with mental retardation. *American Journal on Mental Retardation, 93,* 93–103.

Reynolds, W. M., & Miller, K. L. (1985). Depression and learned helplessness in mentally retarded and non-mentally retarded adolescents: An initial investigation. *Applied Research in Mental Retardation, 6,* 295–306.

Rojahn, J., Warren, V. J., & Ohringer, S. (1994). A comparison of assessment methods for depression in mental retardation. *Journal of Autism and Developmental Disorders, 24,* 305–313.

Ross, E., & Oliver, C. (2003a). The assessment of mood in adults who have severe or profound mental retardation. *Clinical Psychology Review, 23,* 225–245.

Ross, E., & Oliver, C. (2003b). Preliminary analysis of the psychometric properties of the Mood, Interest and Pleasure Questionnaire (MIPQ) for adults with severe and profound learning disabilities. *British Journal of Clinical Psychology, 42,* 81–93.

Royal College of Psychiatrists (2001). *DC-LD: Diagnostic Criteria for Psychiatric Disorders for Use With Adults with Learning Disabilities/Mental Retardation* (Occasional Paper OP48). London: Gaskell.

Ruedrich, S. L. (1993). Bipolar mood disorders in persons with mental retardation: Assessment and diagnosis. In R. J. Fletcher & A. Dosen (Eds.), *Mental health aspects of mental retardation* (pp. 111–129). New York: Lexington.

Senatore, V., Matson, J. L., & Kazdin, A. E. (1985). An inventory to assess psychopathology of mentally retarded adults. *American Journal of Mental Deficiency, 89,* 459–466.

Sevin, J. A., Matson, J. L., Williams, D., & Kirkpatrick-Sanchez, S. (1995). Reliability of emotional problems with the Diagnostic Assessment for the Severely Handicapped (DASH). *British Journal of Clinical Psychology, 34,* 93–94.

Smiley, E., & Cooper, S. (2003). Intellectual disabilities, depressive episode, diagnostic criteria and Diagnostic Criteria for Psychiatric Disorders for Use with Adults with Learning Disabilties/Mental Retardation (DC-LD). *Journal of Intellectual Disability Research, 47* (Suppl. 1), 62–71.

Sovner, R., & Hurley, A. D. (1983). Do the mentally retarded suffer from affective illness? *Archives of General Psychiatry, 40,* 61–67.

Sovner, R., & Pary, R. (1993). Affective disorders in developmentally disabled persons. In J. L. Maton & R. P. Barrett (Eds.), *Psychopathology in the mentally retarded* (2nd ed., pp. 87–147). Needham Heights, MA: Allyn and Bacon.

Sturmey, P., & Bertman, L. J. (1994). Validity of the Reiss Screen for Maladaptive Behavior. *American Journal on Mental Retardation, 99,* 201–206.

Sturmey, P., Burcham, K. J., & Perkins, T. S. (1995). The Reiss Screen for Maladaptive Behavior: Its reliability and internal consistencies. *Journal of Intellectual Disability Research, 39,* 191–195.

Sturmey, P., Jamieson, J., Burcham, J., Shaw, B., & Bertman, L. (1996). The factor structure of the Reiss Screen for Maladaptive Behaviors in institutional and community populations. *Research in Developmental Disabilities, 17,* 285–291.

Sturmey, P., & Ley, T. (1990). The Psychopathology Instrument for Mentally Retarded Adults: Internal consistencies and relationship to behaviour problems. *British Journal of Psychiatry, 156,* 428–430.

Sturmey, P., Reed, J., & Corbett, J. (1991). Psychometric assessment of psychiatric disorders in people with learning difficulties (mental handicap): A review of measures. *Psychological Medicine, 21,* 143–155.

Tsiouris, J. A., Mann, R., Patti, P. J., & Sturmey, P. (2003). Challenging behaviours should not be considered as depressive equivalents in individuals with intellectual disability. *Journal of Intellectual Disability Research, 47,* 14–21.

Tymchuk, A. J. (1993). Symptoms of psychopathology in mothers with mental handicap. *Mental Handicap Research, 6,* 18–35.

van Minnen, A., Savelsberg, P. M., & Hoogduin, K. A. L. (1994). A Dutch version of the Psychopathology Inventory for Mentally Retarded Adults (PIMRA). *Research in Developmental Disabilities, 15,* 269–278.

van Minnen, A., Savelsberg, P.M., & Hoogduin, K. A. L. (1995). A Dutch version of the Reiss Screen of Maladaptive Behavior. *Research in Developmental Disabilities, 16,* 43–49.

Walsh, K. K., & Shenouda, N. (1999). Correlations among the Reiss Screen, the Adaptive Behavior Scale Part II, and the Aberrant Behavior Checklist. *American Journal on Mental Retardation, 104,* 236–248.

Watson, J. E., Aman, M. G., & Singh, N. N. (1988). The Psychopathology Instrument for Mentally Retarded Adults: Psychometric characteristics, factor structure, and relationship to subject characteristics. *Research in Developmental Disabilities, 9,* 277–290.

World Health Organization (WHO). (1992). *International Statistical Classification of Diseases and Health Related Problems (ICD-10), Volume 1: Classification of mental and behavioural disorders: Clinical description and diagnostic guidelines.* Geneva: Author.

Zung, W. W. K. (1965). A self-rating depression scale. *Archives of General Psychiatry, 12,* 63–70.

Part III

Treatment Issues

10

PSYCHOTROPIC MEDICATIONS FOR MOOD DISORDERS IN PEOPLE WITH MENTAL RETARDATION

Kimberly A. Stigler,

David J. Posey,

and

Christopher J. McDougle

This chapter reviews the major classes of antidepressant medications as well as their mechanisms of action and their possible adverse effects. In addition, the mood stabilizers, a category of drugs that help to diminish mood swings over time in patients with bipolar disorder, are reviewed. Mechanisms of action and adverse effects are also described for each of these drugs. Several available instruments utilized in measuring medication tolerability in individuals with mental retardation are discussed. The chapter concludes with a review of the literature on the pharmacotherapy of depression and bipolar disorder in people with mental retardation.

Prevalence

In individuals with mental retardation, the prevalence of comorbid mental illness is estimated to be three to four times higher in comparison with the general population (American Psychiatric Association, 2000). Indeed, it has been suggested that mood disorders are more frequent in people with mental retardation and that depressed mood is one of the most common psychiatric symptoms in mentally retarded adults (Corbett, 1979; Nezu, Nezu, Rothenberg, DelliCarpini, & Groag, 1995). (See Chapter 3 for an alternate perspective on this question). Despite the increased occurrence of mood disorders, little is known regarding the prevalence of use of antidepressants and mood stabilizers in this population. A statewide analysis found that antidepressants were prescribed for 5.9% of individuals with mental retardation (Spreat, Conroy, & Jones, 1997). More recently, two statewide surveys of families who are members of autism societies in North Carolina and Ohio revealed that 21.7% and 21.6%, respectively, of individuals received antidepressant medication (Aman, Lam, & Collier-Crespin, 2003; Langworthy-Lam, Aman, & Van Bourgondien, 2002).

Antidepressants

Nonpharmacological approaches have been found beneficial in the treatment of depression in individuals with mental retardation (Lindsay, Howells, & Pitcaithly, 1993; Matson, 1982; Nezu & Nezu, 1994). (See Chapter 12, by Lindsay, Stenfert Kroese, and Drew, for a review of cognitive therapies). However, treatment with antidepressant medication is also often necessary. Early theories regarding the etiology of depression hypothesized that the disorder was due to a deficiency of serotonin and norepinephrine. These two monoamine neurotransmitters were theorized to interact with a variety of receptors in the brain to regulate mood, appetite, arousal, and vigilance. Although antidepressants are known to swiftly increase monoamine neurotransmitter activity (serotonin, norepinephrine, and dopamine), several weeks of treatment are required for full effect. Thus, the therapeutic action of antidepressants is thought to result from adaptive responses within neurons over time.

Monoamine Oxidase Inhibitors (MAOIs)

Monoamine oxidase inhibitors (MAOIs) are antidepressants that inhibit the enzyme monoamine oxidase (MAO), an intracellular enzyme that metabolizes biogenic amines, such as serotonin and norepinephrine. In addition its presence in presynaptic nerve terminals, MAO can be found in the liver and gut, where it serves the important function of metabolizing amines that are consumed in foods. When MAOIs are taken, the drug not only acts to inhibit MAO at the nerve terminals, but also at the liver and gut. Thus, vasoactive (affecting the caliber of blood vessels) amines, such as tyramine, that are found in foods, are not broken down safely. They can enter the bloodstream, where they may be taken up by sympathetic nerve terminals and cause a hypertensive crisis (Rabkin, Quitkin, Harrison, Tricamo, & McGrath, 1984; Rabkin, Quitkin, McGrath, Harrison, & Tricamo, 1985; Shulman, Walter, MacKenzie, & Knowles, 1989). This hypertensive crisis includes such symptoms as a significant increase of blood pressure, rapid heart rate, irregular heart rhythm, and severe headache. It may be life-threatening. The inhibition of MAO through use of MAOI antidepressants can consequently become very problematic, particularly in individuals with mental retardation, in whom it may be difficult to carefully monitor food intake. Thus, this class of antidepressants is generally not recommended in this population.

Tricyclic Antidepressants

Tricyclic and related cyclic antidepressants inhibit the uptake of norepinephrine and serotonin to different extents. This class of drugs is swiftly absorbed from the gut, with a high percentage metabolized by the liver ("first-pass" effect) before reaching the systemic circulation. Tricyclics are usually administered once daily, with the dosage gradually increased over time to target symptoms of depression. Blood levels are generally obtained 5 days after a change in dosage. Among the available drugs within this class, a therapeutic window has been identified for nortriptyline (50–150 ng/mL), and levels may be helpful in judging response for imipramine, desipramine, and amitriptyline. Blood levels may also be helpful for identifying slow and fast metabolizers. A

Table 10.1. Cyclic antidepressants.

Generic Name	Trade Name	Adult Dosage Range
Amitriptyline	Elavil®	100–300 mg/day
Amoxapine	Asendin®	100–400 mg/day
Clomipramine	Anafranil®	100–250 mg/day
Desipramine	Norpramin®	100–300 mg/day
Doxepin	Sinequan®	100–300 mg/day
Imipramine	Tofranil®	100–300 mg/day
Maprotiline	Ludiomil®	100–225 mg/day
Nortriptyline	Pamelor®	50–150 mg/day
Protriptyline	Vivactil®	20–60 mg/day
Trimipramine	Surmontil®	100–300 mg/day

list of common tricyclic antidepressants, their generic and trade names, and their adult dose ranges may be found in Table 10.1.

Because of the propensity of tricyclic antidepressants to affect the conduction of nervous impulses in the heart, it is important to obtain a thorough history and physical examination prior to prescribing the medication (Roose & Glassman, 1989). Because patients with mental retardation may not be able to provide an adequate or reliable history, it is highly recommended that caregivers provide a supplemental history as well. Individuals should also undergo an electrocardiogram (ECG) prior to treatment to screen for cardiovascular conduction abnormalities.

In addition to the potential cardiovascular toxicity, an array of other adverse effects associated with the tricyclics limits their use in individuals with mental retardation (Janicak, Davis, Preskorn, & Ayd, 1997a). Of particular concern is the propensity of this class of drugs to lower the seizure threshold. In addition, tricyclic antidepressants have been associated with orthostatic hypotension (severe decrease in blood pressure upon standing), thus increasing the risk for falling. Anticholinergic effects, commonly observed with use of these drugs, may include dry mouth, constipation, blurred vision, and urinary retention. Other worrisome adverse effects include weight gain, rapid heart rate, confusion, delirium, and agitation. Finally, this class of drugs can be fatal if taken in overdose, which is a significant risk for people who are depressed and suicidal.

Overall, although the tricyclic antidepressants can be helpful in targeting symptoms of depression, their use in individuals who are mentally retarded is complicated by a possible inability of the person to communicate adverse effects. In addition, as with any drug, but particularly with the tricyclics, access to these compounds would need to be carefully monitored to avoid the risk of overdose or accidental ingestion.

Selective Serotonin Reuptake Inhibitors (SSRIs)

The primary mechanism of action of the selective serotonin reuptake inhibitors (SSRIs) is to selectively inhibit the uptake of serotonin at presynaptic nerve terminals. In addition to their efficacy in the treatment of depression, this class of medication is better tolerated overall, in comparison with the tricyclics and MAOIs. Several SSRIs are currently marketed for the treatment of depression. A list of commonly used SSRIs, their generic and trade names, and their adult daily doses may be found in Table 10.2.

Adverse effects commonly observed with the SSRIs include increased anxiety and behavioral activation (for example, agitation), gastrointestinal upset (nausea, vomiting,

Table 10.2. Selective serotonin reuptake inhibitors and other antidepressants.

Generic Name	Trade Name	Adult Dosage Range
Bupropion	Wellbutrin®	200–450 mg/day
Citalopram	Celexa®	20–60 mg/day
Escitalopram	Lexapro®	10–20 mg/day
Fluoxetine	Prozac®	20–80 mg/day
Fluvoxamine	Luvox®	50–300 mg/day
Mirtazapine	Remeron®	15–45 mg/day
Paroxetine	Paxil®	20–50 mg/day
Sertraline	Zoloft®	50–200 mg/day
Venlafaxine	Effexor®	75–375 mg/day

diarrhea), headache, and sedation (Lowry, 1998). The risk of activation is of potential concern, particularly in individuals with mental retardation who may be unable to communicate their distress verbally, and exhibit increased aggression or self-injury. Antidepressants may also precipitate mania (Santosh & Baird, 1999). No specific medical or laboratory testing is required with the SSRIs.

Other Antidepressants

Bupropion.

Bupropion is an antidepressant drug that inhibits dopamine uptake at the nerve terminal. The drug's unique mechanism of action may target symptoms of hyperactivity and inattention, as well as mood. Adverse effects commonly observed with bupropion include agitation, nausea, tremor, and anxiety. Of note, a report of bupropion in individuals without mental retardation found the drug to be associated with an increased risk for seizures of 0.4% (Rosenstein, Nelson, & Jacobs, 1993). It should not be given to individuals with a known seizure disorder. Furthermore, it is recommended that single and total daily doses of the drug not exceed 150 mg and 450 mg, respectively.

Venlafaxine.

Venlafaxine inhibits serotonin, norepinephrine uptake, and, to a lesser extent, dopamine uptake. Adverse effects include anxiety, sweating, insomnia, sedation, and nausea. In addition, higher doses of venlafaxine have been associated with an increase in diastolic blood pressure. Thus, it is important to obtain a baseline blood pressure and continue to monitor this carefully during treatment (Janicak et al., 1997a).

Mirtazapine.

Mirtazapine increases levels of norepinephrine and serotonin through a unique mechanism of action (blockade at alpha$_2$–adrenergic and serotonin receptors). Increased appetite, weight gain, and sedation are among the more common adverse effects. Orthostatic hypotension has also been associated with the drug. Rarely, severe neutropenia (decrease in a type of white blood cell that fights infection) has developed in individuals receiving the drug (Janicak et al., 1997a).

Mood Stabilizers

Mood stabilizers, including lithium, carbamazepine, and valproic acid, are medications commonly used in the treatment of depression in the general population (Poindexter et al., 1998). A list of commonly used mood-stabilizing medications, their generic and trade names, and their adult dosage ranges are listed in Table 10.3.

Lithium

Lithium is an alkali metal whose mechanism of action is uncertain. The compound

Table 10.3. Selected mood stabilizers.

Generic Name	Trade Name	Adult Dosage Range
Carbamazepine	Tegretol®	400–1600 mg/day
Lamotrigine	Lamictal®	100–200 mg/day
Lithium	Eskalith®, Lithobid®	900–1800 mg/day
Topiramate	Topamax®	100–400 mg/day
Valproic acid	Depakote®	750–1500 mg/day

appears to have acute and chronic effects on serotonin and norepinephrine, as well as on transmembrane ion pumps. Long-term, the drug alters the coupling of several neurotransmitter receptors to signal-transducing G proteins (Berridge, Downes, & Hanley, 1989; Manji & Lenox, 1998).

Prior to initiating treatment with lithium, a medical workup must be completed. In addition to a history and physical examination, the workup should include ECG with rhythm strip, renal function tests (blood urea nitrogen [BUN], creatinine), thyroid function panel, complete blood count (CBC), and pregnancy test in females of childbearing potential. It is important that the patients and their caregivers ensure that sodium and caloric intake is not altered, and that diuretics and nonsteroidal anti-inflammatory drugs not be given without monitoring by a physician.

Lithium therapy can be associated with a variety of adverse effects. Indeed, such effects may occur in up to 75% of individuals treated with the drug, including those with comorbid mental retardation (Pary, 1991a). Among the potential adverse effects, those most commonly observed include weight gain, tremor, increased urination (polyuria), and increased thirst. More specific adverse effects may be divided into renal, cardiovascular, neurologic, endocrine, gastrointestinal, and dermatologic.

Regarding renal adverse effects, polyuria may occur in roughly 20% of individuals treated with lithium (Poindexter et al., 1998). Of concern, the polyuria can become extreme and interfere with lithium blood levels. It is important to ensure that fluid intake remain consistent. More severe renal impairment (for example, interstitial nephritis, nephrotic syndrome), has also been associated with lithium (Wood, Parmelee, & Foreman, 1989). Measures of renal function, including BUN and creatinine, should be obtained every 6 months during the maintenance phase of treatment.

Irregular heart rhythms (arrhythmia) and heart failure have been reported with lithium use, particularly in individuals with preexisting cardiovascular disease. Furthermore, the drug depresses the pacemaker activity of the sinus node in the heart. Thus, it should not be prescribed to people with a sinoatrial node dysfunction ("sick sinus" syndrome) (Mitchell & MacKenzie, 1982).

Lithium treatment may affect cognition, resulting in slowed memory and reaction times. Whereas a postural tremor can occur more frequently, other neurological effects that are considered less common are often associated with lithium toxicity. These include dysarthria (difficulty in articulation), ataxia (lack of coordination), delirium (an acute condition distinguished by impaired consciousness and cognition), and increased risk of seizures (Janicak, Davis, Preskorn, & Ayd, 1997c).

Hypothyroidism is also associated with lithium, with approximately 5% of patients developing this condition with long-term treatment (Jefferson, 1979). Due to this adverse effect, a thyroid function panel is recommended at baseline and every 6 months during treatment. Regarding gastrointestinal effects, nausea and diarrhea may occur with lithium use (Janicak et al., 1997c). Although these adverse effects are typically transient and emerge at the beginning of treatment, they can also be a sign of lithium toxicity. Lithium has also been associated with dermatologic adverse effects. Such effects may include acne or psoriasis (red, dry scaling patches). Rarely, exfoliative dermatitis (a widespread eruption of the skin), which can be life-threatening, may occur.

During titration and maintenance phases of lithium treatment, it is important to obtain blood levels. Levels in the range of 0.5–1.0 mEq/L have been recommended for people with mental retardation and bipolar disorder (Pary, 1991b). It is also important to monitor levels in an effort to prevent lithium toxicity, which may occur at levels higher than 1.5 mEq/L (Janicak et al., 1997c). After a maintenance dosage has been achieved, blood levels should be obtained every 3–6 months during treatment. Signs of lithium toxicity include dysarthria, ataxia, nausea, diarrhea, coarse tremor, confusion, delirium, seizures, coma, or death.

Carbamazepine

Carbamazepine is an anticonvulsant medication that inhibits the rapid firing of neurons through blockage of voltage-sensitive sodium channels (Alvarez et al., 1998). This subsequently inhibits voltage-gated calcium channels, thus diminishing neurotransmitter release. The relationship of this mechanism of action to its mood-stabilizing effects is uncertain.

Carbamazepine has been associated with the emergence of such worrisome, albeit rare, adverse effects as aplastic anemia (where the bone marrow fails to adequately produce blood cells) and agranulocytosis (decreased white blood cells [neutrophils] that results in increased vulnerability to infection), hepatitis, and exfoliative dermatitis (Janicak et al., 1997c; Joffe, Post, Roy-Byrne, & Uhde, 1985). Thus, it is particularly important that the patient and caregiver provide a thorough history regarding blood and liver abnormalities prior to initiating this medication. In addition, baseline and ongoing follow-up tests should include a CBC with platelets, liver and renal function tests, and a pregnancy test, if indicated. A blood carbamazepine level should also be obtained during treatment (target range, 4–12 mcg/mL).

Adverse effects that are considered more common are sedation, dizziness, ataxia, nausea, a mild decrease in the white blood cell count, and double vision. The drug has also been found to slow cardiac conduction. Cognitive effects, such as memory impairment, are typically mild and dose-related. Low blood levels of sodium (hyponatremia) have also been reported secondary to the drug's antidiuretic property (Janicak et al., 1997c).

Valproic Acid

This medication is known to increase levels of the inhibitory neurotransmitter gamma-aminobutyric acid (GABA) in the brain. Prior to initiating treatment with valproic acid, a history and physical examination, as well as a baseline liver function test, CBC with platelets, and pregnancy test, if indicated, is recommended. It is also important to monitor liver function, blood counts, and blood drug levels (target range, 50–100 mcg/mL) during treatment. The drug is generally well tolerated, with more common adverse effects including nausea, vomiting, diarrhea, sedation, tremor, hair loss, mild elevation of liver function tests, and weight gain. A low platelet count can also occur during treatment. In addition, an increased rate of polycystic ovarian disease (decrease or absence of ovulation, resulting in menstrual cycle abnormalities) has been reported in women with epilepsy treated with valproic acid prior to 20 years of age (Isojarvi, Laatikainen, Pakarinen, Juntunen, & Myllyla, 1993).

An adverse effect of concern that is associated with the use of valproic acid includes fatal hepatotoxicity (severe liver damage). However, the majority of individuals in whom this has occurred were under the age of 2 years (Dreifuss et al., 1987; Janicak et al., 1997c). Rarely, a life-threatening hemorrhagic pancreatitis (inflammation of the pancreas) may emerge, more commonly during the first 6 months of treatment.

Lamotrigine

Lamotrigine is an anticonvulsant drug that inhibits the release of glutamate, an excitatory amino acid in the brain. Although the medication is thought to be more effective for treating the depressive phase of bipolar disorder, research is needed to understand its efficacy and tolerability in individuals with mental retardation. The drug is usually well tolerated; however, a life-threatening rash, known as Stevens-Johnson syndrome, may occur, often early in treatment. This may necessitate a slow and cautious dosage increase. More commonly observed adverse effects include sedation, headaches, double vision, dizziness, ataxia, nausea, and vomiting.

Topiramate

The mechanism of action of the anticonvulsant drug topiramate results in an increase in the inhibitory neurotransmitter, GABA, and a decrease in the excitatory neurotransmitter, glutamate. Topiramate has been associated with weight loss (Shorvon & Stefan, 1997). Of concern in a population with mental retardation, the medication has also been associated with cognitive dulling (for example, word-finding difficulty, poor concentration, confusion). Sedation, dizziness, anxiety, and ataxia are among more common adverse effects. There is an increased risk of kidney stones with this drug.

Measurement of Response to Treatment

It is essential that the efficacy of antidepressants and mood stabilizers for individuals with mood disorders and mental retardation is evaluated objectively. Evaluations based on general descriptions from family members and care staff are often inadequate by themselves. Although some individuals with mild to moderate mental retardation can be adequate informants, most people with severe or profound mental retardation cannot be adequate, because of limited or absent language skills. (See Chapter 9, by Finlay, for a review of the measures, some of which may be useful for measuring the response to psychotropic medications). Direct observational measures of behavior should also be considered.

Monitoring Adverse Effects

The use of psychotropic medications necessitates routinely monitoring for the emergence of adverse effects. Adverse effects can be difficult to detect, however, in a population with limited cognitive and language abilities. A systematic approach to the assessment of adverse effects has been recommended and includes careful baseline and follow-up observations, physical assessments, and laboratory screenings (Wilson, Lott, & Tsai, 1998; Zametkin & Yamada, 1993). Educating the patient and caregivers about potential adverse effects is also highly recommended.

In addition to the foregoing, rating scales can be useful in the assessment of adverse effects, particularly in patients with mental retardation who are unable to adequately communicate this information (Zametkin & Yamada, 1993). To date, there remains a need for well-designed rating scales tailored to antidepressant and mood stabilizers for this purpose. There are rating scales, however, that may be used to assess a wide range of adverse effects (Matson et al., 1998; Wilson et al., 1998), including the Dosage Record and Treatment Emergent Symptom Scale (DOTES), Monitoring of Side Effects Scales (MOSES), and the Adverse Drug Reaction Detection Scale (ADRDS) (Corso, Pucino, DeLeo, Calis, & Gallelli, 1992; Guy, 1976; Kalachnik, 1988). In addition, the Matson Evaluation of Drugs Side-effects Scale (MEDS), designed specifically for use with people with mental retardation, has been shown to be reliable and should be considered (Matson et al., 1998).

The Efficacy of Psychotropic Medications for Mood Disorders

The efficacy of antidepressants for major depression in the general population is supported by numerous well-controlled studies (Janciak, Davis, Preskorn, & Ayd, 1997b). In addition, data from randomized, controlled clinical trials of mood stabilizers, such as lithium, valproate, and carbamazepine, support their use as mood-stabilizing agents in people without mental retardation (Janciak et al., 1997c). In contrast to these studies, a dearth of research has been conducted on the pharmacotherapy of mood disorders in people with mental retardation. Thus, practitioners often extrapolate findings from research conducted with the general population. Of importance, mentally retarded individuals may exhibit developmental differences and structural brain abnormalities that could affect response to psychotropic medications. Research has shown, however, that similar neurotransmitter systems may mediate psychopathology in people with, and without, mental retardation (Matson & Sevin, 1994).

Antidepressants

A paucity of research has been conducted on the use of antidepressants in individuals with mental retardation. The majority of publications are case reports that involve subjects with a wide range of intellectual functioning, as well as various antidepressant medications, suggesting a need for well-designed, controlled research in this area.

Tricyclic Antidepressants.

A case report on the use of imipramine (100 mg/day) in a 25-year-old woman with moderate mental retardation and major depression found the drug beneficial (Ghaziuddin & Tsai, 1991). The authors reported a substantial improvement in crying spells, suicidal ideation, self-injury, and associated erotomania. Field, Aman, White, and Vaithianathan (1986) published a double-blind, placebo-controlled case report on the use of imipramine (100 mg) in a 22-year-old woman with moderate mental retardation and chronic major depression. A reversal design was employed, with dosages of imipramine administered in three 2- to 3-week periods, alternating with 2-week placebo periods. Treatment with the drug was found to result in consistent improvement in comparison to placebo. A double-blind, placebo-controlled study of imipramine (3 mg/kg/day) was conducted in five adults with depressive symptoms and profound mental retardation, and five adolescents and adults with disruptive behavior and profound mental retardation (Aman, White, Vaithianathan, & Teehan, 1986). Subjects received 4 weeks of imipramine and placebo, with a 1-week washout period. Whereas drug treatment resulted in behavioral activation in a subject with disruptive behavior, improvement was observed with imipramine in the depressed individuals, who became less active and disruptive.

Ruedrich and Wilkinson (1992) reported on the use of amoxapine, a tricyclic antidepressant with antipsychotic properties, in two patients. The first patient, a 28-year-old woman with mild mental retardation and chronic major depression, was treated with the drug at a dosage of 150 mg/day. The authors noted that symptoms of depression, including affect, concentration, self-injury, and somatic preoccupations, improved significantly with treatment. The second patient, a 35-year-old woman with severe mental retardation, autistic disorder, and chronic major depression, received amoxapine (300 mg/day). Over a duration of 8 months, improvement was noted in crying spells, insomnia, and self-injurious behavior.

SSRIs.

A case series on the use of fluoxetine (20–40 mg/day) reported on six patients with mental retardation [mild (3), moderate (2), severe (1)] and symptoms of depression over a duration of 5 to 20 weeks (Howland, 1992). Three patients were diagnosed with major depression and three with an atypical depression. Five of six patients improved significantly, whereas one patient with severe mental retardation showed a partial response to treatment.

Sovner and colleagues published a case report on fluoxetine in two patients with chronic major depression and mental retardation (Sovner, Fox, Lowry, & Lowry, 1993). The first case involved a woman diagnosed with severe mental retardation treated with fluoxetine (20 mg/day). The drug was found effective and resulted in remission of symptoms of depression over a treatment duration of 15 months. The second case described a man with profound mental retardation who received 20 mg/day of fluoxetine over a duration of 14 months. Symptoms of depression were reported to remit with treatment.

More recently, the effectiveness of citalopram was evaluated in 20 individuals with mental retardation and depressive symptoms (Verhoeven, Veendrik-Meekes, Jacobs, van den Berg, & Tuinier, 2001). The dosage was initiated at 20 mg/day and held constant for 6 weeks. The mean final dosage was 33 mg/day (range 20–60 mg/day). A moderate to marked improvement in depression was recorded in 12 (60%) of 20 patients.

Mood Stabilizers

Although investigators have reported on the use of mood stabilizers in individuals with mental retardation, their main focus has often been the treatment of symptoms of aggression, self-injury, and disruptive behavior (Luchins & Dojka, 1989; Smith & Perry, 1992). Few studies have been conducted on the use of this class of medication in patients with mental retardation and comorbid bipolar disorder.

Lithium.

Rivinus and Harmatz, (1979) published a case series on 5 patients with mental retardation and symptoms of bipolar disorder. Over a period of 3 years of treatment with lithium, symptoms of mood illness and the number of episodes of illness were diminished. An open-label study of lithium, or lithium and carbamazepine, in 10 patients with mental retardation and rapid cycling mood disorder found that 5 improved with treatment (Glue, 1989). In addition, 2 individuals who recovered from their illness were in the lithium-plus-carbamazepine group.

A double-blind investigation of lithium (blood level range, 0.6–1.0 mEq/L) was conducted in 14 subjects with mental retardation, 9 of whom also had bipolar disorder (Naylor, Donald, LePoidevin, & Reid, 1974). The long-term study documented the number of weeks ill on 1 year of lithium versus 1 year of placebo. As a whole, the authors found that individuals receiving lithium experienced a significantly fewer number of weeks of illness. When each person was considered individually, however, no significant differences were recorded in episode frequency.

Valproic Acid.

Sovner published a case report on the use of valproic acid in 5 individuals with mental retardation and bipolar disorder (Sovner, 1989). The author reported that 4 of the patients exhibited a marked improvement, whereas 1 patient had a moderate improvement. Blood levels of valproic acid were considered therapeutic, within the 50–100 mcg/mL range. The author suggested that the drug may have a role in the treatment of patients with mental retardation and comorbid "typical" and "atypical" bipolar disorders. A 2-year open-label study of valproic acid was conducted in 21 subjects with mental retardation as well as affective symptoms (Kastner, Finesmith, & Walsh, 1993). Overall, 14 (78%) of 18 completers were considered responders. However, 3 subjects were withdrawn from phenobarbital, which could have contributed to the improvement observed. One individual experienced acute hyperammonemia (increased ammonia level) during treatment with the drug.

Conclusion

A variety of antidepressants and mood stabilizers are currently available for the treatment of mood symptoms in individuals with mental retardation. As a whole, however, there is a lack of well-designed research demonstrating their effectiveness and tolerability in this population. Frequently, clinicians are left to refer to published studies conducted in people without mental retardation.

Regarding antidepressants, clinicians often begin treatment with an SSRI (Sovner et al., 1998). Other antidepressants, such as mirtazapine or venlafaxine, may also prove beneficial in the treatment of depression in this group. Alternatively, medications associated with more worrisome adverse effects, such as the tricyclic antidepressants, are typically utilized in treatment-refractory cases. In addition to the specific concerns associated with each class of drug, it is important to note that the antidepressants in general may precipitate mania in predisposed individuals (Santosh & Baird, 1999).

Among mood stabilizers, lithium and valproic acid are two drugs commonly utilized in the treatment of bipolar disorder in the general population. Their use, however, requires frequent blood samples and close monitoring for the emergence of adverse effects. Carbamazepine is a drug less commonly used because of concerns regarding adverse effects. It may be used more often in treatment-refractory situations. Although newer anticonvulsant drugs, such as lamotrigine and topiramate, may have a role in the treatment of bipolar disorder, research is needed to understand their use in this population.

Although antidepressants and mood stabilizers are commonly prescribed to individuals with mental retardation and comorbid mood disorders, data are insufficient to support their effectiveness and tolerability. Well-designed, controlled research will serve to build upon a limited knowledge base, thereby positively contributing to the treatment of mood disorders in persons with mental retardation.

References

Alvarez, N., Kern, R. A., Cain, N. N., Coulter, D. L., Iivanainen, P., & Plummer, A. T. (1998). Antiepileptics. In S. Reiss & M. G. Aman (Eds.), *Psychotropic medications and developmental disabilities: The international consensus handbook* (pp. 151–178). Columbus, OH: The Ohio State Nisonger Center.

Aman, M. G., Lam, K. S., & Collier-Crespin, A. (2003). Prevalence and patterns of use of psychoactive medicines among individuals with autism in the Autism Society of Ohio. *Journal of Autism and Developmental Disorders, 33*, 527–534.

Aman, M. G., White, A. J., Vaithianathan, C., & Teehan, D. J. (1986). Preliminary study of imipramine in profoundly retarded residents. *Journal of Autism and Developmental Disorders, 16*, 263–273.

American Psychiatric Association. (2000). *Diagnostic and statistical manual of mental disorders* (4th ed., rev.).Washington, DC: Author.

Berridge, M. J., Downes, C. P., & Hanley, M. R. (1989). Neural and developmental actions of lithium: A unifying hypothesis. *Cell, 59,* 411.

Corbett, J. A. (1979). Psychiatric morbidity and mental retardation. In P. Snaith & F. E. James (Eds.), *Psychiatric illness and mental handicap* (pp. 11–25). Ashford, CT: Headley.

Corso, D. M., Pucino, F., DeLeo, J. M., Calis, K. A., & Gallelli, J. F. (1992). Development of a questionnaire for detecting potential adverse drug reactions. *Annals of Pharmacotherapy, 26,* 890–896.

Dreifuss, F. E., Santilli, N., Langer, D. H., Sweeney, K. P., Moline, K. A., & Menander, K. B. (1987). Valproic acid hepatic fatalities: A retrospective review. *Neurology, 37,* 379–385.

Field, C. J., Aman, M. G., White, A. J., & Vaithianathan, C. (1986). A single-subject study of imipramine in a mentally retarded woman with depressive symptoms. *Journal of Mental Deficiency Research. 30,* 191–198.

Ghaziuddin, M., & Tsai, L. (1991). Depression-dependent erotomaniac delusions in a mentally handicapped woman. *British Journal of Psychiatry, 158,* 127–129.

Glue, P. (1989). Rapid cycling affective disorders in the mentally retarded. *Biological Psychiatry, 26,* 250–256.

Guy, W. (1976). Dosage record and treatment emergent symptom scale. In *ECDEU assessment manual for psychopharmacology (revised)* (DHEW Publication No. ADM 76-338, pp. 223–244). Washington, DC: U.S. Government Printing Office.

Howland, R. H. (1992). Fluoxetine treatment of depression in mentally retarded adults. *Journal of Nervous and Mental Disease, 180,* 202–205.

Isojarvi, J. I. T., Laatikainen, T. J., Pakarinen, A. J., Juntunen, K. T. S., & Myllyla, V. V. (1993). Polycystic ovaries and hyperandrogenism in women taking valproate for epilepsy. *New England Journal of Medicine, 329,* 1383–1388.

Janicak, P. G., Davis, J. M., Preskorn, S. H., & Ayd, F. J. (1997a). Treatment with antidepressants. In *Principles and practice of psychopharmacotherapy* (2nd ed., pp. 243–321). Philadelphia: Lippincott Williams & Wilkins.

Janicak, P. G., Davis, J. M., Preskorn, S. H., & Ayd, F. J. (1997b). Treatment with mood stabilizers. In *Principles and practice of psychopharmacotherapy* (2nd ed., pp. 403–470). Philadelphia: Lippincott Williams & Wilkins.

Janicak, P. G., Davis, J. M., Preskorn, S. H., & Ayd, F. J. (1997c). Treatment with mood stabilizers. In *Principles and practice of psychopharmacotherapy* (2nd ed., pp. 403–470). Philadelphia: Lippincott Williams & Wilkins.

Jefferson, J. W. (1979). Lithium carbonate-induced hypothyroidism. Its many faces. *Journal of the American Medical Association, 242,* 271–272.

Joffe, R. T., Post, R. M., Roy-Byrne, P. P., & Uhde, T. W. (1985). Hematological effects of carbamazepine in patients with affective illness. *American Journal of Psychiatry, 142,* 1196–1199.

Kalachnik, J. E. (1988). Medication monitoring procedures: Thou shall, here's how. In K. D. Gadow & A. G. Poling (Eds.), *Pharmacotherapy and mental retardation* (pp. 231–268). Boston: Little, Brown.

Kastner, T., Finesmith, R., & Walsh, K. (1993). Long-term administration of valproic acid in the treatment of affective symptoms in people with mental retardation. *Journal of Clinical Psychopharmacology, 13,* 448–451.

Langworthy-Lam, K. S., Aman, M. G., & Van Bourgondien, M. E. (2002). Prevalence and patterns of use of psychoactive medicines in individuals with autism in the Autism Society of North Carolina. *Journal of Child and Adolescent Psychopharmacology, 12,* 311–321.

Lindsay, W. R., Howells, L., & Pitcaithly, D. (1993). Cognitive therapy for depression with individuals with intellectual disabilities. *British Journal of Medical Psychology, 66,* 135–141.

Lowry, M. A. (1998). Assessment and treatment of mood disorders in persons with developmental disabilities. *Journal of Developmental and Physical Disabilities, 10,* 387–406.

Luchins, D. J., & Dojka, D. (1989). Lithium and propranolol in aggression and self-injurious behavior in the mentally retarded. *Psychopharmacology Bulletin, 25,* 372–375.

Manji, H. K., & Lenox, R. H. (1998). Lithium: A molecular transducer of mood-stabilization in the treatment of bipolar disorder. *Neuropsychopharmacology, 19,* 161.

Matson, J. L. (1982). The treatment of behavioral characteristics of depression in the mentally retarded. *Behavior Therapy, 13,* 209–218.

Matson, J. L., Mayville, E. A., Bielecki, J., Barnes, W. H., Bamburg, J. W., & Baglio, C. S. (1998). Reliability of the Matson Evaluation of Drug Side Effects Scale (MEDS). *Research on Developmental Disabilities, 19,* 501–506.

Matson, J. L., & Sevin J. A. (1994). Theories of dual diagnosis in mental retardation. *Journal of Consulting and Clinical Psychology, 62,* 6–16.

Mitchell, J. E., & Mackenzie, T. B. (1982). Cardiac effects of lithium therapy in man: A review. *Journal of Clinical Psychiatry, 43,* 47–51.

Naylor, G. J., Donald, J. M., LePoidevin, D., & Reid, A. H. (1974). A double-blind trial of long-term lithium therapy in mental defectives. *British Journal of Psychiatry, 124,* 52–57.

Nezu, C. M., & Nezu, A. M. (1994). Outpatient psychotherapy for adults with mental retardation and concomitant psychopathology: Research and clinical imperatives. *Journal of Consulting and Clinical Psychology, 62,* 34–42.

Nezu, C. M., Nezu, A. M., Rothenberg, J. L., DelliCarpini, L., & Groag, I. (1995). Depression in adults with mild mental retardation: Are cognitive variables involved? *Cognitive Therapy and Research, 19,* 227–239.

Pary, R. (1991a). Side effects during lithium treatment for psychiatric disorders in adults with mental retardation and mental illness. *American Journal on Mental Retardation, 96,* 269–273.

Pary, R. (1991b). Towards defining adequate lithium trials for individuals with mental retardation and mental illness. *American Journal on Mental Retardation, 95,* 681–691.

Poindexter, A. R., Cain, N., Clarke, D. J., Cook, E. H., Corbett, J. A., & Levitas, A. (1998). Mood stabilizers. In S. Reiss & M. G. Aman (Eds.), *Psychotropic medications and developmental disabilities: The international consensus handbook* (pp. 215–227). Columbus, OH: The Ohio State Nisonger Center.

Rabkin, J., Quitkin, F., Harrison, W., Tricamo, E., & McGrath, P. (1984). Adverse reactions to monoamine oxidase inhibitors. Part I: A comparative study. *Journal of Clinical Psychopharmacology, 4,* 270–278.

Rabkin, J., Quitkin, F., McGrath, P., Harrison, W., & Tricamo, E. (1985). Adverse reactions to monoamine oxidase inhibitors. Part II: Treatment correlates and clinical management. *Journal of Clinical Psychopharmacology, 5,* 2–9.

Rivinus, T. M., & Harmatz, J. S. (1979). Diagnosis and lithium treatment of affective disorder in the retarded: Five case studies. *American Journal of Psychiatry, 136(4B),* 551–554.

Roose, S. P., & Glassman, A. H. (1989). Cardiovascular effects of tricyclic antidepressants in depressed patients. *Journal of Clinical Psychiatry Monograph Series, 7,* 1–18.

Rosenstein, D. L., Nelson, C., & Jacobs, S. C. (1993). Seizures associated with antidepressants: A review. *Journal of Clinical Psychiatry, 54,* 289.

Ruedrich, S. L., & Wilkinson, L. (1992). Atypical unipolar depression in mentally retarded patients: Amoxapine treatment. *Journal of Nervous and Mental Disease, 180,* 206–207.

Santosh, P. J., & Baird, G. (1999). Psychopharmacotherapy in children and adults with intellectual disability. *The Lancet, 354,* 233–242.

Shorvon, S., & Stefan, H. (1997). Overview of the safety of newer antiepileptic drugs. *Epilepsia, 38S,* 45–51.

Shulman, K. I., Walter, S. E., MacKenzie, S., & Knowles, S. (1989). Dietary restriction, tyramine, and the use of monoamine oxidase inhibitors. *Journal of Clinical Psychopharmacology, 9,* 397.

Smith, D. A., & Perry, P. J. (1992). Nonneuroleptic treatment of disruptive behavior in organic mental syndromes. *Annals of Pharmacotherapy, 26,* 1400–1408.

Sovner, R. (1989). The use of valproate in the treatment of mentally retarded persons with typical and atypical bipolar disorders. *Journal of Clinical Psychiatry, 50S,* 40–43.

Sovner, R., Fox, C. J., Lowry, M. J., & Lowry, M. A. (1993). Fluoxetine treatment of depression and associated self-injury in two adults with mental retardation. *Journal of Intellectual Disability Research, 37,* 301–311.

Sovner, R., Pary, R. J., Dosen, A., Gedye, A., Barrera, F. J., Cantwell, D. P., et al. (1998). Antidepressant drugs. In S. Reiss, & M. G. Aman (Eds.), *Psychotropic medications and developmental disabilities: The international consensus handbook* (pp. 85–94). Columbus, OH: The Ohio State Nisonger Center.

Spreat, S., Conroy, J. W., & Jones, J. C. (1997). Use of psychotropic medication in Oklahoma: A statewide survey. *American Journal of Mental Retardation, 102,* 80–85.

Verhoeven, W. M. A., Veendrik-Meekes, M. J., Jacobs, G. A. J., van den Berg, Y. W. M. M., & Tuinier, S. (2001). Citalopram in mentally retarded patients with depression: A long-term clinical investigation. *European Psychiatry, 16,* 104–108.

Wilson J., Lott, R. S., & Tsai, L. (1998). Side effects: Recognition and management. In S. Reiss & M. G. Aman (Eds.), *Psychotropic medications and developmental disabilities: The international consensus handbook* (pp. 85–94). Columbus, OH: The Ohio State Nisonger Center.

Wood, I. K., Parmelee, D. X., & Foreman, J. W. (1989). Lithium-induced nephrotic syndrome. *American Journal of Psychiatry, 146,* 84–87.

Zametkin, A. J., & Yamada, E. M. (1993). Monitoring and measuring drug effects. In J. S. Werry & M. G. Aman (Eds.), *Practitioner's guide to psychoactive drugs for children and adolescents* (pp. 86–91). New York: Plenum Press.

Acknowledgments

This work was supported in part by a Daniel X. Freedman Psychiatric Research Fellowship Award (Dr. Posey), a National Alliance for Research in Schizophrenia and Depression (NARSAD) Young Investigator Award (Dr. Posey), a Research Units on Pediatric Psychopharmacology Grant (U10-MH66766-02) from the National Institute of Mental Health (NIMH) to Indiana University (Drs. McDougle, Stigler, and Posey), a Research Career Development Award (K23-MH068627-01) from NIMH (Dr. Posey), a National Institutes of Health Clinical Research Center Grant to Indiana University (M01-RR00750), and a Department of Housing and Urban Development (HUD) Grant No. B-01-SP-IN-0200 (Dr. McDougle).

11

Other Biological Treatments

Peter Sturmey

and

Mohammad Ghaziuddin

The previous chapter reviewed the most conventional biological treatments for mood disorders: psychotropic medication. However, there are a number of other biological treatments that are used less commonly, but nevertheless deserve consideration because they are used in practice, sometimes quite commonly. This chapter reviews three kinds of biological treatments for mood disorders: phototherapy, dietary modifications and herbal supplements, and electroconvulsive therapy (ECT).

Phototherapy

There has been interest in the use of light therapy, or *phototherapy*, to treat depression, especially in people whose mood disorder seems to worsen in the winter and to improve in the spring and summer. This condition is often referred to as seasonal affective disorder. The DSM-IV diagnostic criteria for mood disorders allows a specifier to be added to several mood disorders, including both major depressive disorder, dysthymia, and bipolar disorders, indicating "seasonal pattern" (American Psychiatric Association, 1994). The specifier can be added if the following criteria are met: (a) There is a regular relationship between the onset of a mood disorder and fall or winter; (b) there is full remission during spring or summer; (c) major depressive episodes have not occurred during the summer for the past 2 years; and, (d) there are more episodes of depression related to the winter than to the summer.

It seems intuitively possible that the lack of light might cause the worsening of depression and that the provision of the missing light might in some way remedy the seasonal mood disorder. Based on the hypothesis that the absence of light is a key factor in mood disorders with a seasonal pattern, light therapy has been used for the treatment of these disorders. The treatment involves exposure to light in a so-called "light box." A variety of schedules of intensity and wavelengths of light have been investigated. There is some evidence from well-controlled, double-blind trials in the general population that light therapy can be effective in the treatment of depression (e.g., Kennedy, Lam, Cohen, Ravindran, & CANMAT Depression Work Group, 2001).

Phototherapy and Mental Retardation

Anecdotal reports suggest that some patients with mental retardation also show an increase of mood and behavior problems during the winter months. Indeed, there are some limited data on this issue. Lindblom, Heiskala, Kaski, Leinonen, and Laakso (2002) conducted a study of the sleep patterns of 293 people with mental retardation from late winter to early summer in a setting at 60 degrees north latitude. They found some evidence of changes in sleep patterns over the change of the seasons. They divided the time studied into five periods. They found that there were more wake-sleep transitions during the winter and fewer during the summer. They concluded that the sleep patterns were affected by seasonal change, and they recommended that there should be increased exposure to light during the winter.

The literature on light therapy with people with mental retardation is very limited; indeed, only two, uncontrolled, studies were located. Guilleminault, McCann, Quera-Salva and Cetel (1993) reported on the effectiveness of phototherapy in a series of 14 children with moderate to severe mental retardation and sleep disturbance. Following treatment with phototherapy, 5 of the 14 children were said to have achieved normal sleep patterns, which were maintained at 2-to-5-years follow-up. Two families could not follow the treatment regime, and 7 children did not respond. Thus, approximately one third of the chidlren responded to phototherapy. This study may only be tangentially related to the present concern, because mood disorders were not the focus of the study. This study suggests that sleep disturbance, one aspect of mood disturbance, might respond to phototherapy in a minority of cases. It is unclear if these results are generalizable to people with mental retardation and mood disorders.

Cooke and Thompson (1998) described two patients with mental retardation diagnosed with seasonal affective disorder. Both were treated successfully with light therapy using bright artificial light. The authors concluded that patients with mental retardation who show recurrent mood and behavior changes should be assessed for seasonal affective disorder and treated with bright artificial light. They underscored the need for careful monitoring of behavioral changes, especially in those with poor verbal skills, in order to establish a correct diagnosis. This study was quite limited. It included only two subjects, and it is unclear how the diagnoses were reached.

At this time there is only very limited evidence of the efficacy of phototherapy in people with mental retardation. In order to use phototherapy rationally, the clinician must reliably differentiate in a diagnosis a mood disorder with a seasonal pattern from one that does not have a seasonal pattern, or there needs to be evidence that phototherapy is also effective in nonseasonal disorders. At this time there is very limited evidence that phototherapy is effective, and the side effects of phototherapy are currently unknown. Its use is therefore not recommended as a treatment for depression in people with mental retardation.

Dietary Supplements

Various dietary and mineral supplements and modified diets have a long history in the field of mental retardation and other developmental disabilities. Their use has been recommended for boosting intelligence and modifying behavior, including maladaptive behaviors and psychiatric disorders. However, the history of the effectiveness of dietary interventions is generally a checkered one. (One exception is the modified low-protein diet for phenylketonuria to prevent the development of mental retardation, which is very well supported). Reviews have repeatedly pointed out the lack of well-controlled trials to establish the efficacy of dietary interventions and mineral supplements, despite decades of research in this area (e.g., Ellis, Singh, & Ruane, 1999). Indeed, many might consider dietary interventions as a prime example of a treatment modality that is especially susceptible to treatment fashions and fads, despite the general absence of evidence of effectiveness, or despite evidence indicating the ineffectiveness of such interventions (cf. Jacobson, Mulick, & Foxx, 2005).

There is an absence of evidence of the effectiveness of dietary modifications and mineral supplements. Indeed, there is even the possibility that they may have a variety of harmful effects, such as unknown medical effects and interference with effective programming. For example, dietary modification may restrict access to effective reinforcers and thereby undermine effective behavioral programming. Nevertheless, dietary interventions are used quite frequently. Three recent large-scale surveys of children and adults with autism spectrum disorders illustrate this. Langworthy-Lam, Aman, and Van Bourgondien (2002) surveyed over 3,000 members of a state autism society and just over 1,500 responded. Among those who responded, nearly 6% reported taking a variety of dietary supplements. Aman, Lam and Collier-Crespin (2003) conducted a similar survey of another state autism society and found that 1 in 10 took various over-the-counter preparations, such as Saint-John's-wort and melatonin. Smith and Antolovich (2000) conducted a survey of parents of children with pervasive developmental disabilities receiving early intensive behavioral intervention and found that just over half had tried a gluten- and casein-free diet.

These studies show that the use of various dietary supplements, including those related to mood disorders and sleep disorders, are used quite widely. At this time, we do not have good documentation of the use of dietary and other unconventional treatments in adults with mental retardation and mood disorders.

Saint-Johns-Wort

One of the most popular dietary interventions for mood disorders is Saint-John's-wort (*Hypericum perforatum*), a plant extract used for treatment of depression. It is commercially available and commonly used.

There is extensive evidence from multiple well-conducted double-blind trials supporting the effectiveness of St John's wort for depression. Whisky, Werneke, and Taylor (2001) conducted a systematic review and meta-analysis of the literature on the treatment of depression. They identified 22 randomized controlled trials, including several double-blind trials comparing Saint-John's-wort with conventional antidepressants. They found that Saint-John's-wort, like conventional antidepressants, was superior to placebo. In comparisons of Saint-John's-wort with conventional antidepressants, both appeared to be equally effective, but there were more negative side effects reported with conventional antidepressants. This review indicated that Saint-John's-wort is a plausible treatment for depression with a good evidence base.

It is tempting to imagine that such natural products as Saint-John's-wort are necessarily safe because they are natural. Saint-John's-wort has been associated with a variety of negative side effects, however, including serotonin syndrome, resulting in such symptoms as convulsions. Further, here is some evidence that Saint-John's-wort interacts with a variety of other conventional medications, including antibiotics. It may also act additively with other antidepressants, giving rise to potentially dangerous levels of serotonin (Izzo & Ernst, 2001).

Saint-John's-Wort and Mental Retardation

Although there is some indirect evidence from the survey of Aman and colleagues (Aman et al., 2003) of the use of Saint-John's-wort in people with autism, we were unable to find any published literature on Saint-John's-wort and mental retardation.

Clinicians should assume that a proportion of clients they see are given Saint-John's-wort by their family members. It is reasonable to assume that some adults with mild mental retardation self-medicate with over-the-counter preparations such as this. Clinicians should certainly screen for its use and should also conduct a comprehensive review of any other medications that the client is taking, especially those that increase serotonin.

Electroconvulsive Therapy (ECT)

Electroconvulsive therapy (ECT) is the administration of electric current to the brain in a controlled manner for the treatment of severe mental disorders, mainly depression and some psychoses. ECT is more likely to be used for more severe depressions characterized by psychotic features, catatonia, or stupor, or after a failure of the patient to respond to psychotropic medications. Controversially, some authorities have argued that it is an effective and relatively safe treatment for depression. They point out to potential advantages over psychotropic medication because of faster response to treatment, which might be desirable. Indeed, some reviews have recommended that ECT should be considered a first-line treatment of depression, rather than it being reserved for treating more severe or recalcitrant forms of depression (Wheeler Vega, Mortimer, & Tyson, 2000).

ECT should be clearly distinguished from contingent electric shock, a controversial behavioral technique where painful shock is applied to a limb, usually an arm or leg, to reduce the future probability of a severe behavior problem, such as severe self-injury or aggression. ECT and contingent electric shock are two completely different treatments.

Over time there have been concerns over the use of ECT. These concerns have included possible negative side effects, including memory loss from around the time of the ECT itself, and the possibility of progressive memory loss over time. The latter is controversial, because it can be difficult to distinguish progressive memory loss due to aging and the course of a depression or psychosis from that due to ECT. Another controversy over the use of ECT is the ethical problem of consent for treatment. Because ECT is often used with people who are very cognitively impaired due to severe depression or psychosis, a significant number of people who undergo ECT are neither factually or legally competent to consent to its use. Also, some people who undergo ECT are inpatients in institutions or private mental health facilities when coercion to accept treatment may occur. Hence, the issue of legally adequate consent for ECT is frequently raised. There are now guidelines in place, such as the use of surrogates to consent, and reviews by an independent physician, which attempt to prevent or minimize these problems.

After being shunned and criticized for a long time, ECT seems to be enjoying a surge of popularity, yet, it remains a controversial form of treatment. In some populations, such as the elderly, it may be safer than medications and also more effective. Indeed, Alexopoulos, Streim, Carpenter, Docherty, and The Expert Consensus Panel for Using Antipsychotic Drugs in Older Patients (2004) recommended ECT as a first-line treatment for psychotic depression in seniors alongside other first-line treatments, such as antipsychotic medication and antidepressants.

ECT and Mental Retardation

A growing number of papers have described the use of this treatment in people with mental retardation, including people with autism. For example, Zaw, Bates, Murali, and Bentham (1999) described a 14-year-old youngster with autism and catatonia who displayed symptoms of mutism (not talking), akinesia (not moving), posturing, and rigidity. In addition to these symptoms of catatonia, he appeared depressed and showed nonspecific psychotic symptoms. A course of ECT improved the condition dramatically, although the core symptoms of autism were not affected.

The number of cases of the use of ECT reported in the scientific literature has been modest, but there have been continued reports over time. Van Waarde, Stolker, and van der Mast (2001) reported a systematic literature review of the use of ECT in people with mental retardation. They searched the research literature from 1966 to 2000 and contacted experts in the field. They identified no controlled studies of ECT in people with mental retardation, but they did identify 44 cases of the use of ECT in people with mental retardation. Participants included men and women who ranged in age from 14 to 69 years with varying levels of mental retardation. Most were diagnoses with psychotic, unipolar, or bipolar depression. Less common diagnoses included refractory and nonorganic psychosis, schizophrenia, and schizoaffective disorder, and a small number of people with such nonspecific behavior problems as aggression or self-injury.

In 84% of the participants reported in these papers, ECT was said to be successful, but in 16% there were severe side effects or no response. Side effects included status epilepticus and violent agitation after administration of ECT. In 48% of cases, relapses occurred within 1 week to several years after initial successful ECT.

These results are suggestive that ECT may be effective in treatment of mood disorders in people with mental retardation. The quality of the evidence is very limited, however. First, the bias toward publishing successful treatment studies means that the figure of 84% success rate may not be generalizable to typical populations of people with mental retardation and mood disorders. Second, in almost all cases, the outcome was judged only by clinical impression rather than standardized outcome measures. Standardized measures of outcome, such as measures of mental status, mood, and adaptive behavior, were used in only 11% of the reported cases. In order to strengthen our knowledge of ECT for mood disorders in people with mental retardation, controlled randomized trials of ECT are needed. In their absence, future research should report the outcome of ECT in a series of consecutive cases using standardized measures of mood, behavior, mental state, adaptive behavior, and psychosocial functioning.

One controversial aspect of the use of ECT in people with mental retardation has been its use for the treatment of behavior problems; van Waarde et al. (2001) noted at least two examples of this use. Bates and Smeltzer (1982) reported the use of ECT with an 18-year-old man with moderate mental retardation and multiple behavior problems, such as aggression to others, sleep disturbance, agitation, poor appetite, and incontinence. No formal psychiatric diagnosis had been made. They reported that ECT resulted in an "excellent" outcome with no side effects. The rationale for the use or ECT in such cases is usually given as some underlying mood disorder, inferred from the presence of some symptoms of a mood disorder, such as sleep and appetite disturbance, and perhaps the severity of the behavior problems. Matson (1983) criticized this report, because it did not first explore less dangerous treatment options, such as simple reinforcement-based behavioral interventions, and because the diagnosis was presumed rather than demonstrated systematically.

There have been few reports of the use of ECT for behavior problems at this time. Caution should be exercised over the use of ECT for depression in people with mental retardation, given the availability of other less controversial and, perhaps, safer interventions, as well as the lack of consensus on behavioral equivalents of depression in people with mental retardation (Tsiouris, Mann, Patti & Sturmey, 2003; for a review, see also Chapter 2, by Charlot, in this volume). There is therefore little support at this time for the use of ECT for behavior problems.

Case History

Mr. Koslowski was a 17-year-old Caucasian male with a history of autistic disorder, recurrent depression, and mild mental retardation. He was admitted to the adolescent inpatient unit because of progressive worsening of mood accompanied by a generalized slowing of movements. He had started looking increasingly sad and depressed, and he had also become almost mute, speaking only in monosyllables. His food intake had decreased, and he had also lost weight.

The family history was positive for depression. His mother had depression. His prenatal history and birth had been uncomplicated. All his milestones had been delayed, however. He had been diagnosed with autism and mild mental retardation at about 4 years of age. He had attended a program for children with autism throughout his school years, and he had received social skills training and language intervention.

He had a 3-year history of progressive decline in his level of functioning. Parents recalled that he had been functioning reasonably well till he reached his puberty. After this, he had become increasingly depressed and had slowed down over a period of 6 months. He needed to be prompted to initiate such simple activities as getting dressed and eating. His behavior in the classroom had also deteriorated. He would stand alone or sit for long periods, doing nothing. He would spend several hours in the bathroom, repeatedly washing his hands or looking at himself in the mirror. In addition, his parents had observed many types of abnormal movements, such as eye blinking and eye rolling with a jerking of the neck.

Prior to the onset of his symptoms, he had been described as a well-adjusted youngster with autism. He spoke spontaneously, and he was able to carry on a simple conversation. In addition to English, he spoke and read Hebrew. His school reports described him as being in the mildly mentally retarded range. His parents dated the onset of his symptoms to his trip to an overnight camp for a month. After returning from the camp, his behavior started deteriorating. He seemed to show less facial expression; he appeared somewhat gaunt, and his language became sparse. Over the next 4 months, he became progressively mute, with marked slowing of movements, a depressed mood, and a gradual loss of independence of his activities of daily living.

He was no longer able to function at school. He also showed increased motor tics, consisting of frequent turning his head to the side, blinking rapidly, and gazing rightward and upward. He had a battery of investigations to rule out any physical cause of the condition, all of which were in the normal range.

A diagnosis of depression with obsessive-compulsive features was made. Over the course of 6 months, the excessive slowing of his movements increased, resulting in his dropping out of school. The parents used the analogy of watching a movie in slow motion to describe his extreme slowness. He received several trials of antidepressants, all of which failed. Because of his excessive slowing, and his decline in self-care, he was diagnosed with catatonia and depression.

Mr. Koslowski was admitted and assessed, and recommendations were made after two consultations with separate child psychiatrists for the patient to undergo ECT. He was given a course of 18 ECTs, which proved life-saving. He became increasingly verbal. He started eating his food as before, and his movements became more spontaneous. Although he never regained his past level of functioning, he was maintained as an outpatient on antidepressants.

Conclusions and Recommendations

The evidence base for the use of phototherapy, dietary and herbal therapies, and ECT is weak. No systematic trials with people with mental retardation and mood disorders were identified for this review.

Phototherapy

There is little evidence for the effectiveness of phototherapy with people with mental retardation and mood disorders at this time. Therefore, its use is not recommended.

Dietary Supplements

There is little good-quality evidence supporting the effectiveness of almost all dietary supplements for mood disorders; one exception is the use of Saint-John's-wort. There are many well-controlled trials of Saint-John's-wort in the general population, demonstrating that it is superior to placebo and is as effective as conventional antidepressants. Saint-John's-wort carries with it the risk of some negative side effects, however. Clinicians should screen for the use of Saint-John's-wort and carefully evaluate its use as to its efficacy, possible negative side effects, and interactions with other medications.

ECT

The use of ECT has the strongest evidence base in people of average intelligence and depression. Its use with people with mental retardation is limited to uncontrolled, descriptive case studies. Some clinicians and researchers would view it as an established method of treatment of severe depression, which has been successfully used in people with mental retardation.

There is good evidence for the effectiveness of ECT as a treatment for major depression in the general population. Some authorities have voiced the opinion that it may have some benefits over psychotropic medications for dangerous catatonic depression and depression involving suicide, because some people appear to respond quickly to treatment. Within the general population, however, concerns have been voiced over the excessive use of ECT in the past, and hence safeguards are often in place limiting its use. Others have been critical about the use of ECT when such side effects as memory loss may be significant. If alternative, effective, and lower-risk interventions, such as psychotropic medications, behavioral, and cognitive-behavioral treatments exist, there needs to be a positive reason to select ECT for treatment of depression. There are now reports of the use of ECT for depression in people with mental retardation that establish that it may be an effective treatment. However, because of ethical concerns over consent for treatment and the availability of other treatment options, caution is advised for the use of ECT in this context.

Some studies have used ECT for treatment of behavior disorders, such as self-injury, under the assumption that these behavior problems were behavioral equivalents of depression in people with severe or profound mental retardation. There is little evidence for this use of ECT, and at this time this use is not recommended.

References

Alexopoulos, G. S., Streim, J., Carpenter, D., Docherty, J. P., & The Expert Consensus Panel for Using Antipsychotic Drugs in Older Patients. (2004). Using antipsychotic agents in older patients. *Journal of Clinical Psychiatry, 65* (Suppl. 2), 5–99.

Aman, M. G., Lam, K. S., & Collier-Crespin, A. (2003). Prevalence and patterns of use of psychoactive medicines among individuals with autism in the Autism Society of Ohio. *Journal of Autism and Developmental Disabilities, 33,* 527–534.

American Psychiatric Association. (1994). *Diagnostic and statistical manual of mental disorders* (4th ed.). Washington, DC: Author.

Bates, W. J., & Smeltzer, D. J. (1982). Electroconvulsive treatment of psychotic self-injurious behavior in a patient with severe mental retardation. *American Journal of Psychiatry, 139,* 1355–1356.

Cooke, L. B., & Thompson, C. (1988). Seasonal affective disorder and response to light in two patients with learning disability. *Journal of Affective Disorders, 48,* 145–148.

Ellis, C., Singh, N. N., & Ruane, A. L. (1999). Nutritional, dietary, and hormonal treatments for individuals with mental retardation and developmental disabilities. *Mental Retardation and Developmental Disabilities Research Reviews, 5,* 335–341.

Guilleminault, C., McCann, C. C., Quera-Salva, M., & Cetel, M. (1993). Light therapy as treatment of dyschronosis in brain-impaired chidlren. *European Journal of Pediatrics, 152,* 754–759.

Izzo, A. A., & Ernst, E. (2001). Interactions between herbal medications and prescribed drugs: A systematic review. *Drugs, 61,* 2163–2173.

Jacobson, J., Mulick, J. A., & Foxx, R. (2005). *Controversial therapies for developmental disabilities: Fad, fashion and science in professional practice.* Mahwah, NJ: Lawrence Erlbaum.

Kennedy, S. H., Lam, R. W., Cohen, N. L., Ravindran, A. V., & CANMAT Depression Work Group. (2001). Clinical guidelines for the treatment of depressive disorders. IV: Medications and other biological treatments. *Canadian Journal of Psychiatry, 46,* 38S–58S.

Langworthy-Lam, K. S., Aman, M. G., & Van Bourgondien, M. E. (2002). Prevalence and patterns of use of psychoactive medicines in individuals with autism in the Autism Society of North Carolina. *Journal of Child and Adolescent Psychopharmacology, 12,* 311–321.

Lindblom, N., Heiskala, H., Kaski, M., Leinonen, L., & Laakso, M. L. (2002). Sleep fragmentation in mentally retarded people decreases with increasing day length in spring. *Chronobiology International, 18,* 441–459.

Matson, J. L. (1983). ECT versus behavior modification for self-injurious behavior. *American Journal of Psychiatry, 140,* 667–668.

Smith, T., & Antolovich, M. (2000). Parental perceptions of supplemental interventions received by young children with autism in intensive behavior analytic treatment. *Behavioral Interventions, 15,* 833–897.

Tsiouris, J. A., Mann, R., Patti, P. J., & Sturmey, P. (2003). Challenging behaviours should not be considered as depressive equivalents in individuals with intellectual disability. *Journal of Intellectual Disability Research, 47,* 14–21.

van Waarde, J. A., Stolker, J. J., & van der Mast, R. C. (2001). ECT in mental retardation: A review. *Journal of ECT, 17,* 233–235.

Wheeler Vega, J. A., Mortimer, A. M., & Tyson P. J. (2000). Somatic treatment of psychotic depression: Review and recommendations for practice. *Journal of Clinical Psychopharmacology, 20,* 504–519.

Whiskey, E., Werneke, U., & Taylor, D. (2001). A systematic review and meta-analysis of *Hypericum perforatum* in depression: A comprehensive clinical review. *International Clinical Psychopharmacology, 16,* 239–252.

Zaw, F. K., Bates, G. D., Murali, V., & Bentham, P. (1999). Catatonia, autism, and ECT. *Developmental Medicine and Child Neurology, 41,* 843–845.

12

COGNITIVE-BEHAVIORAL APPROACHES TO DEPRESSION IN PEOPLE WITH LEARNING DISABILITIES

William R. Lindsay,

Biza Steinfert Kroese,

and

Philippa Drew

This chapter describes the application of cognitive-behavior therapy (CBT) to depression in people with learning disabilities. In order to put this type of therapy in context, a brief historical account is presented of how and why behavioral approaches to the treatment of depression have incorporated cognitive components. This is followed by a review of the causative factors of depression in the general population, as well as those associated specifically with the learning-disability population. Finally, the application of CBT approaches for depression in learning disabilities and the available evidence for efficacy are reviewed.

Historical Context

The application of experimental psychology to clinical psychology began in the 1950s and 1960s. Whereas in Britain Pavlovian principles were first used in clinical practice (Wolpe, 1959), North American clinicians were more influenced by Skinnerian operant conditioning. Both approaches were able to produce reasonably successful treatment methods that could be and were subjected to rigorous randomized controlled trials. However, most of the presenting problems that responded so well to these behavioral interventions concerned fear and anxiety. Progress in developing effective clinical applications for depression and other mood disorders was less evident. Although Seligman's (1975) experimental animal work was highly influential in the understanding of depression by showing that uncontrollable adverse events produce an over-generalised sense of lack of control over important outcomes of life, no specific therapy was developed on the basis of these findings.

Lewinsohn (1974, 1975) had also developed a behavioral, contingency-based theory of depression. He proposed that a loss or lack of response-contingent positive reinforcement for "adaptive" behaviors, accompanied by positive reinforcement for attention- or sympathy-seeking "maladaptive" behaviors (for example, crying, complaining, threatening suicide), shapes the depression (Lewinsohn Weinstein, & Shaw, 1969; Libet & Lewinsohn, 1973). He did propose a treatment based on his theoretical explanation. This treatment was designed to increase the rate of positive outcomes contingent on the depressed person's behavior and increase involvement in positive activities. Lewinsohn devised programs for depressed adolescents that included mood monitoring, social skills training, increasing pleasant activities, and relaxation (Lewinsohn, Mischel, Chaplin, & Barton, 1980). Lewinsohn identified deficits in social skills as particularly important.

In these early behavioral interpretations of depression, the focus remains on specific behaviors. If the clients describe themselves as "depressed," the therapist tries to define this in behavioral terms: What *happens* when the client feels more or less depressed. Contextual issues are also emphasized, and the interaction between environmental stimuli and behavioral responses is the basis of the functional analysis.

However, limitations in such an interpretation were soon evident to behavioral clinicians. Depressed people do not just suffer from specific problematic behaviors. It became obvious from self-reports that dysfunctional cognitive strategies when interpreting or explaining experiences were crucial mediating factors (for example, automatically blaming yourself for negative outcomes and not crediting yourself for positive outcomes).

Thus, later models (Lewinsohn, Rohde, Hops, & Clarke, 1991; Lewinsohn et al., 1994) incorporated such cognitive components as cognitive restructuring as another way in which to increase reinforcing experiences and to reduce punishing ones. The introduction of cognitive components was very much influenced by what Rachman termed the "waning prohibition against using cognitive concepts" (Rachman, 2003, p. 590). Particularly, research by Bandura (1977) on observational learning indicated that cognitive mediation takes place during learning. In the clinical field, Kanfer and Karoly (1972) developed a cognitive model of self-control, and Meichenbaum (1975) convinced many that the concept of *mental* operant behavior (coverants) is not only acceptable but essential in explaining behavior change. The 1970s saw other authors introducing the concept of metacognition (Brown, 1975) and specific problem-solving techniques (e.g., D'Zurilla & Goldfried, 1971).

In the field of depression, Beck's (1976) influential work incorporated the notion of cognitive distortions. That is, biased, negative (dysfunctional) interpretations regarding self, others, and the world in general develop through early experiences of loss and rejection. These "schemata" become interpretative filters for understanding events. Certain critical events may activate these beliefs, or schemata, which in turn activate negative automatic thoughts (NATs). These then result in emotional, physiological, and behavioral consequences, which are often interrelated by serving as mutual triggers (see Figure 12.1). The treatment method that Beck devised on the basis of this theory involves five steps: (a) Learn to recognise NATs that are dysfunctional and lead to serious dilemmas; (b) recognize the connections between NATs, the emotions they evoke, and the consequent actions; (c) learn to examine the evidence for and against the NATs; (d) replace NATs with more realistic interpretations; and (e) identify and change the inappropriate beliefs, assumptions, and schemata that predispose a person to NATs.

Like most other CBT approaches, Beck's clinical application retains behavioral analysis at its core. That is, not only does it focus on cognitive components, but it also retains observable behaviors as measures. Accurate, reliable, and continuous recording, as well as clear definitions, have all been transferred from the applied behavioral analysis school of thought. Moreover, cognitive-behavior therapists acknowledge that behavior change itself can generate new insights, feelings, and self-perceptions, which in turn may lead to new, more adaptive behaviors.

Ellis's *Rational Emotive Behavior Therapy (REBT)* is another form of CBT (Ellis, 1973;

Ellis & Grieger, 1977). This approach also assumes that irrational underlying beliefs can cause depression and other types of psychological distress. Ellis stressed that the client's emotions need to be fully involved in order to move from just an intellectual acknowledgment to "emotional insight." The therapist must use "force and energy" by means of stories, mottoes, witticisms, and so on, in order to dispute the client's irrational beliefs vigorously. The significant impact that behavior has on cognitive change is again acknowledged, however, and thus *in vivo* homework, including desensitization and "shame-attacking" exercises, is seen as an integral part of treatment.

CBT, especially Beck's approach is now considered to be an effective and viable alternative to behavioral and biochemical interventions, particularly in the treatment of depression (e.g., Hollin, 1996).

Assessment of Depression-Related Cognitions

This chapter reports only the literature that concerns adults with intellectual disabilities (ID) who are capable of (albeit limited) verbal communication. There are very few reported studies on the assessment of mood disorders in people with severe or profound ID, probably because a number of depressive symptoms are not observable and are reliant on self-report (for example, feelings of worthlessness and inappropriate guilt). Past studies have found third-party reports unreliable (e.g., Clark, Reed, & Sturmey, 1991), although more recently Ross and Oliver (2003) have reported that their 25-item *Mood, Interest and Pleasure Questionnaire (MIPQ)* has good inter-rater and test-retest reliability and excellent internal consistency. This indicates that if people are unable to self-report, the MIPQ can provide reliable information on core symptoms of major depression.

Some of the most robust work in the field of mood and ID has been on instruments to help clients report their feelings, cognitions, attitudes, and problems in a structured systematic manner. Kazdin, Matson, and Senatore (1983) and Helsel and Matson (1988) developed a methodology for employing a visual analog to help the individual with ID understand increasing states of personal arousal, deepening mood, and other internal states normally assessed using Likert Scales. These methodologies and their effectiveness have been described elsewhere (Finlay & Lyons, 2001; Lindsay & Olley, 1998) and are covered elsewhere by Finlay in this volume (see Chapter 9). Thus, there is now a developing methodology for assessing self-rated depression in this client group. Lindsay, Michie, Baty, Smith, and Miller (1994) investigated the consistency of responding across measures of related emotions, such as the *Zung Depression Scale* and the *Zung*

Anxiety Scale, using this methodology. They found a high degree of convergent validity of reported emotions and concluded that this form of self-report was reliable and valid with participants who have mild ID.

Two studies in particular have found that the patterning of responses from people with ID on self-reports of depression show the same lawful statistical pattern as with other client groups. Dagnan and Sandhu (1999) administered the *Zung Depression Scale* (Zung, 1965), the *Rosenberg Self-Esteem Scale* (Rosenberg, Schooler & Schoenbach, 1989), and the *Social Comparison Scale* (Allen & Gilbert, 1995) to 18 women and 25 men with mild ID. The numbers involved in this study are small, and the results should be treated with caution. They reported that the factor structure of these instruments was consistent with that of the original scales. This conclusion is supported by recent evidence from Kellet, Beail, Newman, and Hawes (2004), who administered the 53-item *Brief Symptom Inventory* (*BSI*; Derogatis, 1993) to 335 participants with ID. They had previously demonstrated the efficacy of an assisted completion format (Kellet, Beail, Newman, & Mosely, 1999; Kellet, Beail, Newman, & Frankish, 2003). General instructions were simplified, and responses were aided with numerical, dramatic, and pictorial representations. They found that the BSI factor structure corresponded broadly to that originally reported. With reference to the present chapter, it is notable that six of the scales reproduced the item allocation of the original statistical analysis, with five scales retaining their original labels: depression, anxiety, somatization, hostility, and paranoia. They concluded that there was considerable overlap between the general adult and the ID population factor structures.

In reviews of assessments for use with clients who have ID, Dagnan and Ruddick (1995) and Dagnan and Lindsay (2004) have concluded that relatively sophisticated question formats, such as analog scales, can be used by people with ID with a reasonable degree of reliability. However, Lindsay and Lees (2003) and Lindsay and Steptoe (in review), with particular reference to depression, have found that certain items on the *Beck Depression Inventory (BDI)* require considerable linguistic sophistication: There are subtle changes in concepts across individual items, which may be too complex for clients with ID. The item on self-criticism moves from self-blame ("I am more critical of myself than I used to be") to a concept of universal responsibility ("I blame myself for everything bad that happens"). This requires not only an understanding of increasing degrees of self-criticism, but also an understanding of the nonlogical shift from self-criticism to universal blame, such as a clear cognitive distortion. The item on self-dislike moves from losing confidence in oneself to disliking oneself. These are different concepts and may introduce unnecessary complexity. Therefore, these authors simplified the internal conceptual consistency of each item and employed additional administration instructions.

Using this methodology, Lindsay and Lees (2003) compared anxiety and depression in groups of sex offenders and controls, both with ID. They found that sex offenders reported significantly lower rates on both the *Beck Anxiety Inventory* (*BAI*: Beck & Steer, 1990) and *the Beck Depression Inventory* (*BDI*: Beck, Steer, & Brown, 1995). From the point of view of the present chapter, however, the interesting result is that reported rates of emotion were extremely high for both groups. For both assessments, a score of 0–10 is a nonclinical score, 11–20 indicates mild depression, 21–30 moderate depression, and over 30 severe depression. The *average* score for the control group on the BAI was 20.62 and on the BDI 32.03; for the sex-offending group 8.14 on the BAI and 16.21 on the BDI. Three of these four average scores are in the clinical range, and one indicates severe depression. To have an average rate of self-reported depression in the severe range for a cohort of 16 individuals stands at odds with the low prevalence rates of depression often reported historically and more recently by Meins (1995) and Deb, Thomas, and Bright (2001).

Lindsay and Steptoe (in review) investigated this further with 86 consecutive referrals to a service for people with ID and offending and challenging behavior. They again found high rates of self-reported anxiety and depression on the BAI and BDI, with scores of 19.5 and 19.8, respectively. Again, sex offenders scored lower than did other client categories. However, few participants appeared to report point prevalence of cognitions and emotions as indicated in the instructions. The instructions for most assessments of emotion ask the participant to report on their thoughts and feelings in the preceding 2 weeks or month. Participants with ID have difficulty with the concept of time, and there appeared to be a tendency to report on any incidence the participant could recall. Therefore, what appeared to be point prevalence might actually have been prevalence over a much longer period of time. Here is an example:

Assessor: Do you feel sad?

Participant: I felt terrible at Christmas, because I am still here, and I wanted to be with my family. [The interview took place in May.]

Assessor: Yes, but in the last two weeks have you felt sad?

Participant: Yes, I felt sad all the time, and it lasted for ages, because I don't want to be here and I didn't see my family at Christmas.

Assessor: Yes, that was at Christmas, but how are you feeling now?

Participant: I felt sad all the time.

This response gained a score of 3 on the BDI, and the participant continued to report high scores on a number of items based on historical information. It was difficult to help the individual to report only recent mood states. Although there had been indications of low mood during the Christmas period, there were no current indications that the individual was experiencing low mood; yet his self-report placed him at the top end of the "moderate depression" range. It may be that with clients with ID, it is preferable to have a simple, immediate instruction. One could ask, "Do you feel any of these symptoms now?" Nevertheless, assessment of cognitions and feelings related to depression may result in an overestimate of point prevalence, as there was also a tendency for individuals to respond at the extreme ends of the scale (see also Kolton, Boer, & Boer, 2001). This is crucial for the cognitive behavioral therapist who is specifically interested in self-reports of current cognition and emotion. One has to be aware of the temporal framework in which the client is working during therapy and that any self-reports may be subject to ceiling and floor effects.

Causative Factors

The application of CBT to depression in both the general and the learning-disabled populations have been influenced by social cognitive models that highlight risk and vulnerability factors for depression. The following section considers the ways in which risk/vulnerability factors are thought to contribute to the development of depression. The literature is examined within the general population and the learning-disabled population.

Risk/Vulnerability Factors in the General Population

Within the general population a substantial literature now exists that examines the role of vulnerability and risk factors for depression. Social-cognitive theories of depression highlight the relationship between negative life events, aspects of the social environment, and mediating cognitive processes in the development of depression (Champion & Power, 1995; Oatley & Bolton, 1985). Brown and Harris (1978) originally identified the association between threatening life events and the onset of depression, particularly in the presence of certain vulnerability factors. Subsequent research has highlighted that one of the main vulnerability factors for depression is the lack of an intimate, confiding, or supportive relationship (Oatley & Bolton, 1985). Other functions of social support, such as practical help, information giving, and social companionship, have been identified as helping to protect against depression (Cohen & Wills, 1985). Such adverse social and environmental conditions as poverty, poor housing, and unemployment have also been linked with an increased risk of depression (Champion & Power, 1995). Social-cognitive models of depression have emphasized the availability of valued roles and goals within the context of risk factors. Oatley and Bolton (1985) suggested that negative life events can lead to depression if they disrupt or change a role that has been central to a person's sense of self- identity and self-worth. This could occur, for example, through the loss of a significant relationship, or through a change in circumstances that makes it impossible to maintain a valued role (for example, loss of employment, children leaving home). They argued that it is not simply the loss of a valued role but rather the perceived absence of alternative roles that is a key factor in a person's vulnerability to depression.

Another cognitive process that has been shown to mediate depression is social comparison (Swallow & Kuiper, 1988). According to cognitive models of self-concept, people assimilate information about themselves into a self-schema, which is then evaluated and modified through ongoing social interactions. Social comparison, or the process of comparing oneself with others, is seen as an important means of self-evaluation that can have both positive and negative effects. On one hand, social comparison can help to reduce uncertainty about oneself and act as a source of motivation for self-improvement. On the other hand, it can also reveal negative information that is potentially threatening to self-esteem. Swallow and Kuiper (1988) proposed that in some circumstances social comparison can underpin the negative evaluations that are characteristic of depression. Two factors are thought to be associated with a predisposing vulnerability to depression. One is the complexity of the self-schema, or the ability that a person has to keep various aspects of his or her self separate and distinct. There is some empirical support for the idea that people with a simpler or less differentiated view of self are more vulnerable to depression (Linville, 1985). Arguably a more complex view of self acts as a buffer against threats to a particular role or aspect of self. The second factor is self-schema consolidation, which refers to the extent to which a person can process self-relevant information consistently and efficiently. People with poorly consolidated self-schemas would be expected to be less certain about themselves and their abilities, which may in turn be associated with an increased emphasis on social comparison.

Lewinsohn's early model of depression, which was not specific to ID, relied heavily on a social skills deficit hypothesis (e.g., Lewinsohn, 1974). Lewinsohn and his colleagues later modified the hypothesis (e.g., Lewinsohn & Rohde, 1987) to suggest that poor social skills not only act in the causation and maintenance of depression but may also be a consequence of depression. There is certainly a wealth of evidence that there is a strong relationship between depression and poor social and relationship skills (Segrin, 2000). Treatments that encourage and promote social and relationship skills significantly improve self-reported depression (Bellack, Hersen, & Himmelhoch, 1983; Hersen, Bellack & Himmelhoch, 1980). In his review of the hypothesis, Segrin (2000) noted the conflicting evidence regarding whether social skill deficits proceed, run concurrently with, or are symptoms of depression. He noted two important points: that social skill deficits are unquestionably concomitants to depression and that poor social skills are clearly not specific to depression. Both these points have clear relevance to people with ID. He concluded that "a complete understanding of the interpersonal aspects of depression, and depression more generally, is not possible without a careful examination of the social skills of those afflicted with this psychosocial problem" (p. 397).

How Causative Factors Relate to People With Learning Disabilities

People with learning disabilities are arguably particularly vulnerable to risk factors that have been highlighted in the general population. Reed (1997) suggested that the life situations and experiences of many people with learning disabilities incorporate known risk factors for depression, emphasizing, for example, experiences of repeated failures, stigma and prejudice, unemployment, and lack of social support. A growing number of studies have begun to show that cognitive and social processes mediate depression for people with learning disabilities in much the same way as they do for the general population. Reiss and Benson (1985) found, for example, that low levels of social support were associated with depression in people with ID. They suggested some reasons why social support might be particularly important for people with ID, highlighting that significant others can provide support to solve life problems, accomplish goals, and cope with stressors.

Benson, Reiss, Smith, and Laman (1985) reported the relationship between social skills and depression in people with ID who had been referred to an outpatient mental health clinic for treatment of emotional problems. Clients who had emotional problems were separated into a depressed group and a disturbed but nondepressed group. Depressed participants were rated significantly lower in social skills, indicating that poor social skills were specifically associated with depression, rather than emotional difficulties in general. Laman and Reiss (1987) followed this up in a study of 45 adults with ID. They found depressed mood to be negatively correlated with social support and social skills. Benson and Ivins (1992) found a significant high correlation between negative self-concept and depression.

Nezu, Nezu, Rothenberg, DelliCarpini, and Groag (1995) also found a negative association between depression and social support in people with learning disabilities. However, their findings indicated that it was the presence of negative social interactions that predicted depression, rather than the amount of positive support available. Gender has also been identified as a risk factor for depression in people with learning disabilities. Lunsky (2003) found that women reported higher levels of depressive symptoms than did men with learning disabilities.

Cognitive Processes and Depression

Such concepts as social comparison and stigma have been examined in relation to depression and self-esteem in people with learning disabilities. As a group they could be seen to be vulnerable to the negative effects of social comparison for a number of reasons. In mainstream settings the social comparisons that people with learning disabilities make with nondisabled peers are likely to be unfavorable (Szivos-Bach, 1993). People with ID may also have limited opportunities to develop varied roles and attributes related, for example, to employment or social intimate relationships. As previously identified, having access to a wide range of roles is thought to buffer against negative social comparisons and associated depression (Swallow & Kuiper, 1988). It could also be hypothesized that people with ID may have less complex and poorly consolidated self-schemas, factors that are thought to make people more vulnerable to the negative effects of social comparison.

Dagnan and Waring (2004) have further developed this model in a study linking stigma to psychological distress in 39 participants. They found that scores on stigma scales correlated with negative evaluative beliefs. They concluded that core negative evaluative beliefs about oneself were fundamentally related to the experience of feeling different. Though they did not include a measure of depression in their study, they hypothesized that the negative social constructions associated with ID might be a risk factor for depression.

Support for this hypothesis comes from the carefully controlled study by Richards et al. (2001). Drawing from the Medical Research Council's National Survey of Health and Development (NSHD), and selecting for cases with non-missing values on the relevant psychiatric outcomes, they identified 41 people with ID and 2,119 others. They found that the ID group were four times more likely to be identified as having affective disorder. This was true both at aged 36 years and at aged 43 years. They then went on to consider a number of variables that might account for the increase in risk of affective disorder in the ID sample. Drawing on work by Scott (1995), they investigated four basic factors: medical, environmental neglect or inconsistency, an effect of the ID regardless of cause, and reverse causality (psychiatric disorder leading to impaired intellectual performance). Their data allowed them to discard the first and last hypotheses. In considering the second and third hypotheses, they found some support, although it was not strong. They concluded "adverse circumstances in adulthood did not account for risk of affective disorder in learning disability in the present analysis, just as adverse circumstances in early life did not. However, there may be more subtle factors that were not taken into account, such as coping capacity and self-worth" (p. 526). The social-cognitive processes demonstrated by Dagnan and Waring (2004) certainly give a possible account of these more subtle factors. Nezu, et al. (1995) also found a relationship between cognitive variables and depression in this client group. In a sample of 107 adults, they found levels of depressive symptoms correlated positively with increases in negative automatic thoughts, feelings of helplessness, and rates of self-reinforcement and also (as already mentioned) correlated negatively with increasing social support. Likewise, Glenn, Bihm, & Lammers (2003) found a high correlation between negative affect and maladaptive cognitions in a group of people with ID.

Payne and Jahoda (2004) investigated the associations between social skill and self-reported ratings of depressive symptomatology. Reduced communication skills were associated with increases in self-reported ratings of depression, and, paradoxically, they found a positive association between self-rated social self-efficacy and depression. They surmised that participants may believe in their own ability, but because they are members of a stigmatized group, outcomes in their lives may be determined more by external than by internal factors. This may result in a state of learned helplessness, in which they believe positive social outcomes are unattainable, leading to increased vulnerability to depression. This suggested that feelings of depression may be in response to a realistic appraisal of stigma and marginalization.

McBrien (2003) expressed surprise at the paucity of studies investigating the role of social and cognitive processes underlying depression in people with ID despite the obvious relevance of the range of psychological theories of depression. More recently, a number of authors have investigated these underlying cognitive processes and have produced evidence attesting not only to their importance but also to the possibility that they may be instrumental in the development of depressive symptoms in this client group. Therefore, the development of treatments directed at these cognitive processes is crucial for people with ID.

The issue of whether people with ID have the requisite cognitive abilities to make use of CBT has been open to debate (e.g., Stenfert Kroese, 1997). Recently, more structured procedures for assessing people's suitability for CBT have begun to be developed. In a study by Dagnan, Chadwick, and Proudlove (2000), participants with mild ID completed tasks that assessed their ability to identify emotions, link emotions to situations, and select evaluative beliefs to mediate between emotions and situations. The majority (75%) correctly linked situations and emotions together. However, they had more difficulty recognizing the mediating role of cognitions, with only 10–25% responding at a level better than chance. This study highlighted the potential use of a stepwise approach to cognitive tasks for people with ID, emphasizing a teaching component for skills identified as absent.

The next section describes and discusses how clinicians have interpreted some of these findings and how they have applied them in their clinical work.

Applications

Pioneer Studies

In an early study, Matson, Dettling, and Senatore (1979) reported the effective treatment of depression in a 32- year-old man with borderline to mild ID. He had a 10-year history of social withdrawal, suicidal threats, depressed mood, anxiety, feelings of worthlessness, and sleep difficulties. They used self-monitoring, social reinforcement, and the encouragement of positive self-statements. Treatment was designed to increase positive self-statements, decrease negative statements, and develop increased sociability. The client was praised for positive statements and was asked to evaluate negative statements. The therapist modeled appropriate statements, and the client was asked to praise himself for appropriate, positive statements. Negative and inappropriate statements decreased and remained low during post-treatment and follow-up sessions. Staff reported that he made more positive statements, participated in more social activities, and met a girlfriend.

This study goes beyond a purely behavioral interpretation of depression. The authors employed positive self-statements, which is a method to address dysfunctional cognitive strategies, such as expecting negative outcomes, blaming oneself for negative outcomes, or not crediting oneself for positive outcomes. Benson's (1990) review of these early studies indicated that they should be viewed as preliminary, with significant limitations. For example, they did not include generalization probes to assess behavioral change outside of the therapy session, and they selected target behaviors because of their face validity without providing a clear rationale for their selection.

More Recent Studies

The development of self-instruction techniques by Meichenbaum (1977) and their applicability for a range of problems in clients with ID is discussed extensively elsewhere (Dagnan & Lindsay, 2004; Lindsay 1999).

In addition to this work, case studies using a simplified and revised form of Beck's CBT for depression (Beck, Rush, Shaw, & Emery, 1979) were published. For example, Lindsay, Howells, and Pitcaithly (1993) reported on a 28-year-old man and a 20-year-old woman with measured IQs of 67 and 65, respectively. The methods used were simplified and revised considerably. However, the essential components of CBT—establishing the relationship between thought, feeling, and behavior; setting an agenda; monitoring thoughts; isolating negative thoughts; attempting to elicit underlying assumptions; reviewing the accuracy of these cognitions; generating alternative thoughts and practicing them in reviews, role-plays, and real settings—were maintained. They gave clear examples of each of these stages of treatment, noting the importance of placing a simple, straightforward interpretation on dysfunctional thoughts. Therefore, for one client, thoughts about everyone dying, including his mother and father, revealed an underlying assumption of "I can't cope on my own."

Using principles similar to those underlying social problem solving training, Nezu and Nezu (1994) outlined a model for treatment that employed a number of cognitive operations. This model was both practical and subtle and included five phases: problem orientation, problem definition and formulation, generation of alternatives, decision making, and solution implementation and verification. A number of cognitive principles were included in each phase, such as identifying the beliefs, assumptions, and expectations one has in relation to the problem; clarifying personal realistic goals; generating alternative ways of thinking and behaving; reviewing the personal potential consequences of these alternatives; and implementing solutions and monitoring their effects. Loumidis and Hill (1997) described a successful group intervention using social problem solving based on the work of D'Zurilla and Goldfried (1971)

Unfortunately, this reasonably promising beginning to the development of CBT for depression with this population has not yet shown much development. In two recent reviews, Hatton (2002) and Dagnan and Lindsay (2004) mention only three reports of case studies. This is particularly disappointing, because CBT for depression is now considered to be an effective and viable alternative to biochemical interventions—both with adults (Hollon, 1996) and with children and adolescents (Michael & Crowley, 2002).

Schema-Focused CBT

Beck's theory of depression, which was described earlier, relies heavily on the concept of schemata—that is, thought patterns that develop early on in life and become filters that organize and process incoming information. The work on negative self-image and stigma (Dagnan & Sandhu, 1999; Dagnan & Waring, 2004), the relationship between social development and depression (Payne & Jahoda, 2004), and the relationship between social support and depression (Benson et al., 1985; McBrien, 2003; Richards et al., 2000) indicate that these schemata are of primary importance for this client group. Instability and disconnection refer to the expectation that one's basic needs for nurturance and safety may not be met by one's social support network. This leads to schemata involving abandonment, mistrust, and emotional deprivation. Impaired autonomy refers to a perception that one cannot function independently and adequately within society. This is associated with schematic concepts of dependence, personal vulnerability, and underdevelopment. Undesirability indicates negative social comparisons with others across a range of features including social skills, achievement, socio-economic background, physical and personal attractiveness, and so on. Schemata involved with undesirability are basic beliefs supporting feelings of shame, defectiveness, social undesirability, and failure.

These schemata seem to have resonance with the work of Dagnan and colleagues. Their studies showed that people with ID have heightened feelings of negative evaluation against others (alienation), poor self-image and feelings of stigma (undesirability), and repeated experience of failure resulting in the perception of dependence on others (impaired autonomy, difficulty in self-control). Their structured approach indicated that CBT for depression can be modified to make it accessible and therefore suitable for clients with ID. As with Nezu and Nezu (1994), they emphasized problem definition in the initial stages of therapy and educating the client in the techniques of CBT. Such simple clarity has been found to be extremely beneficial for clients with ID. They go on to recommend that only one or two problems are considered during each session and that, at the end of the session, the therapist asks the client for a summary of the session. The following case studies illustrate the way in which the therapist can simplify therapy, the way in which underlying assumptions and core schemata are of primary importance, and the way in which this therapy is particularly appropriate for clients with ID.

Case Examples

We present two case examples to illustrate some of the ways in which the methods of CBT for depression can be simplified and adapted to suit individuals with ID.

Paul was a 20-year-old man who has a measured IQ of 62. He was referred for aggression and behavioral difficulties within the group home where he was staying. It was said that he was defiant and verbally abusive toward staff members and was also antagonistic, aggressive, and demanding of fellow residents. He had stopped going to his day activities and spent a great deal of time out and about on his bicycle. His behavior had escalated to the point that there was doubt whether he could maintain his ongoing tenancy, and he was referred urgently.

Joanne was a 28-year-old woman with an IQ of 69. She lived on her own in a small apartment and had often been refusing to go to her day activities in the adult resource center. She had previously dropped out of a college course for people with special needs, and the community nursing staff realized that she was spending increasing amounts of time on her own, refusing to go out of her apartment. Two months previously she had been charged with theft of batteries and a toothbrush. There appeared to be no strong motive for the theft, because Joanne had ample amounts of money with which to buy daily items. Following attendance at court, she pleaded guilty and was given a 1-year probation sentence with a requirement for attendance at treatment sessions.

Assessment Phase

Following initial history taking, BDIs were completed by both Paul and Joanne, which revealed important information. Both clients admitted to having frequent suicidal thoughts, and both indicated feelings of worthlessness and uselessness. Paul in particular admitted to feelings of guilt and inappropriate responsibility. Already from a simple assessment, certain areas of therapeutic focus were indicated. Social withdrawal was also a feature of both assessments. Paul had a BDI score of 41, which placed him in the range of severe depression, and Joanne had a BDI of 27, placing her at the upper end of moderate depression range.

The initial assessment sessions returned to the responses on the BDI, investigating the reasons why clients had indicated these levels of problems on particular issues. Paul in particular found this embarrassing and was extremely reluctant to discuss why he felt guilty. It soon transpired during the assessment that he was visiting a graveyard and was stealing small headstones and flower containers. He would put them in his ruck-sack and cycle back home. He would then take the items to his room and hide them, and the increasing feelings of anxiety in relation to being discovered were contribut-ing toward correspondingly increasing feelings of guilt. It did not take much further questioning to make the link between the death of his father 3 years before and these visits to the graveyard. When his father died, he had not been allowed to go to the funeral, because his family had felt it would be too upsetting for him. He did not know which cemetery his father was buried in, and so he visited the local cemetery instead. He said he enjoyed going to the graveyards to feel sad. A second theme began to emerge from the assessment. Three months previously he had gone to collect an application form for a job in a local supermarket, and the manager who gave him the application form had said something that Paul had construed as indicating he was not good enough to apply for the job. It would appear that he ruminated upon this for some time and punched the wall and kicked the door in his room. Following this incident, Paul ap-pears to have developed a number of thoughts related to being a useless or worthless person, and this persisted over the following weeks.

Joanne said she had always been a somewhat anxious individual and had felt that people were talking about her in a disparaging way. Following the court appearance, she be-came further convinced that others were talking about her, and after that she became extremely reluctant to go out of the house. She thought people in the neighbourhood were watching her, did not like her, and were talking about her behind her back. She was quite explicit in her statements that "people are dreadful and they don't like me." The core theme and schema related to feelings of stigmatization were not difficult to uncover. Joanne felt that if she left to live in Glasgow, things would be much better, because nobody would know her there. "I'll move to Glasgow where no one knows me" was a frequent thought during Joanne's day. Previously she had taken a neighbor's dog for a walk but had stopped this activity following the court case, feeling, clearly unrealistically, that even the dog did not like her.

Assessment takes two or three sessions. By conducting a structured interview that cov-ers the main feelings and themes of depression, one can investigate the reasons for and the nature of responses. The structure provides a clear tangible focus to which the client can respond. It also allows the consideration of actual situations that give rise to such responses as "I find it difficult to make decisions most of the time," "I always feel like a worthless person," "I don't look forward to the future," "I feel that things are my fault all the time," and "I sometimes dislike myself." In this way, a picture can be built up of the main personal and interpersonal situations that contribute toward specific symptoms of depression.

Treatment Phase

Setting an Agenda.

Setting an agenda is an extremely helpful way in which to structure a treatment session for an individual with ID. The agenda may be repetitive, but that only serves to help the individual understand the requirements of therapy. The agenda in the first few treatment sessions may be simpler than the agenda in later sessions. In later sessions, the therapist is beginning to investigate underlying assumptions that the individual may have about himself or herself and to review cognitive schemata. In earlier sessions, the main task is to build up an understanding of the link between thought, emotion, behavior, and bodily feelings. Rather than doing this in an abstract context, it is better to use personal events and reactions.

In Paul's case, he drew a number of pictures with linked, circular arrows in the cycle of thought – feelings – behavior – thought. Figure 12.1 shows a series of these simple relationships as he drew them. We have substituted words for his drawings. In the first sequence, an event happens that produces the thought "I am a useless person." This makes Paul feel upset or angry with himself. This leads him to punch the walls in his room or kick the door. This, in turn, produces the thoughts that he is a useless person, but it also increases the thoughts that he is a bad person, which further increases the degree to which he is upset with himself—and so on in a vicious cycle. In the second sequence, Paul drew himself bringing home a graveyard ornament and thinking that he should not be stealing the ornaments and that he will be found out. This leads to him feeling guilty with himself for taking the ornaments and angry that he is going to be caught. In order to avoid detection and feeling aroused by his anger and guilt, he then swears at the other resident, is confrontational with the staff, and tells them to get out of his room. On these occasions he might also kick the door. These behaviors lead him to have thoughts that he is a bad person and increases his general feelings of being upset. If the staff approach his door in order to see what is wrong, he feels guilty again

Figure 12.1. A cognitive formulation for Paul in two sequences.

Sequence 1

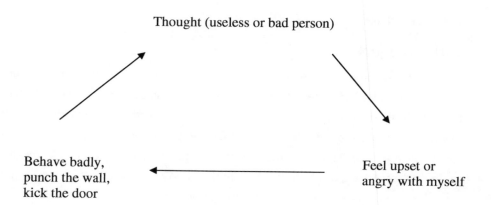

Sequence 2

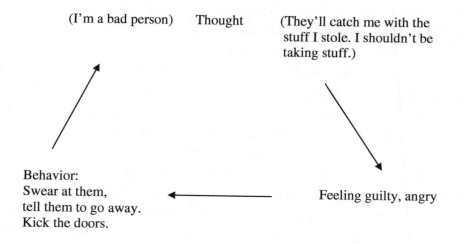

and worried that he will be found out—and the cycle continues.

Joanne was more typical in her expression of negative automatic thoughts, in that they were quite uncluttered. She thought that people were watching her, thought that people disliked her, and thought that she was a bad person who is stigmatized by others because she had had problems with her nerves and had been caught stealing. Similar to the case with Paul, the link was made between her thoughts that people were watching her and her thoughts that she was a bad person, to feelings of anxiety and becoming depressed, to refusing to go out of the house, and to developing a core belief that people disliked her. This in turn made her more convinced that she was stigmatized and that people were watching her, leading to a similar vicious cycle. Early sessions involve a simplified agenda of dealing with homework tasks, reviewing the events of the week, and placing them in the cycle of thought/self-statements, feelings/emotions, and behavior/actions.

Isolating negative thoughts.

Several methods are used for isolating negative thoughts. It is often very easy to identify negative self-statements in clients with ID. Joanne simply said, "I don't go out 'cause people are watching me and they don't like me." Clearly these two negative self-statements—"people are watching me" and "people don't like me"—are powerful disincentives to going out and evoke feelings of stigmatization. Therefore, straightforward interviewing is one of the most important methods for eliciting negative self-statements in this client group. In fact, they are so straightforward that there is a danger of missing them. In one or two quick sentences, clients will sometimes reveal five or six negative self-statements, which if used repeatedly, can be quite debilitating in the individual's everyday life. Therefore, therapists have to be careful to isolate them and make them explicit as the client is revealing them. They can then be analyzed later for their accuracy.

One effective method for eliciting negative automatic thoughts is through role play. Therapist and client can re-enact some of the difficult situations that have taken place in the client's recent past. With Paul, we role-played him coming home and a staff member or client asking him what he had in his bag. His thoughts emerged in a simple uncluttered fashion with statements, such as "Get away from me or I'll hit you," "You're going to think I've done a terrible thing," or "I've got to get out of here to my room."

Sometimes clients will say that they are unable to identify any thoughts. They will say simply that "I don't know what I'm thinking, I just feel bad" or "I don't know what I'm thinking, I just want you to go away." These statements themselves are indeed simple self-statements and can be used during therapy taken at face value. If somebody is saying to themselves "I feel bad" or "Just go away," these self-statements can be dealt with during treatment. Often we feel that the very simplicity of self-statements and feelings in people with ID is an asset to therapy and, conversely, makes them more debilitating to the individual in question. In other words, simplicity should not be taken as an indication that these thoughts are not particularly important; rather the reverse may be the case. In certain cases, it is doubtful that clients will say to themselves "I feel bad" in situations resulting in depression. It may be that the individual self-statements become enmeshed into emotions and do not reach the level of conscious thought, or it may be that the person does not have the language to express their emotional state. It could also be that there is no negative thought or self-statement; people just feel bad and so do not engage with others. However, the fact that mediated self-statements are possible means that they can either be inserted into the chain of responses (the vicious cycle just described) if they are absent, or changed to more adaptive self-statements if they are present in the sequence. In his development of a theoretical framework for self-statements, Meichenbaum (1975) wrote that it is unlikely that clients actively talk to themselves prior to treatment. Nevertheless, he recommended the employment of self-statements as a proactive treatment procedure. By challenging an individual's elicited self-statements, the therapist can increase their importance to a level where he or she may be able to employ them in therapy.

Another technique, reported in Lindsay et al. (1993), is that of role reversal. The client and therapist reverse roles, and the client as therapist has to ask what the "patient" is thinking. We find that the client as therapist may ask a very leading question of the "patient," such as "Do you worry that everyone is watching you when you go out of your house?" In this way clients can either reveal very clearly the nature of thoughts that they consider to be important in their own lives or confirm thoughts that have been elicited previously during interview. This can be the beginning of a more generalized technique, in which the client is asked to review his or her circumstances from the point of view either of the therapist or of a dispassionate observer. This will be dealt with in more detail below.

Monitoring Thoughts and Feelings.

As has been mentioned in previous sections of this chapter and elsewhere in this book, there is a developing technology for the valid and reliable assessment of thoughts and feelings in clients with ID. Figure 12.2 shows a daily diary chart, the kind that Paul and

Joanne each filled out during the course of treatment. If they suffer from restless sleep, night waking, anxieties, fears, or feelings of depression at night, they may fill this section out first thing in the morning. Figure 12.2 shows a fairly typical diary for Joanne. She felt worse in the morning than she did in the afternoon, and she slept through the night. She was able to record that she felt very worried in the morning, quite a lot in the afternoon, and not at all in the evening or during the night. In this way, a picture can be developed concerning the pattern (or lack of it) for each client's emotion. If the client is able to keep sufficiently complete records, they can be developed into a temporal, graphical representation and discussed during treatment. This was certainly possible in the case of Joanne, who could see that she felt worse in the morning than she did in the evening, and she was able to discuss this during treatment. In fact, she felt that there were no expectations on her to go out during the evening, and it was quite in order to sit at home and watch television. Therefore, she did not feel worried about staying in during the evening. On the other hand, she felt there were considerable expectations on her to attend appointments, the resource center, go shopping, and so on in the morning, and so she experienced a far greater level of feelings of self-doubt, stigmatisation, and worthlessness in the earlier part of the day.

Testing the Accuracy of Cognitions.

As has been indicated previously, the simplicity and clarity of procedures is important for clients with ID. The first way of testing the accuracy of cognitions is to review the direct evidence for and against the statements. In the case of Paul, he had the self-statement and feeling that he was a useless person. This was evident from his responses on the BDI. As treatment developed, we were able to set Paul's self-statement on one side of the flipchart, and on the other side we placed a number of competencies against

Figure 12.2. Examples of daily self-recording used in cognitive therapy with people with mild mental retardation.

	Did I Feel Worried?			What Did I Worry About?	What Did I Do?
Morning:			√	Not going out	Stay in
	NOT		QUITE A	People looking at me	
	VERY	A BIT	LOT		
Afternoon:			√	Stayed in	Stay in
	NOT		QUITE A	No one visited	
	VERY	A BIT	LOT	They don't like me	
Evening:	√			Nothing	TV
	NOT		QUITE A		
	VERY	A BIT	LOT		
Night:	√				
	NOT		QUITE A		
	VERY	A BIT	LOT		

this statement. He could ride a bike, work in the day center, cook simple meals for himself, use public transport and get the train to the nearest town, and keep his room tidy. These competencies could be ordered in complexity and difficulty and practiced through homework tasks. Therefore, the generalized catastrophizing nature of his feelings of worthlessness were challenged from the early stages in therapy.

Another common method for challenging the accuracy of cognitions is to employ reattribution methods. This is a commonly used exercise whereby the therapist asks the client to make an appraisal of an individual who has exactly and precisely the same characteristics and circumstances. In Joanne's case, the therapist asked her to make an appraisal of an individual using the following procedure. Joanne drew a girl on the flipchart and gave her a name. She was called Mary. She was then asked to give Mary a number of attributes that included all of the competencies and positive attributes that Joanne considered herself to possess. These were duly written on the flipchart so that they could not later be negated. Therefore, at this stage, a number of positive aspects of Joanne and a number of competencies were quite explicit. The therapist then asked Joanne whether it was sensible for Mary to think "Nobody likes me" or "They think I'm a bad person." There can be two results from this exercise: Either the client can accept the challenges on their cognitions, or he or she may offer further justification of them. If the latter occurs, this is added to the list of automatic thoughts and negative cognitions, which might lead to underlying assumptions and schemata that can be dealt with later in treatment. In general, this method of reattribution can be an effective means to review the evidence for negative self-statements or to develop a clearer picture of the client's matrix of negative cognitions.

Eliciting Underlying Schemata and Assumptions About Self.

Certain themes emerge from the therapeutic processes that identify problematic self-statements, avoiding actions, and emotions in individuals. As therapy progresses, it usually becomes apparent that there are certain schematic representations or underlying assumptions that underpin the way in which the client interacts with his or her world. In the case of Joanne, determining this was not difficult, because she was quite open about the way in which she viewed the world from a very early stage in therapy. Both her self-statements and her underlying assumptions reflected the view that she thought she had been stigmatized from an early age because of her intellectual limitations and her anxiety. It is very common for people with ID to be bullied both verbally and physically at school, because they are relatively easy targets. Suffering from both intellectual limitations and anxiety, Joanne was probably a particularly easy victim for others at school. The first three maladaptive schemata domains outlined above from Young, Beck, and Weinberger (1993) seem particularly relevant to people with ID. Instability and disconnection includes perceived unreliability of support, expectations that others will abuse or humiliate the individual, and an expectation that others will not adequately meet the required degree of emotional support. Impaired autonomy includes a belief that one is unable to handle everyday responsibilities, a fear of harm or illness, and the belief that one will be unable to survive or be happy without the support of another. Undesirability includes feelings of being defective, feelings that one is undesirable, and a belief that one is stupid, inept, and prone to failure. These features correspond all too easily for some clients with ID who have experienced bullying, stigmatization, negative comparison with others, and repeated failure throughout their childhood.

In Joanne's case there were clear maladaptive schemata associated with stigmatization, feelings of abandonment, feelings that society is deceitful, and feelings of incompetence. These maladaptive schemata may have been supported for many years by cognitive interpretations, behavioral avoidance or manifestation, and affective constrictions that make them quite resistant to treatment, especially at the early stages of therapy.

In the case of Paul, eliciting maladaptive schemata was more subtle. It certainly appeared that there was a delayed bereavement reaction in relation to his father in that he would continue to feel low and would visit cemeteries. He said explicitly that he enjoyed feeling sad in the graveyard. These feelings were complicated by his guilt concerning the theft of graveyard ornaments. This guilt led to heightened emotional arousal, which appeared to be linked to verbal aggression in the home and physical aggression toward his surroundings. Teasing out these various psychological strands in the required simple fashion proved quite challenging for Paul. The therapist contacted the local police department and arranged that Paul would be able to return the graveyard ornaments without any penalty. This alleviated some of the feelings of guilt that he experienced. At the same time, we set prosocial homework tasks with other members of the home. Paul was able to use relaxation techniques before and after these exercises, which began to establish him in a more sociable light. After eight sessions, his BDI score had reduced from 41 to 19, and he was clearly beginning to feel better about himself. However, maladaptive schemata are considered to be relatively durable, more resistant to treatment, and they feature prominently in theories of relapse in depression. Therefore, it was considered important to review any maladaptive schemata that Paul may have in relation to death, bereavement for his father, and his exclusion from the knowledge of his father's burial. Although we were never able to set any precise label to the schema, it contained the elements of: "I wish I had known my father better"; "They should have allowed me to go to his burial"; "Everybody needs their family and I miss my dad"; "I feel let down [abandoned]." A further maladaptive schema emerged from Paul's case, which was easier to address. It was related to his interaction with others, his guilt over the thefts, his worry about being found out, and his aggression toward his surroundings. This resulted in an underlying assumption that he was a bad and worthless person.

This point in the process is probably around halfway or two thirds of the way through therapy. The agenda can be extended to include underlying assumptions and maladaptive schemata under the heading "me" or "me deep down," and a further heading added to the agenda concerning evidence for and against these underlying schemata. It is important that the client feels fairly safe within the therapeutic relationship before these very basic personal schemata are reviewed and challenged. However, from the point of view of maintenance of therapeutic gains and relapse prevention, it is important that therapist and client begin to review more basic constructs and the way in which they might affect the client in the future. If they are not addressed, it is likely that negative encounters and obstacles will reactivate these schemata that, after all, have had many years of powerful affirmation and development.

With Paul, we reviewed in detail his relationship with his father, his feelings at the time of his death, and the feelings he has had toward his father since his death. We reviewed the ways in which these were helpful and the ways in which they interfered with his life. Most importantly, we reviewed ways in which he could maintain his father's memory in an adaptive manner that would not hinder or interfere with the rest of his life. We also reviewed hypothetical situations that might occur in the future and that would reinforce any maladaptive feelings he had related to his father. Therefore, the alternative schema was promoted that he would remember his father in a positive way, that he would try to be more comfortable with his memory, and that his dad would not want to interfere with the way he interacted with others in the future. In practical terms, we drew up a scrapbook of memories, which Paul could read and add to at any time. This seemed to prove particularly helpful, and a schema that had been a source of confusion and resentment for him began to be replaced with a much more positive series of references to his father.

For Joanne, the maladaptive schema of stigmatization was addressed in a more straight-forward fashion by encouraging structured activities, reviewing the evidence for a negative view from others using the methods mentioned above, and introducing a greater level of contact with society. While these therapeutic processes were developing, we continued to monitor her thoughts during each period of the day, using the monitoring sheet already described. After a more adaptive view of society had been established, we reviewed in detail a range of situations that Joanne might need and that might undermine this adaptive schema. We also reviewed what she might do if any of them occurred.

Homework

Setting homework tasks is very important, both to monitor the extent of maladaptive thinking that has occurred during the week and to provide situations in which more adaptive responses can be practiced. We have mentioned a series of homework tasks as we have gone through each case. Part of the homework is also to keep a simple record of situations that have arisen and that have provoked an emotional response. This can be done with a single word or picture. The essential aspect is that it can be reviewed at the next session both in terms of the problems that have been experienced and in terms of the progress that may have been made.

Conclusions

CBT for depression is a very practical and structured treatment procedure that is eminently suited for clients with ID. Its very structure and the predictable nature of each session allows for a clarity that is extremely helpful to clients. Experimental work has reviewed depression in relation to stigma, negative social comparisons, poor self-esteem, and the experience of repeated failure. It is important to caution that these findings will not be true for all individuals with ID. However, they must be considered as vulnerability factors for this client group. They certainly correspond uncomfortably with the maladaptive schemata drawn up by Young et al. (1993), in that at least three of the basic domains seem to be common in the upbringing of some individuals. We have noted that the experience of depression at some point in the lives of clients with ID may be relatively common. This might give rise to an overestimate of point prevalence because of the difficulty clients have with their personal judgments and estimates of time. In other words, if asked if they have experienced symptoms of depression in the last month or two they may answer with a time frame of the last year or two. We have emphasized that treatment for emotional disorders may be particularly apposite for this client group and have demonstrated in the two case studies that, with appropriate modifications, people with ID can report and understand the role of mediating cognitions in the causation of psychological distress and consequent behavioral disturbance. It is therefore disappointing that there has not been a greater number of treatment studies over the past 10 years (Hatton, 2002).

References

Allen, S., & Gilbert, P. (1995). A social comparison scale: Psychometric properties and relationship to psychopathology. *Personality and Individual Differences, 19,* 293–299.

Bandura, A. (1977). Self-efficacy: Towards a unifying theory of behavioural change. *Psychological Review, 84,* 191–215.

Beck, A. T. (1976) *Cognitive therapy and the emotional disorders.* New York: International Universities Press.

Beck, A. T., Rush, A. J., Shaw, B. F., & Emery, G. (1979). *Cognitive therapy of depression.* New York: John Wiley.

Beck, A. T., & Steer, R. A. (1990). *Manual for the Beck Anxiety Inventory.* New York: Psychological Corporation.

Beck, A. T., Steer, R. A., & Brown, G. K. (1995). *Beck Depression Inventory – Second Edition.* New York: Psychological Corporation.

Bellack, A. S., Hersen, M., & Himmelhoch, J. M. (1983). A comparison of social skills training, pharmacotherapy and psychotherapy for depression. *Behaviour Research in Therapy, 21,* 101–107.

Benson, B. A. (1990). Behavioral treatment of depression. In A. Dosen & F. J. Menolascino (Eds.), *Depression in mentally retarded children and adults* (pp. 309–330). Leiden, Netherlands: Logon Publications.

Benson, B. A., & Ivins, J. (1992). Anger, depression, and self-concept in adults with mental retardation. *Journal of Intellectual Disability Research, 36,* 169–175.

Benson, B. A., Reiss, S., Smith, D. C., & Laman, D. S. (1985). Psychosocial correlates of depression in mentally retarded adults. II: Poor social skills. *American Journal of Mental Deficiency, 89,* 657–659.

Brown, A. L. (1975). The development of memory: Knowing about knowing, and knowing how to know. In H. W. Reese (Ed.), *Advances in child development and behaviour* (Vol. 10, pp. 103–152). New York: Academic Press.

Brown, G. W., & Harris, T. (1978). *Social origins of depression.* London: Tavistock.

Champion, L., & Power, M. (1995). Social and cognitive approaches to depression: Towards a new synthesis. *British Journal of Clinical Psychology, 34,* 485–503.

Clark, A. K., Reed, J., & Sturmey, P. (1991). Staff perceptions of sadness among people with mental handicaps. *Journal of Mental Deficiency Research, 35,* 147–153.

Cohen, S., & Wills, T.A. (1985). Stress, social support, and the buffering hypothesis. *Psychological Bulletin, 98,* 310–357.

Dagnan, D., Chadwick, P., & Proudlove, J. (2000). Towards an assessment of suitability of people with mental retardation for cognitive therapy. *Cognitive Therapy and Research, 24,* 627–636.

Dagnan, D., & Lindsay, W. R. (2004). Research issues in cognitive therapy. In E. Emerson, C. Hatton, T. Thompson, & T. Parmenter (Eds.), *Handbook of applied research in intellectual disabilities.* Chichester, UK: John Wiley & Sons.

Dagnan, D., & Ruddick, L. (1995). The use of analogue scales and personal questionnaires for interviewing people with learning disabilities. *Clinical Psychology Forum, 79,* 21–24.

Dagnan, D., & Sandhu, S. (1999). Social comparison, self-esteem and depression in people with intellectual disability. *Journal of Intellectual Disability Research. Special Issue: Mental Health and Intellectual Disability, V, 43,* 372–379.

Dagnan, D., & Waring, M. (2004). Linking stigma to psychological distress: Testing a social-cognitive model of the experience of people with intellectual disabilities. *Clinical Psychology and Psychotherapy, 11,* 247–254.

Deb, S., Thomas, M., & Bright, C. (2001). Mental disorder in adults with intellectual disability. I: Prevalence of functional psychiatric illness among a community-based population aged between 16 and 64 years. *Journal of Intellectual Disability Research, 45,* 495–505.

Derogatis, L. R. (1993). *Brief Symptom Inventory: Administrative scoring and procedures manual* (3rd ed.). Minneapolis: National Computer Systems.

D'Zurilla, T. J., and Goldfried, M. R. (1971). Problem-solving and behaviour modification. *Journal of Abnormal Psychology, 78,* 107–126.

Ellis, A. (1973). *Humanistic psychotherapy: A rational emotive approach.* New York: Julian Press.

Ellis, A., & Grieger, R. (1977) (Eds.). *Handbook of rational-emotive therapy.* New York: Springer-Verlag.

Finlay, W. M. L., & Lyons, E. (2001). Methodological issues in interviewing and using self-report questionnaires with people with mental retardation. *Psychological Assessment, 13,* 319–335.

Glenn, E., Bihm, E., & Lammers, W. (2003). Depression, anxiety, and relevant cognitions in persons with mental retardation. *Journal of Autism and Developmental Disorders, 33,* 69–76.

Hatton, C. (2002). Psychosocial interventions for adults with intellectual disabilities and mental health problems: A review. *Journal of Mental Health, 11*, 357–373.

Helsel, W. J., & Matson, J. L. (1988). The relationship of depression to social skills and intellectual functioning in mentally retarded adults. *Journal of Mental Deficiency Research, 32*, 411–418.

Hersen, M., Bellack, A. S., & Himmelhoch, J. M. (1980). Treatment of unipolar depression with social skills training. *Behavior Modification, 4*, 547–556.

Hollon, S. D. (1996). The efficacy and effectiveness of psychotherapy relative to medications. *American Psychologist, 51*, 1025–1030.

Kanfer, F. H., and Karoly, P. (1972) Self-control. A behavioristic excursion into the lion's den. *Behavior Therapy, 3*, 398–416.

Kazdin, A. E., Matson, J. L., & Senatore, V. (1983). Assessment of depression in mentally retarded adults. *American Journal of Psychiatry, 140*, 1040–1043.

Kellet, S. C., Beail, N., Newman, D. W., & Frankish, P. (2003). Utility of the Brief Symptom Inventory (BSI) in the assessment of psychological distress. *Journal of Applied Research in Intellectual Disabilities, 16*, 127–135.

Kellet, S., Beail, N., Newman, D. W., & Hawes, A. (2004). The factor structure of the Brief Symptom Inventory: Intellectual disability evidence. *Clinical Psychology and Psychotherapy, 11*, 275–281.

Kellet, S. C., Beail, N., Newman, D. W., & Mosley, E. (1999). Indexing psychological distress in people with an intellectual disability: Use of the symptom checklist–90–R. *Journal of Applied Research in Intellectual Disabilities, 12*, 323–334.

Kolton, D. J. C., Boer, A., & Boer, D. P. (2001). A revision of the Abel and Becker Cognition Scale for intellectually disabled sex offenders. *Sexual Abuse: A Journal of Research and Treatment, 13*, 217–219.

Laman, D. S., & Reiss, S. (1987). Social skill deficiencies associated with depressed mood of mentally retarded adults. *American Journal of Mental Deficiency, 92*, 224–229.

Lewinsohn, P. M. (1974). A behavioral approach to depression. In R. M. Friedman & M. M. Katz (Eds.), *The psychology of depression: Contemporary theory and research* (pp. 157–185). New York: Wiley.

Lewinsohn, P. M. (1975). The behavioral study and treatment of depression. In M. Hersen, R. M. Eisler, & P. M. Miller (Eds.), *Progress in behavior modification* (Vol. 1, pp. 19–64). New York: Academic Press.

Lewinsohn, P. M., Mischel, W., Chaplin, W., & Barton, R. (1980). Social competence and depression: The role of illusory self-perception. *Journal of Abnormal Psychology, 89*, 203–212.

Lewinsohn, P. M., Roberts, R. E., Seeley, J. R., Rohde, P., Gotlib, I. H., & Hops, H. (1994). Adolescent psychopathology: II. Psychosocial risk factors for depression. *Journal of Abnormal Psychology, 103*, 302–315.

Lewinsohn, P. M., & Rohde, P. (1987). Psychological measurement of depression. In A. J. Marsella, R. M. A. Hirschfeld, & M. M. Katz (Eds.), *The measurement of depression* (pp. 240–266). New York: Guilford Press.

Lewinsohn, P. M., Rohde, P., Hops, H., & Clarke, G. (1991). *Adolescent coping with depression course: Leader's manual for parent groups.* Eugene, OR: Castalia.

Lewinsohn, P. M., Weinstein, M. S., & Shaw, D. A. (1969). Depression: A clinical research approach. In R. D. Rubin & C. M. Franks (Eds.), *Advances in behavior therapy* (pp. 231–240). New York: Academic Press.

Libet, J., & Lewinsohn, P. M. (1973). The concept of social skill with special reference to the behavior of depressed persons. *Journal of Consulting in Clinical Psychology, 40*, 304–312.

Lindsay, W. R. (1999). Cognitive therapy. *The Psychologist, 12*, 238–241.

Lindsay, W. R., Howells, L., & Pitcaithly, D. (1993). Cognitive therapy for depression with individuals with intellectual disability. *British Journal of Medical Psychology, 66*, 135–141.

Lindsay, W. R., & Lees, M. (2003). A comparison of anxiety and depression in sex offenders with intellectual disability and a control group with intellectual disability. *Sexual Abuse: A Journal of Research and Treatment, 15*, 339–346.

Lindsay, W. R., Michie, A. M., Baty, F. J., Smith, A. H. W., & Miller, S. (1994). The consistency of reports about feelings and emotions from people with intellectual disability. *Journal of Intellectual Disability Research, 38*, 61–66.

Lindsay, W. R., & Olley, S. C. M. (1998). Psychological treatment for anxiety and depression for people with learning disabilities. In W. Fraser, D. Sines, & M. Kerr (Eds.), *Hallas' The care of people with intellectual disabilities* (9th ed., pp. 235–232). Oxford, UK: Butterworth-Heinemann.

Lindsay, W. R., & Steptoe, L. (in review). *The assessment of anxiety and depression in a cohort of individuals with intellectual disability* (submitted for publication).

Linville, P. W. (1985). Self-complexity and affective extremity: Don't put all your eggs in one cognitive basket. *Social Cognition, 3*, 94–120.

Loumidis, K., & Hill, A. (1997). Social problem-solving groups for adults with learning disabilities. In B. Stenfert Kroese, D. Dagnan, & K. Loumidis (Eds.), *Cognitive behaviour therapy for people with learning disabilities* (pp. 86–109). London: Routledge.

Lund, J. (1985). The prevalence of psychiatric morbidity in mentally retarded adults. *Acta Psychiatrica Scandinavica, 72*, 563–570.

Lunsky, Y. (2003). Depressive symptoms in intellectual disability: Does gender play a role? *Journal of Intellectual Disability Research, 47,* 417–427.

Matson, J. L., Dettling, J., & Senatore, V. (1979). Treating depression of a mentally retarded adult. *British Journal of Mental Subnormality, 26,* 86–88.

McBrien, J. A. (2003). Assessment and diagnosis of depression in people with intellectual disability. *Journal of Intellectual Disability Research, 47,* 1–13.

Meichenbaum, D. H. (1975). Self-instructional methods. In F. H. Kanfer & A. P. Goldstein (Eds.), *Helping people change* (pp. 357–391). New York: Pergamon.

Meichenbaum, D. H. (1977). *Cognitive behavior modification: An integrative approach.* New York: Plenum.

Meins, W. (1995). Symptoms of major depression in mentally retarded adults. *Journal of Intellectual Disability Research, 39,* 41–45.

Michael, K. D., & Crowley, S. L. (2002). How effective are treatments for child and adolescent depression? A meta-analytic review. *Clinical Psychology Review, 22,* 247–269.

Nezu, C. M., & Nezu, A. M. (1994). Outpatient psychotherapy for adults with mental retardation and concomitant psychopathology: Research and clinical imperatives. *Journal of Consulting in Clinical Psychology, 62,* 34–42.

Nezu, C. M., Nezu, A. M., Rotherburg, J. L., DelliCarpini, L., & Groag, I. (1995). Depression in adults with mild mental retardation: Are cognitive variables involved? *Cognitive Therapy and Research, 19,* 227–239.

Oatley, K., & Bolton, W. (1985). A social cognitive theory of depression in reaction to life events. *Psychological Review, 92,* 372–388.

Payne, R., & Jahoda, A. (2004). The Glasgow Social Self-Efficacy Scale: A new scale for measuring social self-efficacy in people with intellectual disability. *Clinical Psychology and Psychotherapy,11,* 265–274.

Rachman, J. (2003). Eysenck and the development of CBT. *The Psychologist, 16,* 588–591.

Reed, J. (1997). Understanding and assessing depression in people with learning disabilities. In B. Stenfert Kroese, D. Dagnan, & K. Loumidis (Eds.), *Cognitive behaviour therapy for people with learning disabilities* (pp. 53–66). London: Routledge.

Reiss, S., & Benson, B. A. (1985). Psychosocial correlates of depression in mentally retarded adults: I. Minimal social support and stigmatization. *American Journal of Mental Deficiency, 89,* 331–337.

Richards, M., Maughan, B., Hardy, R., Hall, I., Strydom, A., & Wadsworth, M. (2001). Long term affective disorder in people with mild learning disability.

British Journal of Psychiatry, 179, 523–527.

Rosenberg, M., Schooler, S., & Schoenbach, C. (1989). Self-esteem and adolescent problems: Modelling reciprocal effects. *American Sociological Review, 54,* 1004–1016.

Ross, E., & Oliver, C. (2003). Preliminary analysis of the psychometric properties of the Mood, Interest and Pleasure Questionnaire (MIPQ) for adults with severe and profound learning disabilities. *The British Journal of Clinical Psychology, 42,* 81–93.

Scott, S. (1995). Mental retardation. In M. Rutter, E. Taylor, & L. Hersov (Eds.), *Child and adolescent psychiatry: Modern approaches* (3rd ed., pp. 616–645). Oxford, UK: Blackwell Science.

Segrin, C. (2000). Social skills deficits associated with depression. *Clinical Psychology Review, 20,* 379–403.

Seligman, M. E. P. (1975). *Helplessness: On depression, development and death.* San Francisco: Freeman.

Stenfert Kroese (1997). Cognitive behaviour therapy for people with learning disabilities: Conceptual and contextual issues. In B. Stenfert Kroese, D. Dagnan, & K. Loumidis (Eds), *Cognitive behaviour therapy for people with learning disabilities* (pp. 1–15). London: Routledge.

Swallow, S. R., & Kuiper, N. A. (1988). Social comparison and negative self-evaluations: An application to depression. *Clinical Psychology Review, 8,* 55–76.

Szivos-Bach, S. E. (1993). Social comparisons, stigma and mainstreaming: The self-esteem of young adults with mild mental handicap. *Mental Handicap Research, 6,* 217–234.

Wolpe, K. (1959). *Psychotherapy by reciprocal inhibition.* Stanford, CA: Stanford University Press.

Young, J. E., Beck, A. T., & Weinberger, A. (1993). Depression. In D. H. Barlow (Ed.), *Clinical handbook of psychological disorders* (pp. 240–277). New York: Guildford Press.

Zung, W. W. K. (1965). A self-rating depression scale. *Archives of General Psychiatry, 12,* 63–70.

13

PSYCHODYNAMIC COUNSELING AND PSYCHOTHERAPY FOR MOOD DISORDERS

Nigel Beail

and

David Newman

This chapter outlines the evidence base for and the basic principles of psychodynamic counseling and psychotherapy. It describes the basic techniques of psychodynamic counseling and psychotherapy, and it illustrates them through case material. The focus of the chapter is the method and modifications made to increase the applicability and usefulness of psychodynamic counseling and psychotherapy with people who have mental retardation.

Introduction

All forms of psychotherapy and counseling aim to bring about positive changes in a person's psychological functioning. Where the presenting problem is one of mood disorder, psychotherapy aims to assess and formulate the onset, nature, and meaning of the disturbance of mood and to support the client in working through his or her difficulties, if possible to a point where the disorder of mood is alleviated. There is a range of therapeutic approaches that place differing emphases on the focus of feelings, thoughts, attitudes, or behaviors in the therapeutic encounter. In psychodynamic work, the therapist is concerned with the patient's mental representation of him or herself within the world and seeks to identify the origin, meaning, and resolution of difficult feelings and inappropriate behaviors. The work entails making links between early life experiences and how these experiences influence unconscious and conscious expectations of relationships in the present day.

Until recent years, psychodynamic approaches have not been routinely offered to people with mental retardation. This reticence perhaps stems from Freud's (1904) assertion that "those patients who do not possess a reasonable degree of education and reliable character should be refused" (p. 263). This single sentence may have had a significant impact on the basis of selection and exclusion for psychotherapeutic treatment for a century (Bender, 1993). For example, Rogers (1957) stated that person-centred psychotherapy was not suitable for people with disabilities. Tyson and Sandler (1971) stated that mental deficiency is a contraindication for psychoanalysis. Being of average intelligence became an attribute for suitability for counseling and psychotherapy (Brown & Peddar, 1991). A professional consensus grew to the point where most health professionals believe that mentally retarded individuals cannot benefit from psychotherapy (Hurley, 1989). Probably as a consequence of negative professional views toward counseling and psychotherapy, services did not develop despite a growing evidence that people with mental retardation are subject to the same range of psychological problems as are other sectors of the population (Deb, Thomas, & Bright, 2001; Moss, 1999). Psychodynamic models would predict that people with mental retardation would be more vulnerable to depressive disorders due to the fact that they spend their lives in a dependent relationship to some degree. Thus, the loss of a significant caregiver has more catastrophic consequences. Klein (1975) also identified the feelings aroused in young children about their fear of loss of their mother or father. Similarly, people with mental retardation may have significant anxieties concerning their fears about what would happen to them if their caregiver left them.

Psychodynamic counseling and psychotherapy has a massive literature; so this chapter can provide only a brief and selective outline. Since its earliest days, psychoanalysis has been the subject of numerous disputes resulting in splits into various schools of thought. Today, counselors and psychotherapists find their own therapeutic home—whether Freudian, Kleinian, Jungian, Object Relations, or Rogerian. In the field of mental retardation, several practitioners have developed their own style, informed by a theoretical base, but informed and refined by their work with people who have mental retardation (Fletcher, 1999; Prout & Strohmer, 1998; Sinason, 1992).

The Evidence Base

The research literature to date on the effectiveness of psychotherapy with people who have mental retardation is limited (Beail, 2003; Prout & Nowak-Drabik, 2003). Sinason (1992) found that the earliest reports of such work amounted to a few moments of curiosity dating back to the 1930s. Prout and Nowak-Drabik (2003) recently reviewed research on psychotherapy with people with mental retardation covering the period 1968 to 1998. Their definition of psychotherapy was fairly broad and included counseling and a range of behavioral interventions. They found 92 reports with interventions. Psychotherapy accounted for only 15% of these reports. The psychodynamic literature was dominated by case studies or uncontrolled pre-post studies (e.g., Beail, 1995; Hurley, Pfadt, Tomasulo, & Gardner, 1996; Nezu & Nezu, 1994). The 92 studies were reviewed by an expert panel, which concluded that psychotherapy effects are modest with persons with mental retardation. The review compared only effects across theoretical approaches, such as psychotherapy and behavior therapy; it did not compare different forms of psychotherapy.

Beail (2003) reviewed five case series and outcome studies of psychodynamic psychotherapy with people who have mental retardation. Frankish (1989) reported reductions in behavior problems for series of seven therapy recipients. Beail (1998) reported the outcome of weekly outpatient psychoanalytic psychotherapy with 20 men with mental retardation, who presented with behavior problems. The problem behaviors were eliminated in most cases. Change was maintained at 6 months follow-up. Beail (2001) reported on recidivism rates among 18 male offenders with mental retardation. Of the 13 who completed psychodynamic psychotherapy, the majority remained offense-free at 4 years follow-up. Of the 5 men who refused treatment, all had reoffended within 2 years. Beail and Warden (1996) and Beail (2000) reported a study of the outcome of psychodynamic psychotherapy with 20 adults with mental retardation who had comorbid mental health problems. They found significant reductions in symptoms of psychological distress, improvements in interpersonal functioning, and increases in self-esteem. A study not identified in Beail (2003) or Prout and Nowak-Drabik (2003) was carried out by Bichard, Sinason, and Usiskin (1996). They evaluated change on the Draw-a-Person Test for seven adults with mental retardation who were in psychodynamic psychotherapy for 2 years. In their design they had an age- and IQ-matched control group. They reported statistically significant improvements for the treatment group but no change in the control group.

The evidence base is small, but it is an improvement on the situation a decade ago. Available evidence suggests that people with mental retardation do make gains during psychodynamic psychotherapy, gains that are maintained at follow-up. The range of clinical presentations of recipients was limited, with most presenting with problem behavior, including offending, and a range of mental health problems. Further, assessment and outcome variables were small in number and narrow in focus. Despite the limited evidence for the effectiveness of counseling and psychotherapy with people who have mental retardation, a case for its provision can be made on grounds of equity (Sinason, 1992). Certainly, we must not forget that the absence of evidence for efficacy is not evidence of ineffectiveness.

Preassessment

Many people with mental retardation are dependent upon the support of professional caregivers or family members if they are to attend psychotherapy or counseling sessions. It is often the case that these outside supports have been integral in making the referral. A preassessment meeting with supporting agencies can serve several useful purposes. First, as the therapist, you will hear firsthand about the issues or concerns of the referrer. Second, you can probe into issues regarding the client's ability and willingness to consent to psychodynamic assessment. You can also address expectations regarding the frequency and length of treatment and give information regarding the boundaries of confidentiality. The meeting also serves to inform you of the reality of the client's social situation, the stability of his or her home life, and the degree of social support. This information can prove useful in formulating whether psychodynamic work is indicated in any given case.

Boundaries

Counseling and psychotherapy require a safe and private space. If undertaking weekly sessions, you should use the same room consistently at the same time and day of the week. Traditionally psychoanalysts used a room that contained a couch and a chair. Today, in most service settings counselors and psychotherapists sit with their clients in comfortable chairs, where they are able to see each other, but not face to face. This creates a less threatening situation, where eye contact is reduced so that the client does not feel under scrutiny. The risk of outside interruptions should be minimized. Clients are offered a set session duration—usually 50 minutes—for each session they attend. However, some people with mental retardation find the 50-minute duration hard to tolerate, and sessions lasting only 30 or 40 minutes may be offered initially. Risks to your personal safety are usually low but still present. Therefore, prior to any session, you should take into account risk issues by implementing personal alarm procedures and placing yourself near the door, with a clear exit from the therapy setting.

The Therapeutic Relationship

As the therapist, you need to seek to establish a "working alliance" with the client (Bugental, 1987). Different schools of psychotherapy emphasize different aspects of the alliance. The factors identified by the client-centered school as necessary and sufficient conditions for patient change are accurate empathy, positive regard, nonpossessive warmth, congruence, and genuiness. Today these are accepted as essential aspects of all counseling and psychotherapeutic endeavors. Psychodynamic counseling and psychotherapy involves working within a process that begins with an assessment. If the outcome of that assessment is that counseling or psychotherapy is appropriate and if the client consents, then the intervention begins.

In psychodynamic work, you should refrain from revealing anything personal about yourself. The safe setting, the clear boundaries, and the therapeutic relationship are all designed to facilitate the client's exploring and clarifying his or her psychological reality. Furthermore, they function to contain the client and therapist in a manner whereby previously intolerable psychological states can become held within the session, clarified, and—where possible—resolved and reintegrated in a tolerable form by the client.

Assessment

Prior to engaging a client in counseling or psychotherapy, you need to assess the client's problem, circumstances, and treatment needs. You must also obtain the client's consent to any proposed intervention. The treatment must be described in simple terms. For example, you might say, "This treatment involves coming to see me each week to talk about any difficulties you are having. Together we will try to understand your difficulties and overcome them." As people with mental retardation may have expectations, such as your giving them drugs, it may be important to say that you will not be giving them any pills. You also need to inform the client about the positives and negatives. This includes telling the client that the treatment may help reduce his or her symptoms and improve his or her quality of life with reference to the difficulties and possible outcomes. The negative aspects of therapy include that it is a difficult process, involving talking about painful or upsetting things. You need to check that the client has retained and understood this, weighed the positives and negatives, and made a choice. Some clients may not be able to do this. If you believe that treatment is in the client's best interest, you should follow the legal procedures and guidance for your state or country for providing treatment for adults who cannot consent.

In the case of people with mood disorders, we are interested in how the client communicates their difficulties. People with mental retardation often have limited communication skills and so may have more difficulty communicating their symptoms. Verbal statements, utterances, nonverbal behaviors, and the use of expressive materials, such as paper and crayons—all are seen as valid modes of communication. When working with people who have mental retardation, you need to work within the expressive and receptive communication skills of the client. You need to ask questions and make your interventions in clear and nondemanding language. You may also have to help your client to label objects, feelings, and behaviors. As in child analysis, you may have to include an educational element and make provision for the use of such materials as paper and pens and such representative objects as figures. People who have mental retardation often have difficulties in constructing a chronology around autobiographical memory. Therefore, part of the work in assessment and treatment may involve the construction of chronology. Pictorial images, such as a timeline illustrating key moments in the client's autobiographical history, can be used to provide a concrete representation and aid this process.

The assessment is the beginning of the therapeutic relationship. Part of the assessment involves evaluating whether you and the client can work together. Does the client appear to trust you, or can some preliminary work be carried out to build a trusting relationship? The nature of the relationship between you and the client—the working alliance—has been found to be a significant factor in outcome for a range of psychological interventions, including counseling and psychotherapy (Roth & Fonagy, 1996).

The aims of counseling are more limited. Therefore, counseling tends to be more problem-focused, goal-oriented, and time-limited. Psychotherapy, on the other hand, is not problem-focused or goal-oriented and is more open-ended. Counseling is usually attended weekly, but psychotherapy could be more frequent. Clients suitable for counseling should have a problem of recent onset that has clear possible reasons. They should have some relationships, should be functioning well in some aspects of life, should tolerate disturbing feelings, and should not act out. They should also have a wish to understand themselves and have a desire to change.

Clients who are more suitable for psychotherapy would have long-standing problems with unclear reasons. They should have difficulties with relationships, an inability to trust, and an excessive concern about the self. They should experience severely disturbing thoughts and acting out. However, there should be a desire for change and understanding. The assessment phase may therefore extend over a number of sessions, as the therapist obtains as detailed and accurate history as possible.

During the assessment phase, the therapist also looks for possible reasons that suggest against a psychodynamic approach. Clinical judgment is required for each individual case, but common contraindications include where a person is abusing drugs or alcohol, where an organic brain disease inhibits the cognitive integration of the material raised in therapy, and where the person is experiencing an acute psychotic episode. In the case of a psychotic episode, psychodynamic therapy can begin after the acute phase of psychosis has passed. It is good practice to make such a decision in conjunction with both the client and a psychiatrist. A further contraindication for psychodynamic counseling or psychotherapy in mainstream service settings is where the client habitually acts out distress in the form of significant violence to self or to others. Psychodynamic work may be offered in such cases in specialist settings that are equipped to manage the risk of violence.

Some practitioners also advocate the use of psychometric assessments to further supplement the clinical picture, both at assessment and at discharge from treatment (Newman, Kellett, & Beail, 2003). However, some counselors and psychotherapists object to the use of such scales, because they believe that the introduction of an evaluative element into the treatment impacts negatively on the therapeutic relationship.

Case Example

Alan, a 20-year-old man with mental retardation, was referred due to behavioral problems, low mood, public crying, and manic episodes. His manic episodes were associated with pressure of speech, grandiosity, and psychomotor agitation. When he was out of the house, he had frequent falls to the ground, which never occurred at home. In the assessment sessions, Alan initially said he could not understand why there was concern about him falling down. As the assessment progressed, he acknowledged the problem and said he did it when he was upset. He could not tell the therapist why he felt upset. However, when asked to say whatever came into his mind when he thought about being upset, he said he needed to talk about men and men's things. This was accompanied by sexualized behavior toward his male therapist. The reasons for Alan's difficulties are unclear. Therefore, Alan was offered a course of psychotherapy.

Gathering Information

Psychodynamic counseling and psychotherapy involves a continuous process of exploration. Throughout psychotherapy, the therapist gathers information from the client. Psychodynamic sessions begin with the therapist providing the client with space to free-associate. This involves inviting the client to say whatever is in his or her mind and whatever comes to mind. The counselor or psychotherapist will be interested in anything that the client says, including information on their current problem, circumstances, current and past relationships, dreams, fantasies, and so on.

In psychodynamic work, the therapist resists giving the client information about him or herself. The therapist presents him or herself as a type of screen onto which the client can project imagined perceptions of the therapist. However, the way in which this is done with clients who have mental retardation needs special care. So, if a client asks about what the therapist is doing that night, the therapist may say, "That's an interesting question. You are thinking about what people might do at night time." Thus, the client's question is used as a vehicle to refocus on his or her own psychological material. Some therapists ask for dream material and fantasies. However, clients with mental retardation may not experience dreams in the same way. For example, some people with mental retardation believe that any person who appeared in their dream would also know about it. Also, some cannot distinguish between dreams, fantasies, and reality (Beail, 1989).

Developmental understanding of representation (Bruner, 1972) suggests that adults with mental retardation would possess a better visual record of their experiences, but would not possess the symbols, such as words, to communicate their visual recall. Such cognitive difficulties may lead to frustration in the therapeutic relationship, where the client tries to communicate and the therapist struggles to understand. This may lead to the client acting out in the session as a means of communicating an experience. This may be particularly the case for victims of sexual assault who do not have a sexual vocabulary. People with mental retardation often fail to achieve levels of development that enable a capacity for full perspective taking or for feeling empathy. Thus, the therapist has to work within the limits of the development of the client. This may mean working with clients who interact with the world from a singular perspective of self-interest (that is, narcissism).

Basic Techniques

The therapist uses a number of methods to enable clients to tell their story. Most of these methods are common to both counseling and psychotherapy. Psychodynamic psychotherapy differs, in that it also involves the formulation of interpretations aimed at accessing and making sense of unconscious content.

Information-Giving Responses

Clients need information about their treatment and about such matters as the time left in the session and so on. In working with people with mental retardation, this is particularly important, because they may forget information about their treatment much more easily. They may agree to attending for a number of sessions but may be unable to retain that information over time and also may not be able to keep an internal log and count down remaining sessions. Thus, the therapist needs to provide this information more regularly and provide concrete representations of time, such as crossing out each completed session on the client's appointment card. Also, the reason for the referral may become lost as the therapy proceeds, so this may need to be revisited from time to time to help the client evaluate his or her progress or lack of it. However, advice and instruction are not usually within the remit of the psychodynamic model.

Listening and Observing

The therapist listens carefully to the client's verbal communications, attending to what the client says in terms of the factual content, the words used, and also what is not said. With clients with mental retardation, the therapist attends to the extent of the client's expressive language skills to make sure to work within them. The therapist clarifies the personal meaning to the client of certain words used within topics and clarifies words that contain ambiguous or double meanings. The therapist also observes the client's mood, as communicated through what he or she says, the way it is said, and how the client behaves. The therapist should also remember as much as possible. The client may talk about a range of things, and the therapist does not interrupt. Points that need to be taken up and further explored have to be held in memory. The therapist also observes the client's nonverbal communications, including facial expression, gestures, and posture. People who have mental retardation are additionally more likely to act out what they cannot communicate in words.

While listening to the client, you as the therapist need to monitor your own feelings, fantasies, and reactions in response to the client's material. You must be prepared to accept these as meaningful elements in the communication between the client and you. This is referred to as the *counter-transference*. You need to distinguish between different aspects of the counter-transference. You need to pay attention to whether the client's communication triggers unresolved issues in your own life. Such matters should be explored in supervision and then with your own therapist. Counter-transference proper refers to those feelings that have been communicated, stimulated, or induced by the client and play an important role in understanding the client's problems. This may provide some insight into how the client makes other people feel and also what the client may be doing to make them feel that way. Thus, attending to the counter-transference enhances empathy with and understanding of the client.

Reflecting

At various times when the client is telling his or her story, you may reflect back, paraphrase, or précis what the client has been telling you. In therapy with people who have mental retardation, you may also reflect back your observations of nonverbal behavior. This type of response indicates to the client that you have been listening and paying attention. Observations in long periods of silence let the client know that you are still attending to him or her and thinking about him or her. It also helps you to check that what you have observed or heard is accurate. Reflections are also considered as helpful to the client in developing what he or she is communicating.

Exploratory and Information-Seeking Responses

Exploratory responses attempt to draw out more information from the client. These are generated from hypotheses about what the client may not be saying in words but may be hinting at through behavior or tone of voice. Information-seeking responses are aimed at clarification. Clarification helps sort out what is happening by questioning and rephrasing. These often constitute direct questions, which seek to elicit more information about what the client is saying. Kebbel and Hatton (1999) carried out research on people with mental retardation being witnesses. They concluded that they can provide accurate accounts of events they have witnessed when interviewed appropriately. Thus, people with mental retardation can provide accurate accounts of past events, particularly when questioned using open questions about central information, rather than closed questions about peripheral information. In seeking information from people with mental retardation in therapy, we need to take account of these finding when we are inquiring about their past experiences.

Linking Responses

Psychodynamic counselors and psychotherapists also make linking responses. Here words and or actions are linked together as a tentative interpretation to try to understand the nature of the client's anxiety in the session. These responses differ from the others in that they aim to elucidate unconscious feelings and ideas.

Case Illustration

In the following abstract from a session with Alan, some of these basic psychodynamic techniques are illustrated.

TH: Where would you like to start today?

ALAN: *(Behavior: Looks therapist in the eye. 2 minutes).* *[Observation]*

TH: You are looking at me. *[Reflecting response]*

ALAN: *(Behavior: His head is bowed down. He looks at his legs and groin. Periodically he looks up at the therapist. There is a slight smile on his face. 5 minutes).*

TH: You are smiling at me. *[Reflecting response]*

ALAN: Yeah. *(Behavior: Looks at therapist and smiles slightly. He places his hands on his knees and looks down at his groin. He moves his hands slowly up his thighs. His hands reach his groin. He looks up at therapist and smiles slightly. His face flushes red. He moves his hands slowly down his thighs until they reach his knees. 5 minutes).*

TH: You are looking at me. You are smiling at me. You are touching your legs. *[Reflecting response with linking]*

ALAN: *(Shaky voice)* Yeah.

TH: It feels nice to touch your legs like that. *[Exploratory response]*

ALAN: Yeah.

TH: I wonder if you could tell me more about that feeling. *[Information-seeking response]*

ALAN: *(Behavior: Looks at his hands as he moves them up and down his legs. He repeats these actions several times. His hands rub his legs and penis through the fabric of his trousers. His penis appears to becoming erect. He looks up at the therapist and smiles slightly. The smile dissipates, and his lips quiver. 5 minutes).*

TH: You are rubbing your legs. You are feeling excited inside. *[Exploratory response]*

ALAN: *(Louder, shaky voice)* Yeah.

TH: Sometimes when you feel excited, you also feel anxious, feel nervous. *[Linking response]*

ALAN: Sometimes.

TH: You feel nervous now. *[Exploratory response]*

ALAN: I don't, I don't know. . . .

Alan then went on to tell his therapist that he did not know what to do when he became aroused this way. He also continued to be aroused and exhibit extreme anxiety and frustration.

Understanding the Unconscious Content

Psychodynamic therapists seek to understand with the client the latent or unconscious meaning of the client's communications. In order to do this, they recontextualize the manifest content of the communications as transference. Freud (1912) described transference as occurring when psychological experiences are revived and, instead of being located in the past, are applied to dealings with a person in the present. The client transfers positive (love and gratitude) and negative (anger and hate) feelings and experiences from the past into his or her relationship with the therapist. The transference is acknowledged to be the terrain on which all the basic problems of a given analysis play themselves out. In psychodynamic psychotherapy, the establishment, modalities, interpretation, and resolution of the transference are in fact what define the cure (Laplance & Pontalis, 1988).

Transference conceptualizes the individual's problems within the realm of the interpersonal. It recognizes that interpersonal problems with or negative feelings toward significant others in the past and present, and it can be enacted with the therapist as well. Transference within therapy allows the therapist to identify interpersonal issues and deal with them as empirical data in the here and now. This process allows early traumatic experiences and empathic failures on the part of parents and other caregivers to be relived and corrected.

Psychodynamic psychotherapy also seeks to understand unconscious communications through models of the internal world. Most significantly, we all have an ego, which is the location of the anxiety caused by unconscious material. It is the ego that employs a range of defenses to ward off anxiety. There is also a range of psychodynamic theories of development that the therapist may also employ to understand the origins or development of difficulties and conflicts, as well as coping styles.

Psychotherapy offers a range of possibilities whereby the therapeutic relationship can facilitate change. Clarkson (1993) highlights the reparative/developmentally needed relationship and defines this as the intentional provision by the therapist of a corrective/reparative or replenishing parental relationship (or action) where the original parenting was deficient, abusive, or overprotective. Such a relationship modality is a further facet of the therapist's intervention and style. It is particularly relevant to working with many clients with mental retardation. It is sensitive to the needs of the individual who may have experienced deficient or abusive, emotional, physical, or sexual relationships with caregivers. Often such experiences occur in relation to the vulnerabilities or perceived qualities of the mental retardation itself. The holding environment of Winnicott (1958) is an example of such a provision, as are the re-parenting techniques of Schiff et. al. (1975) in transactional analysis.

Malan (1979) depicted the aim of psychotherapy in the form of the "Two Triangles" (see Figure 13.1). The two triangles describe the process of psychodynamic psychotherapy. Each triangle stands on its apex. The aim of the therapeutic endeavor is to reach beneath the defense and anxiety to the true feeling. At this point, the true feeling can be traced back from the present transference location—the therapy room—to its origin in the past, usually to the relationship with parents or significant caregivers. Malan (1979), states that "the importance of these two triangles is that between them they can be used to represent almost every intervention that a therapist makes; and that much of the therapist's skill consists of knowing which parts of which triangle to include in his interpretation at any given moment" (p. 91).

Figure 13.1. Malan's two triangles.

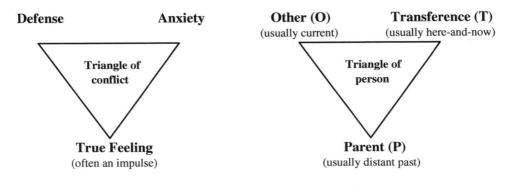

Defense   **Anxiety**   **Other (O)**   **Transference (T)**
                                          (usually current)   (usually here-and-now)

Triangle of conflict   Triangle of person

True Feeling   **Parent (P)**
(often an impulse)   (usually distant past)

Alan's therapist hypothesized that the content of the session represented a transference of a sexual relationship from the past being acted out in the session.

TH: You are unsure about these feelings. You are unsure . . . what these feelings mean.

ALAN: (*Behavior: He holds and rubs his penis through the fabric of his trousers*).

TH: You are rubbing yourself, in between your legs.

ALAN: Yeah.

TH: Can you tell me what you call that?

ALAN: What is . . . between my legs?

TH: Yes, what name do you give that?

ALAN: Have you got one?

TH: You want to know if I have got one.

ALAN: I don't know . . . I don't know how to . . . (*Loud voice*) I don't know how to do it. (*Behavior: Looks at therapist and pinches his penis through his trousers. His face is flushed and red. He moves his legs so that they open and close in fast succession*).

TH: You feel sexual, excited, turned on. [*Information giving*] You also feel anxious or nervous. You are holding your penis and pinching it. You are saying, "I don't know how to do it." I wonder what it is that you do not know how to do. [*Exploratory response*]

ALAN: I don't know how to do it. Please, I don't know . . .

TH: You are looking at me and holding your penis. You are telling me that you don't know how to do it. [*Reflecting response*] It feels to me . . . right now, that you are wanting me to hold your penis. [*Linking to the therapist's counter-transference in response to the transference*]

ALAN: (*Behavior: Looks at therapist, his hands and body still*). Yeah. (*Behavior: Looks at therapist intensely. His face is becomes very flushed with color. He rocks his body back and forth on the chair. He opens and closes his legs in a frantic manner. He puts his hand down his trousers and increases the intensity of his masturbation*).

Here the therapist is working with the "here and now" corner of Malan's triangle of the person. In the here and now, the client is acting out in a sexual way. The therapist works with the triangle of conflict in which "acting out" represents a defense. Defense mechanisms are viewed as psychological processes designed to give the most effective compromise expression to the varying external and internal, past and present, needs of the individual at each point in time (Wallerstein, 1983). Such processes operate largely within the individual's unconscious mental functioning but are capable of being extrapolated and understood within the conscious realm. Perry (1990) defined "acting out" as an episode wherein "the individual deals with emotional conflicts, or internal or external stressors, by acting without reflection or apparent regard for negative consequences. Acting out involves the expression of feelings, wishes or impulses in uncontrolled behavior with apparent disregard for personal or social consequences. It usually occurs in response to interpersonal events with significant people in the subject's life, such as parents, authority figures, friends, or lovers" (p 6).

For Alan, this defense mechanism allows him to discharge and express his feelings and impulses, rather than tolerate them and reflect on the painful events that stimulate them. In therapy the therapist reflects upon his erotic actions as they occur. However, Alan bypasses the awareness of his actions by ceasing to attempt to delay, reflect upon, or plan a strategy to handle the impulses or feelings. Rather, he directly expresses these impulses in his behavior. This results in his expression of raw sexual impulses that do not appear to take possible consequences into account.

At one point following his acting out, Alan momentarily reflects on his feelings and behavior. His mouth quivers and twitches as his anxiety presents in the form of guilt. At this point he looks at his therapist, expecting punishment for his behavior. His experience at this point lies on a boundary that expects punishment from the transference relationship—that is, patient/child–therapist/parent. But the therapist does not act out by punishing the breaking of the boundary. The therapist works to contain the client's anxiety as well as the therapist's own anxiety, thus allowing the transference relationship to develop beyond therapist as parent. This results in a new transference situation, in which Alan's sexual impulses become discharged through the mechanism of "projective identification." He experiences his sexual impulses as unacceptable and projects them into the therapist, as if it was really the therapist that originated the impulse. This defensive process is paramount to the formulation of Alan's difficulties. It is a defense that signifies Alan's irrational responsibility for a past sexual trauma. Perry (1990) stated that projective identification "is called into play when interpersonal cues stimulate memories of traumatic situations or interchanges" (p. 15). The therapist interprets the projective identification ("It feels to me . . . right now, that you are wanting me to hold your penis"), and in doing so, gives the ownership of these feelings back to Alan, who then integrates the impulses as his own and contains them for a moment. The interpretation reaches beyond the defense to elevate Alan's anxiety as outlined in Malan's triangles. Alan is unable to contain his anxiety for long enough to access the true feelings. He returns once more to the defense of acting out. Alan's defensive functioning in this form is maladaptive. It does not mitigate the effects of his internal conflict. Furthermore, in other settings, perhaps even with other therapists, his acting out could bring serious, negative, external consequences.

In this session Alan is provided with the experience of his impulses and feelings not destroying the container—that is, the therapist. This experience is presented in successive sessions. It is a therapeutic strategy designed to strengthen the client sufficiently until he can withstand and contain his previously intolerable experiences. As the patient becomes empowered to contain himself, he is enabled to lower his defensive structures. At this point he can hold, own, examine, and eventually understand his true feelings. The holding environment is a necessary space in which Alan can experience empowerment and integration over his psychic conflict. These processes within the therapeutic relationship parallel the infant's earliest experiences. As such, the analyst is a container for the client's intolerable experiences, just as a good-enough parent is the container of the baby's nameless fears (Bion, 1959).

As Alan's therapy progressed, the therapist began to offer interpretations linking Alan's presentation in therapy to a past confusing sexual relationship with a man. In response, Alan continued acting out by asking his therapist for sexual contact. He also talked about "pain" and stated, "It will not be as bad this time." Subsequently, Alan's past sexual relationship with one of his care staff became the focus of therapy. A key issue for Alan was the loss of the relationship as well as coming to terms with the issues of power imbalance and exploitation in the relationship. In his therapy, he went on to mourn the loss of that relationship, develop an understanding of appropriate relationship boundaries, and develop new relationships.

Technical Considerations

In psychotherapy with people who have mental retardation, the therapist should make all interpretations in clear language the client can understand. The therapist should also take into account memory difficulties of the client. As some interpretations involve linking together several pieces of information, they should be delivered in parts and built up often over the course of many sessions. As the interpretation is delivered, the therapist should check what the client has heard and understood. Opinions vary as to whether interpretations should be given when the transference is negative. Freudian approaches give interpretations only when the client is in a state of positive transference. Kleinians depart from this approach and see the act of interpretation as dealing first and foremost with the negative transference. Klein (1975) found that the maximum point of anxiety was reached during negative transference, and interpretations shifted the feelings for the therapist in a positive direction. In work with people with mental retardation, Klein's approach appears more appropriate for pragmatic reasons. First, it avoids the risk of clients forgetting some features of the content due to memory difficulties. Case studies suggest that people with mental retardation defend themselves against anxiety through more primitive mechanisms, such as splitting and disowning aspects of themselves and their experience (Beail, 1989; Sinason, 1992). Thus, deferring interpretation runs the risk of material being lost and disowned if only temporarily.

Ending Therapy

All treatments come to an end. With people with mental retardation, this needs to be managed with great care. Clients are in a constantly dependent state and go through life losing people due to the very nature of staffing in care organizations. The therapist therefore needs to manage issues that arise from the temporary nature of the therapeutic relationship and keep termination issues on the agenda.

Following successful psychodynamic work, clients will be better equipped to manage negative mood states and understand how to develop and maintain relationships with peers and caregivers. Such indicators of progress from the world outside therapy inform client and therapist that gains in psychological and social functioning have occurred.

Summary and Conclusion

In this chapter we have provided a brief overview of the process of psychodynamic counseling and psychotherapy with people who have mental retardation. This has been illustrated through work with one client. All people with mental retardation should have equal access to counseling and psychotherapy, in line with service provision that is afforded to people without mental retardation. Now that the case for equal access has being made, the need for research on outcome is paramount. Only a handful of studies have been published. But the weight of the evidence so far has been positive. We are unable, however, to answer a range of questions about the comparative effectiveness of treatments and a range of issues about treatment length and what treatments are best for what disorders. Progress will be made only if we continue to empathize with the psychological needs of people with mental retardation and respect their right to have access to counseling and psychotherapy.

References

American Psychiatric Association. (1994). *Diagnostic and statistical manual of mental disorders* (4th ed.). Washington, DC: Author.

Beail, N. (1989). Understanding emotions. In D. Brandon (Ed.). *Mutual respect* (pp. 27–44). Surbiton, UK: Good Impressions.

Beail, N. (1995). Outcome of psychoanalysis, psychoanalytic and psychodynamic psychotherapy with people with intellectual disabilities. *Changes, 13,* 186–191.

Beail, N. (1998). Psychoanalytic psychotherapy with men with intellectual disabilities: A preliminary outcome study. *British Journal of Medical Psychology, 71,* 1–11.

Beail, N. (2000). *An evaluation of outpatient psychodynamic psychotherapy for adults with intellectual disabilities.* Paper presented at the 11th World Congress of the International Association for the Scientific Study of Intellectual Disabilities, Seattle, WA. *Journal of Intellectual Disability Research, 44,* 204.

Beail, N. (2001). Recidivism following psychodynamic psychotherapy amongst offenders with intellectual disabilities. *British Journal of Forensic Practice, 3,* 33–37.

Beail, N. (2003). What works for people with mental retardation? Critical commentary on cognitive behavioral and psychodynamic psychotherapy. *Mental Retardation, 41,* 468–472.

Beail, N., & Warden, S. (1996). Evaluation of a psychodynamic psychotherapy service for adults with intellectual disabilities: Rationale, design and preliminary outcome data. *Journal of Applied Research in Intellectual Disabilities, 9,* 223–228.

Bender, M. (1993). The unoffered chair: The history of therapeutic disdain towards people with learning difficulty. *Clinical Psychology Forum, 54,* 7–12.

Bichard, S., Sinason, V., & Usiskin, J. (1996). Measuring change in mentally retarded clients in long-term psychoanalytic psychotherapy. *National Association for the Dually Diagnosed Newsletter, 13,* 6–11.

Bion, W. (1959). Attacks on linking. *International Journal of Psychoanalysis, 40,* 308–315.

Brown, D., and Peddar, J. (1991). *Introduction to psychotherapy*. London: Methuen.

Bruner, J. S. (1972). The nature and uses of immaturity. *American Psychologist, 27*, 687–708.

Bugental, J. F. T. (1987). *The art of the psychotherapist*. New York: W. W. Norton.

Clarkson, P. (1993). *On psychotherapy*. London: Whurr Publishers.

Deb, S., Thomas, M., & Bright, C. (2001). Mental disorder in adults with intellectual disability. I: Prevalence of functional psychiatric illness among a community-based population aged between 16 and 64 years. *Journal of Intellectual Disability Research, 45*, 495–505.

Fletcher, R. (1999). *Therapy approaches for persons with mental retardation*. New York: NADD Press.

Frankish, P. (1989). Meeting the emotional needs of handicapped people: A psychodynamic approach. *Journal of Mental Deficiency Research, 33*, 407–414.

Freud, S. (1904). On psychotherapy. In. J. Stratchey (Ed.), *The standard edition of the complete psychological works of Sigmund Freud* (Vol. 12, p. 263). London: Hogarth Press.

Freud, S. (1912). The dynamics of transference. In. J. Stratchey (Ed.), *The standard edition of the complete psychological works of Sigmund Freud*. (Vol. 12, pp. 97–108). London: Hogarth Press.

Hurley, A. D. (1989). Individual psychotherapy with mentally retarded individuals: A review and call for research. *Research in Developmental Disabilities, 10*, 261–275.

Hurley, A. D., Pfadt, A., Tomasulo, D., & Gardner, W. I. (1996). Counselling and Psychotherapy. In J. W. Jacobson & J. A. Mulick (Eds.), *Manual of diagnosis and professional practice in mental retardation* (pp. 371–378). Washington, DC: American Psychological Association.

Kebbell, M. R., & Hatton, C. (1999). People with mental retardation as witnesses in court. *Mental Retardation, 3*, 179–187.

Klein, M. (1975). *The writings of Melanie Klein. Volume 3*. London: Hogarth Press.

Laplanche, J., & Pontalis, J. B. (1988). *The language of psychoanalysis*. London: Karnac Books.

Malan, D. H. (1979). *Individual psychotherapy and the science of psychodynamics*. London: Butterworth.

Moss, S. (1999). Assessment: Conceptual issues. In N. Bouras (Ed.), *Psychiatric and behaviour disorders in developmental disabilities* (pp.18–37). Cambridge, UK: Cambridge University Press.

Newman, D. W., Kellett, S., & Beail, N. (2003). From research and development to practice-based evidence: Clinical governance initiatives in a service for adults with mild intellectual disability and mental health needs. *Journal of Intellectual Disability Research, 47,* 68–74.

Nezu, C. M., & Nezu, A. M. (1994). Outpatient psychotherapy for adults with mental retardation and concomitant psychopathology: Research and clinical imperatives. *Journal of Consulting in Clinical Psychology, 62,* 34–42.

Perry, C. J. (1990). *Defense Mechanism Rating Scales.* Cambridge, MA: Cambridge Hospital.

Prout, H. T., & Nowak-Drabik, K. M. (2003). Psychotherapy with persons who have mental retardation: An evaluation of effectiveness. *American Journal of Mental Retardation, 108,* 82–93.

Prout, H. T., & Strohmer, D. C. (1998). Issues in mental health counseling with persons with mental retardation. *Journal of Mental Health Counselling, 20,* 112–120.

Rogers, C. R. (1957). The necessary and sufficient conditions of psychotherapeutic personality change. *Journal of Consulting Psychology, 21,* 95–103.

Roth, A., & Fonagy, P. (1996). *What works for whom: A critical review of psychotherapy research.* New York: Guildford Press.

Schiff, J. L., Schiff, A. W., Mellor, K., Schiff, E., Schiff, S., Richman, D., et al. (1975). *Transactional analysis treatment of psychosis.* New York: Harper & Row.

Sinason, V. (1992). *Mental handicap and the human condition: New approaches from the Tavistock.* London: Free Association Books.

Tyson, R. L., & Sandler, J. (1971). Problems in the selection of patients for psychoanalysis: Comments on the application of "indications," "suitability" and analysability." *British Journal of Medical Psychology, 44,* 211–229.

Wallerstein, R. S. (1983). Defenses, defense mechanisms, and the structure of the mind. *Journal of the American Psychoanalytical Association, 31* (Suppl.), 201–225.

Winnicott, D. W. (1958). *Collected papers: Through paediatrics to psycho-analysis.* London: Tavistock Publications.

14

Behavioral Formulation and Treatment of People With Mental Retardation: Formulation and Interventions

Peter Sturmey

Behaviorism and Depression

Emotion and cognition are often said to characterize depression. People *feel* sad and *feel* that they lack energy. They *believe* they lack self-worth or a sense of purpose. Their *underlying* core schemata formed in childhood and activated by stressors *cause* depression. Underlying biochemical irregularities reduce the value of reward. It is often said that behaviorism focuses on behavior, not on feelings and thoughts; it might be adequate for teaching a child to pull up his or her pants or to suppress aggression through manipulation of punishment and reward, but behavioral approaches are inadequate for complex problems. Surely cognitive therapy can change how a depressed person thinks? Surely psychotherapy will identify the root cause of the person's depression in his or her childhood, and this uncovering of hidden trauma will result in the relief of the depression? Surely psychotropic medication will elevate the person's mood?

So, behaviorism might seem an especially infelicitous approach to depression! This chapter, however, argues that a behavioral approach can easily formulate depression and be used to develop behavioral treatments for depression. In this chapter I outline some of the core features of behaviorism and then go on to outline behavioral formulations of depression. In the next section I describe a number of behavioral approaches to depression, including applications to mood disorders in people with mental retardation. The final section makes specific recommendations for the behavioral therapies most likely to be effective for depression in people with mental retardation.

Skinner's Account of Behavior

B. F. Skinner undertook an ambitious program of research with application to human behavior and society generally. It began with his studies of basic learning processes in nonhuman animals and in the 1950s went on to speculate on the implication of this basic research to applications to human and broad societal problems. From the foundation of the *Journal of Applied Behavior Analysis* in 1968, a whole field of applications of behaviorism to socially significant problems began, which continues to this day.

Skinner (1953) emphasized that behavior comes from three sources: biological evolution, cultural evolution, and evolution of behavior within the person's lifespan. In biological evolution, a species acquires a variety of physiological, physical, and behavioral adaptations that allow future members of the species to function more effectively in future environments. Effective, adapted variations in different members of the species are selected by the environment, and ineffective forms are extinguished. Variations in the organisms and the selecting environments are the engines that propel natural selection.

Cultural evolution occurs as variations in cultures arise and permit the survival of the group by avoidance of famine and starvation and by propagation of the culture. Societies that cannot avoid various lethal disasters cannot survive. Many cultural practices are seemingly arbitrary and ossified: "Always take your hat off in church!" or "Always cover your head before God!" as you or your culture wills. Some societies drive on the right and some on the left. Some societies prohibit eating pork and some prescribe it on certain occasion. A person acquires their culturally specific behaviors by being a member of a linguistic community that rapidly and efficiently passes on practices through language ("If you do that, you will go to hell!"). Whatever their origin, many cultural practices remain relatively fixed, but incremental variations in cultural practices occur. Some, such as the printing press, the car, and the World Wide Web, are selected and spread rapidly. Others, such as raising food for yourself and your family, and walking to work, are extinguished (Diamond, 1997). Inasmuch as selection of variants of cultural practices lead to the future survival of the culture, the environment will select these practices.

The third form of evolution is the selection of the operant during the organism's lifespan. Reflexive behavior is limited because of the more invariant form of the responses and the relatively invariant form of the relationship to the environment inhibits flexibility in the behavioral repertoire during the lifespan. Hence, blinking when there is dirt in your eye is relatively invariant in its form throughout the lifespan and in its relationship to the range of stimuli that elicit blinking. Although some learning can occur, so we may learn to blink to stimuli paired with dirt being blown into out eye, it is limited: The blinking reflex is unlikely to be the basis for learning to look for a book or for learning to roll your eyes at your mother. Operant learning occurs when the environment selects through reinforcement some variations in the behavior that the organism emits, a selection that results in the future probability of that behavior increasing. Simultaneously, other forms of behavior that were once reinforced are no longer reinforced and are extinguished. Other forms are extinguished as reinforcement if withheld from previously reinforced behaviors. Over time reinforcement can gradually lead to complex behavior and novel forms of behavior being learned.

Human behavior seems to present behaviorism with a special case. Human behavior usually evolves quickly during the lifespan, and adult humans sometimes learn complex response repertoires or exhibit old repertoires in novel situations very quickly. Thus, although operant leaning accounts for some important aspects of human behavior the role of language in self-instruction and in passing on cultural practices is perhaps a crucial difference in how most humans learn compared with animals and nonverbal humans. Skinner's (1957) *Verbal Behavior* gave an account of how language affects behavior in humans.

Private Events

Skinner did not deny human thoughts and feelings; entire chapters of *Science and Human Behavior* are devoted to self-control and to private events, such as thinking, perception, and the self. The controversy arises over the status of private events as causes of human behavior. There are at least two objections to private events: methodological and conceptual. The methodological objection is that private events can be observed by only one person—the one who is doing the thinking and feeling. Thus, objectivity and a science of thoughts and feelings is impossible, because the observations are not verifiable by a second observer. Thus, when someone cries out "My back hurts!" we do not know if we are measuring something about the person's back, some other organ, or something about the person's history with social consequences after saying such things.

A more important objection is the status given to private events as the causes of behavior. When we can determine that the person's depression has been caused by some private event—his or her mood, cognitive schemata, depressed personality, incomplete psychic development, anger at his or her mother, or unobserved levels of neurotransmitters—we are elevating private events into causes of behavior. Skinner objects to this and characterizes this explanation as an *explanatory fiction*. Skinner rejects private events as causes of behavior, because of the circular nature of such explanations. We say, "He eats because he is hungry" (Skinner, 1953, p. 31), but we cannot measure his hunger. We can only infer his hunger from his eating. Worse yet, we then elevate the unobserved construct of hunger to be the cause of his eating. Science, including a science of behavior, must be based on measurable variables that can be manipulated to infer a functional relationship. Hence, in order to observe a reliable function between the environment and behavior, we might measure the relationship between the number of seconds—1 s; 10 s; 100 s; 1,000 s; 10,000 s—since the previous meal and the latency to eat after 10 g of bread have been placed 0.1 m in front of the person. Likewise, if we wished to conduct a functional assessment of depression, we might measure the probability of crying given the presence of a spouse, a child, or a stranger as a partial analysis of that problem. So, behaviorism seeks to find functional relationships between environmental events that can be measured, on the one hand, and behavior that can be measured, on the other hand. Private events, if we could measure them, are covert behaviors to be explained, but they are not an explanation of observed behavior.

Skinner and Therapy

Skinner (1953, Chapter 24) placed psychotherapy, along with government, law, religion, economic control, and education, as one of the societal agencies engaged in controlling the behavior of individual people. These controlling agencies are well organized, and they manipulate environmental variables to control the behavior of individuals. For example, a university may deny students registration for their courses until they produce a vaccination certificate and then reinforce the students with the opportunity to engage in registration for the courses. A local government may punish a wide range of its citizens' inappropriate behaviors, such as placing garbage out on the wrong day, driving dangerously, and parking illegally. A state government may increase its available resources by reinforcing its citizens into giving money to the government by buying lottery tickets with intermittent reinforcement through cash prizes. Therapy is another societal agency for behavioral control.

Skinner (1953) speculated on a number of behavioral processes that might underlie traditional therapy, and he made a number of recommendations for therapy based on a behavioral analysis of therapy. Unfortunately, society's practices for controlling the behavior of its members are often suboptimal. Individual members may escape society's punishment by cheating, by revolting, and through passive resistance—such as refusing to carry out duties previously done voluntarily, calling in sick, and going out on strike. Society's inappropriate efforts to control the behavior of individuals may produce emotional by-products, such as freezing in the presence of stimuli associated with punishment. A mild case may be when we drive more slowly or straighten up in the presence of the police. In a more extreme case, we may be unable to return to the scene of previous punishment, though the emotions of shame and guilt.

Skinner construed depression as one example of passive resistance. Behavior is not emitted, because of the presence of aversive stimuli associated with previous punishment. Thus, in the presence of a person or situation similar to previous experiences of punishment, the person may show much less behavior. Protracted extinction may also be analogous to depression in some occasions. Not only do we see gradual reduction in adaptive behavior during extinction, but we also see emotional side effects, perhaps analogous to the behavioral excesses, such as crying and complaining, associated with some forms of depression.

If psychotherapy, then, is a controlling agency to modify client behavior for the benefit of society, and perhaps of the individual, then what are the processes underlying traditional therapy? Initially therapists have little at their disposal when first working with their clients: The client has no learning history with that specific person. However, some headway is immediately made in the professional garb, certificates, and authoritative paraphernalia that are similar to other sometimes-effective sources of relief from pain and distress. Perhaps the client has had a history with similar stimuli in the past. To the extent that the therapist's behavior brings about relief of the client's distress, or perhaps to the extent that the therapist delivers other reinforcers, then turning to the therapist for help will be reinforced. Over time, the therapist may establish himself or herself as a powerful reinforcer for client behavior. If the therapist gives effective advice on how to rearrange the environment to reduce stress, then the client's behavior may change. Early on, the therapist's instructions control the client's behavior. Later, the natural contingencies that the client experiences after changing his or her behavior may come to control that behavior.

In traditional psychoanalysis, the therapist ostensibly does very little, but rather passively reflects the verbal and sometimes nonverbal behavior of the client. The therapist does not criticize or even make suggestions for solutions (see a classic exposition of this approach in Chapter 13, by Beail and Newman). Skinner construed this as a nonpunishing audience. What will a person with a history of punishment in other environments do when faced with a nonpunishing audience? He or she will eventually start emitting the previous suppressed behaviors. Over time, the client speaks words he or she has not spoken for many years and perhaps describes traumatic events that have been too painful even to think about. By the client's repeatedly describing emotional and traumatic material, stimuli that have previously elicited negative emotional reactions become less likely to elicit such reactions, through the process of classical extinction. With a little differential reinforcement of client reports of progress in the form of contingent grunts and nods from the therapist, which the therapist may be unable to describe (Truax, 1966), traditional psychotherapy may, under certain circumstances, be able to change client behavior.

Surprisingly, Skinner's own suggestions for therapy do not contain particular prescriptions for specific forms of therapy: he does not recommend contingency management or desensitization. Rather, Skinner emphasized that effective therapy involves three things: First, because the client's adaptive behavior is not under the control of effective stimuli, his or her effective behavior must be identified, and the stimuli that control that effective behavior must be manipulated to bring about an increase in the client's adaptive behavior. Second, the therapist must teach the client an effective set of behaviors to avoid punishment and the stimuli associated with punishment. Skinner specifically recommends teaching the client methods of self-control. For Skinner self-control means emitting a controlling response—for example, setting an alarm clock—to ensure later emission of some desired behavior—for example, getting out of bed on time. This form of self-punishment is reinforced by avoidance of more powerfully punishing consequences—social criticism at work and loss of a job and associated resources. Hence, the therapist must teach the client self-control skills that make it more likely that the client will engage in healthy, nondepressed behaviors. Skinner's third and perhaps most insightful recommendation for therapy is that the therapist, even if he or she has a solution at hand, should refrain from providing the solution to the client. One reason is that solutions offered from others may well be rejected out of hand, even if they are effective solutions. More importantly yet, Skinner suggested that a client who has identified the solution independently has done much more than merely generate a solution. Rather, the client has also engaged in new behavior that allows him or her to identify and analyze the problem and identify the environmental variables that control his or her own behavior. Skinner put it this way: "Therapy consists, not in getting the patient to discover the solution to his problem, but in changing him in a such a way that he is able to discover it" (p. 382). Skinner's approach to therapy is not merely that it is not driven by specific techniques; his approach is strongly grounded in teaching self-control to the client.

Behavioral Formulations of Depression

Behavioral models have been used to account for a variety of forms of psychopathology (Sturmey, 1996), including psychopathology in individuals with mental retardation (Sturmey, Lee, Reyer, & Robek, in press), that at first glance seem to be a challenge to behaviorism. Self-injurious behavior, psychotic behavior, anxiety disorders, addictions, personality disorders, and indeed depression have all been formulated from a behavioral perspective. Behavioral approaches have been used to explain how psychopathology, including extreme forms of psychopathology, might be acquired (Sturmey et al., in press). These models have been used to derive novel and idiographic treatments (Sturmey, 1996). The efficacy of other treatments, such as cognitive behavioral treatments and some form of psychotherapy, may seem to challenge behavioral accounts of behavior. However, the efficacy or nonefficacy of various kinds of therapy are merely something for behaviorism to explain, but are not direct challenges to behaviorism. Nonbehavioral therapies may often contain explicitly or implicitly behavioral mechanisms for change (Skinner, 1953, Chapter 24; Sturmey, 2004; Truax, 1966). The next section describes behavioral models of depression.

Ferster (1973); LeJuez, Hopko, & Hopko (2001); and Lewinsohn (1975) have all developed a number of variants of behavioral models of depression. They include a number of common elements, including clarification of depressed and healthy behaviors, the nature of reinforcers in depression, and the nature of contingencies in depression.

Depression, like other forms of psychopathology, can be characterized by behavioral excesses and behavioral deficits. Behavioral excesses are behaviors that are shown in the wrong context, or too frequently for their context. Thus, pacing up and down, complaining, crying, and anger might be construed as examples of behavioral excesses associated with depression. Behavioral deficits are behaviors that are not shown when they should be, or are shown too infrequently for their context. Behavioral deficits are probably the most salient feature of depression. In depression, the overall behavioral repertoire is reduced, behaviors are emitted more slowly and with greater than usual latency. Avoidance and withdrawal characterize depression. Many descriptions of depression emphasize the lack or absence of effective social, assertive, and problem behaviors.

Behavioral models of depression also emphasize the identification of and the enhancing of an appropriate repertoire of behavior to replace unhealthy behaviors. (Recall that Skinner emphasized the development of self-control skills as the key to therapy). With help from the therapist, the client must learn how to arrange the environment to make engaging in healthy behavior more likely to occur and to make depressed behaviors less likely to occur. Both Lewinsohn's work and that of Lejuez and colleagues emphasize increasing appropriate behaviors that are effective in recruiting reinforcement from the environment (Lejuez, Hopko, & Hopko, 2001; Lewinsohn, 1975). These healthy behaviors include social skills, for example.

Another important characteristic of depression is the reduction in the number of effective reinforcers in the person's life. People with depression complain that things they used to enjoy are no longer enjoyable. Things are just no longer worth the effort they used to be. Food does not taste good. Other people who were interesting are now irritating. Additionally, various forms of negative reinforcement—the removal of aversive stimuli—are powerful and may reinforce depressed behaviors. Complaining is negatively reinforced by the termination of aversive social demands, and psychosomatic complaints are negatively reinforced by the removal of work and responsibilities. Clients' depressed behaviors punish other people's social behavior and have the effect of removing demands and other people from the affected person's life. Many of the stressful life events associated with depression are events characterized by the loss of available negative reinforcers, such as unemployment, loss of significant others, or an illness or chronic disability that involves the loss of reinforcers.

One point of intersection between behavioral and pharmacological treatments is that one of the effects of antidepressant medications is to increase the reinforcing value of stimuli and the number of available reinforcers that the client and therapist has to work with. Hence, carefully coordinated behavioral and pharmacological treatment could work synergistically to complement each other.

There may also be problems with the social contingencies of reinforcement that inadvertently maintain depressed behavior and fail to support healthy behavior. Coworkers and family members offer support, sympathy, and apparently helpful solutions to the client's problems. Others, wishing to be helpful, take on responsibilities that were formerly the client's. The helpful boss may suggest that the person take a few sick days to get over the current period of stress. All these may be examples of inappropriate contingencies of reinforcement that maintain depressed behavior and fail to maintain healthy behaviors.

Matching Law

Some behavioral models of human behavior often emphasize how organisms choose between two or more possible response and the variables that control such choosing. This area of behavior analysis is known as *matching theory*. It refers to the way in which the organism matches its rate of responding to the availability of reinforcement (Herrnstein, 1961). For example, if a pigeon can respond on two schedules available at the same time (a concurrent schedule), it will distribute its responses in proportion to the available reinforcement. For example, suppose two variable interval (VI) schedules are concurrently available. If the pigeon pecks the red key, it is reinforced after about 30 seconds. If it pecks on the green key, it is reinforced after about 60 seconds. After exposure to the two schedules, the pigeon will learn to switch back and forth between the two schedules and distribute approximately two thirds of its responses to the VI 30-s schedule and approximately one third to the VI 60-s schedule (Fisher & Mazur, 1997).

Several variables can influence matching. Reinforcer delay and reinforcer magnitudes are important variables that control performance in matching. If an animal is given two concurrent schedules, one of which delivers an immediate but small reinforcer and one of which delivers a large but delayed reinforcer, then the animal usually selects the immediate, small reinforcer. This self-control choice situation is used to model impulsivity and the development of self-control. Under certain circumstances an organism can learn self-control and will refrain from the immediate gratification and wait for a later larger reinforcer. Although humans do show matching like nonhuman animals in some circumstances, not all do. Some research has indicated that the rules that humans use to describe schedules may influence matching in humans (Fisher & Mazur, 1997).

The matching law has been demonstrated in human adaptive and maladaptive behavior. Martens, Lochner, and Kelly (1992) demonstrated that fourth-grade students distributed their time on task according to the matching law. The matching law has been used to model a variety of problematic human behaviors, such as drug usage (Madden, Bickel, & Jacobs, 1999), impulsivity in children with attention-deficit/hyperactivity disorder (Murray & Kollins, 2000), and the behavior of children with learning disabilities (Mace, Neef, Shade, & Mauro, 1996). The matching law has also been used to model how children with mental retardation choose immediate versus delayed reinforcers (Dziadosz & Tustin, 1982) and how people with mental retardation distribute their responses between appropriate communication and problem behaviors (Borrero & Vollmer, 2002). Thus, the matching law can be used to model a variety of human psychopathology, including problematic behavior in people with mental retardation.

Matching Law and Depression

LeJuez, Hopko, and Hopko (2001, 2003) used the matching law to model depression and to develop behavioral treatments of depression. The matching law hypothesizes that there should be more reinforcement for depressed behaviors than for healthy, nondepressed behaviors. Thus, the rationale for *Behavioral Activation Treatment for Depression (BATD)* is that reinforcement for depressed behaviors should be reduced or eliminated and reinforcement for healthy behaviors should be increased.

The matching law also has other implications for the formulation and treatment of depression, some of which have yet to be explored. The matching law is consonant with a number of features of the natural history of depression. Many people with depression have poor social, problem-solving, and other interpersonal skills. One way to construe this is that they have fewer ways, other than depressed behaviors, to recruit reinforcement from the environment, including from significant others. Hence the ratio of reinforcement for depressed behavior to reinforcement to healthy behavior is reduced. Many people with depression live lives characterized by punishment for adaptive behaviors. Chronic illnesses, for example, deliver punishment contingent upon each adaptive response. For some people with certain illnesses or disability, every step, every reach, and every breath may be punished with contingent pain. For others, assertive responses are consequated with verbal punishment from an abusive significant other or from demanding family members. For still others, depressed behaviors are inadvertently reinforced by helpful others who do the chores, assist the person to bed to rest, take responsibilities for the daily hardships, and provide comfort or helpful suggestions contingent upon complaints and distress. A history of punishment—as shown by poverty, abuse, personal loss, injury, victimization, and stigmatization—

may reduce the overall rate of many appropriate behaviors. This may reduce the overall number of appropriate, healthy behaviors in the person's repertoire, and hence place the person at risk for fewer healthy behaviors to recruit reinforcement. Many biological models of depression emphasize the loss of pleasure in food, sex, and association with others. These biological changes can be considered reductions in the number reinforcers available for healthy behaviors.

The self-control choice situation may also be considered to be a model for depression. Depression could be construed as the person making a choice between emitting a depressed or a healthy behavior. The depressed behavior, which may be low effort and highly practiced, is followed by an immediate, contingent, small negative reinforcer of removal of aversive demands or other people. A healthy behavior is effortful and less practiced, and may be followed by some larger reinforcer in the distant, perhaps very distant, future.

Other Behavioral Models of Depression: Functional Assessment

Sturmey (1996) proposed that functional assessment could be used as a general framework for assessment and treatment of any form of psychopathology including depression. Preintervention assessment is used to identify individual target behaviors, functions, replacement behaviors, and interventions. Thus, two ostensibly similar problems might have very different formulations and hence very different interventions based on those different formulations. For example, a school phobia maintained by avoidance of bullying might be treated with assertiveness training, whereas a school phobia maintained by avoidance of travel-related anxiety might be treated with relaxation training and graded *in vivo* exposure to traveling.

To date, there is no such research to guide practice in the area of depression. One might speculate as to whether preassessment formulations make any difference to intervention for depression. If one person's depression is the result of a punishment in the current environment, one might retrain others around them to refrain from criticism and offer only encouraging comments. If another person's depression is due to a lack of self-management skills, then one would teach the client how to identify the environmental variables that control his or her mood, to arrange the personal environment to engage in initially modest tasks that result in somewhat delayed reinforcement, and later to engage in more effortful tasks that result in more delayed reinforcement. Thus, functional assessment might guide clinicians in developing individually tailored, behaviorally based interventions for depression.

Behavioral Treatments for Depression

There is an extensive literature on behavioral treatment of depression dating back to the 1970s. Interest in behavior therapy for depression waned as psychologists adopted cognitive behavior therapy and as new classes of psychotropic medications have become widely used. Nevertheless, behavioral treatments for depression are currently making a minor comeback. Jacobson et al. (1996) reported a comparative study of activation therapy versus cognitive behavior therapy in a group of 150 outpatients with depression. At 6-month follow-up, activation therapy was just as effective as cognitive behavior therapy on all measures of depression, *including cognitive measures.*

Relatively little is known about the efficacy of behavioral intervention for depression in people with mental retardation. The following sections review a variety of behavioral interventions. There is extensive evidence for the efficacy of behavior therapy and applied behavior analysis in a wide range of areas of application (Didden, Duker, & Korzilius, 1997), including some aspects of mental health problems in people with mental retardation (Sturmey et al., in press). However, the evidence for effectiveness is very limited in both quality and quantity. It is not the case that there have been treatment evaluation trials and behavior therapy has been shown to be ineffective. Rather, there is a general absence of well-controlled research. Thus, behavior therapy for depression does not rise to the level of an evidence-based practice at this time.

Skills Acquisition

Based on the notion that strengthening healthy behaviors to compete with depressed behaviors, behavioral studies have addressed the teaching of a variety of skills to people with depression in order to treat depression. Examples of this approach include Lewinsohns' behavioral package to treat depression, including social skills training; Matson's early studies; other skills training approaches; Behavioral Activation Treatment for Depression (BATD); and relational frame theory, including Acceptance and Commitment Therapy (ACT).

Lewinsohn's Behavioral Package

Based on his behavioral model of depression Lewinsohn developed the *Coping With Depression (CWD) course,* a psycho-educational treatment run in twelve 2-hour groups over an 8-week period. There are also 1- and 6-month follow-up meetings. Emphasis is placed on teaching skills to cope with each person's own set of problems related to his or her own depression (cf. Sturmey, 1996). Booster sessions can be used.

The treatment consists of social skills training, modifying inappropriate patterns of thinking, increasing pleasant activities, and relaxation training. The treatment is very structured, and manuals have been published for clients and therapists as well as a text.

The CWD course has been evaluated with a wide variety of populations, including adult outpatients, adolescents, seniors, and a variety of ethnic minority participants. (See Antonuccio [1998] for a concise review).

Social Skills Training.

Several studies have evaluated the efficacy of social skills training to treat depression. Bellack, Hersen, and Himmelhoch (1983) conducted one of the more interesting studies, which compared four treatments for depression: an antidepressant medication (amitriptaline), social skills training combined with amitriptaline, social skills training alone, and psychotherapy combined with placebo. Out of 72 women with unipolar depression who participated, there were 52 who completed the treatment. Surprisingly, all treatments produced statistically significant reductions in depression, but there were no differences in effectiveness between the four types of treatment. There were large differences in participant dropout, however; more than half dropped out of the amitriptaline group, whereas only 15% dropped out of the social skills training group. This study suggested that social skills training may be as effective as some forms of psychopharmacology and is associated with better participation. (It should be noted that amitriptaline is no longer widely used because of problematic side effects and because of the availability of SSRIs, which have a better side-effect profile).

Provencal (2003) reported an experimental study that taught social skills to adolescents with autism and increased positive relationships with their peers. Ten received social skills training, and nine received treatment as usual. Social skills training positively impacted not only the symptoms of autism, but also the self-reported sense of adequacy, depression, normalcy, and anxiety. Thus, social skills training may be an effective way to improve mood in adolescents with autism.

Matson's Studies

Matson and colleagues conducted several studies demonstrating that skills training, including social skills training, could be beneficial to people with mental retardation and depression. Matson, Dettling, and Senatore (1979) used a variety of behavioral interventions, including modeling, self-monitoring, social reinforcement, and the prompting of positive self-statements to increase positive statements, decrease negative statements, and increase appropriate social behavior in a 32-year-old man with borderline to mild mental retardation. This man had a 10-year history of a variety of mood and anxiety problems. The treatment resulted in large changes in his speech and desirable social outcomes. Matson (1982) reported similar results with a 10-year-old child with depression and mental retardation.

Benson (1990) correctly pointed out the limits to these studies. Specifically, these studies did not address generalization across either responses or settings. Hence, it is not clear whether the changes that occurred were limited to the specific target behaviors and settings or whether other nontargeted behaviors characteristic of depression also changed. It is also not clear whether the target behaviors changed in other settings. Unfortunately, despite these early promising studies, this line of research has not been taken up over the past 20 years. Future research should do so, and respond to Benson's (1990) important critiques by addressing response and setting generalization, changes in self-report, or other behavioral manifestations of depression.

Other Skills

Most behavioral treatment research on mood disorders has been limited in the range of skills that it has addressed. Although social skills and target behaviors most closely related to the core features of depression seem the most likely place to start, there is no reason to assume that these are the only or the most important skills to address. Teaching problem solving to reduce stress, vocational skills to increase autonomy and income, parenting skills (Feldman, DuCharme, & Case, 1999), and self-control skills (Dixon & Holcomb, 2000) may all be viable, but they are as yet unexplored approaches to reduce depression in people with mental retardation.

Behavioral Activation Treatment for Depression (BATD)

Behavioral Activation Treatment for Depression (BATD) is a development of Lewinsohn's behavioral approach to behavioral treatment of depression, which has been standardized through the use of a treatment manual (LeJuez, Hopko, & Hopko, 2003). There are two phases in BATD. In the first phase, the therapist presents the rationale for focusing on increasing activity and healthy behavior gradually, rather than focusing on feeling better. In BATD, cognitions and affect are monitored as a *consequence* of increased activity. Unlike cognitive therapy, BATD does not attempt to change cognitions and emotions directly. The therapist presents educational information on recognizing depression. The treatment phase begins with preparing for treatment by completing baseline mood ratings that monitor activities using standardized forms and creating a healthy environment by asking friends and family to focus on healthy behavior and not on depressive symptoms, perhaps using a behavior contract. During the early stages of treatment, 10 domains of activities, such as family relationships, education, physical health issues, and spirituality, are reviewed to identify activities that are specific, preferred, and meaningful to the client. Clusters of functionally related activities that go toward achieving some long-term goals are also identified. For example, instead of "feeling better," an appropriate goal might be to walk on a treadmill at the gym twice a week for 20 minutes each time. In order to work toward that goal, subsidiary goals, such as finding out about local gyms, joining a gym, purchasing clothes, and walking for 10 minutes twice a week might be identified. The client then identifies 15 activities that are ranked from easiest to most difficult. The client writes these on an activity log and works to record progress on a weekly basis. Once the first three goals are met, two or three additional goals are added while activity on the first goals is maintained. The number of activities completed each week is graphed.

Treatment sessions should be weekly and take 45 to 60 minutes. Initially the therapist should be quite directive and specific. Over the course of 10 weekly sessions, help is faded in order to promote independent goal setting and attainment.

LeJuez and colleagues have published both case studies and a controlled trial to evaluate BATD. Lejuez, LePage, Hopko, and McNeil (2001) and Hopko, LeJuez, and Hopko (in press) reported four examples of the application of BATD to three adults with depression. In all three cases, activity levels were increased, scores on the Beck Depression Inventory changed from clinically significant to nonsignificant levels, and all three reported improvements in mood and cognition. All three participants achieved several personally significant goals, such as quitting their old job and gaining a better job, losing 20 pounds in 3 months, and improving marital relationships.

Hopko, LeJuez, LePage, Hopko, and McNeil (2003) conducted a randomized controlled trial of BATD. Participating were 27 adult inpatients with a principal diagnosis of major depressive disorder. Approximately half also had other disorders, such as substance abuse, anxiety, and personality disorders. The experimenters randomly assigned the participants to either BATD or supportive psychotherapy. Therapists used the BATD manual to guide treatment but used three weekly 20-minute meetings as the therapy format. Tokens from the unit token economy were used, contingent on completion of the activities assigned in BATD. Clients in the supportive psychotherapy group met with their supportive and facilitative therapist three times per week, and they participated in a nondirective discussion of their problems. The therapist also encouraged the participants to gain social support from their psychiatrist, unit staff, and peers. The mean scores on the Beck Depression Inventory decreased from 35 to 19 in the BATD group and from 37 to 30 in the supportive psychotherapy group. At the end of therapy, the group receiving BATD was statistically significantly less depressed than the group receiving supportive psychotherapy. The effect size was large ($d = 0.73$). There are currently other ongoing trials of BATD for other populations.

BATD and Mental Retardation.

There are no reports of the use of BATD with people with mental retardation. Hence, at this time BATD is unevaluated with this population. However, several features of BATD make it a promising treatment. First, the treatment does not depend upon sophisticated verbal skills. Rather, it focuses on increasing activity. Second, the treatment is clearly operationalized in a treatment manual. Masters-level therapists can administer it effectively in a time-limited fashion. Third, it includes active participation with the client on identifying and achieving personally meaningful personal goals and is thus ideologically compatible with current service trends, such as client-centered planning. Finally, by using a behavioral paradigm that many services are familiar with, the treatment may be readily acceptable to services.

The current version of BATD probably requires some significant modification to use it with people with mental retardation. For example, many people with mental retardation would need additional help in using the various forms of self-recording that are currently part of BATD. Some simplified forms or photographs and pictures as activity schedules might be needed. Some of the measures used might require modification to be suitable for this population. Some people might also require more frequent monitoring and reminders to engage in the agreed activities than would the general population.

Relational Frame Theory

The most stereotypical forms of behavior therapy involve contingency management and skills training. However, recently some behavior analysts have moved into the realm of verbal therapy based on relational frame theory (Hayes, Barnes-Holmes, & Roche, 2001). Relational frame theory seeks to understand human behavior by incorporating a Skinnerian analysis of language and how language and cognition may produce psychopathology.

Wilson, Hayes, and Zettle (2001) reviewed a number of new behavior therapies based on relational frame theory, such as *Acceptance and Commitment Therapy (ACT)*. ACT teaches clients not to fight and avoid the aversive nature of their personal experience of their psychopathology, but rather to accept it. Fighting and avoiding suffering is seen as part of the problem, an ineffective coping mechanism that has failed to relieve suffering. The aim of the acceptance phase of ACT is to accept that avoidance of private events is hopeless. Attempts to control psychopathology are seen as short-term solutions that make psychopathology worse rather than better in the long-term. Client private verbal behavior is seen as problematic, so clients are taught through metaphor, paradox, and other methods to view their private language as furniture in a house, but not as the house itself. Clients learn that the self is distinct from one's thoughts and feelings. After private events are accepted, the client identifies valued life goals. Traditional behavior therapy methods are used to achieve these goals.

ACT and other verbally based behavior therapies require considerable verbal abilities. No trials of these therapies have yet been conducted with people with mental retardation, so at this time they are not recommended.

Modifying Affective Behavior

Several studies have investigated increasing happy behavior and decreasing unhappy behavior in people with mild through profound mental retardation and/or autism. Green and Reid (1996) developed an observational measure of happy and unhappy behavior in five people with profound mental retardation. They compared the effects of preferred and nonpreferred stimuli on affective behaviors. Preferred and nonpreferred stimuli were identified by repeatedly presenting two or more stimuli and observing which stimuli the client approached and which they avoided. Stimuli that were frequently and consistently approached were identified as preferred stimuli. Green and Reid showed that presentation of preferred stimuli was associated with increases in happy behaviors and decreases in unhappy behaviors, and that this association was reflected in caregivers' ratings of client mood. Subsequent studies have shown similar effects (Ivancic, Barret, Simonow and Kimberly, 1997; Lancioni, O'Reilly, Singh, Oliva, & Groeneweg, 2002), including increases in happy behavior in problematic situations previously associated with unhappy behavior, such as physical therapy (Green & Reid, 1999), and stimuli that had been associated with bad mood and combinations of bad mood and demands that precipitate problem behaviors (Carr,

McLaughlin, Giacobbe-Grieco, & Smith, 2003). These studies have shown that affective behavior in people with severe and profound mental retardation is a function of the presence or the absence of preferred stimuli. Further, environmental enrichment with preferred stimuli can be used to increase happiness. These studies are limited for the present purpose in that the participants were not diagnosed with mood disorders. However, these studies do suggest that these methods are promising.

Lindauer, DeLeon, and Fisher (1999) extended this earlier work to the treatment of self-injurious behavior (SIB) and negative affective behaviors in a 23-year-old woman, Candy, with severe mental retardation, major depression, and autistic-like behavior. She was also treated with carbamazepine throughout the study. Her negative affective behaviors included frowning, crying, whining, and saying such things as "I am sad." A functional analysis of her SIB demonstrated that it functioned to avoid demands but was present across all conditions. Lindauer et al. informally observed that her SIB was most likely when she was left alone, and therefore they developed a program of environmental enrichment in order to reduce her negative affective behaviors and SIB. They selected her 12 most preferred items for the environmental enrichment program based on paired stimulus preference assessments. A simple hands-down procedure was in operation throughout the experiment for Candy's SIB. They compared a baseline, when Candy was alone in a room, and an environmental enrichment condition, when the 12 preferred items were in the room with Candy. Lindauer et al. found that Candy consistently exhibited high rates of negative affective behavior and SIB during baseline sessions. When preferred items were present, Lindauer observed high rates of positive affect behaviors and near zero levels of SIB and negative affect behaviors.

This study shows that behavioral manifestations of depression, such as negative affect behaviors and accompanying SIB, can be effectively treated in individuals with severe mental retardation by increasing the availability of preferred activities. This study extends the earlier work of Green and Reid (1996) on management of happiness in people with severe and profound mental retardation without mood disorders to the treatment of diagnosed major mood disorders in this population.

Comment.

Environmental enrichment using preferred stimuli appears to be a relatively simple and fairly robust technology to increase happiness in people with mental retardation and other disabilities. Thus, it may be an appropriate method to prevent negative mood in people at risk for mood disorders, to prevent relapse in people with a history of a mood disorder and to manage negative mood in people who do not or who only partially respond to psychotropic medication. Although there has been only one demonstration of the application of this technology to one person with a diagnosed mood disorder, it does appear to be a promising approach when such other approaches as counseling, psychotherapy, and cognitive therapy would not be suitable.

Behavioral Treatment for Suicide

Suicide and suicidal attempts in people with mental retardation have been reported relatively infrequently in the literature, although several recent reports contradict this observation. Lunsky (2004) conducted interviews with 98 adults with mental retardation and their caregivers. One third reported thinking that life was not worth living "sometimes" or "a lot," and 11% reported suicide attempts in the past. Those who reported suicidal thoughts were more likely to also report loneliness, stresses, depression, and lack of social support. Patja, Iivanainen, Raitasuo, and Lonnqvist (2001) conducted a 35-year follow-up of 2,369 people with mental retardation from a Finnish case register in 1962. They found that women with mental retardation were at equal risk of suicide as were women in the general population and that men with mental retardation were only a third of the risk of suicide compared with men in the general population. People with mild mental retardation and those who had been admitted to a psychiatric hospital were at greater risk of suicide.

Despite these and other reports of suicidal ideation and attempts in people with mental retardation, there have been few attempts to behaviorally analyze and treat suicidal behavior. Sturmey (1994) reported a behavioral intervention to better manage suicidal threats and gestures in a man with moderate mental retardation. This man had been frequently admitted from his developmental center to a psychiatric hospital for suicidal gestures and threats. Observation and a review of records suggested that access to medical and nursing staff and being placed on one-to-one staff may have been important consequences in maintaining suicidal behavior. Therefore, his psychiatric monitoring was modified to minimize access to these consequences. The number of pleasurable activities at the home was increased. The psychiatric monitoring procedure was changed so that instead of being placed on a nursing unit, he was placed in a boring individual room with no TV and minimal social contact for 12 to 36 hours. This procedure was effective in eliminating admissions to a psychiatric hospital and keeping him safe.

Contingency management is not the only and perhaps not even the most appropriate form of intervention for suicidal behavior. A Skinnerian analysis would suggest teaching self-control strategies to manage depressed mood and teaching appropriate behaviors to replace suicidal behavior.

Summary and Recommendations

Both the quality and quantity of the evidence for behavior therapies for depression in people with mental retardation and depression is very limited. For people with mild and moderate mental retardation, BATD seems promising. There are trials of BATD and similar Lewinsohn-style interventions that show it is effective with the general population. The high degree of structure and the emphasis on engaging in activities to promote health behaviors seems pragmatic, likely to make maximum use of client strengths, and likely to tailor intervention to each client's personal interest.

For people with severe or profound mental retardation, there are now a number of studies that have shown that increasing access to preferred activities identified by the client him or herself is reliably associated with improvements in mood. However, only one paper with only one subject has applied this method to someone with a diagnosis of mood disorder.

Future research should conduct both pilot work and controlled studies to evaluate the use of BATD to treat depression in people with mental retardation. Further work should also be done using Skinner's (1953) self-control model of therapy for psychopathology and how it might be adapted for people with mild or moderate mental retardation. Finally, the work on preferred items to promote positive mood in people with severe or profound mental retardation should be extended in two ways. First, the technology should be packaged in such a way that direct-care staff and family members can use it to promote positive mood in people with severe or profound mental retardation. Second, evaluation research on its applicability to depression in people with mental retardation should be conducted.

References

Antonuccio, D. O. (1998). The coping with depression course. A behavioral treatment for depression. *The Clinical Psychologist, 51,* 3–5.

Bellack, A. S., Hersen, M., & Himmelhoch, J. M. (1983). A comparison of social skills training, pharmacotherapy and psychotherapy for depression. *Behaviour Research in Therapy, 21,* 101–107.

Benson, B. A. (1990). Behavioral treatment of depression. In A. Dosen & F. J. Menolascino (Eds.), *Depression in mentally retarded children and adults* (pp.

309–330). Leiden, Netherlands: Logon Publications.

Borrero, J. C., & Vollmer, T. R. (2002). An application of the matching law to severe problem behavior. *Journal of Applied Behavior Analysis, 35,* 31–27.

Carr, E. G., McLaughlin, D. M., Giacobbe-Grieco, T., & Smith, C. E. (2003). Using mood ratings and mood induction in assessment and intervention for severe problem behaviors. *American Journal on Mental Retardation, 108,* 32–55.

Diamond, J. (1997). *Guns, germs and steel. The fate of human societies.* New York: W. W. Norton.

Didden, R., Duker, P. C., & Korzilius, H. (1997). Meta-analytic study on treatment effectiveness for problem behaviors with individuals who have mental retardation. *American Journal on Mental Retardation, 101,* 387–399.

Dixon, M. R., & Holcomb, S. (2000). Teaching self-control to small groups of dually diagnosed adults. *Journal of Applied Behavior Analysis, 33,* 611–614.

Dziadosz, T., & Tustin, R. D. (1982). Self-control: An application of the generalized matching law. *American Journal on Mental Deficiency, 86,* 614–620.

Feldman, M. A., Ducharme, J. M., & Case, L. (1999). Using self-instructional, pictorial manuals to teach child-care skills with mothers with intellectual disabilities. *Behavior Modification, 23,* 480–497.

Ferster, C. B. (1973). A functional analysis of depression. *American Psychologist, 28,* 857–870.

Fisher, W. W., & Mazur, J. E. (1997). Basic and applied research on choice responding. *Journal of Applied Behavior Analysis, 30,* 387–410.

Green, C. W., & Reid, D. H. (1996). Defining, validating , and increasing indices of happiness among people with profound multiple disabilities. *Journal of Applied Behavior Analysis, 29,* 67–78.

Green, C. W., & Reid, D. H. (1999). Reducing indices of unhappiness among individuals with profound multiple disabilities during exercise routines. *Journal of Applied Behavior Analysis, 32,* 137–146.

Haynes, S. C., Barnes-Holmes, D., & Roche, B. (2001). *Relational frame theory. A post-Skinnerean account of human language and cognition.* New York: Kluwer.

Herrnstein, R. J. (1961). Relative and absolute strength of response as a function of frequency of reinforcement. *Journal of the Experimental Analysis of Behavior, 4,* 267–272.

Hopko, D. R., LeJuez, C. W., & Hopko, S. D. (in press). Behavioral activation as an intervention for co-existent depression and anxiety symptoms. *Clinical Case Studies,* in press.

Hopko, D. R., LeJuez, C. W., LePage, J. P., Hopko, S. D., & McNeil, D. W. (2003). A brief behavioral activation treatment for depression: A randomized pilot trial within an inpatient psychiatric hospital. *Behavior Modification, 27,* 458–469.

Ivancic, M. T., Barret, G. T., Simonow, A., & Kimberly, A. (1997). A replication to increase happiness indices among some people with profound multiple disabilities. *Research in Developmental Disabilities, 18,* 79–89.

Jacobson, N. S., Dobson, K. S., Truax, P. A., Addis, M. E., Koerner, K., Gollan, J. K., et al. (1996). A component analysis of cognitive-behavioral treatment for depression. *Journal of Consulting and Clinical Psychology, 64,* 295–304.

Lancioni, G. E., O'Reilly, M. F., Singh, N. N., Oliva, D., & Groeneweg, J. (2002). Impact of stimulation versus microswitch-based programs on indices of happiness of people with profound multiple disabilities. *Research in Developmental Disabilities, 23,* 149–160.

LeJuez, C. W., Hopko, D. R., & Hopko, S. D. (2001). A brief Behavioral Activation Treatment for Depression. *Cognitive and Behavioral Practice, 8,* 164–175.

LeJuez, C. W., Hopko, D. R., & Hopko, S. D. (2003). *The brief Behavioral Activation Treatment for Depression (BATD). A comprehensive patient guide.* Boston: Pearson.

LeJuez, C. W., Hopko, D. R., Hopko, S. D., & McNeill, D. W. (2001). A brief Behavioral Activation Treatment for Depression treatment manual. *Behavior Modification, 25,* 225–286.

Lewinsohn, P, M. (1975). Engagement in pleasant activities and depression level. *Journal of Abnormal Psychology, 84,* 729–731.

Lindauer, S. E., DeLeon, I. G., & Fisher, W. W. (1999). Decreasing signs of negative affect and correlated self-injury with mental retardation and mood disturbances. *Journal of Applied Behavior Analysis, 32,* 103–106.

Lunsky, Y. (2004). Suicidality in a clinical and community sample of adults with mental retardation. *Research in Developmental Disabilities, 25,* 231–234.

Mace, F. C., Neef, N. A., Shade, D., & Mauro, B. C. (1996). Effects of problem difficulty and reinforcer quality on time allocated to concurrent arithmetic problems. *Journal of Applied Behavior Analysis, 29,* 11–24.

Madden, G. J., Bickel, W. K., & Jacobs, E. A. (1999). Discounting of delayed rewards in opioid-dependent outpatients: Exponential or hyperbolic discounting functions? *Experimental and Clinical Psychopharmacology, 7,* 284–293.

Martens, B. K., Lochner, D. G., & Kelly, S. Q. (1992). The effects of variable-interval reinforcement on academic engagement: A demonstration of matching theory. *Journal of Applied Behavior Analysis, 25,* 143–151.

Matson, J. L. (1982). The treatment of behavioral characteristics of depression in the mentally retarded. *Behavior Therapy, 13,* 209–218.

Matson, J. L., Dettling, J., & Senatore, V. (1979). Treating depression of a mentally retarded adult. *British Journal of Mental Subnormality, 26,* 86–88.

Murray, L. K., & Kollins, S. H. (2000). Effects of methylphenidate on sensitivity to reinforcement in children diagnosed with attention deficit hyperactivity disorder: An application of the matching law. *Journal of Applied Behavior Analysis, 33,* 573–591.

Patja, K., Iivanainen, M., Raitasuo, S., & Lonnqvist, J (2001). Suicide mortality in mental retardation: A 35-year follow-up study. *Acta Psychiatrica Scandanavica, 103,* 307–311.

Provencal, S. C. (2003). The efficacy of a social skills training program for adolescents with autism spectrum disorders. *Dissertation Abstracts International: Section B: The Sciences & Engineering, 64 (3-B),* 1504.

Skinner, B. F. (1953). *Science and human behavior.* London: MacMillan.

Skinner, B. F. (1957). *Verbal behavior.* New York. Appleton-Century-Crofts.

Sturmey, P. (1994). Suicidal threats and behavior in a person with developmental disabilities: Effective psychiatric monitoring based on a fundamental assessment. *Behavioral Interventions, 9,* 235–245.

Sturmey, P. (1996). *Functional analysis in clinical psychology.* Chichester, UK: Wiley.

Sturmey, P. (2004). Cognitive therapy with people with intellectual disabilities: A selective review and critique. *Clinical Psychology and Psychotherapy, 11,* 222–232.

Sturmey, P., Lee, R., Reyer, H., & Robek, A. (in press). Applied behavior analysis and dual diagnosis: Behavioral approaches to dual diagnosis. To appear in N. Cain & P. Davidson (Eds.), *Dual diagnosis.*

Truax, C. B. (1966). Reinforcement and non-reinforcement in Rogerian psychotherapy. *Journal of Abnormal and Social Psychology, 71,* 1–9.

Wilson, K. G., Hayes, S. C., & Zettle, R. D. (2001). Psychopathology and psychotherapy. In S. C. Haynes, D. Barnes-Holmes, & B. Roche, B. (Eds.), *Relational frame theory. A post-Skinnerean account of human language and cognition* (pp. 211–239). New York: Kluwer.